THE BRIDGER:
A SECULAR HUMANIST ODYSSEY

A SEMI-FICTIONAL AUTOBIOGRAPHICAL NOVEL

BY JACK WISE KENNEDY

**WITH POLITICAL, RELIGIOUS & ECONOMIC ESSAYS
ATTACHED FOR CLARITY**

brid.ger /ˈbrij-jer/ n 1: a person who builds bridges to connect broken circles of thought 2: a person who can perceive hidden social structures after reflecting on seemingly random, unrelated material 3: a realist 4: a philosopher

PYRAMID WORKERS PRESS • GRASS VALLEY, CALIFORNIA

Pyramid Workers Press
P.O. Box 2505
Grass Valley CA 95945

A subsidiary of
Scanlan Publishing Services
P.O. Box 2065
Nevada City CA 95959

First Edition
ISBN 0-9626280-4-2 (Soft)
ISBN 0-9626280-1-8 (Hard)

Also available on disk:
ISBN 0-9626280-2-6 (Mac)
ISBN 0-9626280-3-4 (MS-DOS)

EPIGRAPH

AND IF THEY SAY THIS LOVE HAS NO MORTAR
AND IF THEY SAY IT HAS NO ORDER
TELL THEM WE WILL NOT DESPAIR
BECAUSE THIS LOVE AMONG THE TOPPLED STRUCTURES
WILL BE LIKE THE OPENING OF A PETALLED FLOWER
LIKE THE RECREATION OF A FABLED TOWER

Music by Ray Donat
Lyrics by May Summers

PREFACE

This novel is not only a story of romance, mystery, and my fall into political and economic adventurism, but contains a humanistic philosophy that is intended to be read and used as a primer for understanding our lives. Due to the circumstance that I was not privy to events that had taken place out of my hearing and sight, many of the suppositions and motives attached to people and events in this book are strictly created from my imagination. I also feel compelled to point out that mostly for the literary effect, but also to protect myself and others in the future against an unknown alignment of the far right, I have intentionally blurred and entwined both truth and fiction so that they bleed into each other without a clear demarcation line. Where this manuscript can be documented or confirmed by another source, it is the truth; where it cannot, consider it a work of fiction. I also state that the fictionalized people and events in this book were devised, fabricated and composed, not to deceive anyone, but for the sole purpose of dramatizing the truth.

TABLE OF CONTENTS

DEDICATION

To see what others have not seen, an author must, in the true sense, become alienated from the crowd, must always observe from the outside of a class, a culture; must always be a stranger, a visitor in his own country. The following made my sojourn in Washington, California, less lonely, less alienated: "Tepee" Steve and Pattie, who did the first editing, and "Mama Su" for helping me with one of the critical chapters; and especially for telling me that she cried when she came to a part of my book that moved her. This gave me confidence that as a writer I was able to convey my experiences and feelings to a reader. That's important for an author to know. And I wish to thank "Big" Steve, whose only failure in life was that he couldn't beat me consistently in Backgammon, and "Chick", the best boulder mover in the world, and "Little" Steve, for carrying on the traditions of the third floor, and Diane Petty, who represented what was best in tribalism and held the town together for years by sacrificing herself for its unity, and David Petty, who I envied because he had Diane, and "Doc" who deservedly received the Silver Star in Vietnam and confirmed what truly happened there, and Charley Brown, because he was Charley Brown, and Paula, because just hearing that she was in town for the day made me feel less isolated, and Susan, a writer, who we almost lost. And all those who, at one time lived on the third floor of the Washington Hotel, and to the River Rest and Pine-Aire Camp Grounds summer people and those residents of the resort town of Washington, California, who for years shamed me and kept me writing by continually asking if I had finished my book. And thanks, too, to Dan Scanlan for his editing skills and for marshalling this project through the publishing process.

CHAPTER I

NARRATIVE: CONVERGENCE

Yes, I remember — diary of my mind. These pages are proof of those remembered incidents. Although my youthful memories have aged and regressed, the fog of time has only intervened to soften the harsh contours on some of my more lamentable recollections, not to conceal them. Even today, my mind still recalls how elated I was when my eyes, following Janet's pointing finger, beheld Lili's shadow being cast on the surface of a small, translucent window. A window that filtered and dimmed the harsh light of day for her; a window that separated and screened the world of reality for her; and sadly, for me, a window that did not allow me to intrude into her austere, nine by seven feet, structured world.

Lili! Lili! Recalling her name brings back suppressed memories of love and seduction in the days of my youthful gestures; it also brings with it a feeling of sadness; a deeply felt sadness. It is still hard for me to comprehend that there will be some unfortunate people who will never meet someone like her. Not to have known a Lili in one's lifetime can restrict your knowledge of the frailty of transitory youth, of the alchemy of the innocent, of the common denominator of youth — love.

I remember calmly thinking that since I had found Lili again, I must try to extricate her; to remove her physically from those who make their living erecting road signs from inaccurately drawn maps. At the time — still beguiled by the events that were occurring around me — I had just begun to think that within a few months I would be able to come to a state of rest. Not for an extended period, you understand, but just for a brief time. Be assured, I truly needed the rest, as I had been, and still was fighting with hydra-headed dragons and tilting with black knights on their home turf.

What? You say that you do not believe they inhabit this modern world? That might be because they are much more cunning than in the days of old. These days they hide their modern form under the guise of respectability, under the cloak of propriety, under the projection of other facades. Some of our current dragons wear stiffly starched, three-quarter length white coats with large buttons running down the front, and the black knights have been known to hide their stainless steel armor under long, black flowing robes. For the vigilant, listen well, and be not deceived by those disguises; underneath those ostentatious facades the essential forms of old remain hidden from the unwary, the unobservant, the careless.

Back then, I even found myself quietly dabbling in the old, the hidden, the cryptic world of spells and incantations to see if I could vanquish the dragons and black knights that patrol the corridors of our minds. I did not know if I could conquer these modern manifestations with magic words from the law books that I was relentlessly examining, but I knew that I must try or I would surely end up in the black knight's dungeon, my screams muffled by the thick walls of injustice that would surround me.

You might be wondering who is speaking? I am a Darwinian observer, and the chronicler of those observations. In this book you will find out that I play a dual role. I am not only the writer of this fiction, but also a factual participant in the nonfiction.

When growing up in San Francisco, it seemed to me that I would be eternally denied a significant speaking part on the stage of life. Once in a while, I would be recruited as a stagehand where my duties would require me to knock on a stage door; but in answer to the words, "Come in," spoken on stage, another actor would stroll through the door. Only my bruised knuckles and the echo of the knocking would let me know that I still was not participating fully in life's ongoing drama.

Time eventually changed that. There came a day when I found myself in a road production where the lead role was being played back stage, and only I knew that it was the undistorted drama. The play appearing on stage was just a visual deception created for the audience; in it, I was still just a bit player. Finding Lili had made me aware that I now had to expand my role to include her. Just because we were a couple of bit players trapped inadvertently in a side eddy of a larger drama, did not mean that we could not dream. After finding her, my dream included not just appearing in a nonspeaking background part, but the masculine and feminine leads were my goal for us. My problem was that I had to convince fate — which controls the daily casting — that it should allow us the opportunity to rewrite the script so that we could play those lead roles; to rewrite the script so that we could control our entrances and exits. I felt that if I could postpone the opening of that deceptive drama being written by those who would like to control us, then by the time we were programmed to appear on *their* stage, Lili and I would be blowing in the wind, where we would be free and unencumbered by much of society's excess baggage, free of the burden of our past collapsed visions.

At this point we must change the scenery because this is near the ending. To better understand the story we will have to intersect it in the year 1954. It began when, on a fogless autumn day in San Francisco, I was aimlessly strolling through the Tenderloin District.

Many events in 1954 had already been noticed, recorded, and inserted into the tapestry of time, where they formed common reference threads that were shared by the living when these events became printed words and pictures. The Army-McCarthy hearings began, the detonation of the first Hydrogen Bomb occurred, Dien Bien Phu fell to the Viet Minh, and the CIA sponsored a right-wing coup in Guatemala, which led to the overthrow of an elected government that had nationalized the property of the United Fruit Company. Those were just a few of the threads worth mentioning, but there were other events that were woven into the tapestry that year, and only the participants who did the original weaving can accurately describe those inserted threads.

The following is an interval of remembered weaving: This day, unknown to me, was to become a time I commemorated, a time I celebrated, a time that I would never have to mark on a calendar to remember. Its vivid impressions were to be forever stigmatized on this molecular structure that encompasses my thoughts. It turned out to be a day of good omens when lead filled balloons overcame gravitation; a day when a myriad of mescaline induced worlds converged into a single vision; a day that turned out to be a time of perfect alignment, when only one shadow was cast by two lovers. It was all this and more, because this was the day that Lili and I met.

I was playing my assumed role of a street person when I first saw Lili lightly tripping down that San Francisco sidewalk. As she frolicked up to me, her Madonna face radiated a smile of confident youth. She did not realize that I had seen her on a movie screen just a few days before. She was being played by Leslie Caron in the movie *Lili*. Do you remember Leslie Caron walking down that carnival row and meeting the puppets? If you do, you can visualize my Lili, if you do not, then a description of a virgin meadow filled with wild flowers will have to suffice.

"Have you seen my girl friend around here?" were the first words I heard expelled through Lili's unadorned lips. "She was carrying all our money, and I am getting dreadfully hungry," she said.

We stand amazed before the pyramids, astonished by the Grand Canyon, awed by life itself, but a simple meeting of lovers is the natural miracle that surrounds us. In reflection I can see that a simple little distraction — such as my looking at a window display — could have changed the future for the two of us. Then Lili would have been only a momentary reflection in a store window as she passed behind my back. How close was that fragile meeting. If we had passed without recognition, then this story would be incomplete. You cannot change reality by using the word *if* so the word is used here to show amazement, to show astonishment, to show the beguilement in nature's arrangement of our meeting.

Lili's ingenue hairdo and Catholic school girl uniform could not hide that adult imagery that was trying to blossom out to attract the honey gatherers. To this day, by following similar patterns that cross my field of vision, my impudent eyes look for what was imprinted on my mind that day. It has been written that your first love predominates in your memory; and so it has been with me.

"Lili?" I hesitatingly asked this incarnated figure who had used some form of human metamorphosis to turn her image from common celluloid into a sorcerer's dream.

"Oh! You do not know me, Sir. My name is ..."

"Sir? Sir? You address someone of my age as Sir? You must be one of those persons from another time dimension that the science fiction people have been speculating about through the ages. Tell me, how did you circumvent the time barrier that separates us?" I teasingly asked her.

Her response was a little school girl's giggle; which betrayed her for what she was — a truant school girl playing grown-up in the city. Lili and her girl friend had taken off from the nuns that day. Their purpose; their quest? To see first hand the snares and traps that intrigue the minds of the young and innocent. Lili and her girl friend — the one who had the money and their return ticket — were separated in a game that had rules only understood by the youthful players. These rules are not translatable into the language of the nonplayer or to those who live in a different age sphere.

Lili did not understand that she was surrounded by predators that day. Predators who could be attracted by her truant cry of, "I am getting dreadfully hungry," just as a coyote is attracted by the screams of a rabbit caught in a trap. The Catholic Church, for its lack of foresight that day, should be condemned. Why does it not tell their students about the traps and snares encountered in the game of living? To allow a person to stumble through their early experiences without this knowledge is cruel. Can they not see that their fledglings will not always remain safe and protected behind those walls of long black cloth?

I was soon made aware that Lili and her girl friend had gained entry through the time barrier and into my dimension by simply riding a Greyhound Bus from Redwood City to San Francisco. When I first met Lili, I was still not sure that I could play a major part in life's daily dramas, but there was surely nothing to stop me from falling in love with the heroine on stage. It was a pure love of youth; a love of butterflies and flowers and trees and lakes and mountains; a love that did not intrude upon the acting on stage. Is time playing "games" with my memory? Was there ever an authentic time to love like that, or was this segment of my life attributable to simply another programmed tape that nature introduced into my brain center to stimulate it, another of nature's inherited panaceas for the survival of the species?

On that fateful day of our first meeting, I took Lili to my room to feed her and keep the street predators at bay, ignoring in my youthful arrogance that I was also a predator. She seemed fascinated with the way I lived, with someone who actually slept on a mattress on the floor. Lili thought that she had come in contact with a true beatnik that day, one who could put her on one of those stages that the grown-ups played upon. I did nothing to dispel the myths that she had read about the beatnik's way of life. In the 1950s, this folklore — which would produce the "Hippie Movement" in the 1960s — had already infected Lili and a small, restless group of young people from the middle-class. Lili, in her protected innocence, did not understand that an observer's pay is exceptionally small, and that my long hair, old clothes, and the mattress on the floor were to be equated more with poverty than to an unknown movement or cause.

Lili came along willingly and trustingly to my room that day. If you cannot see the snares and traps, then what is there to be afraid of? Instead of committing a simple seduction that day, it was to become for me a day of postponed dreams, a day of wonderful awakening, a day of exploring the grandeurs of love. It was a new and unexpected experience for me when I first realized that our vibrations had meshed; that we shared a global covenant with other lovers. The universal attractor — love — is one thing that youth uses in its original primitive design. This primeval kaleidoscope of emotions engulfs us when, deep within us, a signal comes from the genes, thus, awakening within us the desire for fusion with another. This early sexual desire is usually pure, because it has not had the time to be corrupted by duty, by status, by eligibility, by financial security, and on and on, until it becomes just another transaction to be recorded and filed in its proper place. Love, a common emotion to all, guides a person's passage through life; surely, life must be incomplete without it.

Parents fear this time of life because this is when the beautiful unite with the homely, the poor with the rich, the sane with the crazy, the educated with the dullards; and all the adding, subtracting, multiplying and dividing of the above categories into all feasible combinations will ensure that grown-ups become elevated to the supreme height of paranoia. These paranoid parents come to believe their children are deliberately trying to convert them into smoke so they might dispose of them by running them up the nearest flue pipe. Essentially, what is worrying them and causing them this anguish is just a simple arrangement in the body of some microscopic genes. Tormented and irritated by a lack of knowledge, parents have not been able to manipulate these genes, but they are not going to give up the hope of eventually rearranging those bits of matter so their children's future choice will be more compatible with theirs.

Trying to capture a short interval of time is fascinating. A tapestry can do it, a painting can do it, even a sculpture can do it; but a book produces a finer weave and gives a larger panorama than can be captured by something that remains static. Even as events are being recorded, there is a change going on in time's tapestry. What is being described is no longer there; it quickly passes away. A writer must, from a great volume of remembered impressions, try to capture and distill a few drops of time, and from this distill an essence that will make those images pertinent to those who will come after and might wish to glimpse a few moments of eternity frozen in prose. If the participants do not tell their own, true story, then the truth might be distorted and lost. That would be sad because every thread in the tapestry of life is worth recording truthfully so that the living can go on learning from the past.

Only novice writers believe that they must travel to a far place to seek unique subject matter. There is nothing going on in New York, London, Paris, Hong Kong, Moscow, or Tahiti that is different than what is happening in the smallest out of the way place. What is going on in all locations is human beings striving to search out and reconcile — in their unknown and undesignated allotment of time — a meaning to their usually unconsciously adopted tenets and illusions.

Because many people's minds are so obscured and clouded by their daily struggle to exist that they cannot imagine the true shape of stars, it is the duty of a writer to describe those stars, and to portray by whatever means they are capable of, that time they have lived through. So, this book is my interpretation of the truth as I have observed and lived it. Yes, these pages are the recorded memorabilia of my mind.

CHAPTER 2

NARRATIVE: INTRIGUE

You are now going to join me in a two and a half year journey that I embarked on in 1961. We will explore the byways as they were before and after, so you can understand why I ambled down some, ran down others, and refused to take some confirmed intellectual paths, even though they were distinctly marked on known maps. I have the documentation that the journey took place; no one will dispute that. What is in contention, and you will have to decide, is when I resort to speculative fiction because of a lack of validation, whether the unverifiable parts of the journey took place as described, or were they calculated deceptions I dreamed up then, or later? In other words, could this book be just another hoax novel, or is the improbable true — that I am telling the truth? From the evidence that I will present, each reader will have the opportunity to make that determination.

I was about 12 years old when there occurred at the Fox Theater in San Francisco, an unexpected event. Because of our seating arrangement, some theater patrons and I observed an illusion, which was the disappearance of a live elephant on stage, fall apart. The show began with the entire back of the stage draped in shimmering black velvet. When the magician diverted our attention away from the elephant, three large curtains of identical black velvet were to drop down between the audience and the elephant. This would blend with the background to attain the illusion of a disappearing elephant. When the magician spoke the appropriate words, a stagehand released the curtains as planned, but the side curtain facing me hung up a couple of feet from the floor, where it remained suspended for a few seconds before dropping down and completing the visual deception.

The audience sitting in the center and to the far right of me, saw the completed trick and began clapping loudly for such a splendid illusion, while a part of the audience and I, could still see the elephant's feet. This incident made a great impression on me. Not the exposure of the deception, for even though I was young, I still knew that it was a trick, but the realization that two people viewing the same event could have different perspectives when describing what took place on that stage.

On April 22, 1961, I had again observed somebody's created illusion, which would, within a few hours, cause the disappearance of my mentally created world. A world comprised of 35 years of impressions and beliefs that I regarded as so true, so persuasive, that I was willing to sacrifice my life for them. Because of my former experience at the Fox Theater, I knew that someone had misdirected the attention of the participating audience, but much to my regret I did not see the side curtain hang up this time. I did not know how the illusion was carried out, but later, I would reconstruct from memory the stage before the curtain dropped, and speculate from that how someone had created the conditions that made my former world disappear.

We will begin by following my movements and my thoughts on the morning of April 22, 1961: I had made the decision to return to Los Angeles, just the night before. I decided to go back and fight what was happening deep within the underground structure of the political party that I belonged to. By the time the sun had dropped below the horizon on that April day, I could lament on the foolish human beings who feel that their plans, actions, or destinies are controllable, without taking into account the plans, actions, and destinies of others we do not even know exist, and therefore cannot even guess about or take into account the results they will have on our lives.

When examined, scientists find there is an uncertainty principle in nature. The intervention of that attribute found me, on that spring morning of 1961, driving down a lonely stretch of back county highway. Suddenly, my mind was alerted to a dangerous situation as a passing automobile came to a screeching halt in front of me. All this commotion led me to think that the driver must have tire trouble and I should stop and see if he needed help. Could anyone predict from a simple incident such as that, a change in a person's destiny, in a person's perception of the society he has grown up in? I do not believe anyone could; and nether did I.

The driver of the car was already out and walking back toward me before I had set my hand break. Expecting him to ask me for a tire jack, I innocently greeted him with a noncommittal, "Hello. Need some help?"

Instead of a similar greeting, a hand came into the window and a commanding voice of authority addressed me.

"I am John Marchi, Special Agent of the Federal Bureau of Investigation! Here is my identification. Would you mind answering a couple of questions?"

To my surprise, he proceeded to explain why he was on this back county highway at 7:30 in the morning. It seems that, the day before, there had been a bank robbery in the little town of Cotati, California. He said he was on his way to Santa Rosa to work on the robbery and had noticed my old, tan, 1949 Plymouth Station Wagon as he passed it. Because the automobile used in the bank robbery was described as a brown, 1949 or '50, Plymouth Station Wagon, he had turned around and stopped me for questioning. The antic with his automobile was just to attract my attention and have me pull over for questioning.

"Where were you about 11:30 yesterday morning?" was the first question he asked me.

Unconcerned, I told him that I was probably on my way to the movie theater in Santa Rosa, or, because I was not sure of the time of my arrival, I might have even arrived there.

"Where did you start from?" he asked in a calm, professional manner.

I told him that I had started from Bodega Bay where I had been camping alone on a nearby beach for a couple of weeks.

He said that he was familiar with Bodega Bay, then mentioned that a license plate had been reported stolen in that area, and it was observed on the automobile that was involved in the bank robbery. He proceeded to the back of my car to see if I had changed license plates recently. He came back and informed me that the rust showed that the license plate had not been removed for some time, but I could have attached the stolen plate in such a way as not to disturb the old, rusted bolts on my license plate.

"When is the last time you shaved?" he asked.

I told him that I had shaved just before starting for the movie theater yesterday, after not shaving for the two weeks that I was camped at the beach.

"Do you ever wear contact lenses, and can you see without your glasses?" he asked.

I told him that I did wear contact lenses, but I did not have them with me because I had left them in Los Angeles as they were too much trouble to wear when you are camping out; and yes, I needed the heavy thick glasses I was wearing as I could not see without them.

"Do you have a handgun with you?" he cautiously asked.

"No, all I have is a pellet gun for shooting BBs."

"May I see it?" he asked.

"Certainly," I replied. Feeling that I had nothing to hide, I reached into the glove compartment and handed him the pellet gun, which looked exactly like a .22 automatic pistol when viewed from the rear. The only way you could tell the difference was if you were looking down the barrel, and then you could see by the small bore that only a BB could exit through it.

Then he told me that the gun in the holdup was described as a .22 caliber automatic pistol, and how some people might think my pellet gun was one, especially in the excitement of a robbery.

After I had opened the glove compartment to show him my pellet gun, I could see all the paraphernalia needed to clean and insert contact lenses into the eyes, plus an extra container to carry them in, but I knew the container was empty.

When I had time to think about our encounter, I concluded that it was not planned. The facts were undeniable: he was alone in his private automobile, he was without radio communication, and the questions he asked, the manner of his approach, all made me think that there must have been another plan; a plan by others that went completely amiss someway, somehow, somewhere. Those other planners did not, and could not, take into account what was about to happen on that lonely stretch of county road between the FBI agent and me. Also, the questions he asked enabled me to recreate, when I had the time, a possible explanation of what had gone wrong with the plans of that other group of people who had managed to intrude into my life without me even suspecting that they existed. This analyzing would give me important clues to predict the actions that someone had to carry out to have the knowledge that I wore contact lenses, but still not realize that I did not have them with me, and to think that I had a .22 automatic pistol when it was just a BB gun.

When John Marchi had shoved his FBI identification through the window and in front of my face, the first thought that entered my mind was that the FBI had found out about the internal security operation that I had been running from the Los Angeles area. As a consequence of some previous actions that I had participated in — an underground operation of a Marxist-Leninist political party — I unintentionally deluded myself into making some false assumptions. All the questions he subsequently asked, I thought, were being made-up for the sole purpose of having an excuse to question me. I firmly believed that I was to be brought to the local FBI office, and once there they could try to find out what knowledge I had about what had happened to certain people in the San Francisco and New York City area. Even if he had been competent, I do not believe that it would have changed anything. My mind was on something more serious than bank robbery. The death of two human beings, which I felt responsible for because of my actions, was my worry. I knew that if the FBI had found out about those deaths, that my former colleagues and I were going to be charged with conspiracy to commit murder.

Not satisfied with my answers, he asked if I would mind following him into Santa Rosa where we could have the time to straighten out a few things. I innocently agreed. You must remember that even when he was through questioning me, I still had the belief that the bank robbery story was a pretext. I assumed that the Southern California Office of the FBI had put out a description of my automobile stating that they wished to question me, and that was the reason he had stopped me. But when he began questioning me about a robbery, I jumped to the conclusion that they lacked enough evidence to issue a warrant to bring me to their nearest office for questioning; therefore, a bank robbery was being used as an excuse. Secure in my innocence, and knowing that they could not entice information from me about my activities down south, I agreed to follow him to his office in Santa Rosa.

Everything that was happening on the road into Santa Rosa led me to further believe that they just wanted to question me about what had happened down South. As we were going down the freeway, John Marchi was about 300 feet in front of me, and anytime I wished, I had the option of taking an off ramp (we passed at least 20 of them). By the time he turned his automobile around, I could have easily disappeared into one of the many side roads. It just did not seem sensible to me that If I was a suspected bank robber that he would have me following behind him. At the time, I presumed that if I were a true suspect when he stopped me, he would have locked up his car and had me drive him into Santa Rosa. If I were the bank robber, he would not have wanted to leave my automobile at the side of the roadway because there might have been evidence that could have, if someone had come along and broken into it, been lost. And if they had found evidence in my car that would link me to the bank robbery when they returned for it, I could claim it was put there when he was driving me to Santa Rosa. He also had another option: to wait for another automobile to come along, stop it, and have them call for assistance while he waited with me. And he was telling the truth when he said that he was driving his own automobile because he had no radio in it or he would have been able to call for help. In retrospect, I realized later that it was just plain sloppy police work that had led me into believing something that was not true.

The closer we came to Santa Rosa, the more confident I was that I was going to their office to be confronted with someone from down south. I told the FBI agent to go slowly as my station wagon was old and I did not want to push it over 40 miles an hour. It was too early in the morning to be held up by heavy traffic, so the few automobiles that were on the freeway, were passing us. A couple of cars even intervened between us, giving me even more chances to evade the FBI agent by going off an exit ramp, but I suspected that he might not be alone. When we had driven onto the freeway ramp, I watched behind me and noticed another car come up that ramp. It was the same late model automobile that I saw parked in the underpass where we entered the freeway. I observed it in my rear view mirror as it followed us all the way into Santa Rosa. It remained behind us although we were going only about 40 miles an hour.

Beguiled by my false assumptions, they left me no time to plan an escape when I finally realized what had occurred on that highway was not a created deception of the FBI agent, John Marchi.

NARRATIVE: THE GAME

To understand why I was deluded by what was going on around me, you should know that I am, and always have been, a game-playing person. On that day when I first met Lili on that San Francisco street, I understood the innocent game that she and her girl friend were playing. In my youth, I also played games that were innocent of motive. Now, I play adult games. I play games that entangle the mind in many contradictions, games that have hidden trap doors that open unexpectedly on well-traveled paths, games that have no winners or losers, and games in which the winners lose and the losers win.

As you will see, I have entered you into one of my games; a game that mimics one of those parties in which they call a person up at the last minute and tells them that they must come as they are, dressed or undressed. My goal is to catch some of you not without clothes, but intellectually naked. In this game, you will have my assurance that it will remain open-ended; a game that closely parallels life itself; a game in which I will try to give you the psychological tools to become civilized. However, this last statement has a shadowy existence; there is an ambiguity here, a contradiction here, because my view of a civilized person might be dubious. You see, I am a diagnosed schizophrenic which complicates the adult game we are playing. To ease your burden, we will begin with a question you should eventually answer: which is whether you will agree with the findings of several doctors that I am a schizophrenic, or go against the preponderant amount of evidence and find that the truth cannot be disguised by verbal labels tattooed upon the victimized. I believe I know the answer already, but then if I am a schizophrenic, what I believe might be just a compilation of illusions created by my illness.

I consider myself sane; not absolutely sane, you should understand, but reasonably sane; while I consider the world surrounding me completely and hopelessly mad. This does not preclude me asking, "Am I not also of this world?" Just because I cannot seem to find any way to divorce myself from this world that I inhabit, does that prevent me from acting sane in an insane world? It also brings up some fundamental questions: who will diagnose those who do the diagnosing; who decides what is abnormal until the norm is ascertained? What am I to think when I observe somebody yelling "Freedom!" yet my eyes see that person fastening chains on a fellow creature? Should I not ask myself, "Is this part of my illness; is my view of the world being obstructed by my sickness?" Perhaps the person shouting "Freedom!" means the freedom to shackle their fellow human beings? Has my diagnosed sickness distorted the true meaning of freedom? It seems, for some unexplained reason, that whenever my mind enters a fantasy state to explain these inconsistent observations, I continually find myself running through tunnels that have been excavated by rabbits. There I meet these strange inhabitants created by Lewis Carroll, who tell me that peace means war, that love means hate, that killing means life. When I argue with them, they say I do not understand; that I am mentally ill.

Then in a most condescending tone of voice, they tell me that it is a simple concept, that when they use words, those words mean just what they choose them to mean — neither more nor less.

These relationships between deeds and words do not appear to me to be stable; they keep cropping up in various disguises. When people pull off a mask exposing a false image, this deceptive image simply reappears under a new definition. This is why I am not sure whether the world is totally mad, or whether I have this aberration, this sickness that leads me to believe that the truth can only remain constant and cannot change with every single toss of a coin. I keep asking myself, "Is this world to remain an asylum forever?" These strange inhabitants in these rabbit tunnels keep telling me that I cannot go back to that simpler way of living, but could they be wrong? Are they just saying that to protect their interest as keepers of the asylum? If you retain a building plan in your mind, can you not also pass on that plan to others? Then what is to prevent them from taking those blueprints and rebuilding from those toppled structures of society something that would be closer to an architect's heart?

Sometimes I do perceive shapes and sounds differently from those around me, and this worries me. It leads me to believe that their diagnosis could be correct, that I might be truly mentally ill. Early in life I could see that our view of this world can be restricted by our language if we do not make a concerted effort to distinguish between descriptive words and the world that we are trying to describe with those words. For example, when we say that the sun rises or sets, it can prejudice our view of reality because it does neither. The earth spinning on its axis just gives a visual deception of a rising and setting sun. Until this was pointed out scientifically, it was not comprehended as a true condition, as a fact; we had to rely on our animal senses. Neither could a human being describing and acting on this false animal perception be faulted for the harmful results caused by this false view. I assume that you would not find fault if a prairie dog jumped into its burrow because it could not distinguish between a genuine hawk and a kite shaped like a hawk, for it is acting under instructions from its genes. There is no way that nature can encode reality (an authentic hawk) from perceived reality (a paper kite shaped like a hawk) in our genes. This forces human beings to use a language to pass on to others that some of their perceived reality is false. Still, if someone is informed: "It is just a paper hawk, being controlled with an unobserved string," can they be faulted if they ignore this information; then, acting on their animal perceptions, run through the streets warning of an approaching hawk? To find fault here, you need to condemn an animal because it acts like an animal, and this is just one contradiction that you must come to terms with while playing our game.

My present endeavor? I want to describe a factual world and not the illusions that surround us. So, In this game, the investment I ask of you is small, just a few hours of your time. If you can understand what I am going to try to convey to you, then you might be able to control a future that has a limited need of delusions.

Before language developed in *Homo sapiens*, natural selection was the major determining feature of who or what would survive to become the future. Since the development of language, we human beings have gone outside the limited corridors of natural selection and have intro- duced human selection into the equation. This gave *Homo sapiens* the ability to say who and what is to survive on this planet. Your survival can depend not only on your physical inheritance, but among other things, your race and culture and your religious or political beliefs. If you can accept this, then the truth might give you and your descendants a future without need of delusions; but you should be wary, because truth has no guarantee in reality either; all it can do is to give you a favorable percentage in the grandest game of all — life.

I have been intrigued by Science Fiction stories in which time travelers go back in time to the formation of life. Once there, one of them accidentally steps on and kills a direct link in human evolution, thereby changing the evolutionary characteristics of life and eliminating the human species. The flaw exposed here, is to explain the human time travelers if human beings did not evolve. Today we find historians in some countries duplicating these Science Fiction writers, trying to change the future by changing the past. They too keep ending up with unexplained time travelers (like Trotsky and Bukharin) in their history books.

When this story ends, you must ask yourself if I have also left one or more unexplained time travelers in this narration. If you cannot detect one, then you might be able to perceive if my description of what happened was accurate. If you find one or more, then you can legitimately find that I am truly mentally ill, and have just engaged you in a game that a schizophrenic might play. A game where I am trying to rearrange your mind to control the illusions in it, and later in the story, to manipulate your view of morality. A sense of balance, however, must inform you that the problem is that even the sane can and do play these games. Even the sane, at one time, believed the delusion caused by a rising and setting sun was true, believed in a sun driven across the sky by Gods. If you have no knowledge of gravity, then how else can you explain the movement of the sun without the use of a Supreme Being intervening in your explanation?

My present aberration? I want to explain to you that just like the natural law behind gravity, there is one behind morality; and by knowing about it you can excise your need for a supernatural explanation for it. We are going to explore and learn about a reality without the need of delusions. This is the true game we are playing.

CHAPTER 3

NARRATIVE: QUESTIONING

Concretely, who am I? Can one ever know the true person behind the mask that society demands we wear? I doubt it, because although at times I have universal thoughts, there are other times when they can be described as provincial. There are times when I feel that I am encompassed in a blowing grain of sand, and at other times the essences of me might feel constricted in a spinning galaxy. You have met me and will continue to meet me in many places, in many time periods, and hiding under many disguises. You would have recognized an emotional part of me in that Texas book tower, while another part of me on that faithful hour, was watching a rectangular box in California, just as the pale horse disguised as a lead missile approached from the East. Ignoring the untold number of pyramid workers who took their final bow on that November day of 1963, the spotlight handlers, during the next few months, focused their bright lights on that lone figure on stage, thus allowing me, in the far west, to get off another stage unseen, unnoticed, and to remain off that stage, hiding mentally and physically, until this recording day.

Having a clear, decisive relevance to life's game, you should know that if you ever meet me, I possess the ability to have you believe I am lying when I am telling the truth, and telling the truth when I am lying. If I declare the rules by which I play beforehand, I feel under no additional obligation to warn you further. Just know that this is not how I entertain myself in an insane world, but just a diversion, a ruse I use to try to obtain the hidden, the recessed, the primeval memories from you; yes, it is to help remove the mask that society demands we all wear. I assure you it is not done with malice, it is not done for spite, but for the reason given: the seeking of truth that might only be revealed when you put aside your protective covering. Consider: If in seclusion, when you remove your mask, you cannot recognize yourself, then how can you know me with my disguise in place? Also, be forewarned that as a writer I wear a mask underneath my mask to further confuse the unwary.

In this reality I was conceived, the third in a lineage of five, by a father who escaped from the Pennsylvania coal mines to become a copper miner, earning $30 a month in California, and by a mother who escaped from being the daughter of a cowboy who earned $30 a month, to become the wife of that copper miner. It turned out that my Lili was also a resident of this dimension. Like the rest of us, she had no control over her conception, so, when she was rewarded by being born into a family who were so prosperous that they were able to ignore the great depression of the 1920s and '30s, she could not be assigned a debt for her good fortune. Consequently, Lili's burden of a mother who had brought into the family marriage a fanatical belief that the Catholic Church was the foundation of modern civilization, could not be assumed to be in payment of an incurred debt.

The distance in age between Lili and me might have been seen as the main barrier between us, but there was a wider cultural gap that separated us than either our age or the short distance up from the San Francisco Peninsula. That latter separation was just in mileage, which could be overcome with the correct transportation. The cultural one was in the mind, and much more difficult to overcome. Love alone could not save us from that medieval moat that we had to cross to protect ourselves against Lili's parents. Their parental wrath was about to push us over that part of a corrugated society that could bruise forever the mind of an innocent such as my Lili. Even if she had those years of experience to catch up with me, she would not be able to bridge that gap that separated us, because she was encumbered by a burden that once assumed by a young person is difficult to ever put down.

I was released from that burden, a belief in a Supreme Being, early in life, and the last vestige of it went when the death camps in Germany, Japan, the Soviet Union, and in other countries, were laid before the altar of humanity by the Christian world as the result of a small mistake made by a Supreme Being. It seemed that their God had produced an angel with character defects that were not apparent at its formation; nor apparently, could the results and consequences of its formation be seen beforehand by its creator. Although the revelations of the death camps were later to be passed off as nations gone mad, I clearly saw and heard Americans bleat out their true feelings, which were no different from the nations that were supposed to have gone insane. To seek the truth here, we will later delve into these inconsistencies and see if they can be dovetailed into a single encompassing irony.

Because I never could reconcile a loving, caring God with the horrors of the concentration camps, the final demise of a personal God brought me a feeling of relief, a feeling of being freed from an imposed cultural burden. In the Christian Bible, we are confronted with a God that kills when It is displeased, One that is angry, that is vain, that brings, without distinguishing between them, the same plagues and disasters to the innocent and guilty. Much earlier, I had put behind me the belief in a vengeful God, in a jealous God, in a God full of anger, because I understood these were just emotions that human beings are heir to, and could not be attributes of a Supreme Being. I could never comprehend a small, petty God (described in *Numbers 15*) that could give an order through Moses to have a man stoned to death because he was gathering sticks on the Sabbath day. Surely a designer God that permits the murder of millions of innocent men, women, and children in concentration camps, either by Its presence or Its absence, cannot be assigned the task of determining morality. So, when the time came, I had no fear of putting down my disquieting cultural encumbrance.

I already knew by the early 1950s that if I had been born into an uninformed cannibalistic society, I much more likely would have adopted their beliefs without questioning them, than I would have adopted Christianity. (Cannibals raised in a closed cannibal environment cannot be blamed for their actions. They have no control over the supplied information, which form the beliefs that they act on. Therefore, if they unknowingly accepted false information that they have no way of verifying, how can they be held accountable for their harmful actions?) As an educated outside observer, I can see that cannibalism came about because of the way people view and try to interpret life without the benefit of scientific facts, but if I had been born and then raised in that culture, there would be no way for me to reject it. I would not have had the information that cannibals are simply a product of their society when cannibalism is institutionalized into a religious belief. For this argument, it is immaterial how they arrived at the idea that by eating a person — in fact, or symbolically in a wafer — the person doing the eating will receive some kind of benefit. It is enough to say that all cannibals will be handicapped (just as all religious believers are) by an adopted religion if they move out of the cultural environment that produced and disseminated it. They can never become civilized until they understand how the false ideas arrived and are reproduced in each generation. These religious persons can never do, always, what is good for the human race, because they will tend to make decisions for what is best for their selective religious beliefs, and that does not always coincide with what is best for the human race. A belief in a God or Goddess is always a regional and tribal belief, just as language and culture are; and this will ensure that all decisions will be regional and tribal. As a result, the religious person will have a restrictive view of the world. This analytical reasoning applies not only to all religions, but as you will see later, to all political beliefs as well. There are no exceptions.

I truly cannot say when I first realized that my mind was alien to the various cultures I lived in and came into contact with. It was difficult for me to admit that people do not care to be disturbed by proven facts that go against the preordained notions that were inserted into their minds when they were unable to reason because of their youth. It took years for me to learn that you do not flaunt knowledge in front of the ignorant, just as you do not display money in front of a thief. People do not want to give up their instilled program of hatred, their misinformation, their prejudices, or their fanatical belief that time spent making money confers a special dispensation toward qualifying the truth. These persons cannot accept that they do not have absolute control over what they learn, nor do they believe they can be manipulated without their consent. It is sad, but true, that prejudices are sometimes the only things that hold some people together mentally. Without them they could disintegrate in an acid bath of truth.

NARRATIVE: LILI AND I

Lili and I met about the time the coffee houses in San Francisco's North Beach area had begun to expand and draw the fad seekers who were curious about a group of people living without materialistic attachments. The poverty culture of the blacks, with their jive talk and hip ways, had already invaded the white slums; which in turn, because of the mass media focus, would spread it to the white middle class, who would read this propaganda and become fascinated by the seemingly unrestricted freedom and lack of restraints on the beatnik's way of life. To a middle class person restricted by a watch, calendar, and programmed time, the coffee house scene seemed to be a truly whimsical way to exist. These coffee houses were staged for the benefit of all the "Squares" who bought their admission tickets (a cup of coffee for $2) to watch life in another culture. When new coffee houses opened, there were not enough beatniks to go around, so they had to be manufactured to meet the demand of customers to see live beatniks at play. If you were poor and willing to enter into a hoax, by dressing up and acting the part you could get free coffee and sandwiches. For a short time Lili and I became participants in this little masquerade. The customers never did catch on that the same production company that had brought them the speakeasies in the 1920s, had staged, produced, and directed the coffee houses; so they remained ignorant to the end that it was a manufactured production they were seeing. To this day, I remain mystified by the way the news media were seductively able to make the dirt, squalor, and poverty of the slum dwellers exciting and romantic to the young from the middle class. This propaganda put out by the news media is one reason that Lili and her girl friend were lured to San Francisco. In retrospect, I could see that Lili heralded the coming of the middle class "Flower Children" to the Haight-Ashbury, bringing with them a fascination with the forbidden street life.

Why is a different culture so fascinating to our children? A partial explanation can be observed in the way nature requires us (like the other animals) to break from our parents at puberty. We are not taught why we look for a new culture, so, we do it without understanding that nature is behind it. If you were, like my Lili, taught by your religion that human beings are divorced from nature, how could you explain a natural break of the parental bond? Every culture that observes the young people, at puberty, dressing differently, adopting different music, different life styles, is horrified by their actions. How soon we forget our own puberty, our own rebellion, our own parental break.

The middle class white children on safari to the North Beach in San Francisco thought it was so easy to become a rootless, wandering beatnik. Just move into the slums, throw a mattress on the floor, wear old clothes, and then let hair grow upon your face if a male, or iron your hair straight if you were a female. The young girls and women were also expected to dispense loveless, guiltless sex to prove they were free and emancipated from society's morals; to show that they thought sex was just a natural biological function, not something to make a big fuss over. To give sex to affirm sexual liberation proved to be a cold existence to many. This culture tore apart the Romeo and Juliet syndrome, but had nothing to substitute for it; which, after its destruction, left a void in the relationships of the young.

The news media failed to inform the white middle class youngsters that the unbounded "street people" were on those streets to make a living. They were the front runners that only a harsh environment can produce. They were the natural selection of the slums where no compassion is shown toward the fragile. They were the ones culled out through the most rigorous grading sieve known to mankind since the original screening was done on those grassy plains adjacent to the old jungles. Only one born into and surviving in a poverty culture can understand that you must prepare yourself to enter a different culture as you would prepare yourself to make an expedition to Africa in the time of Stanley and Livingstone.

The unbounded "street people" saw the young people from a different culture descending on them as the farmer views fertile ground and its produce. They saw them as a resource to be exploited and used, as something to be eaten and digested, as something to be celebrated and enjoyed. Lured by the news media into what they thought was a better, freer way of living, the youth of another culture found they were exceedingly vulnerable when caught out of their environment. The slaughter of egos that was to take place in the 1967 "Summer of Love Festival" in San Francisco, turned out to be the modern version of the "Children's Crusades." You could discern that the middle class children were listening to the same melody that caused the crusading children to believe they were following the sound of a pure golden bell. However it was only the same Judas Bell, on the sheep in front of them, that they were following to the prepared slaughter ground, the ground that was to be named the "Haight-Ashbury." "Spare me the delight of those city lights" was to be the refrain after the slaughter. The survivors dispersed, usually in pairs, to the country, to small villages and towns in the foothills; they attached unflattering names to those they left behind, to those who had crushed their egos. Do not blame the "street people" because they made their kill just as other animals do — to survive; and they are just as free of guilt as a lion is when it kills to meet its needs. Remember: Strangers had invaded their territory, had contested their ground, so they set the rules; and those rules have always been that the invaders must pay the price when they lose.

Later, I was to lose many times, but I never cried because I knew the rules before I entered the game. I never contested the strong to be able to make those rules, what I have always contested was their presupposing that there was a moral right behind the force they used.

There are short periods of lucidity even in those who fall in love. "Phone home," I begged Lili. "Write," I pleaded. "Get in touch through friends," I urged. I could hear the first few notes of the cavalry's bugler in the background, and I knew the call was going to be charge. I also felt that I was going to be an Indian on foot in that coming scenario.

Many times in your life, when you find yourself in a situation that leaves you uneasy, all you can do is question yourself. If I had only been more insistent, if I had only done this instead of that, if I had not taken Lili to my room that day, what would have been my life's co-ordinates? I knew even then that you cannot change or move the starting line after you arrive at the finish line. Lili and I tried to steal a few weeks of getting high on life, but it seems that in most cultures, happiness is a commodity that has to be paid for. To our detriment, when the bill finally arrived, we could not plead that we had not received it or had not used the merchandise, as the reflection of love in our eyes betrayed us to the bill collectors when they arrive, unannounced, at our door.

ASSERTIONS

In this book, you may encounter what you consider miscellaneous and extraneous material. I use this method because it allows me to separate fictional and nonfictional material, to staple together the story line, to describe my former and present economic and political beliefs, and to justify (because of their incompatibility with nature, science and civilization) my rejection of all religions. The main story line will proceed without the need of you reading this material, but if your mind is not allowed to register the concepts included among them, then you will not have the knowledge of my credibility or the reasons behind my actions. A warning: Throughout this book, the majority of the quoted material is either paraphrased or simulated.

When a person questions a political or religious philosophy and the philosophers and theologians whose words are used to claim infallibility for those beliefs — especially when they claim to have ascertained the philosophy of life — what plausibility can you assign to those authors without knowing the other beliefs that were held by them at the same time they claimed through divine or historical intervention to know the truth about the philosophy they were expounding? You might better grasp what I am saying by examining some of the roots of Saint Augustine (354-430 C.E.), who was raised to believe in the Roman Gods, and later rejected them and adopted Christianity. Saint Augustine claimed, because of his adoption of a close, personal relationship with his Christian God, that he was immune from the errors he could observe in those who still clung to their old, imperfect beliefs. He believed he could perceive the divine intervention of his God into his personal life, and this allowed him to discern and advise the world on what is the true structure of reality. Fifteen hundred years later, some of his philosophy is still quoted by the Catholic theologians as germane to the present, and viewed by many Catholics as incontestable truth.

You should know that his God did not enlighten him by giving him knowledge that could transcend the past and be valid for all times. Saint Augustine believed the earth was flat and had four corners, believed it was the center of the universe, and that the sun, stars, and the moon revolved around a stationary, flat earth. He declared that heaven was directly overhead and hell directly below his feet. He asserted that the body was composed of four elements: earth, fire, water and air. He affirmed that creatures were born from inanimate things, that spontaneous generation was producing new life. He also believed in demons, which he thought were wicked angels controlled by the devil; and although he repudiated the art of divination when he joined the Catholic Church, he still believed:

> *That many things in the past and future are made known, and turn out just as they are foretold.*

However, he believed it was a pact between human beings and the devil that produced the results. He also believed that some numbers were exalted above others and had hidden meanings that could be ascertained by study; yes, he believed:

> *Many numbers and combination of numbers are used in the sacred writings, to convey instructions under figurative guise.*

His books are a compilation of these and many other superstitious errors too numerous to include here. All these false beliefs were just the common beliefs of his time, so we cannot fault him there; but if he claims that because of his belief in a Christian God, he can discern truth outside the boundaries of the common knowledge of the times, then these false beliefs of his will leave doubts about the validity of his writings and pronouncements on what is true and what is false. Especially, when there were a few persons, even in his day, who believed the earth was round and that there probably was land and people on the other side of it. He even had a friend named Nebridius who was more enlightened and gave him a more modern explanation about divination that even today with our advanced knowledge could be accepted; and that was:

> *That there was no such art whereby to foresee things to come, but that men's conjectures were a lottery, and out of many things, which they said would come to pass, some actually did, unaware to them who spoke it. They accidentally stumbled on it through their speaking so often on many subjects.*

At one time Saint Augustine leaned toward this explanation, but joining the church entangled him in and with the superstitious concepts of angels, demons, ghosts, and devils, and as a result, he was never able to extricate his mind from these entanglements and thus be able to explain the world without using them. I do not view this as a fault either, because he or anyone else cannot explain Christianity or other religions without conjuring up these desperately needed, insubstantial images.

Saint Augustine was not entirely unenlightened because by comparing the lives of twins with identical horoscopes, and using another example of comparing two unrelated persons born at the same time (one born into a slave family, and the other into a noble family), he proved that astrology was illogical and absolute nonsense. He believed that just because human beings had identical horoscopes, did not mean that their lives (when observed through life) would match.

Still, because his religious beliefs interfered, Saint Augustine categorically denied that Jesus plagiarized many words and passages that Christians consider sacred, from the books of Plato (427?-347 B.C.E.). He did not deny that they were in Plato's books, but speculated that Plato must have plagiarized them from a prophet of the Old Testament. Beginning with the destruction (by a Christian mob in 390 C.E.) of the great library at Alexandria, the Christians, enclaved in their monasteries, proceeded to gather, sort and revise or destroy all the manuscripts of antiquity they could gain access to that disputed or contradicted the Christian theology. Because the Catholic Church inherited Plato's manuscripts and made copies of them for a thousand years or more, to this day we do not know how much editing and revision they did on those manuscripts to exclude passages that exactly parallel the words of Jesus in the New Testament. We are left in doubt about how closely the manuscripts that survived reflect the original manuscripts of Plato.

Saint Augustine also castigated the people for their beliefs in the Roman Gods (which was correctly done); and showed by valid arguments that they were false Gods (also correct); and the belief in them in no way prevented the tragedies and misfortunes that the Roman Empire encountered in their present or previous history under the Roman Gods (also true). He also pointed out that these Roman Deities could not even protect the city of Troy from being destroyed by the Greeks who worshiped the same Gods, so how come they believed that Rome could be saved by them (a valid question)? But because of his beliefs, he could not comprehend that every true point used against the Roman Gods could be used to point out that the adoption of the Christian Faith would not alleviate the abuses he accused the Roman Deities of being unable to influence. Eventually, the millions and millions of Christians killed by others who believed in the same Supreme Being, was to expose his false belief that when the Christians came to power, they would not use "fire and sword" against others that believed the same as they did, as just another delusion. It would prove that a change of Gods did not and could not change the animal behavior of human beings; would prove that we are influenced more by our genes and environment than by a nonexisting concept.

This is why it is important for you to know my beliefs and understand how, why, and under what conditions those beliefs were formulated. I can assure you that they were not arrived at by accepting the cultural beliefs held by most Americans. I am not handicapped by the beliefs of the majority when viewing the past and present, and only the passing of time will tell if my interpretation of what controls and runs the "Grand Unified Engine" (that seems to be continually running in the background) is erroneous because of my present beliefs.

CHAPTER 4

NARRATIVE: ACCUSATIONS

After coming off a downtown exit ramp, I followed the automobile containing the FBI Agent, John Marchi, into the Santa Rosa Police Station. When I had arrived at the Roxy Theater the day before to see the movie *Elmer Gantry,* I had parked in the theater's parking lot, which was directly across the street from the theater. I had not, when I left there about fifteen hours before, taken particular notice that the police station's parking lot and the theater's parking lot were adjacent, and only separated by an open wire mesh fence. The two lots were wide open to pedestrian travel and were only separated from the sidewalk by a foot high curb. Anyone entering or leaving the back door of the police station or driving by the street could see all of the cars that were parked in both lots because the automobiles were not concealed.

Parking my car in the police station's parking lot this time, I calmly followed the pointed finger of John Marchi and entered the back door of the station. Once inside, the first inkling that my assessment of what was happening was totally wrong came when I was asked to empty my pockets of everything they contained onto a desk. John Marchi then proceeded to search me after first notifying the police officer on duty that he had a suspect in the Cotati Bank robbery. In emptying my pockets, I found that I still had, because I was wearing the same clothes, a ticket stub that I had received the day before at the theater. A little later, I called his attention to it when he was questioning me about my whereabouts the morning of the bank robbery. I told him about attending the movies and being parked in the theater's parking lot for about five hours. This jarred his memory that my car in the parking lot had been unattended for around thirty minutes, so he had a police officer sent out to guard against anyone removing evidence from it. What did not seem to enter anyone's mind, including mine, was that someone might want to plant evidence in it.

Trying to figure the exact time that I entered the theater, I told him that I believed that it would not be that difficult to determine as the usual procedure was for the ticket seller to start the day by recording the numbers of the first tickets sold, in each price category, on a prepared sheet of paper. This was a permanent record, and they could match my ticket number and find out that I was close to the first, if not the first person, to buy a ticket when the box office opened at 12:45P.M.. I could not correlate this time with the exact time of the bank robbery until I decided to write this book. My research in 1980, of the newspaper accounts of the robbery, showed that it had occurred at exactly 11:36A.M. As it only takes about ten or fifteen minutes on the freeway, there was ample time for the bank robber to shave, change his clothing, drive from Cotati to Santa Rosa and be at the box office by the time it opened. Because I told them that I was on the road to Santa Rosa from the beach at Bodega Bay, it would seem that I was without an alibi. With the information that I gave them about where I thought I was and the timetable of when the bank robbery occurred, they also thought that I did not have an alibi, and that allowed someone to act in a manner that was to be detrimental to me.

I was never sure who was doing the interrogation that followed my arrival at the police station because they had me in an office where faces kept changing as different people scurried in and out of it. Sometimes three or four were present, sometimes just a single person, and sometimes I was left all alone while they conferred out of my hearing. From their conversation, when they were close enough to hear, I was able to learn that they were searching my station wagon, which I had no fear of, and they were trying to get hold of the bank employees to see if they could identify me. This worried me as I knew the unreliability of witnesses under stress, and knew how law enforcement people were able to manipulate them. I do not know if they let me hear what they were saying as an interrogation tactic to elicit feedback from me, or if they were just trying to convince those around them that they had the right man. Whichever it was, it enabled me to make an assessment of my true chances of escaping from what I first thought was just an unlikely set of coincidences, but which was turning into a bizarre nightmare. Truthfully: I did not like my chances. I knew something was absurdly wrong, but could not get my mind to align what I knew into a coherent explanation. There were just too many coincidences pointing to me as the guilty person.

They debated how my BB gun could be mistaken for a .22 automatic pistol, and agreed that under stress it was possible. They had evidently found out that I did not have my contact lenses in that little container in my glove compartment, and were speculating if I still had them in my eyes. I, however, knew that the only pair I owned was with my things at my brother's house in Los Angeles. Although I have not used them for years, I still keep that lone pair to remind me that I was not hallucinating, that the facts I knew were concrete facts just as I remembered them.

I lost track of time, but I must have been at the police station for about two hours when I awoke to the movements of one of my interrogators as he entered the room where I had been left alone for a while. He came into the room and walked over to the water cooler and proceeded to take what I assumed were a couple of aspirin. Casually turning to me, he commented about how I must be under stress and wanted to know If I wanted a couple of his aspirin? I assured him that he had guessed correctly. He then handed me the pills and the water to drink them down with. From that point on things began to get confusing as passing time enabled my captors to slowly close all exits.

I do remember arguing about some of the conditions they wanted to impose in the line-up, and being searched again because they did not want me to have a chance to pass anything to the prisoners in that line-up. A lone police officer, evidently unknown to someone who was probably searching my automobile, even had me remove my shoes and socks, and checked them for contraband before I was allowed in the line-up. A half hour after taking the so-called aspirin, I felt myself becoming withdrawn. My eyes became very heavy and I found it increasingly difficult to keep them open. I could not keep my head upright and my speech began to blur. I knew what I wanted to say, but could not express myself in words. These abnormal actions were noticed by my questioners, and they became alarmed and called in the jail doctor. By the time he arrived, I was completely helpless. Although I could reason and hear everything that was said around me, I could not speak or communicate intelligently. When the doctor was examining me, someone kept asking him to check and make sure that I was not wearing contact lenses. That person seemed worried; only later would I be able to theorize why. I listened to the doctor explain that under stress, some persons are subject to a mental breakdown, and although he was not a psychiatrist, he did not feel that I was pretending. This sounded reasonable to me, except that I was not under that much stress because I knew I was innocent. Then someone mentioned to the doctor that after several hours of searching my station wagon they had just found the bank robbery money, about ten thousand dollars hidden in a large thermos jug that was partly filled with water. Even under the influence of the drug, I could hear them as they gathered tightly around me in the small interrogation room and, while ignoring my presence (which stuck me as odd behavior), speculated if someone had told me about finding the money, and perhaps that had caused me to break down.

Before that conversation, everything that had happened could have been a coincidence, but from that moment on I knew that I was being framed. I also realized the significance of those supposed aspirin. I had been drugged. The trap had been sprung, and there was no escape. Who? What? Where? Why? How? All these questions would have to wait, as I was in no condition at that time to speculate on them, let alone to try to solve them.

After some discussion of what to do with me, I was taken to a locked hospital room in the Sonoma County Hospital. There I was examined by another doctor whose opinion was that I was definitely faking, but thought it best that I remain there for the night. He told the police officers that he would give me a shot to relax me, and I would be fine after a night's rest.

The drug that I had already ingested in my system had a hypnotic effect. I understood commands and was able to carry them out, to the extent that it was easier to carry them out than to think of a good reason as to why I should not. Later I looked it up in medical books. There is a psychological state called "automatic obedience", and evidently the drug mimicked that state.

They had to remove my clothes to put me to bed as I was in no condition to do it. When someone removed my socks, I heard a surprised exclamation, "Look what I found in his sock! Some of the missing bank money." (Four hundred and eighty dollars in twenty dollar bills was reported in the newspaper.) Only that lone police officer who had searched me before the line-up and I, knew that there was no money in that sock before it was removed. Someone by a sleight of hand trick had planted and then produced that money; that someone in that cell was in a conspiracy to frame me.

By then, I was completely beyond being amazed. Allegorically, once a person has talked to a werewolf in Transylvania, then for that person, life has no further surprises. In that Santa Rosa Police Station I had met my symbolic werewolf. Consequently they could have pulled J. Edgar Hoover out of the other sock and I would not have been surprised.

There was just a light discussion among the persons who had crowded into the hospital's prison cell with me, about how I had managed to conceal the money through two searches and the need for better search procedures. Then I was injected with a drug, which must have reacted with the drug already in my body because I quickly passed into oblivion.

ESSAY: UNIFYING THOUGHTS

It has been noted that we live in a culture where we build in the flood-plains, then cry when the water covers our physical and mental structures that we build there. Not wanting to blame ourselves, we blame an unjust system, an unjust God or Goddess. It seems that the human brain is genetically limited in the information that it will accept. All information that contradicts its original acceptance, requires great effort by the recipients to realign their thinking. Human beings cannot be faulted here, because the cosmic irony is that we are all a product of our misperceptions of reality. We all have our cherished axioms; one of which is that most of us do not believe our thought processes is materialistic. To understand me, you should know the facts that allowed me to conclude that we need materialistic brain cells to hold the information that we use to think with.

If we all gather, store and process information the same way, then we are who we are because of the information we have accepted or rejected. Some insight will tell you that sight, sound and touch all produce minute electrical impulses that human beings utilize to read and write to their memories. If you recall the story of Helen Keller, you know that because she lacked the ability to see or hear, she was able to be taught a language and to express herself through touch alone. From this we can deduce that the electrical impulses received by the brain can all be programmed with a similar function, whether they come from one or a combination of the senses.

Scientists tell us that the human brain has approximately 100 billion brain cells, and they estimate that there are 100 trillion connections between neurons in it. Those who have studied the human brain have informed us that learning is to make a new physical synaptic connection in our brain, which is an actual, physical alignment of molecules. When we learn, our nerve cells sprout more branches and form new synapses. They tell us that thinking is not an abstract process separated from the body, that the mind is not independent of the brain, that you always need a live physical body for thought, because information in a biological system always has a materialistic form. We are informed that thinking causes a physical movement within the brain of electrically charged matter that can be measured. They also tell us that the conception of a number or a word cannot be implanted in a person's brain until such a physical connection is made and accepted by the individual.

Confined to numbers, where there is an agreement to their truth and arrangement, there is little conflict with reality. The trouble arises when we try to make a connection that does not agree with other connections. The average brain does not allow us to hold that 2+2=4 and also that 2+2=5, or we would have a brain unable to function correctly, and could conceivably lead to a person with a multiple personality. To avoid a result such as that, if we wish to implant a new connection over an older one, we must break the old connection and completely replace it with the other to avoid having ambiguous numbers with more than one possible meaning. We have the further problem that if we wish to say that 2+2=5, then it does not conform to other branch connections that we have made with the number "two." Therefore, we would have to rearrange all the other branch connections to conform to that new connection. Furthermore each branch broken also has branches that need realigning.

When we grow up, there is no reason for human beings to change the meaning of the number "two" or the connection 2+2=4 because they agree with our taught, structured reality. They are not ambiguous. But where human beings get into mental trouble is with the use of abstract words, because unlike numbers, these words can have more than one plausible meaning, and it is readily observed that two opposite and contradictory abstract connections can be held at the same time. Words like *Freedom*, *Liberty* and *Justice* have connections and branches just like numbers, but they have no universal, agreed meaning. We know that 2+2 does not equal 5, but words such as *Freedom* are abstract words and can be interpreted by different people as either 2+2=4 or 2+2=5; therefore there is no way to limit the word *Freedom* to a single meaning.

For most of us there will come a time when we want to change a definition of an abstract word such as *Justice* because it does not agree with our observed reality. However, just like changing numbers, we cannot just change the one word because it also has millions of branch connections that we must also change. Unlike the other animals that have no other choice than to depend on their genes for instructions, our use of language permits us at puberty to question connections that we made before we gained the ability to understand their implications. As young children, we are forced to accept many connections without reasoning. This is observed in all young primates, and was, and is needed for the survival of a species in a natural state, where unless they accept without questioning the information received from their genes, they will be at a disadvantage in surviving to become adults. These early connections in animals are later broken and replaced with new overriding connections by their genes when they reach puberty, because new information is needed to mate and make adult decisions. The remnants of this system can be observed in human beings today. When they reach puberty, young people will revolt and question their parents' teachings, and then form new branch connections by overriding those beliefs instilled by their earlier acceptance of ideas that were germane to early childhood, but which will not allow them to make adult decisions.

Just like numbers and abstract words, political and religious beliefs also cannot be broken by just one simple disconnection when a single philosophical statement or idea is proven true or false. That will be because these new, single ideas or statements are intertwined with other connections that were made and held over a period of years, and each of these connections has to be broken and realigned just to fit in this one new true or false concept. The crux of the problem is that for the majority there seems to be only a limited time at puberty to accomplish this overriding and get rid of our false connections so that we do not pass them on to the next generation; thereby hampering our future descendants with the possibility of false information that could prove fatal to them. If at puberty, we do embrace our parent's teachings in an uncritical manner, then we will, unless confronted by an astronomical contradiction that our senses cannot deny, have them throughout our lifetime. I have consistently found that while you can cite facts that prove you are correct in your argument, that you still cannot convert or sway your opponents over to your side. They are unable to break all the incorrect connections that were made. There is strong evidence that the older you get, and consequently the older the connections are, it goes from difficult to impossible to change a person's religious or political beliefs. Once we learn something (make a connection), our minds become less flexible; the more we use and reinforce the adopted information the harder it becomes to erase.

An example: In the 1970s, before metal bending was exposed as a fraud, Uri Geller, the magician, claimed his psychic abilities enabled him to bend and break metals by merely stroking the object. At the time, there was elation among the parapsychologists over the prospect of verifying this psychic feat, and thus proving to the world that their belief in ESP was true. Soon after this, in England, a horde of children also claimed this ability, and after observing many children performing this feat, author John Taylor wrote and published a book celebrating and extolling this common ability among children. Later, it was proven by watching and photographing the children through a one-way mirror that *every child* was cheating by bending the metal object when they thought that they were not under observation. This proof was ignored and had no affect on the beliefs of most parapsychologists. They continued to believe that metal bending was caused by a person's psychic ability. Using excuse after absurd excuse, they tried to explain away this reality of children cheating and making fools of the experimenter. It has been well documented that once the brain has been programmed with a set of beliefs, it loses the ability after that to be neutral in accepting facts that contradict its deep-seated beliefs. After a person has dedicated years to a study of a philosophy, that person's brain will not and cannot accept information that will contravene those beliefs. The brain can only accept facts that agree with its beliefs.

When examined, we find that our basic emotions, drives, and behaviors such as hunger, thirst, pleasure, pain, stress and sexual arousal are hard-wired connections in our brains, but do not think that I am also describing a hard-wired, deterministic fate for learning when we become adults. Further on you might come to agree with me that because of inequalities in our genes (we are not all created physically and mentally equal), that when some of us grow up, all is not completely lost. That for a few, no matter how ingrained a false connection is, those false beliefs can be changed during our lifetime if we are willing to look uncritically at information that contradicts our beliefs.

CHAPTER 5

NARRATIVE: TRIBULATIONS

Six weeks of time had eroded away while Lili and I gratified and explored our intuitive love. A love that I had no control over; a love whose outcome could not be preassigned by those dice of uncertainty which fate controls. Endlessly, fate rolls the dice, and all probable combinations of numbers will eventually be revealed by them. The last alignment of the dice had brought Lili's parents and a private detective knocking softly on our door. Opening it, I could distinctly hear in the background the words of Poe's Raven echoing from the past through that open door: "Your deeds are exposed for all to see; so your fate is sealed evermore; evermore."

Sentences; sentences; completely untranslatable to those who think in a different dialect.

"We understand our daughter is living here? ..."

"Oh my poor child! ..."

"Why didn't you get in touch with us? ..."

"Is there something we failed to do? ..."

"We don't blame you! ..."

"What are we going to do about this situation? ..."

"Are you in love? ..."

"You are not that way, are you? ..."

"Do you want to get married? ..."

"...a quiet wedding in the church; family only ..."

"...a house, a new car, a honeymoon trip to Europe ..."

"...connections in a brokerage firm; room for advancement ..."

"Did you know that she is only sixteen? ..."

"You know, we can have you arrested if you do not cooperate."

My assessment of what Lili's parents offered me: you cannot put on the trappings of wealth without becoming the guardians of those privileges. You only have to ask the few successful "Okies" who came to California during the Great Depression, how they now cast their votes after becoming the owners of the land on which they formerly groveled in when pleading for a chance to work. Ask them if they remember singing the Wobbly Songs, saluting President Roosevelt's WPA and NRA flags; and ask them why they are now so ardently waving the banners that they previously despised, and using the rhetoric of their former enemies.

Solitary moments were easy to come by as I wandered through the crumbling and disintegrating structures of society. I would take these moments and relive every experience, every hope, every dream that Lili and I shared. Lili's parents did not understand that if they had allowed the candle to burn, it would have gone slowly out, as time quenches all flames. However, to extinguish it before its time was to ensure that it would be remembered by Lili and me as a bright, clear flame that for a short time lit up our drab world. Separate two magnets and that attraction will lessen. Separate two human beings in love and their attraction will persist across the furthermost distances that can be perceived by the human mind. Only later was I to learn that after our forced separation, Lili was to embark on an incessant search for the light that she remembered so well, only to discard candle after candle because she could not ignite them in the heavy wind that societies continually produce to limit the light needed to dispel the shadows that surround us.

Most of my views on the environment had been influenced by the seven foreboding years I had lived with death; death that was so near and final. I was just twenty years old when in December of 1946, I was flown several thousand miles from the Admiralty Islands in the South Pacific to the Marine Hospital in San Francisco. My first night at the hospital was to lift that hidden shroud that surrounds us, to show me how close the ever-waiting, permanent darkness was. Lights on my tuberculosis ward were put out at nine o'clock; ten minutes later, a loud cry of, "Oh my God! I am hemorrhaging!" brought on the lights from individual bed lamps. They revealed a frightened face that was obviously unprepared for life's final journey. Within seconds a nurse was there with a wash basin to catch the blood, but a pitiful cry of, "Please! Help me," were the departing words of this patient as he fell back, lifeless, on his blood drenched pillow; fell back to dream no more. A life had ended because some microscopic bits of living matter had picked the wrong place to lodge and release their deadly acid. That acid had slowly etched away at the membrane of a blood vessel until a barely audible cough had broken a paper thin vessel, releasing a flood of unbreathable red fluid into his lungs. Who might we put on trial here? A bit of living matter; perhaps the acid that did etch; maybe the light cough that did rupture; or can we trace the fault, our frailties, back to that brew that first formed in the Alpha Sea? Every single living individual can trace his or her direct lineage back to that first molecule that formed in the Alpha Sea; every single living being is related to every single living organism. Might this be the assigned truth: that the guilty culprit is a chemical brew?

That person who had died that first night I arrived at the hospital was a young civilian construction worker, who was captured by the Japanese on Wake Island and spent the war years in a concentration camp in Japan. I do not even have a name to attach, let alone blame to place. His dreams and plans (all prisoners have them) went unrecorded, but his death is noted here. All his hopes and plans became naught in a few fleeting seconds of measured time. He was but a stranger to me, but how much more is the symbiotic pain when time allows you to watch and record and observe your comrades take that final trip, take that journey that needs no advance booking. Some of my friends eroded away slowly, and some, like the returned war prisoner whose story I would never fully know, would exit by spewing their bright red life forces into a gleaming, sterilized, stainless steel bowl.

After six years of hospitalization, I, too, was to find myself in the Hemorrhaging Room; a room that was reserved for the hospital patients whose departure was imminent. Telegrams were sent, telephone calls were made, and the family clan was gathered for a final good-bye before the body was released to the morgue. My body enclosed in an oxygen tent, and four quarts of whole blood dripping at the same time, into my arms and legs was what greeted my family. Nobody talked about it, but they surely knew that I understood what this all meant. The unlimited morphine injected into me, to make the passing easier, was the final clue that the hospital staff did not expect me to live through the night. The nurse looked surprised when I refused an injection of morphine. How could I explain to her that she should reserve it for the elderly who had lived their life, or for a child in pain; that I did not feel that I should go sedated and blissfully into that long night, but should go in pain and cursing and struggling, and angry at the fate that had dealt me a hand that only time would allow me to play correctly?

How did I survive that night? What alchemy did I master that could prolong existence? I will reveal this: I threw into that pot of life, tokens that I did not own, promissory notes that I could only repay if I lived, obligations that I could only pay off by a personal sacrifice and dedication, by a personal devotion to seeking the truth. And deep in the interior of my being, I also knew that if in my future I could influence just one person into becoming a civilized person, then my betting markers would be paid in full, and I could make that final journey (that we all must make) prepared and out of debt.

One year later, resurrected and proclaimed the miracle of the ninth floor, I walked out of the Marine Hospital in San Francisco. After seven years of confinement, I was cured of tuberculosis. In a period of six months, the abscessed holes in my lungs had closed and been covered over by concrete patches. Far from the blessed, the consecrated, the supposed healing waters of Lourdes, I had drunk the unblessed, the common, the ordinary tap water from the faucet, I had openly cursed, had openly challenged the close and ever-present darkness, and through it all I lived. The light from my candle remained lit, although, seemingly unprotected from the winds blowing from the East, the direction from which the pale horse of death is reputed to arrive to claim its prey. I firmly believed that my commitment to the truth would keep me alive until I repaid those borrowed chips, which I noticed had time stamped on them when I threw them into the pot of life. Some of it was to be hard times, some of it was to be brutal times, but most of it was to be reflective times. Whatever it was, it was all usable time, and I had only myself to blame if I had not used the gift correctly.

That is why I knew that I could not make my markers good by accepting the lures that Lili's parents dangled in front of me just five months after leaving the hospital.

ESSAY: DREAMS

One does not have to sleep to dream, as there are more vivid dreams that intrude upon those awake than were ever evoked by the restless night sleepers. Young people are sometimes beguiled by those dreams that persist and prevail; and sometimes they are wrecked on the shoals of society when their dreams become contagious and epidemic among them. Then the magnificent dreams of youth are turned into frightful caricatures by the imponderable circumstances that can arise to challenge all movements that try to change our parents' social order for one that would be more pleasing to the young. To give up a secure reality for a persistent dream of mankind is a prerogative of youth. It is a line we cross to establish the difference between the generation past and the "Now Generation." Young people do not believe it — and rightly so — when they are informed that the divisions that our ancestors made are the immutable and final divisions, and that you can be excommunicated from the established society if you try to question that division.

Life is transitory. It is of brief duration, compressing and shortening that time in which youth is allowed to dream. Life is incomprehensible to the young if they are not allowed to try to correct the mistakes of the past, not allowed the time to try to make a future for their descendants that are not ruled by the mistakes of the past.

To spend one's allotted youth at a Walden Pond while planning a new society, or on the French Riviera while planning next week's society dance is equal under nature's laws. Only a human being can weigh and judge the value of each. If you remember this, you will not spend needless time worrying about those who would falsely judge your actions because they can only judge you personally and not by some natural law. There will always be critics, and you will be criticized whether you spend your allotted time at the seashore making those sand castles that will be wiped out by the next high tide, or building castles on impregnable cliffs that nature, with its timeless force, will eventually destroy. It will make no difference in the scheme of nature's tapestry, which of these you attempt to build, as it is only the struggle as we go through life that counts. Nature can have no goals; only people have goals. These goals can be disappointing, but you will always have the satisfaction of remembering the struggle that nature demands of all those who hope to keep unbroken their chain of descent. Reflecting on this, I came to believe that youth should dive for shells of the Nautilus in frigid Arctic Waters; go waterless to the desert; fly with wings attached with wax. Because nature does not recognize triumphs or defeats, there is nothing to commemorate either. Reflect: If we do not engage in struggle, we are left with this yearning, this craving to achieve an objective, to fulfill by our actions an unperceived goal that must be accomplished in an unknown allotment of time. This unfilled yearning will be a heavy burden if, when you near the end of your journey, you can look back and see that you left no footprints, and so no one will ever know that you passed this way.

Therefore, as you make your way down different paths of life, playing the roles forced on you or assumed by you, set no snares or traps, and dismantle and expose those you stumble on so that those who follow you do not have to destroy to create new trails. Markers placed along trails and paths that you have examined and become familiar with will be useful and appreciated. I, myself would like to post the following lines from Catherine Hester's *Anonymous Designs*:

I dreamed that I deeply scratched my mark upon a rock;
Knowing that time, endless time, will devour it by erosion.
Although that rock, will eventually weather into sand
And flow into the sea,
I know that deep down in the bowels of the earth,

It would once again, in its endless cycle,
Become compressed into solid rock.
A rock that, in its time, will rise to the surface
So that someone else can carve their marks upon it.

I want to add that to those who strive to prominently chisel their mark on the largest boulder conceivable, be reminded that it, too, will eventually become sand and flow into the sea. However, if you have scratched "truth" on that rock, worry not for its destruction as there will always arise someone to carve the message afresh. Truth is eternal; it cannot be disguised under a different name, a different language, a different tongue. It will always be recognizable, and if there remains a future, someone will always be marking it, and someone will always be there to decipher it.

Meanwhile, remember me while my mark is still readable, as it is not easy to weigh mountains and measure the depths without a scale. But if you do forget, I will not worry because truth is a struggle that cannot be lost, even in defeat.

ESSAY: INTERRELATED THOUGHTS

For a thousand years the search went on for the Philosopher's Stone, which was supposed to transmute all base metals into silver or gold and produce the *elixir of life* which would give a universal cure for disease and prolong life indefinitely. The art of alchemy captivated and produced many learned and clever human beings who wasted their time, health, money, and energies in this vain pursuit; it produced quacks and charlatans who wrote hundreds of books on this subject, some of which even claimed success in this "Grand Hunt." Do not be hasty in your condemnation of this foolishness. The errors and foolish actions and conduct of our predecessors in the pursuit of truth, can never be uninstructive. Without that fruitless search, we might still have not stumbled into the age of science, or come so close to the true nature of the universe.

Today we know: when all the known elements are added together, they can be arranged into an astronomical amount of lottery combinations. Add sufficient time, and then an impersonal causal sequence, that we call chance, to reach the necessary combinations, and the possibility for its appearance was there. Consequently, life is proof that the correct combinations for life did happen. If, like me, you accept this simple, informal biological explanation that in the beginning life developed from a combination formed from the known elements, then because of this law of chance combinations, which is still in effect today and can be observed in a mathematical form, you should also be able to put aside a need for a Supreme Being to bring those elements together.

A scientific definition of life is a chemical combination that can consume other chemicals, uses these chemicals to grow, and then duplicate its form. Life needs duplication to survive; otherwise, all harmful elements or chemical combinations that might come in contact with a lone, newly-formed combination that produced life, would immediately eliminate it. Natural selection came about when there developed a chemical combination that was better able to compete for the limited amount of chemicals needed for duplication, thereby allowing the genetic material to multiply in competition with other patterns.

Every day, new scientific proof is being uncovered to show that complex life forms evolved from the lower forms of life. When scientists are able to trace specific genes back to the formation of bacteria, they observe that some gene combinations, once produced, are passed on to higher forms of life. The discovery that some bacteria have built-in magnets that they use to navigate with, started a search in larger animals to see if this would also explain their ability to migrate over long distances. These magnets were found not only in birds, but in other animals needing a navigational system. Other scientists have found in a single-celled alga, a visual system which is composed of the same pigments used in vision by human beings and other animals. This indicates that the pigments for vision have descended from some ancient single-cell life. These discoveries tend to show that we still have a few remnants of the first gene combinations ever produced, and from this we might speculate that a gene combination once produced in life, can lie dormant and recessed, but they are never completely lost. When that gene will help a life form to better adjust to its environment, then by natural selection it can resurface in that life form.

Life as we know it needs competition, yet is dependent on not entirely eliminating that competition. If you place an organism, alone, in a closed test tube — one that uses oxygen to survive and duplicate itself and that expels carbon dioxide as a waste product — it will eventually use up all the oxygen and suffocate in its waste product. Place another life form in that closed test tube with it — one that uses carbon dioxide to survive and duplicate itself and expels oxygen as a waste product — and you will reach an equilibrium where each is dependent on the other to sustain life. You have an intertwined ecosystem. From this we should grasp the simple explanation that this planet earth is just a large, closed test tube that mirrors life in a small test tube. Like life in a small test tube, it can be unbalanced. It takes longer, it is true, but the finality is that it can be done.

This still implies though that life is just an aimless game where the seedpods produce more of their kind until they come to the physical boundaries that exist on earth. Then they are either exterminated by competition, or they learn to live in harmony in a balanced ecosystem. For millions and millions of years, life had no choice or control over its destiny. It was a lottery of uncertainty. This all remained true until natural selection introduced the new equation of a seedpod able to examine its singularity. Some of these examining seedpods found out that they did carry within their bodies this programmed genetic material, a material aimlessly plying an endless ocean of reproduction. An assumption might be made that just the act of recognizing this fact can give an advantage in natural selection. In this new game, persons who recognize they are just seedpods, can know that they were forced, by natural limits from the past game, to play the game with animal genes that were molded when most of the information was carried and passed down to the next generation in the genetic material of genes. By recognizing these limits, those persons that acknowledge this can gain an advantage, because they have the ability to organize a compatible system that does not intrude on those natural limits.

All living organisms have a biological clock which is used to detect and measure what is physically going on around them. If you ship a dwarf fruit tree in a container from Australia to the Northern Hemisphere, where they have winter when we have summer, the tree will acclimatize to its surroundings. In its new home, the tree will not go dormant in the summertime because it is winter in Australia. It is attuned to nature; it detects its new environment. A fruit tree can sense that it is the longest day and shortest night by the amount of stimulation on its light receptor cells, but it cannot know when the Fourth of July arrives because it cannot comprehend human abstractions. Through cells composed of concrete chemicals a fruit tree can perceive time and release other chemicals that tell it that it is time to put out leaves and blossoms, but the cells cannot tell a fruit tree to produce blossoms on the first day of spring because this is a human, abstract measurement that needs an outside source to determine, and the tree is limited to internal, concrete measurements. What we are examining is just the chemicals in the tree's cells reacting to an environmental stimulus, thus causing them to excite other cells into producing other chemical substances that perform a certain function. It is always concrete things (chemicals) that are measuring a concrete environment (electromagnetic radiation, motion of electrons, and so forth). A tree's perception is always chemicals controlling chemicals; its perceptions are always physical where each chemical combination is limited to performing a set function. In a fruit tree, when the environment tells it to put out leaves and blossoms, these chemicals cannot make a conscious decision to not produce the substance that tells a tree to put out leaves and blossoms. The biological clock in animals (including the human animal) is also restricted and confined to chemicals, in reaction to the environment, telling chemicals what to do. When human beings control their environment, and then observe the reaction of other human beings to it, then they can, with the correct interpretation, gain some understanding and control over their biological clocks.

The transformation of human beings from an animal existence into a complicated culture could not have come about without language. Before language we had to depend on our genes to pass on information to the next generation. Human beings can change the physical attributes of a fruit fly by tampering with the fruit fly's genes, and that change can be passed on to the next generation, but we cannot manipulate the mental behavior pattern of animals and have them pass abstract ideas on to the next generation, because they need language to do that. The problem here is that the gene information can only be passed on by the production and release of chemicals inside the body of animals, and this precludes passing on abstract ideas because chemicals are comprised of concrete matter that does not feel. It takes language to pass on information about spiritual beliefs, and all ideas that you cannot physically measure.

We can trap a wild coyote, and through aversion training make it fear sheep, and release it back to the range, but there is no way that it can pass on this aversion to its descendants through its genes. Even if it could pass on this artificial information, this abstract idea, it would be harmful because a source of food would be denied those descendants. They would then be handicapped when in competition with other coyotes that did not have this aversion training.

We can also take an animal caged in a zoo and through physical restraints prevent it from mating with another member of its species until a specified time after the female comes into heat, but it would have to be controlled physically by a human being because only our species can conceive of future and past time as a measurement. This is caused by time being a nonmaterial concept, and needing a person to define it through language. Gene information has to be passed through the physical structure of the body to be of use to the recipient. This information cannot be vague, obscure, scrambled or jumbled, and it surely cannot be unintelligible or incomprehensible to the user. Theoretically, by using our senses of observation, gene information can be logically explained, interpreted, and decoded by language.

Being a thinking human being, I had consciously protected Lili, when she was living with me, against becoming pregnant, and told her father that when he (who I could see was embarrassed by the question) shoved me into a corner of the room and keeping his voice low asked me if I had protected her. After Lili reached home, she was dragged off to the family doctor to make sure that she was not pregnant. When the test came back, this put her mother's mind at rest, but she was unable to tell Lili which was the worse sin: intercourse without marriage or the use of contraceptions to block a pregnancy.

The problem they did not want to face was that genes cannot instill morality. A simian male knows when a female produces an egg ready to be fertilized because it produces a chemical change that can be detected by the male; but genes cannot tell the male animal to wait, when a female comes into heat, until a specified birthday. The gene has no way of encoding that information because it has no perception of historical time, no perception of birthdays, no perception of life, liberty or the pursuit of happiness, or of other nonmaterial concepts. It can only pass on specific, coded information to the physical structure of the living.

If an act is widely dispersed, and if it persists in our genes, then it must have an advantage in natural selection. Human beings can make laws to punish males for mating with underage females, but should accept that information implanted in the genes sometimes is a greater compeller than the law is a deterrent.

You readers will have to make your own determination of whether the above could be just a rationalization by me to the charge of statutory rape. However, you should also know that I feel reality must always be expressed truthfully by a writer; that an approval or disapproval of reality can only be a culturally biased statement on my part, and will not change or influence it.

CHAPTER 6

NARRATIVE: COVERT OPERATIONS

Different outlines are formed on city sidewalks during the day, than by those who cast their shadows upon them under artificial light. To the observant, the changing of the shapes, forms, and patterns is just as apparent as different breeds of cat are to those who judge those events.

It was the summer of 1960 when an underground party member, whom I had sent to San Francisco, came back to report on his activities. He informed me that he had inadvertently found out that a person who we had exposed as an informer had died in a car accident. He jokingly remarked, "If this happened enough times, I would begin to think that there might be a God after all."

I immediately felt uneasy about that accident, as I do not believe a spiritual avenger is out there "tramping out the grapes of wrath." So the next time I sent a co-worker (who did not know of the other accident) to New York, I had her investigate the present location of those we had exposed in that area. I was emotionally bewildered when she reported that another person, who we had exposed back there, had died in a similar accident. After mentally debating what I should do, I decided to confront those who I believed were responsible for the accidents by typing up a report stating my views and expressing my disapproval for their actions if the accusations were true. Although I addressed the report to my only underground contact, I intended for him to give it to the elected leadership to see what their response was.

When I handed my contact the written report and query, I turned my back and slowly walked away. If I had stayed to explain my actions in person, I knew that I could not have trusted myself to act in a rational manner. Two and a half years of my life had been sacrificed to prove —

to a person I had thought was in charge of the underground operation —
that I was not one of those who came into the Party to betray it from within.
The same amount of time spent in the Los Angeles area, had gone into
learning to expose those who had became and who would become a
member, so as to betray us from inside the Party's structure.

I mentally felt like a thinking grain of sand wondering about its future
relationship with other grains of sand that it could see being washed away
from an eroding beach. Some of the grains of sand would surely find other
beaches, but what would become of me? Was it my destiny to end up in
an ocean trench, to be covered, grain by grain, and never see the bright
sunshine again? This gloomy mental reflection came about through the
discovery that the bright sunshine of mutual goals, efforts, conduct, and
morality had, for me, become overcast with dark connotations. The
knowledge that I had been misled, hurt. It hurt like hell! Sadly, I came to
realized that there was a good chance that those responsible for the death
of those two infiltrators would be sent to stage another accidental death.
One that would incorporate me as the victim. Death had been an intimate
companion that had attended me on a slow, seven year stroll through the
corridors of the tuberculosis sanatoriums in Fort Stanton, New Mexico
and San Francisco, California, so death held no fear for me. Time would
show me that that expectation was not to be realized, that my punishment
was not to have an assassin hand me one of the short straws of life.

There were no copies saved of my written criticism, so this is a partial
paraphrasing of what I handed him that day, and some of my thoughts as
I was writing it. It also includes some beliefs and some conclusions that
I had not included in the original because they had not crystallized in my
mind at that time. Because of the many complications that implicated
innocent people in my entanglement, I have tried — without compromis-
ing those innocent persons involved with me — to duplicate my words as
coherently as I could. An important thing to know is that I deliberately
handed my contact with the Party's elected leadership, a carbon copy of
my complaints, and that was the only copy I had. I did this so my contact
had no way of knowing if I had kept the original or had given it to someone
else to keep. To protect the people working with me and myself, I had
immediately destroyed the original document when I had completed it.
Later in this narration, you might find this as a further indication of a
paranoid personality, but you should eventually find that it was a justified
action which probably protected me from the earlier mentioned dissolu-
tioners.

The document that I handed him in the summer of 1960 began:
Comrade?

Yes, the question mark is deliberately placed there because I find myself unable, after five years of a clandestine alliance, to know how to address you. This turning point in our relationship has come about because of my accidentally finding out what has happened to two former members that I exposed as infiltrators from right-wing organizations.

When I joined the underground of the Party, I fully understood the need of devising methods of exposing those who would be sent in from the FBI, the CIA, the Communist Party, and from the ultra right organizations; especially these last two groups, as they would come into the Party to destroy it with dissension. You know the method used to establish that I was to be trusted at the highest level of our organization to fight these groups, because I received my clearance directly through you.

I still remember the day I first met you. It was in Golden Gate Park in San Francisco, and it was Comrade Z who brought me to see you.

"There he is, the one sitting on the bench near the children's slide. He is waiting for you. This is far as I go," were Z's words.

"Will he know me?" I asked hesitantly.

"Yes, he knows I was to bring you. He knows me, that is sufficient."

So few words spoken, but the change in my life was to be enormous. I thought my arrival at the park bench was to usher in my rise from being a lowly pyramid worker to an exalted position of telling someone else how to shape and place each individual stone. Instead I found myself recruited for a puppet show that was to extend five years into the future. In all my dealings with you, I was made to feel I had asked for those strings, so adroitly attached and pulled, that made me perform for you. Manipulated by you? Yes, of course, I was. My excuse: a young person who believes in a better system of government, as I did and still do, is malleable material for molding and manipulation into a form more beneficial to those who claim to be the designers of new structures.

You did not tell me about the other underground then. You only hinted that there were hidden rooms in the structure that did not appear in the plans that the ordinary cadre was shown. When recruited, I knew that there was a small underground element, but thought that it extended in the direction pointed out by the person who had recruited me into the Party. Later, I deduced that the hidden room was added by another group so that they could isolate the leadership from disclosing methods used to protect the Party's internal structure from infiltration by its enemies. Until recent events cast some doubts on it, I have, for the last five years, been going on that assumption. So when I joined the underground, I obeyed your requests, your suggestions, and your orders under the assumption that I was dealing with the known elective leadership through you, the leadership that was responsible for the protection of the underground activities.

I can still remember your words at that first meeting in Golden Gate

Park. They were, "We know what you have been doing, and have set up this encounter to find out your motives for your actions; actions that could do great harm to the Party. We have been following you for several weeks as I was suspicious of where you obtained the money that you were donating. We at first suspected that you might be a plant; but some of your observed actions do not coincide with the actions of a provocateur; nor does your life-style suggest that you are personally profiting by your actions."

As you know, I confessed everything. I admitted, after our long discussion, that an individual stealing and robbing for funds for the Party was not only committing an irresponsible act but a needless one. Finally, I agreed with you that a revolution would happen regardless of how much money we had to spend on organizing and recruitment. I could only plead youthful ignorance; which was the truth. After listening to my confession, you advised me to resign from the Party to protect it, but not to mention the reason or our confrontation. You then arranged to have further meetings with me to see if you could use me in some conventional way. You claimed, at that time, that you admired my determination to help, but thought that I needed to work under a disciplined person.

Remember our third meeting, where you told me that you agonized about even asking me to perform an act that you yourself would not do; but the officials above you insisted that I prove myself; so you asked me to do it? You told me that I should go to the police and confess to all the robberies and burglaries that I had committed to obtain money to give to the Party, but not to tell them my motives or to implicate the Party or even admit that I had belonged to it. When I had agreed to quit stealing and robbing after our first confrontation, and because of my method of operation (I worked alone and had no contact with known thieves), you and I agreed that the authorities had a meager chance of discovering my past indiscretions if I had truly stopped. I realized that by accepting your terms and taking on the social burden of a convict, I would forever cut myself off from a world that I despised and disavowed, but a world that I felt I might succumb to if I did not build an unforgivable social gorge to separate myself from it. (I had just had an offer from Lili's parents that I almost accepted; and that worried me.)

For two and a half years, your last words echoed off the Folsom Prison walls: "Trust me; you will not be wasting your time if you accept this verification. Then, when you are released, we will have complete faith in what you say, and we will have a place for you in our underground. Think of yourself as a political prisoner when you serve your time, but do not espouse socialism while you are behind those bars, because we want those who might be assigned to watching you, to completely lose sight of you by the time you are ready to be released. Learn how to hide underground by finding out from your fellow prisoners how they evaded the law when on the run. Learn the interrogation methods used against them, learn how they blended with their background, how they obtain counterfeit identification, and how to enter protected areas. Try to learn all the methods you can of living underground, because we need programs and someone to set up those programs if a fascistic government gains control of the United States."

I do not know if your group had hoped that the sacrifices I made would forever bind me to the Party and obligate me to perform duties that were against my moral and ethical senses. If you and the underground you represent thought this, then I want to assure you that those years I spent to prove myself do not hinder me from speaking out.

I cannot speak for you, but I did not want to make the same futile mistake of blind loyalty that could be observed in the purge trials inside the Russian Communist Party in the 1930s and '40s. Some of those purged members had devoted their entire adult lives to the Party, and their payment was the contention of Stalin's torturers that it was better to accept the false accusations of their Party than to split it with dissension. It produced the tragic scene of old Communist members not yet accused by Stalin, desperately clinging to Party discipline to try to find some reason, some meaning, instead of admitting that the Communist Party should be subservient to the Party members. It took me many years of analytical reasoning to not feel sorry for those discards of history. Professed carnivores cannot ask the historians to pass judgment on other carnivores who viewed them as meat, and proceeded to devour them using the same laws they helped pass to control other carnivores. If you espouse no morality, then you cannot ask to be judged by morality.

It was these old Communist members who claimed that there were no rules; that they would not be hampered by rules, laws, and moralities created my the bourgeoisie. They did not understand that these were rules, laws, and moralities made by men and women for the protection of all human beings, and were not freely handed down from the ruling classes, but obtained over and over again in struggle against all ruling classes. They cannot be circumscribed as bourgeoisie or religious rights, but must be seen as human rights that were meant to apply to all human beings. So the old Communist Party members renounced the protection of traditional structures and gave their lives into the hands of those who thought the same as they did. We know the results. This came about because the statement: "What you sow, is what you reap," is observed wisdom. Just because a passage like this is sometimes found in a religious context, it does not make it false. This observation, and many like it, has nothing to do with Gods or Goddesses or the religious belief of the human beings who wrote them. It has to do with observation of human actions, and then observing the good or bad results of those actions. It is profound reasoning for a political party or government to adopt a morality of not becoming involved in political murder, because once they condone the killing of another person for an imposed reason, then anybody who shares their belief is endangered of being killed by another person or group for their reasons. All the acts of violence you advocate give another person or group the same right to use them against you. You can, the same as those old Russian Communist Party members, become your own executioner.

When I came out of Folsom Prison and joined the underground, I truly understood the reason for secrecy and the isolation of each individual from each other in a cell, with only the knowledge needed to accomplish the goal or carry out an assignment. The greatest fault that had arisen is that communication was a one-way affair, so I had no knowledge of what was being done with the information that I was delivering to you. Although I had to prove my reliability, you and those who you were reporting to were not cleared. The factual truth is that I did not know the names of the underground leaders, as I have always reported to you. I think that was a basic mistake. I was surprised when I found out that I was not trusted completely when I suggested that I should investigate and clear all top underground Party officials, first. I was informed by you that they believed they were above suspicion. But from their actions in this matter, I now believe they were infiltrated by some extremists who are taking the same road that the Stalinists took, and that they are responsible for what happened to those two exposed infiltrators.

Were all our clandestine operations necessary? You know when we discussed it that I thought we were too cautious. We agreed that our main work would be to educate the cadre so they would lead the people in the right direction, and to counter the propaganda hurled against us so we could educate the workers to the true benefits they would derive from socialism.

Did we have secrets to protect? Yes, and that was our membership list of people who had joined us but wished to remain outside the Party's structure because of harassment received by those persons belonging to a leftist organization; especially, if they had a government-derived or supported occupation. When I had joined the Party, you had already started a practice that tried to protect these members. That was by having the person who recruited them and one other trusted person knowing who they were and keeping in contact with them. This narrowed down the possibility of exposure, but could not guarantee against it. However, for the main membership list, there is no way in our modern technical society to assemble and keep a membership list secret if somebody, such as the United States Government or a far right organization, has the money and time to unearth it. This we agreed on at the time we discussed it.

What we in the underground had to do, while waiting for one or more of the contradictions of capitalism to arrive and make the common people into radicals, was to keep out infiltrators so they would not damage the internal integrity of the Party's structure, and prepare for all members to go underground if the "Ultra Right" seized control of the government. Even here, we both agreed that it was the height of arrogance and snobbery for us to believe that our destruction or some other political party's destruction would stop a revolution, or, for that matter, was even needed for a revolution to happen.

Early in our search to unmask infiltrators, I tried, as you well know, direct access to the suspects' living spaces when they were absent from it by internal orders. This was a complete failure as we were not working here with spies, in the sense of what we think of as foreign spies, with all the paraphernalia they would need to carry out their assignment. And the right-wing and fascist literature could be there because we believed in studying our enemies to keep abreast of what they were up to so that we could have the time to try to counter that danger in advance. These infiltrators did not even need a secret drop for their information; all they would need was a telephone number to call or a post office box to mail in their reports, and either one could be concealed in the mind.

I remember my recruiter telling me about two Communist provocateurs who came to the leadership and admitted that they were sent into our Party to spy and create dissension among the members, and that when they found out that what they were told about our political motives and actions were not true, they repented and were going to quit the Communist Party. They wanted to know if we would accept them, knowing as we did that they were sent in to spy and disrupt us. Of course they were accepted. With this experience, when I entered the underground, you put me in touch with an FBI informant who had gone through the same transformation. She gave me valuable information about what the FBI was seeking and how she was reporting it; thereby allowing us to set up our countermeasures that brought our first success. Considering this knowledge, I came to believe that it would do no harm to let those I exposed to you, remain in the Party until they became a direct threat. I thought this was your belief too. We knew that no matter how many we exposed, they would keep sending people to spy, but if they did not rise to the leadership or introduce policies that would endanger the Party, we could have taken advantage of them because of their wish to please and convince us that they were true believers. Then there was the possibility that some of them would have become true believers and come and confessed that they were spying, which would have been to our advantage.

As you well know, exposure is a slow procedure. When we finally found their weak link, things went much faster; still, because of time and financial reasons, it remained a slow method. In my two and a half years of working on the problem, my cell members and I were only able to expose five people as infiltrators and clear about fifteen. That was the total from the east and west coast, and why, early on, we deduced that because of our limited time and resources, they could send spies in much faster than we could unmask them.

As a professed atheist, I do not believe in a heaven or hell; so I believe death is final. Those with religious beliefs think they adopt different standards than an atheist. They contend that their religious belief is fixed and immutable, but they find they are living in a world where everything around them is constantly changing, so they can never reconcile their beliefs with the world they live in, nor can they make the changes that are needed in a world that mutates before their eyes. Because of their beliefs, their minds must deny that what they see is what is happening, whereas an atheist knows that all standards accepted by human beings were made by human beings; and that future standards will also be made by human beings. Knowing this, they can always change the value systems to meet the needs of the people. This is denied to those who believe an ethical code is forever fixed, and is imposed from an outside source.

Atheism will always arise in a world that evolves to the point that it produces thinking pods. However, the proof of this can probably only come about if or when we come in contact with aliens from another solar system. If we ever meet this species from space, the religion of these space travelers will have been, in the early stage of their civilizations, as varied as those we have had on earth, but because they will have to pass through a scientific era to produce space travel, they will have always arrived at the truth of atheism. Until we do meet a different intelligent life form to prove this statement, atheism will remain a belief in competition with other beliefs.

Atheists do act differently. They know life is the first and last chapter combined, know that a human being is just a specialized mammal, but an animal that can transcend and reach a higher code of ethics than can be imposed on us by our animal genes; know that they can reach this plateau without the trappings of religion. Some even understand that atheism is not regional, is not national, is not even earthly, but is universal. It is pure reasoning. It will remain a constant in the universe, and in time will transcend and incorporate all religious teachings and beliefs that are valid and true, thus outlasting all religions.

Still, a look at history will show that to become an atheist does not guarantee that you will become a civilized person. Most of them through history have also participated in the same uncivilized acts that religious believers are heir to. Atheism does not obliterate our animal behavior; it does not alone raise us above the condition of the brutes. To deny religion and become an atheist is not sufficient; one must also adopt moral principles.

Civilization is not factories, automobiles, or the ability to send rockets to the moon, but is an ethical code that a person assumes. Ethical codes are adopted by some atheists even when they know that they will not be rewarded or punished in a future life for accepting them. They understand that nature is always neutral and does not have the knowledge of good or evil, so nature cannot judge in that sense. An atheist can become a moral person without the rewards or punishments that religions promise them. In the finality of it all, we will judge each other because that judgment is the only number represented on the wheel.

It follows that governments are also subject to the judgment of individuals. If a government informs its prisoners, "We are going to execute you for breaking our laws that have been promulgated and enforced for thousands of years," it is following a natural law. But if under different circumstances the prisoners become the victors and the jailers, then they have as much right to condemn you to death under laws that were made up after they had you in captivity. This is attributable to the fact that there is no Supreme Being, so the victors will decide and determine what justice means. All systems of government are equal under nature. If you have internal laws saying that you do not kill or torture prisoners, but lose to a group that does kill and torture their prisoners, then it is still all right for them to do it under the natural law that the winners make the laws. Philosophically, you, by your human declaration of, "We do not murder or torture prisoners," have set up a standard; you have promulgated a law made by human beings to try to define what is civilized or uncivilized conduct. By this act, you have introduced morality into the world. Understand: This conduct is not binding on nature because nature is always neutral, and only after the battle can one perceive whose side it is on. You will find out that nature is always on the side of the living, on the side of the survivors, on the side of the victors.

All true information can help you to survive and gives you an advantage over those who act on false premises; but a false belief held by others can lead to and be the cause of your premature death. An example: Hitler and the German society believed that the Jews were an inferior race and were responsible for the economic problems in Germany. It can be proven that these were false beliefs, but this will not change the fact that millions of people died because of those false beliefs. The only control you have is to see that all false beliefs are exposed and abolished from the mind, before they cause harm.

The Jews also had a false belief that contributed to their destruction in Europe, to their deaths, and that was a belief in a nonexistent God who had chosen them as the chosen people. This was what set them apart from most of the population, set them apart from the majority that is always willing to blame a minority for their problems, that will readily accept the most outrageous false claims against a minority. But the greater fault was that the Jews in Germany had taught their children to obey the law, to obey it even if they thought it was wrong. They did not teach them to distinguish between good laws and oppressive laws — a human distinction made by thinking human beings. The cost: millions of lives to pay for this false belief that human beings could not distinguish between good law and bad law; that only outlaws broke the law. Thus they had to obey a bad law regardless of the cost. In contrast, an atheist can adapt to the world better than someone who limits their actions by holding a false belief that they cannot take an action to solve a problem because that action is usurped, and so therefore denied them by a Supreme Being. Another debilitating effect of religion is that the believers do not believe that they can be on the losing side, while most atheists know better.

We humanistic atheists are not simply do-gooders. We are not exhibiting altruistic genes when we fight for a better world. We are realists. Some of us are Darwin Historians, and we know that we have selfish motives when we fight to end the death penalty for prisoners, to stop the torture of prisoners, or to eliminate the assassinations of those who do not agree with us. We fight because we know that often in the short time that nature allots to us, we will be on the losing side, so we need the protection of morality. We know: if we allow an act of injustice to be used against another person, then it can be used against us at another place, at another time.

Some persons with religious beliefs can and do use their beliefs as an excuse to torture, to kill, to assassinate. And just because I can prove to others and myself that it is false reasoning, descending from a false belief that was instilled in them before they were able to reject it as false, does not invalidate that they have an excuse, a reason to believe that they are doing something that will please their Supreme Being. "Forgive them, for they know not what they do," is applicable here. Just like the evil perpetrated under the banner of the "Inquisition," they kill and torture, not knowing that there is no devil, no evil one to prod them, no vengeful God to sanction their worthless acts of cruelty. But you my former comrade, you as an atheist know there is no Supreme Being, no evil forces commanding you, so with this knowledge you are denied this excuse for what you did to those exposed by me. You took the wrong path here, and these are the paths that can diverge until one's moralities can become fragmented and useless, so this precludes me from following your leadership anymore. I do not want to be governed by a lynch-mob, or have them make rules and laws for me to follow. A political party that advocates and allows its members to take the life of a prisoner or assassinate an opponent is not fit to govern or make laws for others to follow.

A Marxist usually believes that the mass movement of people acting in unison to overthrow a government, is produced by the environment and the times they live in. They believe the leaders of these mass movements are also a product of the times. Leaders do not produce the times and environment, but only reflect the wishes of that mass movement. If a Socialist form of government is going to be the future in all countries, it will be the future without the need to kill or torture or assassinate individuals who now control the government. However, if the forces that control our life, are personal acts of a leader or leaders, then all we would have to do is to eliminate designated individuals for the revolution to be made. Theoretically and historically, we can see that this is incorrect. So, my former comrade, there is no excuse for you here. Once again, I ask you why?

I noticed and wondered that nothing happened to the three FBI informants whom I exposed, but it was the two persons from the "Ultra Right" who were involved in the fatal accidents. I cannot understand what you based your decision on. As a Marxist you should not advocate assassinating someone born in China, solely because they spoke Chinese, or someone born in Saudi Arabia, solely because they are Moslems, or someone born in Finland, solely because of their skin color. You should realize that they have no choice in these matters of where they were born, their skin color, the language they speak, or the religion or politics they have thrust on them. The sons and daughters born to the wealthy have no choice either. If you believe in dialectical materialism, then you must believe that the wealthy persons are just as conditioned by the environment and times as the workers. If you assassinate the wealthy or their menial servants before the revolution, then you are killing someone in a group (who cannot help what they became) before a revolution comes and changes them. After the revolution, if you have taken the power away from them, then what is the threat of those individuals? Remember: If the rich could correct the contradiction of capitalism, we would be superfluous.

As atheists, we should know that the wealthy person, just as the poor person, is not being ruled by a Supreme Being, but by genes and environment. You cannot condemn them because they act on their false beliefs, as they are unable to recognize their beliefs as false or they would not have them. But as an atheistic socialist, you know they are false beliefs, so you can be held accountable if you perpetrate acts that you know violate morality. There is nothing here to give you power to destroy another human being's life. So why did you do it?

It is obvious that you did not have them killed as a warning to others because it was done in secret and made to look like an accident in the two situations. Because there is no legitimate excuse for a socialist party to assassinate spies who can be ignorant of their wrong doing, then the only reason I can think of is that you did it for vengeance. I can see the individual, shaped by the environment and their genes, resorting to assassination as an act of vengeance, but not a party that claims the future; especially when they had time to inquire into it and see the consequences of such an act. The intrusion of personal vengeance into a party's structure is inexcusable; it can never be justified.

When an organized atheist government or political party kills or tortures a prisoner or assassinates an enemy, it is making the statement: because there is no God, all acts cannot be judged to be right or wrong; that standards set up by those who believe in a Supreme Being can be ignored. But this statement goes even further, because if there is to be no judgment, no standard, no ethics or moral principles, then it is obvious that we are saying that we rule by force. If there is no one to judge the atheistic socialist government, then who judges the individuals and their acts? Certainly not the government that denies there are rules that they are obligated to follow; because we have to ask, "Where would they receive their authorization to judge people?" If it is no crime for a Communist country to kill or torture a prisoner, then what right have we to judge the capitalists for their misdeeds? To reject standards set up by religious groups because there is no God, is faulty judgment. Truth cannot be rejected solely because of its religious origin or because it is held by a capitalist government. All morality, all standards of freedom are human standards meant to protect human beings, and can, even under the false delusion of being handed down from a Supreme Being or obtained from a capitalist country, be valid if they prove to make a more civilized person or government out of those who follow them. The wave of the future does not need immorality to succeed in its mission. Behind the barricades, in the trenches in a righteous war or rebellion, or to protect one's life against an aggressor, I can see taking the life of another, but never a prisoner in chains. Until you understand how the Stalinists arrived at their position of killing helpless captives, you cannot avoid the same path.

Where does this lead us? I want direct confrontation with all those who participated in this bad decision. I want to know not only who they are, but how they could arrive at this absurd position. I want complete autonomy to investigate their background if I feel it is necessary, and to bring what I find to the notice of the membership through a special tribunal of the leadership. This can still be corrected and stand as a warning for the future leaders who might fall into such a mistake. We cannot claim to be the future if we have not learned the lessons of history. The fault of the Inquisition and Stalin have much in common. We do not want to add our names to that list. We must now, before a revolution, clarify what our morality will be if we succeed in taking power.

Because there is no God, there is no place to appeal the verdict other than to other human beings, to other living human beings, and so I am appealing directly to you. The dead will stay dead; the living will go on making the rules we live by. You can uselessly curse the dice, but once they have stopped flat with a number showing, then that will be the number you have to play with. Men and women can write civilization on those dice, but until they do, the winning side can ignore and disclaim with impunity that there is such a word for conduct.

EPILOGUE

The following excerpts were taken from various news sources: The FBI was forced to make the following disclosures in "discovery proceedings" arising out of the damage suit (for millions of dollars) filed by the Socialist Workers Party against the FBI. They admitted that between 1960 and 1976, the FBI paid out about $1,700,000 to some 300 people to become members and spy on the Socialist Workers Party and the Young Socialist Alliance, a youth group affiliated with them. These two groups had a combined membership list of around 2,500 people, which makes the 300 FBI informers about 12 percent of the organizations strength. The FBI paid another 1,000 persons who did not join, but sent in reports on the Party's activities.

This means that one member in eight was paying dues and working exceedingly hard to advance to leadership positions. These infiltrators were selling the Party's newspaper, organizing for the party, recruiting for them, and defending its integrity. The FBI had the Socialist Workers Party under surveillance from 1938 to 1976, without discovering a single instance of criminal or treasonable activity.

It can be adduced by this writer that some of the infiltrators did report some criminal activities, but these could not be prosecuted because the persons reported were probably also working undercover for the United States Government.

CHAPTER 7

NARRATIVE: PRISON

To the methodical mind, imprinted with an alien view of nature, there always seems to come a time to number people, to separate people, to distinguish between them and us. This will continue until time mutates away this obsession that "they" are not like us.

Like all things, the numbering had a beginning. It started with a hundred thousand numbers, without a designating letter, being distributed to the prisoners in California; then, the series starting with the letter *A* proceeded to have a beginning. New inmates arrived, and the days passed, and the seasons rotated, until the number A32147 arrived and was assigned to a prisoner at the San Quentin Guidance Center. This number was to be forever tattooed on the mind of that person who in 1955 had walked into the Taraval Police Station in San Francisco and informed the police officers on duty that he wished to confess to several crimes that he had committed. That person is the author of this book.

If you perceive human beings as descendants of evolution, then perhaps you might be able to understand my motives and actions in turning myself in to the police in San Francisco. You will believe in my sacrifice because we — the living — are all at the terminal end of evolution; because of this, our actions and motives can be traced, metaphorically, to nature's original implanter of information, our genes. My motives were to prove to my political Party that I was not an informer, to prove that I had not joined it to betray it from within, to prove to them that I would sacrifice everything, even my life, if I thought the Party, if it came to power, would represent Liberty, Justice, and the Truth.

If, however, you believe that *Homo sapiens* were created by a

Supreme Being, then, with the same facts, you will not be able to explain my actions. Your opinions, sometimes to the point of direct opposition of some other believer's opinions, can never be reconciled with reality. As an example, I am going to contrast the views that arise when two groups, the religious and non-religious, try to explain homosexuality.

To explain my neutrality, I am going to inform you that I have never had an urge to have sex with another man. Furthermore, when growing up, I was taught by my fellow heterosexuals — and believed them — that what homosexuals were doing was something that was disgusting and unnatural. It was only when I had the time to mature mentally (and thus was assured of my heterosexuality), did I lose my fear of associating with homosexual men. This allowed me to devote some time to talking to them and reading their literature so that I could try to understand how they were produced.

The latest scientific thought about homosexuals assumes that they are born with the traits to become homosexuals; it is in their genes. Studying the literature on natural selection, immediately brings one to the conclusion that male homosexuals defy or even overturn the law that states: Those who produce the most offspring will perpetuate their genetic qualities. Two known facts are: homosexuals do not produce more offspring than heterosexuals, and when they do have children they do not produce more homosexual children than heterosexuals. If I believe that natural selection is true, then to explain those two facts it must follow that because of its survivability, male homosexuality must have come into being because it was a positive benefit for a heterosexual couple to produce one or more, and the genes must also be handed down through heterosexuals to explain why homosexuality has not been eliminated by natural selection.

We cannot discover what that benefit is by observing it in a current culture. We have to return to the culture where it probably originated, which must have been when we were hunters and gatherers. It takes hundreds of thousands of years for nature to blindly adopt a beneficial trait and the same amount of time to lose it if it is no longer a benefit. Scientific studies have shown that we can sometimes improve our chances of passing on more of our genes by helping our siblings to survive, than by mating ourselves. We can assume: when a heterosexual couple in a hunting and gathering culture, produced a homosexual son, it gave that family an edge in survivability. A guess would be: by not setting up a competing family, the male homosexual helped his close relatives to pass on more of his genes than if he had mated. Simplified: Whatever the reason for homosexuality's success in natural selection is, it had to be positive or those homosexual genes would not have been passed on.

Homosexuality as an imposed sacrifice, is not an isolated episode in nature. It has other ways that animals can sacrifice their sexuality for the benefit of the group. An examination of a wolf pack will show that it also has members that subvert their sexuality to improve the survivability of that pack. This is done by usually allowing only the alpha male and female to mate and produce offspring. Still, if anything happens to the alpha male or female, they can be replaced by a subordinate that is next in line. That wolf will assume alpha status, mate and produce wolf cubs. Those genes that compel the other wolves to subvert their sexuality are (like homosexual genes) passed down through those that produce the most offspring. The alpha wolves in one example, the heterosexual couples in the other.

What is true for the male is also true for the female. In an example of polyandry, the alpha female tamarin (a small monkey) takes many mates, and the males take care of her offspring. Usually only one female, the alpha, is sexually active, and this will suppress ovulation in her female cohorts. The subverting of the female's sexuality in the tamarin is also passed down through the genes of the alpha female.

What is important here, is that in wolves, tamarins, and homosexuals, even though their sexual traits are passed down through the genes, the roles are not permanently fixed, they are not locked in for everyone, and they can be changed by certain conditions that arise in the environment. Just as the non-alpha wolves and tamarins can — when the need arises — overcome a previous status and assume the role of an alpha, so can a homosexual male or female override their genes and mate with the opposite sex and produce offspring, if they feel the need to, because that option also resides in the genes.

Those who believe in Divine Creation can only judge and blame the male and female homosexual for their actions, and each judgment will be different, but they cannot ever integrate him or her into the human family. They cannot explain their birth and presence in the environment as just another method nature uses to obtain the perpetuation of a species. For a religious person to condemn homosexuals for not being heterosexual and producing children, is the same as condemning non-alpha wolves for not mating and having cubs, or condemning the non-alpha female tamarins for not ovulating, taking a mate and producing offspring. Their religion forbids them from understanding that we are all limited by our genes, that Nature cannot judge, cannot reject, so it uses all mechanisms that arise to increase survivability of a species.

So if you view my actions from a belief contingent on a false view of reality, then it is almost impossible for you to understand me. You will have a handicap that will not allow you to understand your motives or actions; and if you do not know yourself, then how can you hope to know or judge me correctly? You are trapped in a dream world that can never entirely coincide with the true world. And just because you can claim that there are more of you in that dream world than there are in the world that I inhabit, it still does not change the relationship. An antigravity machine of the mind does not allow you to escape from a concrete world.

Early in my life, I came to the conclusion that all religious views, past and present, tend to separate a person from reality. This separating effect can be historically observed by looking at a belief, once held by most of the educated Christians in the world, that the earth was the center of the universe and that all other celestial bodies, such as the sun, the moon, the planets, the stars and comets, revolved around a fixed, flat earth. Except for the moon orbiting the earth, this fabricated belief had no bearing on the true movement of those bodies, nor could it change the natural law by which those bodies moved through our heavens. No matter how many divine proclamations were made, how many Gods or Goddesses were consulted, how many people were forced to repudiate their observations, or how many were tortured and maimed in mind and body for having a contradictory opinion, the fact remained that this religious view was not an accurate conception of how the universe around us worked. From many such observations, you can deduce a natural law, which reads: Reality will never conform to a false belief.

Let us look at another observable — Darwin's Galapagos Islands' Finches. These birds, isolated by nature, buffeted by the elements, and most important, being undisturbed by human beings, the alterers of environments, filled by adaptation several of the open bird niches in the islands' habitats. An accumulation of these types of observations led Charles Darwin, when he returned to England, to speculate on our origin, as there were too many unexplained observations that did not mesh with a Creator forming a permanent line of unalterable species, nor did they fit in with the bible's account of the length of time the earth has been in existence.

There is definite proof that we evolved; what is still in dispute is how it was brought about. Whether it was by a slow selection, by a quick leap, or a combination of these, it will eventually be resolved. However, this does not invalidate Darwin's observation of natural selection as a conveyance of special survival or as the instrument of the extermination of individuals and groups, and through observation we can extend that belief to include the extermination by human beings of competing ideas and beliefs. Natural Selection exists as a force in nature, and your belief or disbelief has no relevance to its existence. However, unlike the movements of the celestial bodies through the heavens, human beings can, and do affect natural selection because of our participation and ability to produce changes in our environment.

This can readily be observed in modern farming where a planted crop of cotton will increase the food supply of the boll weevil. In a natural setting, without the interference of human beings, the cotton plants would be widely dispersed and in competition with other plants for space and nutrition, therefore limiting the food supply of the boll weevil. The farming of the cotton plant negates this, so that we have an increase by human selection of the boll weevil (above its natural selection) by our intervention. Associating a similar situation, it can be observed that human beings are not immune to a created environment where, just as the boll weevils do, they also multiply out of control. Although we cannot eliminate natural selection, we can change many of the ways that it can affect us and other species. This comes about because if you have a true or false belief, and act on it, it can change the environment, which can change the way natural selection selects. From this, you can deduce another natural law, which reads: You do not have to believe in a natural law for it to have the power to have a good or negative influence over you.

This can be proven by observation. If you belong to a religion where you take the most unselfish individuals in that religion, those willing to sacrifice their lives for others, and do not permit them to breed, you are, by using their unselfish actions, producing a culture that produces selfishness. Unknowingly, you are unintentionally breeding for selfishness. The same thing happens when you draft for intelligence and for physical strength, then send those draftees off to be killed in a war before they have a chance to breed. This will eventually produce a less intelligent and less physically fit population.

In 1955, I was unable to understand why some of my actions were dependent on natural laws, but I could, with my meager understanding, eliminate the false starting point that a philosophy based on the falsehood that we were made by a Supreme Being, is forever foredoomed to repeated failures. We can only start from the knowledge of the truth, which is that we are direct descendants of the animal kingdom. Even if some readers do not accept this, it no longer worries me, because I know that time, which seems to me to be but an agreed on measurement of the deteriorations of past errors, will always be on the side of truth. So no matter how long a truth is denied, time will always be on its side; that the passage of time will eventually correct all misinformation, is one more observable law of nature.

Therefore, at the police station in San Francisco, where I had given myself into the hands of those who claimed to be detectors of flawed human beings, my actions were not burdened by a false view of reality — religion. I could not be bribed by a Christian heaven, because I had scrutinized their heaven and ascertained that what they were offering was a permanent fix, the ultimate fix; yes, Huxley's *Brave New World* of soma; with God as the heroin invading your veins forever and ever. I had already spent several years reading history books, and had come to the conclusion that religion had created disabilities in those who believed that were indistinguishable from those that effected drug addicts? Were they not both hooked; were not the design of their crutches interchangeable; were not the two of them trying to escape the harsh realities of killing and butchering their own meat? You could readily see that reformed drug addicts on religious methadone were still hooked, were still dependent on a drug meant to obliterate reality, and so were not cured. The religious person is also an addict, also gets high; it is only that the drug administered to reach that intoxicated high is different.

Because I was not culturally independent of my environment in 1955, I was still under the influence of many false beliefs. So, at the police station, my lies and my actions promulgated on those lies gave symmetrical balance and betrayed me — the user of those lies — as an exceedingly young and vulnerable mortal. Because of this, I was afraid they would see through my shallow pretenses, and was especially worried because I knew that "they" would come to question me; "they" being the FBI.

Remember: I was raised when the FBI was believed to be composed of infallible minds that relentlessly pursued the deviant, and no trail was ever completely obliterated once they were in pursuit. My worry: I had already been informed by friends and sympathizers that the FBI had taken notice of my presence and had begun the gathering of evidence that my actions and views, according to J. Edgar Hoover, had shifted out of the narrow spectrum that had been assigned by them. Before I had left the Marine Hospital in San Francisco, two friendly nurses and a doctor had personally warned me that the FBI had questioned the doctors and nurses on my hospital ward about my activities and my visitors, and especially wanted to know which patients I associated with.

When I turned myself in, I had no trouble convincing the San Francisco Police Department detectives that I was just a repentant thief. However, I gave more credit to the FBI to see through my actions and wonder about those actions. It was only after the FBI interview, which occurred the day after I turned myself in, that I perceived that there are some people who cannot connect a picture of random dots to perceive the picture that those dots represent. These people go through life seeing nothing but unconnected random dots; whereas the astute will look for and perceive the underlying picture.

Although I had been well coached by the underground of my Party, I found it unnecessary, because I found out that the FBI trained mind could not grasp the distortions that I had simply created by assuming human cryptic colorations; a technique of surviving by learning to blend with ones surrounding. Understand: I was not just portraying a criminal, but was one. The FBI could not see that thieves are not separated from the rest of humanity; they are ruled by the same natural laws that we all inherit. It follows that criminals are also willing to sacrifice their lives for a belief. Because I did not have a criminal record, and the courts usually give probation for the first time offender, the FBI offered to guarantee that probation if I would cooperate with them. This was a useless gesture on their part. Even if they knew, their conditioning would forbid them from understanding my reasoning of why I had to go to prison to prove to the party that I was not a FBI informer or a right-wing provocateur.

Within a few days after pleading guilty and turning down a probation report, I found myself on a bus heading for the Guidance Center at San Quentin. In 1955, this is where the Northern California prisoners were sent for diagnostic evaluation and screening. What you learned in those ninety days that you remained at the center, especially if you were a first timer, would determine how you survived in the system. It was a crash course in adaptability where you learned to play the repentance game.

We are all programmed, imprinted, and conditioned, so the art of educating yourself is to be able to detect the false programming, imprinting, and conditioning. I found out early that the prisoners and the jailers that I was about to meet could not see that they were just another animal species filling the open niches created in our human-made environment. Just as Darwin's Finches would not have been able to see — if they had developed language and were able to communicate — that they were just filling those open niches because it was easier than fighting for a part of an established one.

On entering San Quentin, the first thing I noticed was the obsessional need of the guards and the prison staff to be treated as dominants by those they controlled. They failed to understand that the conflict was caused by these appointed dictators trying to impose their will on a reservoir of genes that have the ability, through natural selection, to recognize true dominance and know when it has no validity; know that without the club and gun these guards would be subservient to a majority of the prisoners. The mean and petty acts committed on prisoners will always be senseless and without purpose; acts that can achieve no constructive goal. Nature has made no provision for appointed dominants. It is a cultural invention and cannot be cited as proof that there is a difference between the guards and the guarded. An impartial outside observer could readily see that there was a symbiotic relationship between the guarded and the guards.

I was appalled to see that most of the prisoners' minds, as well as their bodies, were being held behind those bars. By rejecting their conditioning, I rejected their rules whereby they interfered with reality, and so remained a free man all the time I was behind bars. My rules went back to a time on earth when no verbal noises broke the stillness, when no tangible lines were drawn on the surface of the earth to separate us, when the hunter and the hunted were the same, and when the meat eaters and the grass eaters prayed to different Deities, because they knew their heavens had nothing in common.

There is ample proof, readily obtainable, to show that we are descendants of other primates and have retained many behaviors and reactions from outside stimulus that they have. Even those who acknowledge that we are true descendants, would still like to believe that most of our animal behavior patterns have been obliterated by natural selection or have atrophied by not being used; and even if they are passed down in a milder form, that we should be able to overrule this inheritance by reasoning. From personal observations and scientific studies, I do not believe this.

Many irrational behaviors seen in human beings can also be observed in primates placed in similar situations. We are living in a world where Ivan Pavlov and B. F. Skinner's animal experiments are accepted, but their findings are rejected by the majority when they relate to the animal in human beings. In observing primates, we can readily see that the same thing that creates a stable structure in their cultures is valid in human societies. We should assume that anything that prevails in the animal kingdom, and is so widely spread throughout that kingdom, must have come about because it was a success that obliterated less successful experiments that nature had made. Although, because of mating practices of the dominant primates, the offspring of the dominants are favored to succeed to the hierarchy, still, the positions are open to all who aspire and can meet the requirements, and they are even open to a primate that enters from another troop. This trait, so successful in the primate world, has produced us and still rules our life.

History is replete with the continual struggle, at all levels of society, to attain the dominant role. Those who succeed to it can readily be discerned to do their utmost to circumvent and interfere with the natural order of open accession by using all the resources at their disposal to pass on to their direct descendants, even if their descendants did not receive the dominant genes, the power they achieved by being a true dominant. History documents that those who tried to use inheritance to hold on to the dominant positions, even insisting that God or destiny was on their side, could not stave off the inevitable. This just leads to further struggle, and eventually to the collapse and overthrow of those who want to close the hierarchy to outside influence. The new leaders will in their turn impose their restrictions on accession, and by doing that start a new cycle.

A close parallel can be seen in George Orwell's paraphrased observation: Under Communism, all comrades are equal, but some comrades are more equal than others. The Russian Communist Party became a true class when it began to perpetuate itself. This is evident in the behavior of a political party that limits its membership and gives special privileges to its hierarchy — the ruling class. The sons and daughters of the nobility of the party are now granted special dispensation that allows them to be admitted over more qualified students into the universities that produce the future rulers; they are also admitted into the restricted Russian Communist Party without questioning, and quickly advance into the hierarchy because of the position of their mothers or fathers in the ruling political structure.

Our short span of life distorts and ignores eternal time, which shows that just a few seconds have elapsed during that time that we view as a long epic struggle for existence for the human race. One lesson learned from history is that when the road to dominance is closed to a group or individual, if they are true dominants, they will emerge and do their utmost to pull down the interfering system. The insertion of different breeds of unicorn —"they are different from us" and "there is more of us than there are of you, so we are right" — does not give validity to closing the door to dominants. The social structures that so far have survived the longest, seem to be those that remain open to advancement to all classes.

On my arrival at San Quentin, I had as one of my goals the understanding of my fellow inmates. I found out that my preconceived reasoning did not mesh with reality. My socialist party did not understand that the convicted felons were not something outside society, but were similar to them: a group of people contending for the right to reproduce through individual methods instead of united as a party. My life in prison was a continuing session of learning not to point my finger, but just observe and try to relate what I observed with the natural world. This was to be a valuable aid to my survival in prison.

I came to the conclusion that most convicts were imprinted with information that did not coincide with the information that was passed down through their genes. When criminals find themselves in a harsh, alien created environment, their actions will coincide with what their genes tell them is correct behavior for that circumstance, and not what the created culture demands of them. Remember: That all cultures are alien until they are allowed to survive over an extended period, allowed the time for useful mutant genes — that give us the ability to live in a new culture — to become dominant and be incorporated into the species.

Assuming all other aspects remain the same, and with the understanding that these are dreadfully simplistic answers, as no one can take into account the many shapes and sizes in the blades of grass that make up a lawn, I cannot say that I have exhausted all thoughts on the subject of criminality. I will, however, point out that because the human genes were produced by an environment that no longer exists for most of us, then anyone who is willing to think about it can understand why many prisoners are bent, twisted, and manipulated into grotesque shapes when they live in one of these artificially created environments.

Eventually I came to realize that my time in prison was not wasted; realized that truth can be found on either side of the prison walls; realized that walls will imprison the body, but, as of this time, that the jailers are unable to limit the mind by holding the body in confinement.

CHAPTER 8

NARRATIVE: DIAGNOSIS

Silence, as in a deep cavern, had engulfed me for an unknown amount of time. Something had disturbed that silence, which had brought me to a state of consciousness. It came again! It was a familiar but frightening sound that my mind remembered from the many movies that I had seen in my youth. The remembered sound conjured up the picture of heavy metal doors clanging shut and sealing the doom of some innocent, errant knight as he was being flung into a damp dungeon far below ground level.

My mind, for a brief period, was occupied by the unmistakable sound of water rushing and gurgling from an unidentified source. I tried to focus my thoughts on that cool, refreshing sound, because my throat was dry; exceedingly dry. I estimated, later, that I had been without water for three days. Opening my eyes, without moving my body, I found that I was lying completely nude upon a hard, bare concrete floor. Enticed by the sound, my eyes wandered to the center of the floor to solve the mystery of the running water. The entire concrete floor sloped downward to the center where there was a six inch opening. This small, round void had running water squirting into it from the sides. Although I knew they existed by their description given to me by prisoners confined to strip cells for punishment, this was the first time I had observed one. Modern plumbing techniques had removed the dirty, smelly task of carrying out the human waste, and the washing down and cleaning up of those unfortunate persons obscenely embraced by these cold, indifferent concrete walls and floors, could now be achieved with a minimum of labor. The zoo keepers could enter the room with a fire hose and wash everything, including dignity, down through that center bore.

In my cell, I could also see that the darkness of the old style dungeon had been replaced by a two hundred watt light bulb that, I found out later, remained on day and night. For what purpose? With a little thought, it became self-evident. The only opening in my cell was the ponderous metal door with a one-way observation window. The light was kept on so you could be observed without your knowing it. Turning the light on and off would alert the prisoner that he was being watched.

When I realized that I was no longer under the influence of a mind altering drug, the thought that immediately came to me was that my intransigent opponents must now want me to appear normal. That could only mean they had achieved a set goal that must have been a benefit to them; and it could benefit them further if I now appeared recovered.

Although I did not know the exact location of where I was, I immediately speculated that it was a mental institution, and felt sure that it was where somebody had planned for me to be. Only later — by listening to casual remarks when being examined — did I have the answer. I was a prisoner in the mental ward of the California Medical Facility at Vacaville. In retrospect, I could not believe that any of the animals that met their deaths in the claws or beaks of a predator that day, had the free will to choose not to be at that point of time and place when the predator and the prey met. I had no choice of where I was either, and neither did those who watched over me.

After being given the drug at the Santa Rosa Police Station by my unknown questioner, the injection at the hospital combined with it to place me in a state where I lacked full comprehension of what had been happening to me. Every time I regained a little awareness of my surroundings, I was re-drugged, to keep me docile, and then moved. From the talk around me at the police station, I knew that those observing my actions, and not knowing about the drugs that I had ingested, thought I was acting like a person in a catatonic trance. But when I awoke from the drugs, in my cell at Vacaville, my mind was perfectly clear about what had happened before I was drugged.

In my mind, I went over everything that had occurred since I was stopped by the FBI agent near Santa Rosa, to see if there was a way of proving to a jury that I was being framed. Despite all my previous knowledge of the operational methods of the FBI, CIA, and far right organizations, had I been on a jury in the 1960s, my mind would have been overtaxed to believe that they or former members of these government bureaus were capable of deliberately planning to frame me. Talk about blowing one's mind in the 1960s! Imagine the enormous amount of time and money that was needed, the monumental plotting required, and the risk involved to go into a plan as complex and sinister as this, merely to frame a little clog of annoyance. Instead of using a little Drano, they had inserted a stick of dynamite to remove the obstacle — me. It was truly mind shattering! What was more awe inducing was the power that they must have thought they controlled. Power that had to reach to the highest level in our government for them to even contemplate acting in the manner that they did. A last glimmer of McCarthyism was to be my final judgment.

Their choosing *me* as their object of revenge, gave me some hope; it showed that the persons making the decisions were insulated in a world of their personal creation, where the accuracy and interpretation of their intelligence gathering was on the same level as a grade B spy movie. Somewhere, somehow, somebody had suckered them into a farce, into believing that I was responsible for the deaths of their comrades. I knew this now, and evidently they did not. I thought that if I could come up with a counterplan of action to confuse them, then I might have a chance of extricating myself from their plot. This assessment had led me to conclude that I should play catatonic for the time being and see what developed as time passed. I was not playing in a game that was entirely foreign to me. I knew that I was playing against some form of bureaucracy; and I had seen some of their cards, and could guess how they were going to play a few more. My main handicap was that I did not know that I was going to play in such a deadly game. They in turn, did not know that I had stashed away a few high cards from preceding games that I could use in this one. Unless you looked carefully, all the cards seemed to be from the same deck.

Having previously read some literature on psychiatric treatment, I remembered that they gave shock therapy to bring people out of their catatonic trances, but only to physically healthy persons. I felt sure that because of my poor physical condition (eight ribs removed on one side of my body, which left only about forty-five percent of the normal breathing capacity of an adult), they would not take a chance of giving me shock treatment. My reasoning for this was that the normal, healthy human body is subject to great strain under shock treatment, and even a healthy body sometimes breaks down and either death occurs, or the body is totally incapacitated. You become a vegetable. I thought: if they had wanted me dead, then I would not be in this cell. I *did not* contemplate that they might have lost control of the situation; that I was no longer in their direct control, but had just become a pawn in a mindless system.

My weight, about one hundred and fifty pounds on a six foot frame, was a problem. I had kept myself at this weight because I found it easier to breathe, but this left me with little fasting potential. I knew that I could hold out for only a month at the most without endangering my life. The catatonic trance was the easiest to fake as I had the knowledge from experimental use of self-hypnosis of how to control my bodily functions. I was sure, even with my limited knowledge of mental illness, that I could fake the symptoms if I wished to.

While I was lying on that concrete floor, my mind made clear by my unintentional fasting, I realized something that would be of immense help to me in my unequal combat with my shadowy nemeses. That was that the psychotherapists had no way of telling if you were a true paranoid unless they were privy to information that could prove otherwise. If I had informed the doctors, when I regained consciousness, that I thought that I was being framed by a group of people that I suspected were members or former members of the CIA and FBI, and this group was probably financed clandestinely by some right-wing radical group, then they would say, unless they had the knowledge of the plot, that I was suffering from paranoia. There is no way you can tell the actions of a person that just thinks that he or she is being plotted against — a true paranoid — from someone who becomes the victim of a true conspiracy, unless there is some way to prove that the conspiracy is taking place. It was also clear to me that as a defense it was a dead end; because if I had asserted that there was a scheme to frame me, then I would remain in a mental hospital until cured of that delusion. I could not prove the intrigue without exposing some innocent comrades and revealing that I was guilty, according to the conspiracy law, of a greater crime than bank robbery.

I concluded that I had to use other ways to convince an examining doctor that I was mentally ill. So, with the meager information that I had, I came up with a plan of action that I hoped would allow me to regain some type of control over my surroundings. The plan was to fake being a catatonic, and then slowly come out of it. I would then claim that I had no knowledge of what had happened during my illness. After coming out of the faked catatonic trance, I intended to exhibit a schizophrenic and paranoid personality, as I believed this would prevent them from putting me on trial for a crime of which I was innocent.

An unknown amount of time passed while I tried to think of all my possible options. A healthy person can go without food for an extended period, but only without water for a short time. Lying there on that concrete floor, I knew that I had to have water, now. So, the show began. To alert someone that I was awake, the word "water!" came out of my parched throat, every few seconds. This lasted until I heard what I was listening for, a key being inserted into the lock on my cell door. Without delay, the heavy iron door to my cell clanged open and a man dressed in hospital green entered and proceeded to question me. I answered all his questions with a pleading cry for water. When the man could get no other reply, he departed, then returned with a cup of water, which he administered to me. He asked more questions, but received no reply from the now inert and silent me.

He again departed, and I laid there knowing that the observation would begin through that one-way window in the door. So, I put myself into a deep self-hypnotic trance and waited. Time passed, but eventually sound alerted me to the movement of life outside my cell door. Soon after that, the door opened and a large group came in, filling the small cell so full that they were forced to lift me to my feet and hold me up so they could all maneuver around without stepping on me. One of them, dressed in a doctor's white coat with the large buttons down the front, pulled out a small flashlight. Holding one of my eyelids open with one of his hands, he proceeded to shine the light into one of my eyes. With my mind under hypnotic control, I was ready for it. Instead of seeing the bright light, my mind told me that I could only see darkness. The other eye received the same treatment, and received the same answer — darkness. Someone in the group asked, "Do you think that he is in a catatonic stupor, or is he faking it?"

"I don't think it is an assumed state. His eyes show little reaction to the light; and contractions and dilatation of the eyes are hard to counterfeit," came the doctor's reply.

With that reply, act one, scene one was primarily over. I had played a high card from a different deck, and they did not even bother to turn it over to see if the back of the card matched the same deck that they were playing with.

ESSAY: ANALYZING

My examiners, like modern societies, were also handicapped by other false information that leads to delusions. They did not understand that the laws that a society makes, are not inescapably the explicit laws of the universe. That the different roles that men and women are forced to play by economic and religious considerations in society, are not necessarily the roles they would like to play if they had a free choice in the matter. Societies keep trying to instill into the individual the notion that what those societies want is also what the person wants. We are all participants on the stage of life, but in our delusions, most of us speak and act on that stage not the way we wish to, but the way we think other members of a society want us to act and speak. We should come to realize that the men and women who we worry about are also caught in this social trap. They are acting and speaking the way they think we want them to. The few who have the strength to revolt against some of the different roles thrust on them by society, are called rebels. Although the rebels reject some stereotype roles that human organisms assume simply for the convenience of social communications, we find few of them understanding why they are revolting against their system. Rebels in Russia would be those who would argue for the capitalistic system of economics; rebels in the United States would induce you to believe that the communal system of economics is the answer. In the United States they would be atheists, and in Russia they would believe in a Supreme Being.

To find a common ground for these totally opposite rejections, we find that many assumed roles, fostered on us by cultures, come into conflict with the human created environments. Apparently neither capitalism nor communism prevents these conflicts, so we turn to the many ways we have of seeking relief from them. We seek it in mass entertainment, in alcoholism, in drug addiction, in loveless sex, and in the many other social rebellions that we become entwined with. When all else fails, we, involuntarily, seek relief in psychosis and neuroses, which leads to psychiatric treatment. I do not even exclude here mental illnesses that can be incorporated under the name of "schizophrenia," which most of the psychiatric community believes to be untreatable by psychoanalyzing the patient. These aberrations are possibly caused by the patient's brain involuntarily inducing a chemical imbalance that stress, in a perverted environment, has been known to produce.

Inasmuch as there is no underlying master plan, which we need to explain the buildings that we construct in our minds, we keep trying to make sense out of a world that does not make sense. These mental structures cannot stand for long in our cultures without breaking down; they lack a blueprint that takes into account the true world that surrounds us. Continually, we try to instill in our created blueprints, false laws that have no foundation in reality, false laws built by someone's religious, legal, or political beliefs.

Because they have assumed a role that societies have thrust upon them, the psychiatrists who try to cure human beings are handicapped in the treatment they administer. They defend their work as science, but are not able to cure many more patients than a faith healer with a good understanding of human behavior. Psychiatrists cannot even agree among themselves as to what is the true theory or even the terminology of psychiatry, let alone how to treat people. Sometimes, they do not even know when patients are cured or when they are sick. They have to work with a multiplicity of conflicting theories and divergent techniques. Some of these, including lobotomy and shock treatment, are methods used apparently without understanding that the people they are being used on are human beings, not experimental animals that can be caged in the back rooms of mental hospitals if something goes wrong with the experiment.

This incompetence and lack of agreement can be seen in the conflicts that show up in our courtrooms, where the defense psychiatrist claims the person on trial is insane, while the prosecution's psychiatrist will claim that the person on trial is a perfectly normal human being, even though that person's genes and environment have created a monstrous caricature of what a human being should be. You pay your money and tell the psychiatrist what side you want him to appear on in a court case.

The *major fault of psychiatry* is that the doctors cannot divest their minds of the mass delusions that they suffer from; which are the religious, economic, and social duties that they feel compelled to recommend and tout to their patients. What I am saying is that it is impossible for most doctors to be neutral as they cannot divorce their treatment from their earlier encoded mental perceptions. What we have is the sick psychiatrist, suffering under the same delusions that societies are suffering from, trying to cure sick patients of their delusions by trying to persuade the patients to embrace the mass delusions of societies. And although we sometimes send individuals to mental institutions when they have delusions, we do nothing when the majority has a mass delusion; especially when those who do the treating, also have the same mass delusion. The social repression that societies inflict on human beings, has not been the main concern of the psychotherapist. They take the stand that society is right, and their work is adjusting the human organism by coaxing it into social respectability. By doing this, they become the obedient tool of governments, churches, and all other agencies that have power, and seek to adjust the brain of human beings into ignoring millions of years of evolution so that the patient can accept the psychotherapists and their propaganda as gospel and as ordained truth.

If psychiatrists had been allowed into the concentration camps of Dachau and Auschwitz during World War II, I am convinced that they would have spent their time trying to convince the inmates that they should not diet so much and should work harder for the German war effort. Certainly, there were many mentally ill persons being created by the concentration camps, but the psychotherapist was not needed. It was already too late by the time the camps were built. The creators of these environments, the keepers of these asylums, the builders of these concentration camps were the ones needing treatment. They were the true mentally ill. The created environment was the cause of the inmates' troubles in the concentration camps, and it was useless to cure them so they could go cheerfully into those gas chambers.

Oh how I wish I could tell you that this is just a disorder of my mind, instead of a reality of our times. The lonely therapist who sees through these delusions and tries to help the individual is forced into criticizing society. He or she knows that it is useless to cure a person and then put that person right back into the same environment that produced the psychosis in the first place. They understand that society must be changed to bring about a more natural, a more harmonious, and closer relationship between society and the individual human being.

The examination being concluded in my cell at Vacaville, the doctors left with what they assumed was knowledge of the facts. They truly believed that I was in a complete, involuntary, catatonic trance. The truth: they left my cell conned by the false belief that they were too educated to be fooled by a layman. Once again they were diverted by the magician's hand; a diversion that plays, you will later see, a most prominent part in our life. For your information, this all took place before biofeedback was widely known; at that time, most psychologists and psychiatrists did not believe that people were able to control their automatic body functions with their minds.

I will not tell you what it was, because someone might have a legitimate need to fool a doctor, but I found out later, when I met some truly mentally ill patients, that my actions during the observation and examination period exposed me so that a competent psychiatrist or psychologist could have realized and diagnosed my catatonic trance as an outright fraud. And you will learn later that an inmate who had me under observation and cared for the mental patients in Vacaville, also thought that my illness was contrived.

I do not want to clutter your mind with superstitions, still to convey a specific image, an author must sometimes resort to descriptive words in common usage to describe images that might unintentionally have these connotations already attached. Because I pledged not to lead you astray by compounding previous misconceptions you might have, I must confess that when I use words such as *hypnosis*, *self-hypnosis*, and *hypnotic sleep trance*, they are just being used to convey to your mind a subject in a relaxed, slumped-over, entranced, deep-sleep that your mind might associate with a stage performance. Even when I know that there is no such thing as a trance state and that these words were passed down from previous false interpretations of what hypnosis is, still, I must use these words to describe a condition. What they are describing are not the occult, the mystical, or the supernatural, but just an ordinary response to suggestion that can be achieved in our normal, wide-awake state. This relaxed, slumped-over stage trance is used by the subjects undergoing hypnosis as a psychological aid to buttress and focus their minds. It informs their minds through feedback that they are in an altered state; otherwise the mind cannot tell the hypnotic state from an ordinary, normal, wide-awake state, where it can accomplish the same effect. It has been proven that when people are awake, they will produce the same brain-wave patterns on the electroencephalograph that they would produce if they were under hypnosis. They are aware of everything that goes on around them, and are manifesting a normal and natural human response to simple suggestion. Because we are all susceptible to self-hypnosis while we are wide-awake, all learning in our everyday routine is manifested under this condition without us having to be in that stage created sleep state. As individuals, or as a mob, we are all vulnerable to suggestive learning, even when we do not recognize it as hypnosis.

Acupuncture is another form of hypnosis. It is used daily in China and other countries to perform some minor surgery without anesthesia. The suggestions to the patients are the same as under hypnosis. They are informed that a part of their body is going to go numb and they will feel no pain in that area where the minor operation is going to take place. The needles used in acupuncture are used by the mind for the same purpose as the mind uses the slumped-over posture of the body to tell those under-going hypnoses for the first time that they are now hypnotized. The posture fortifies the mind to the belief that it is under the influence of a special state; and under the acupuncture needles, it tells the patient's nervous system to remain numb and without pain in a specified area until the needles are removed. They are just a feedback to keep us in touch with our subconscious mind.

Why can the mind be fooled so easily? Mainly, because the mind is not perfect. It has developed through evolution, and so must adjust to new environments, but since the environment is constantly changing, it must use previous adaptations to develop for each new situation; and some-times there is a residue of a former adaptation that does not make sense when viewed in a different environment. Hypnosis might be part of the automatic obedience system that we inherited from our animal ancestors. This is exhibited by a signal whereby some animals, when they have to leave for things like water or to hunt, will put their offspring into a wide-awake trance where they remain motionless until the parent returns.

Some of us have the ability to use this natural state of higher awareness for our advantage. If you concentrate your mind and eliminate outside sources of distractions, then you can use suggestion to retrieve mental pictures that you have stored in your memory. Because the mind is restricted by former implanted information, you can only retrieve infor-mation that you know and have experienced. When a hypnotist tells you that a part of your body is becoming numb, you cannot retrieve numbness if the body has never experienced it, and so you do not have that word in your mind's dictionary.

If we analyze the stigmata (the bodily wounds that represented where nails were driven into the crucified to hold them on the cross) that have appeared on some exuberant, passionate, zealous Christians, we can see that there is no religious significance to these sympathetic wounds. There is no mystery here, as no supernatural or outside force is needed to produce this effect. The stigmata can be duplicated and controlled by hypnosis. If the mind alone is capable of producing the stigmata associated with the crucifixion of Christ, then it is most likely that self-hypnosis produces this aberrant result. We can see the mind at work here by stating again that the individual mind cannot retrieve and use information that it does not have. For hundreds of years the crucifixion of Christ was always depicted in paintings, on religious icons, on marble and plaster statues, and on carvings on wooden crosses, by showing the nails in the palms of the hands. New information tends to show that the nails were driven into the wrists of the crucified. The minds of Christians that produced these stigmata did not have this true information, or their wounds would have also appeared on their wrists instead of the palms of their hands. If their bodies were being subjected to this by a true supernatural force, then that outside source would have had the knowledge to produce this effect in the correct part of the body. Men and women will continue to delude themselves like this until they realize that there is no supernatural source from outside that can contact and control their minds.

It has been thought that self-hypnosis cannot be learned from reading a book on the subject; nor have stage hypnotists had much success in hypnotizing themselves. How then do I claim that I was able to teach and use self-hypnosis on myself if experts in hypnosis are unable to do it? It was because I was able to overcome the misconceptions and handicaps involved in the art of self-suggestion. A person who wants to learn self-hypnosis must first be hypnotized and conditioned by a competent person who can be trusted, and in a setting conducive to that trust. The ideal setting would be to be hypnotized by a stage hypnotist in front of a crowd, but a classroom setting should give the same results. The only reason to look for a hypnotist is to learn what the hypnotic sleep trance is, and when you are under it. When you read a book or watch a movie, and focus your mind so that you can ignore extraneous background noise and become so engrossed that you lose track of time, you may not realize it, but what you are experiencing is the hypnotic state.

When I first tried to hypnotize myself, I tried the over-used patter of the stage hypnotist. I kept repeating to myself, "I am relaxing; I am getting drowsy; my eyes are getting heavy; I am going into a deep, deep, restful sleep." Over and over, I tried it, but it did not work. What was missing, I finally found out, was that the hypnotist was communicating by voice and gestures to the physical senses of sound and sight of the persons they were hypnotizing. Self-hypnosis could not be communicated without using one or more of the physical senses, and that was what was missing in the equation. I tried talking out loud to myself, but it was distracting and seemed to interfere with the trance, so I tried another method. Impressed by Helen Keller's ability to use the physical sense of touch to learn with, I used touch to successfully develop a language that I used to tell my subconscious that I was communicating with it. An important facet was that I understood (years ago) that the brain was divided into right and left hemispheres, and each side controlled only one half of the body, so I had to program my two hands exactly alike. If the letter *A* was programmed for the little finger on the right hand, it was also programmed for the little finger on the left hand. I developed the ability to use in unison this touch language — that I developed for each hand — to communicate to my subconscious mind. This put me in a state in which I could use self-hypnosis on myself.

To the doctors examining me in the Medical Facility at Vacaville, I exhibited the slumped-over posture, suggesting a deep sleep, seen on stage, but this was also what a person in a catatonic stupor would project, and so the doctors mistook it for that state. Later, I found out that I could by self-suggestion, obtain the same results with my eyes open and using a normal posture. It was in this state that I was able to further mislead the doctors I came in contact with.

CHAPTER 9

NARRATIVE: THE AUTHOR

When you arrive at a train station, you do not have to describe each railroad tie you passed over to understand how you arrived at that station; and so it is with my schooling. My educational ties were and are the extent of thousands of books and magazines that I have read, thousands of movies I have seen, and uncountable radio programs that I have listened to. When growing up, I never had the chance to be raised in a stable culture; so, my morality was not passed down and filtered by tribal lore nor by family traditions. My mentors were there for all to see; they were more than the printed pages, more than flickering celluloid images, more than the voices and music that came out of a speaker. They were preceptors that allowed me to travel to far places and fight the battle of the just, to live a million printed pages and participate in a thousand dramas. To my mind, the emotions I felt were as substantial and true as the other elements that surrounded me, but they were emotions without a barrier to confine my mind. The dream can only be interpreted by the dreamer; the path taken only by those who have made the journey. What can be described by an outside observer as "unfortunate" can be the best of times for the participants. Looking back at my seven years of hospitalization for tuberculosis, I began to consider this a most auspicious occurrence, and eventually came to believe that I was the most fortunate of persons to have had this experience.

Because of our restricted time to realize all the different emotions attainable by human beings, no one can form all their ethical attributes from direct experience. The small difference between the emotions you can know and realize through imaginative and sympathetic participation in the made-up or true experience of others in a book, movie, radio, or TV program, and being a true participant, is of little consequence to the mind. Whether the moon is seen directly or reflected from a mirror, the mind still records an image of a moon. If we evaluate the influence of the difference innermost feelings that were conveyed to me by watching the movie *The Grapes of Wrath*, you would find that the movie would have given me a wider perspective and had more influence on me than if I had been an actual dust bowl farmer participating in a trip to California. Such a trip would have only given me a restricted and meager view. Today, when watching old movies on TV, I can still see how I used them to mold and shape my every thought. For years, and especially from age ten to twelve when I was most impressionable and forming my morality, I can say that I was fortunate to see every motion picture that was nominated for an Academy Award for best actor, actress, or best picture. The movies that were vividly remembered and influenced my character the most, were not the thousands of B pictures I watched, but the Academy Award movies such as *The Good Earth* and *Captain Courageous*. When I first saw these two movies in 1937, I was only eleven years old, but the emotions I felt, when viewing these and hundreds of other notable movies, were to leave a lasting impression on me.

In 1933, when I was about seven years old, I began selling newspapers on the corner of Haight and Fillmore Street, where I became part of San Francisco's street scenery. At that time, the price of the daily newspaper was three cents. The newsboy received two cents of this and the distributor one cent. I had a good day when in two or three hours I sold ten papers and received twenty cents. One big thrill, that made my day and happened a couple of times a week, was to be handed a nickel and told to keep the change. Today, many cannot envisage that depression economy where the customers were so poor that they waited for their two cents change because it represented a major expenditure when contrasted with a salary of about a dollar a day. The economics of this time was to leave its mark on me, and later I tried to understand why the depression happened, and if such adversities could be controlled or even be eliminated by correct governmental action.

Those years were also the time when my character was being formed by listening over the radio to "Little Orphan Annie" "The Lone Ranger" and "Jack Armstrong the All American Boy." Unlike real life, justice always triumphed over evil on these programs. This was the time of giveaway premiums, of Ovaltine mugs and secret decoder rings; and the beginning of being lied to; lies that, because we were children, we were unable to detect. We were told that Jack Armstrong was able to perform his brave and valiant deeds because he ate Wheaties; that "Little Orphan Annie" was victorious over her adversaries because she drank Ovaltine;

and "The Lone Ranger" was a straight-shooter because he ate the correct bread. That also was when my sense of humor was being implanted for life by listening over the radio to comedians like Jack Benny, Fred Allen, Bob Hope, Red Skelton, and George Burns and Gracie Allen. Most of the children growing up today and watching TV are cheated out of the experience that I had of being able to use and train my mind to visualize the people and events portrayed in these radio programs. The good or bad effect on society of not having this opportunity cannot be calculated, but I feel that it was important in shaping my view of the world.

My first incapacitating illness occurred in 1936 when I was about ten years old. The doctors diagnosed a rheumatic heart condition and pre-scribed complete bed rest. It was the middle of the depression; and being on welfare and unable to care for me, my mother allowed the welfare agency to put me in a foster home. Because I was bedridden and had the all this time at my disposal, another facet of my education started. I found that I could escape from my bed by reading books and listening to adult soap-operas over the radio. When I went back to school, I kept on reading books, but abandoned the soap-operas for the movies.

And while on bed rest, I came to appreciate the music of the great classical masters such as Beethoven, Brahms, Liszt, and Chopin. My fondness for this music developed because it had a narcotic like effect that relaxed and mesmerized me. This soothing response to music only made sense to me in the last few years. Scientific investigation found: that under some types of emotional stress, the body is capable of producing a natural narcotic secretion (an endorphin) similar to heroin. Classical music is evidently able to alter my mood and produce this narcotic. Even when I was allowed to go to school after a year of bed rest, I spent many hours lying in bed and getting high by listening to the great symphonic orchestras of the world. I developed such a fix for this music and the mood that it produced, that later in my life, I had to place a limit on listening to it, because I came to believe that it was a weakness on my part to be hooked on something that gave so much pleasure.

If I was mentally examined, it would be found out that I do have a true mental derangement, a mania. All my life I have had this compulsion to continually analyze and try to explain what has puzzled, perplexed, and bewildered me. When I became engrossed in deep thought and began conceptualizing and reflecting on the unexplained, I came to recognize that under these conditions I was also producing this narcotic endorphin. My mind was getting this heroin rush; was experiencing this glorious high when absorbed in solving a problem.

Once explained, you can recognize that this natural heroin is also responsible for the highs experienced in other situations. If you have the chance to watch the propaganda movie *Triumph of the Will*, look at the faces of the observers. See the exhilaration, the happiness that those faces show when the German people are listening to Hitler and watching those huge, fascist rallies, where there is a great spectacle of thousands of banners waving, thousands of flags flying, and thousands of troops marching. They are being stimulated; they are being inspired; they are all getting high on the excitement; they are producing that endorphin; they are all high on the natural heroin that their bodies are producing. This explains to me the adoration and worshiping of Hitler by the German people, the secret of his success, his popularity. What happened was that most of the German people had become addicts, had become hooked on a natural secretion of the body. We cannot find fault here; nature can make no judgments here; it has no method of assigning good or evil to a substance produced by the body, no way of restricting or reserving their usage to a beneficial legacy.

In six years, I had been confined in five different foster homes, where I was buffeted and shuffled around by an uncaring system that I had no control over. Soon after Pearl Harbor, I tried to gain some control by talking my father into allowing me to come to San Francisco and live with him. I had just turned sixteen, but looked and acted much older. Quitting school, and lying about my age, I got a job in a warehouse as a stock-boy, where within six months all the young men, except me, were replaced by women. Because of the shortage of male workers caused by the war, within a couple of months I had advanced to become the head stock boy. When the company I worked for began to ask to see my draft card, I registered for the draft by lying and telling them I was eighteen. I then used that false registration to enlist in the California State Guard where I was assigned to guarding the San Francisco waterfront. That enlistment lasted about four months, and when the California State Guard was disbanded, I joined the Merchant Marines. That was in June of 1943 when I was seventeen years old.

On one of my overseas trips, I signed on as an able-bodied seaman, was broken down to ordinary seaman (for insubordination), and then because someone else was demoted, I was again made able-bodied seaman. (In World War II the Merchant Marines had civilian status when in the United States but came under military law when outside those borders.) As time passed, I was upgraded to become the ship's carpenter, and then, at eighteen years of age, was made boatswain for the last six months of the voyage. It is true that I could have controlled my actions in the first instance, but the subsequent promotions were caused by the misconduct of others that I had no control over. This was enhanced by having a third mate who was promoted to ship's captain because of the war, using his authority in an arbitrary way. This shows the capriciousness and the buffeting that a person can receive in life, without being able to control it. Down the road, you will see that being unable to control the actions of others, even when their actions had an effect on my life, was to be a major theme in my life.

During the war, I had dropped anchor in many familiar World War II ports. I visited Australia, New Guinea, New Caledonia, and the Solomon, Mariana, New Hebrides, and Philippine Islands, and after the war, Japan and Korea. When James Michener's *Tales of the South Pacific* was published, I was amazed and delighted to find out how accurately an author could portray and bring to life a period of my life so that I could read his book and recall the sights, sounds, and smells of those times.

My first encounter with our fighting soldiers began when a ship I was on anchored offshore from the island of Guadalcanal. It was just a couple of months after the soldiers had finished mopping up the island. This gave me the opportunity to talk to and interview some of the soldiers who did the fighting. Like other Americans, I had been raised to hate and despise the Japanese by watching them being portrayed in the movies as beasts without honor; whereas our soldiers were always honorable and without fault. It was there on Guadalcanal that I heard the firsthand stories of atrocities committed by our side. Soldiers from the front lines bragged about killing or watching the killing of Japanese soldiers who had surrendered; boasted about the mutilation of the bodies of Japanese soldiers; and one soldier even offered to trade me a necklace of dried ears cut off the dead bodies of Japanese soldiers. Many years later, talking to the men who participated in the Vietnam War, I was not shocked or surprised to hear them tell of the atrocities they had seen, heard of, or had committed. I had years ago formed the opinion that under the harsh environment of war, a minority of soldiers, no matter what their religious or political background or what side they were on, would revert to a heritage where torture, mutilation and atrocities against other tribes were the norm.

After the war, I remained in the merchant marines; then in late 1946, I found myself on a ship that was anchored off the Admiralty Islands. For six months I had been plagued with a bad cough, was always tired, no matter how much sleep I had, and had developed pleurisy. There was no doctor aboard the small freighter that I was on, so the captain was usually responsible for giving first aid and treating the common cold and influenza that occurred at sea. Unfortunately the captain did not have the experience to recognize from my symptoms that I was extremely sick. However, the minute I coughed up blood in my sputum I knew, and went to the captain and told him that I probably had tuberculosis. My ship was anchored offshore of an Island that had a military hospital, so when I was taken ashore, they soon confirmed my self-diagnosis, and made arrangement to fly me to a Hospital in San Francisco.

There, just three months after I entered the Marine Hospital in San Francisco, my twenty-first birthday was dimly acknowledged. No one could predict that I was to remain hospitalized there, and in the hospital in Fort Stanton, New Mexico until I was released as an outpatient in January of 1954. Under all circumstances, seven years spent in a hospital will influence a person's thinking and outlook on life. For those seven years I was encased in an artificial cocoon that had no purpose of its own, but accomplished the same thing as a natural one — it transformed my boy's mind into a man's. There was a perceived difference though, as I had retained the memories from before being wrapped in that cocoon, of being a butterfly. My seven year stay in the hospital was to become the equivalent of going to college, but with an unsurpassable advantage over attending one. I was free to pick subjects to study that interested me; I had no tests to perform, no grading to worry about; and did not trouble myself about what fraternity to join or whom to date. While in the hospital, all my physical needs for food, clothing, and shelter were taken care of. It was a world of pure socialism where everyone was treated equally.

Soon, after returning to the Marine Hospital in San Francisco from the hospital in Fort Stanton, New Mexico, I was recruited into a Marxist-Leninist Party. When I met him, my recruiter recognized me as an atheist and a person who might be sympathetic toward socialism. He proceeded to educate me by giving me access to hard to obtain socialist's literature. Most of the time while I was in the hospital, I had educated myself by reading at least a book a day. Allowing for periods when I could not read, I estimated that I read about two thousand volumes in the hospital and at least that many before I entered. I read: history and fictionalized history books, biographies and autobiographies, fictionalized and true adventure novels, science and science fiction, religious and irreligious books, current and past philosophies, and the humorous side of life. I came to believe that if you do not develop a sense of humor you cannot be truly human. I also kept up with what was going on outside my cocoon, by reading every well known weekly and monthly magazine that was published. For example: I received the view point of *Time*, *News Week*, and later when it began publishing, News and *World Report*. I was completely democratic in my reading, as I read the magazines put out by the far left, the far right, and everything between. Even then I could see that you cannot educate yourself by reading only one side of an issue, and so I tried to read and study all the major religious, economic and political books that I had access to. Some books influenced me more than other's.

One set of books, that enabled me to see history as small individuals caught up in a larger panorama that they contribute to but have no control of, was John Dos Passos' trilogy *USA*. Another important lesson was obtained from reading the book and seeing the movie *Oil for the Lamps of China* by Mrs. A. T. Hobart. From this book and movie I was able to realize that many people, each having a small effect on his or her environment, when working in concert for their individual benefit, can blindly contribute to producing a larger effect on their environment than they realize they are producing.

I read, I studied, I believed. Reflecting on those years when I was growing up, I could see that my morality was shaped and influenced, and my ethical parameters set, mostly by reading and observing images produced by a strong light being passed through a strip of celluloid. Even when I realized that movies and literature had a great affect on me, that they were somebody's one-sided propaganda, it never entered my mind that others, according to their cultural upbringing, would view the identical reading and viewing material in a different light; that it would match their previous cultural experiences, not mine. How simple it seemed in my youth: just give the poor an education by putting the correct cultural information at their disposal to learn from, and the ills of the world could be cured. If everyone was able to read the truth (what I thought as truth), the problems of the world would be solved. This was a dream that was hard to wake-up from; it sounded so reasonable, so probable.

Among others, that educational dream was shattered when I found a book on General Semantics (S.I. Hayakawa's *Language in Thought and Action*) that helped me clarify my thinking. After finishing this Semantic Bible, I could see many false assumptions that I had made; could see that words mean different things to different people, and that my definitions were not canonized, that my interpretation of words was not sanctified, hallowed, or even necessarily right. Imagine that you were born and grew-up below a stagnant, putrid, polluted stream, a stream filled with all the garbage produced by a modern society. Then, one day when you were about nine years old and the sun was shining brightly, you were taken into the mountains above the pollution and saw a stream in its natural beauty; saw pure, crystal clear water for the first time in your life. That was my introduction to S.I. Hayakawa's book on semantics. After reading it, I was surely prepared to follow this man anyplace; this was a mortal god worth following, I thought.

Then, one day my God became President of San Francisco State University, and spoke. He spoke in a tongue that I did not understand, in a dialect that was completely foreign. Every explanation he used in his book to expose the use of words to uphold unjust cultures against the truth was being used by him to defend the existing state, to support the University's status quo. My explanation for what I thought was his betrayal of his book, for him using every day expediency to solve the problems of the 1968 student's strike: He could not have been the author of that pure, crystal clear book because his words in it did not match his actions. For an explanation, I even fantasized that some unknown author (a recluse, maybe) had sent Dr. Hayakawa his only copy of the manuscript for review, and then suddenly died in an accident without anyone else knowing about it, and so Dr. Hayakawa had it printed under his name. (Trying not to mislead you: because of its traceable roots, anyone who reads his books will immediately know that Dr. Hayakawa wrote them.) This is to show how foolish we are when our Gods disappoint us. The fault, of course, was not with my human god, Dr. Hayakawa, but with me. I expected every person's words to match their deeds, and this was a false assumption on my part. From then on, after adjusting my way of thinking, I was able to view human animals in their natural setting, and not expect them to always be above their animal inheritance.

When you find that you have been traveling in a desert, surrounded by hostile religious and political groups, and so are unable to say what you truly believe, then, when you meet your peers, there is a euphoric rush of proportions that can be compared to other highs. Like religious people, when I joined my Socialist Party, I accepted on faith most of their tenets, principles, doctrines, and beliefs. Later, looking back on the experience, I could see that when I met others of my kind, it became an addiction, I became hooked on comradery. When you find yourself surrounded by people who think like you, who believe like you, and act like you, it produces this euphoric high that can cause you to overlook some obvious flaws in your beliefs. Later, I could see that this high must also be the reason other religious and political groups acted as they did. They also became hooked and accepted blindly the doctrines and beliefs of their group.

When recovering in the hospital, my fear of McCarthyism was a major reason for my joining a far-left group. Many, including me, rejoiced when Edward R. Murrow in his program "See It Now" and Joseph Welch in the Army-McCarthy hearings totally discredited and destroyed Senator Joseph McCarthy. In retrospect, most Americans came to believe that these two men were responsible for the defeat of McCarthyism. This is where simplicity can be misleading. Much later, I was able to analyze what happened in that time reference, and understand that what they destroyed was a man named Joseph McCarthy, and I give full credit to them for that. But McCarthyism survived the death of Senator McCarthy, just like Stalinism and fascism lived on after the death of Stalin and Hitler. All these "isms" share the same cloak, and because they express an idea that has no physical attributes, they are not killed off when a human body dies. Because of my beliefs in cause and effect, I can tell you that McCarthyism did not prosper in America because the economic climate was not right. After World War II, the prosperity that came with it (and is still with us in 1989) held in abeyance its effect, but believe me it lives on, waiting for the right conditions to reappear. When it reappears in America, the name might be different, but it is not the man behind the symbolic name who you will be in contention with; it will be the American form of fascism underneath the cloak that you will have to defeat.

While still in the hospital, I came to believe that socialism would offer all workers a fairer opportunity in the competition for jobs. That this was not a true belief can be abruptly brought into focus when you see a western camera reporter recording a sleek, black, luxurious, chauffeur-driven limousine, with the curtains pulled to hide the occupant in the back seat, going through the gates of the Kremlin. Then, having the camera swing over and record for contrast, the elderly women sweeping up the dust created by the passing limousine. Do you believe that each of these elderly women sweeping up Red Square made a free choice to spend their life sweeping and cleaning up for the benefit of the Soviet upper class? To try to find the truth, these questions must be asked of these women: When growing up and going to school, did you major in street sweeping; was that your goal in life; was this your dream of success? When you were a child, did you whisper into your best friend's ear, "Oh, how wonderful it would be to dedicate my life to keeping the streets clean for my comrades?" I am sure the answers would be no!

Does a socialistic system, like the capitalistic, need an underling class, an exploitable class, an inferior class, a subordinate class to do this type of labor? Is this a built in flaw in socialism that can prevent us from reaching equality, or can we adjust the environment so that everyone (picked in a lottery, where everyone is entered) must dedicate a portion of their life to performing this type labor? Looking at the problem, it seems that only when you have an oversupply of labor — where to make a living, a person must accept these odious jobs — can you force a person not only to accept distasteful labor, but to bid on it. Without these surplus people bidding for the limited work, government would need to offer the street sweepers the benefit of limousines to keep the streets clean.

Throughout this book, when I attack socialistic governments, it is with the understanding that the paths that they have taken have not evolved into socialistic states, let alone the visualized final stage of socialism — "Communism." Although some countries that use the title socialism or communism have in some sections of the economy, a more equal distribution system than it had before, still, to evolve into a democratic form of socialism, it must recognize its true past, so it will not go on repeating its mistakes.

While hospitalized, I had time to study the history of the Spanish Civil War in the 1930s, which played an important part in alerting the public to fascism. When I found out that those fighting under the Communist Party's banner had (in the national interest of Russia) betrayed, purged and even murdered other socialist party members, and especially those fighting under the Trotsky banner, I could not at that time understand why they did it. It was problematical whether the Republican government would have won against the military power of the fascists, but the betrayals, purges, and murders under the label of "ideological purity" surely dissipated what little chance it had, so there had to be a logical deduction to explain the Communist Party's motives for their actions. Rather than search for a flaw in the Dictatorship of the Proletariat, I, like many other socialists, accepted for many years an un-Marxist explanation by blaming most of the failure of the system in Russia on a single man — Stalin.

Further on, we will explore and go beyond this simplistic assumption that historical events can be assigned to prominent individuals; thus making them responsible for either the good or evil of those recorded events (history). I will contend: shaped by the environment, prominent, historical persons cannot divorce themselves from their culture; no accepted belief (that controls their actions) can be shown to have been introduced from a source outside their environment without first being filtered by previously adopted beliefs. Cannibals raised in a cannibal environment cannot be blamed for their actions, because they have no control over the supplied information, which form the beliefs that they act on; therefore, how can they be held accountable for their actions if they unknowingly accept false information that they think is true, but is false and produces evil.

CONDENSED FABLE: ASPIRE TO

At this juncture, I am going to delve into fantasy to explain a misconception displayed by all forms of government. This fantasy is included because it has meaning for those who believe that they are the last revolution. It begins:

There is a narrative, source unknown, that recounts an episodic search for a meaning to the development of a great empire on an obscure planet in our galaxy. This empire had as its Overseer a mighty conqueror who had defeated and subjugated all the nations on the planet. This Overseer lived in great splendor. All his acknowledged desires were fulfilled except what all species lacked, the knowledge of the future. Sometimes, the Overseer was puzzled about what all this great accumulated wealth, power, and splendor portended. To explain his world, the greatest philosophers on the planet were sent for, and they came. There was about one philosopher for each subdivision in the empire, and they all told the Overseer what they thought he wanted to hear. They told him that he would be remembered as the "Greatest Ruler" of all times, and that there would never be another domain such as this seen again on his planet; that the sons and daughters of the ruling class would produce heirs who would inherit this mighty empire forever and ever.

The Overseer was uneasy about the answers received. Word was sent out to convey back to the capitol each new philosopher who appeared among the people. Years passed, and word finally came that a new voice was heard; a voice that denied being a philosopher, but claimed the title of "Bridger" — a person who builds bridges to connect broken circles of thought so that the circle is unified. Summoned before the Overseer, the Bridger was asked the same questions that his predecessors were asked.

"What you see is just temporary," were his words. "All this you see before you will disappear, as in time, all this will pass away and be remembered no more. All the books of the empire will be condensed to a chapter, which in time will become a paragraph, which in turn will become a sentence that will eventually be erased from our species records."

The Overseer heard this and knew it as the truth, but was sad because he could not comprehend another way of life. His mind could only accept the one he was living in.

The words of the Bridger drifted down to those who bore the burden of the empire, and they were elated because they believed that they were the inheritors of this wealth, power and splendor. Knowing the truth, the Bridger tried to explain what they could not understand, which was that all apexes must rest on a base. A pyramid, a mountain top, or an empire must have a base to rest on. This law is inflexible, and reads: the higher the apex the larger the base needed for the support of a pyramid, a mountain top, or an empire. Only, when a species is willing to build without apexes can everyone bear the same burden. Otherwise we will be continually introduced to small minds aspiring to be on the pinnacle of a pyramid, and these individuals, eternally, closing their minds to the crushing burden sustained by those making up the pyramid base.

We are all heir to dreams that become much larger than just the individual, and I am no exception. Since reading this short, science fiction story, my goal in life has been to look for those broken circles of thought — that I have observed in different cultures — and then, to try to unify as many as I can during my allotted time.

To seek the title of "Bridger" — a human being that builds bridges to connect broken circles of thought so that the circle is unified — is surely vanity. But am I not also a human being? Am I not just another animal temporarily residing on this earth? I do not claim to be above vanity; to do so would deny my humanity. Once again, I must warn you that this could be part of my illness. You should remember that I have been diagnosed as suffering from delusions of grandeur by reputable doctors who have made a study of delusions in human beings. So, you readers will have to decide and give a verdict as to what is the truth.

CHAPTER 10

HISTORY AS SEEN THROUGH
QUESTIONS AND ANSWERS

EXTRANEOUS INSERT #1

Query: "Why are you throwing that woman into the water when she is tied up like that?"

Priest: "We are trying to find out if she is a witch."

Query: "What will happen if she is a witch?"

Priest: "She will not drown, but will float to the surface of the water."

Query: "How many have floated to the surface that you know of or have heard about?"

Priest: "None; but you must understand that these cunning witches would prefer to die by drowning than use their black powers to come to the surface and be unmasked and burnt at the stake."

EXTRANEOUS INSERT #2

Query: "We understand that when you attacked that peaceable Indian village, you and your troops castrated, beheaded, and scalped the men and male children that surrendered, and that there was torture and rape of the women and little Indian girls before they were also killed and mutilated by the troops under your command. Is this true Captain?"

Captain: "But sir, all civilized American people, like us, have a Christian right and duty to protect ourselves and our civilization against the incursion of these unchristian savages."

EXTRANEOUS INSERT #3

Query: "We understand that you bombed, mortared, and shelled that friendly Vietnam village for two weeks, until it was a pile of rubble and all the friendly inhabiters were dead. Can you tell the American public why, General?"

General: "Yes, because it was occupied by the enemy."

Query: "Did you not realize that most of the men, women, and children were our allies, and you were condemning them to death?"

General: "Yes, we took this all into account; but looking at the village from all sides, we came to the conclusion that we had to completely destroy it if we were to have a solid chance of saving it."

EXTRANEOUS INSERT #4

Query: "Why are you beating those poor people so unmercifully?"

CIA: "Because we do not want the Communists to take over."

Query: "What would happen if the Communists took over?"

CIA: "They would beat these poor people unmercifully."

EXTRANEOUS INSERT #5

Query: "Is the Christian God a loving and caring God, a truly merciful God?"

Priest: "Yes, definitely! and you should always believe that He is merciful and loving and caring because you will be tortured for eternity if you fail to believe it."

NARRATIVE: HIDDEN HISTORY

The past, recorded truthfully, is essential to understanding why sequential events are similar to the origination and placement of the threads in a tapestry. By studying the historical threads, we can trace and understand why events take place in the order and arrangement that they do. By that, we gain insight into the finished tapestry, and recognize that previous events, like previous threads in the pattern, had to be inserted before the new events had a meaning in the picture that the tapestry is trying to convey.

Before World War II, there had arisen in the American public's mind the belief, mostly obtained through listening to the radio, watching movies, and reading books and magazines, that the valiant hero should always give the cowardly ruffians and desperadoes ample latitude in their encounters of good against evil. This unintentionally instituted a widely accepted code that read: A virtuous person should never fight "dirty" or strike the first blow in combat, never draw their gun first in a duel, never spy on or take unfair advantage against the villain no matter how much they are provoked by them, and should always treat women with courtesy and dignity. By the heroes doing these things, the reading, listening, and viewing public would be able to distinguish, to a greater or lesser degree, the actions of the righteous from those of the wicked. It is sufficient to say that it was used to portray the heroes in a nobler light than the situations in the observed world were or ever have been.

Later in the American intelligence field, this code became a hindrance when it was applied against villains who had not read the book, and so they did not know that they were expected to lose the battle in the final chapter. In the late 1930s, the British Security Agency began an effort to alert the American governmental agencies, and especially the FBI, to the danger of fighting an enemy with attitudes that had been mindlessly engineered by plots inherited from the entertainment world.

When William Stephenson, the head of the British Secret Service, came to the United States before our entry into World War II, he brought with him precepts that were to seep into and permeate the FBI, and later to contaminate the OSS when it was formed. After the war was over, the CIA was to fall heir to those precepts when it replaced the OSS. The main concept that he brought over was that victory over an enemy, *sometimes*, required that men and women in governmental service go outside the legal and constitutional restrictions placed on government and set up quasilegal agencies to act in a summary and illegal manner. Mr. Stephenson, whose code name was "Intrepid," taught that if the government was not acting in the best interest of its people (Being a capitalist multimillionaire, he surely meant his interpretation of what was best for them.), then you could set up an agency outside your government with private money to perform acts that were counter to the prevailing government polices. (Since finishing this chapter, we have been confronted with "Iran-Contragate," where a portion of the government disagreed with an official policy of Congress, and so they set up some private, quasilegal groups that used the cover of legal government bodies to mask their illicit operations of subverting a legal government policy.)

In the late thirties, Mr. Stephenson introduced into the mind of
J. Edgar Hoover and his cohorts in the FBI, the idea that money was readily obtainable outside the United States Government structure for illegal operations against a common enemy of the FBI and those who would supply the funding. Because William Stephenson was a multimillionaire, he financed some of the early British Secret Service operations out of his personal funds. He also knew and socialized with other millionaires in the United States who were willing, even anxious, to

donate money. They saw it as an investment in their future; a future that would allow them to use the influence they derived from giving money to attack their common enemies — Germany and Russia. (Russia had not become our ally at that time.) Some of these contributions are well documented, others less so. Nelson Rockefeller was a well-known contributor of money for one of these early quasilegal agencies, which he set up under the title of "Coordinator of Inter-American Affairs." The FBI controlled and used it to obtain information in South America before our entry into World War II, even though they had full knowledge that the law allowed them no jurisdiction outside the United States' borders; therefore they knew their actions were illegal. Government agencies will continue to break the law, the constitution, or other written or spoken agreements when they feel threatened by circumstances that they cannot control.

When William Stephenson set up Camp X in Canada to train British spies in guerrilla warfare, the FBI and later the OSS were introduced to professional safe-crackers, forgers, bank robbers, and smugglers, as people who had the expertise in an arena that had to be mastered to defeat an enemy. Common causes will form common bonds when common efforts are expended. Few people realize it, but the so-called criminal classes are not immune to patriotism as they are also of this culture; they are also taught to blindly salute the national flag and march to patriotic tunes. They see the flag and hear the tune, and react to it, just as you and I do.

After World War II and the rise of McCarthyism, organized crime and the common criminals became — like most of the United States citizens — extremely anticommunist. Little difference could be perceived between a religious group and a group of prisoners in their sentiments toward communism. Inside many prisons, it became dangerous even to admit that you sympathized with some of their ideas.

Through contacts developed during World War II, the FBI and OSS and later the CIA organized communications between their agents and organized crime leaders. Early cooperation between organized crime and the intelligence people could be seen when, after World War II, Charles "Lucky" Luciano was released from a life sentence in a New York prison by being pardoned and deported to Italy. It was hinted in the news stories that appeared after his release, that his pardon was due to his cooperation in the war effort. Apparently, he used his connections in the Mafia to obtain information and cover for OSS' agents in the Italian sector of the war. When questions were later asked about how close organized crime and the OSS were, there was a temporary outcry that those who were asking the questions were trying to blemish the memory of the OSS and hurt the CIA by association; they were implying that the OSS had cooperated with organized crime and that the same parallelism still existed.

By studying history, you can see that the FBI and CIA did not understand the mentality of the criminals they were dealing with. If they had, they would have known that they could have received the same cooperation without giving anything up to organized crime. To show their patriotism and devotion, most of them would have accepted assignments strictly for the privilege of showing what good members of society they were. Some of them though, had other personal and selfish motives for their fight against communism. They were horrified when Fidel Castro took over Cuba and eliminated prostitution, drugs, and gambling; then proceeded to deport those who were running these free enterprises. They could not understand a form of government where you could not bribe the policemen and politicians to look the other way while they proceeded to plunder the uninformed. They felt more secure with a government that was willing to make deals for their expertise.

At Camp X in Canada, the British and Americans taught their combative forces and secret services methods of killing that were silent and quick, but most important, so as not to alert the opposition that they were also killing noncombatants, methods that would look like an accident. William Stephenson, the top man in the British Secret Service, admitted executing in cold blood and without a trial, a British spy working in the United States. Although the FBI knew about it, they took no legal action against him.

After the war, the FBI and CIA did not hesitate in recruiting professional killers from organized crime, to kill people on the political left that they believed were a threat to capitalism. It takes no Sherlock Holmes to discern where the thread in the tapestry began when it came out that the CIA had hired Mr. Robert Maheu, a former FBI agent and an employee of the extreme right-wing millionaire Howard Hughes, to contact the Mafia. The object of that meeting was to negotiate a CIA contract to kill Fidel Castro. You can then realize why for years no effort was made to try to eliminate organized crime.

As World War II was drawing to a close, there came the realization by the Rockefellers and others in the intelligence agencies that their true enemy — a socialistic society — had contaminated the OSS because of their close association with groups that they were working with to defeat fascism. People such as Tito in Yugoslavia, Ho Chi Minh in Indo-China, and Mao Tse-tung in China were putting doubts in the minds of the OSS' people who were sent to those countries to set up drops for military supplies and gather information about the enemies' strength and movements. Deliberations at the highest commands found no way to decontaminate the OSS, so there arose a group consensus that the OSS had to be completely disbanded and replaced with a new organization to fight the true enemy of capitalism — the political left. Money was to be given by different capitalists to be used to investigate and clear OSS' members. So, in September of 1945, the OSS was disbanded; and in September of 1947, the Central Intelligence Agency came into being, composed mostly of cleared members of the OSS.

The seeds that were given to the FBI and OSS during the war by the head of the British Secret Service, William Stephenson, were to fall on ground that was to be plowed by the strife of our times. They would be recognized by the men at the head of the United States Justice Department, the FBI, and the CIA as correct seeds to plant when planting time came to the United States after World War II.

Witness such crops as "Watergate" and "Iran-Contragate" that came from the concepts that were introduced back in the late 1930s. Still, you are only seeing the misdeeds that were recorded. There were other secret organizations that were so far outside the law that no records were kept or needed because they were financed by private money supplied by the Ultra Right Wing Groups. I came to believe that it was one of these organizations that was responsible for my plight.

ESSAY: ASSOCIATED THOUGHTS

Another recognized thread in nature's tapestry is mathematics. Mathematics cannot be separated from nature. It is intrinsically and permanently bound up in its matrix. By observation you can see that success in life is a mathematical percentage game. ("Success" used here, means the survival of a set of genes.)

When observing a school of fish, it seems that almost instantaneously they turn and act as a unit. Although fish use schooling for the advantages it gives to individuals that belong to a group, each fish is seeking, within it, its explicit selfish interest by belonging to the school. Life in a school of fish is one of nature's percentage games played by individual fish. To prevail, you must become a better "prevailer"; to be a successful player requires you to be in the center of the school at least fifty percent of the time when the predator attacks. The most vulnerable position is on the outside. A professional gambler knows that a very small percentage in your favor over a long period will usually make you a winner. Because (through evolution) each living fish has come from other successful fish that have been able to protect their entities until they reproduced, they are almost equal in their ability to stay in the center of the school. Thus, only a small percentage point over fifty percent is needed to be successful. So, the uncertainty principle — that some call fate — must intervene and play a part in selection. A fish can be at the center of the school ninety-nine percent of the time, but if it happens to be in a vulnerable position and killed when the predator attacks, then there is nothing to intervene or nothing to appeal to from this unjust (to the victim) result. The opposite is also true, because a fish can also be on the outside of the school ninety-nine percent of the time, and still survive by being in the center when the predator attacks.

This can all be related to the human condition. Just because you played the percentage game to your utmost ability, it cannot or does not confer success or failure. Since there is no Grantor, there can be no guarantees in life. This is the reason that those who succeed over great odds cannot claim that a miracle has occurred. Success to nature is being alive and able to reproduce and is the only criteria that can be observed in nature.

Schooling is not an isolated creation by nature. You can observe it in a herd of animals under attack from predators. A herd of animals is a herd because it is preyed on by meat eaters, and the outside position is again the vulnerable one. If the outside animal is killed because of its position, then given enough time, selection takes place and the outside animals will tend to drift toward the safety of the center of the herd, thereby creating the herd. The victims of the predators have no choice in their environment. If they graze on the open plains, then that will be where the predators hunt them. The hunted cannot go to the mountains or the desert to escape, because there is no subsistence for them there. Still, the value of belonging to a school of fish or a herd of animals far outweighs the disadvantages of being outside that school or herd.

Human beings have their variations of the school of fish and herd of animals, and we join our groups for the same reasons — there are survival benefits in belonging to them. However, within the group we are (like other animals) forced by nature to act in our selfish interest. This is because nature is only able to control individuals through their genes. There are no such things as communal genes that have independent status outside those of the individual member. All survival benefit from belonging to a group has to be passed on through the individual. If there is no benefit to belonging to a group, then the grouping will eventually disappear.

From the above information we can ask: if a group of intelligent fish organized a school, and then ordered that those designated by the majority of the organizers must always be on the outside of it, would the designated not be better off if they left that school of fish and fended for themselves? Do they owe any loyalty toward that school? I do not believe so. A government has, like a school of fish, only the rights granted by the formation of that group, which is to offer equal protection against going it alone to all segments within it. When a segment is arbitrarily chosen to receive more benefits than what a natural allotment of chance would bring (we must all have the same chance to swim to the center of the school), then that government is allotting to themselves something that was not granted by its natural formation.

Those who study animal behavior, warn us not to ascribe human emotions to animals or to interpret their behavior in human terms. This is true, because animals do not exhibit human emotions or human behavior, it is we who exhibit animal emotions and animal behavior. After all, we descended from other animals, and not the reverse — that they descended from us.

Many religious people will see a natural success of winning over great odds as a miracle. Winning over great odds, even when with regard to those great odds, a life is saved, does not mean a miracle. It usually means that we are viewing a natural law from the wrong perspective. Imagine a lottery where one billion and one individuals put up a dollar each and there are to be only two winners. If the first person whose number is drawn receives one dollar, and the second person receives one billion dollars, then many, including the one billion dollar winner, would tend to declare, if they believed in miracles, that one had taken place. Although the odds were almost the same, the person who wins a dollar back would not be seen as the beneficiary of a miracle. From this we learn that the payoff on the odds has nothing to do with those odds; the payoff on the billion to one odds can be one dollar, a billion dollars, or a life, but they are all equal, and no miracle has occurred because a life is involved. Odds have no comprehension that there is a payoff, that a life is involved.

Another part of this natural law of probabilities can be explained by an experience of the author. During World War II, when I was on a ship anchored off a Pacific island, a couple of crew members and I were playing five card draw poker. Being nineteen years old, I had probably played only about two thousand's hands in my life, so when I was dealt an ace, king, queen, jack and ten of diamonds — a Royal Flush — I was surprised, as it is only dealt about one time in 649,000 hands. Because I do not believe there is a Supreme Being lurking behind probabilities, then I must attribute it to luck. Cards are inanimate objects; they have no memory of how many hands of five card poker were played that day, so they had no way of choosing me. Yet, if you were able to tally all the hands of five card poker that were played around the world in a year, you would find that a Royal Flush would come out to the correct odds. From this, I must infer that there is a natural law that is behind probabilities, because it can be mathematically demonstrated over and over again.

It is hard to check out the probabilities of a Royal Flush occurring in a poker game because of the high odds against it happening. You can, however, find out that the statement that inanimate objects have no memory is correct by taking two dice and keeping track of the numbers thrown. The prior probability of throwing a selective double, say two sixes, is thirty-five to one; which means that if you keep track of 3,500 throws, it will appear about 100 times. Casinos only pay thirty to one if you throw two sixes. They make their money by paying less than the calculated odds. There are gamblers who believe that if they wait ten times, and no double six comes up, that the odds will change in their favor. They believe that the two sixes will *now appear* on the average of one time in twenty-five, because they waited those ten times before they bet. Dice, like cards, have no memory, and you cannot substitute your memory of what transpired in those ten throws to those inanimate dice. Your memory and beliefs do not influence the natural law of probabilities. To prove this statement, take the 3,500 numbers you have put on paper, and cross out ten numbers after each occurrence of double six, and you will find out that two sixes still come up, on an average, one time in thirty-five times. You can use the same numbers and see that this applies to all doubles; and if the series of recorded throws of the dice is extensive enough, you can check by waiting fifteen, twenty, thirty, or thirty-four times before you start your calculation or make a bet, and the prior probabilities remain the same. What is overlooked in the computation is that when you are waiting (say ten times) for double six to be thrown, the number may come up before ten throws, and you are forced to start counting again from the beginning. Dice or cards have no memory of the last throw of the dice or the last dealt hand, nor do they have knowledge of what the dice or cards are doing at the next table or anyplace in the universe.

Many natural disasters, where the living proclaims that it was a miracle that they survived an earthquake, a hurricane, a flood, the eruption of a volcano, or some other natural disaster, cannot be calculated until after the event has occurred. For instance, on May 8, 1902, a volcano exploded on the Island of Martinique, which killed about 30,000 people in the city of St. Pierre. Only two persons survived. One was a prisoner confined in a dungeon that was built partly below ground, which gave him some protection, and the other was a madman hiding in a damp cellar near the waterfront. Here, probability cannot be calculated either in advance or after the event because those who survived have nothing to do with the natural law of probability. You can only calculate the percentage who survived after the event, but there was no way to tell in advance how many were going to be adequately sheltered to survive this volcano explosion. Note: Because there was an adequate warning, the entire city had time to completely evacuate the town. In fact, a few of the frightened inhabitants did leave the city for other parts of the Island and survived. Even if the entire city of St. Pierre had payed attention to the warnings and had evacuated the city, I still would not have considered it a miracle that they survived. It would just show some common sense on their part.

And what can we make of the priest who told the inhabitants of St. Pierre that no harm would come to the flock if they put their trust in the Lord; informed them that if they trusted in the Lord they would survive? This priest believed implicitly that prayer was a panacea for all their troubles; he told his parishioners that if they believed in prayers, they were in no danger. The result: we observe the Roman Catholic Church crammed full of parishioners beseeching their God to save them, who were all killed when the volcano exploded. If we contrast that with the Negro prisoner, who was condemned for killing a person, and the insane man hiding in the cellar, both of which were saved, what are we to think about that? Do you believe that a Supreme Being deliberately saved the prisoner and that insane person and then condemned those who were praying in the Cathedral of Saint Pierre to die a horrible death? I, personally, can only view their surviving as just the result of the capricious act of a volcano explosion, not something that would have some religious significance.

And what was the later fate of this prisoner, Auguste Ciparis? He was pardoned from hanging the day before the volcano exploded and eventually given a full pardon because he had so miraculously escaped death. He later earned his living by becoming an exhibit in the Barnum and Bailey's Circus; spending his days in a replica of the prison cell that saved him. He was considered by the circus and the public as just another freak of nature, just another dog-faced boy, another fat woman, another rubber man; just something to be exhibited to the public, not someone who was saved to preach that a Supreme Being was in complete control of the universe and his survival was the proof of this.

When the prisoner, Auguste Ciparis, and the madman, Leon Leandre, were found by a rescue party looking for survivors, they had no profound wisdom to impart to their rescuers, nor could it be observed that the remainder of their lives served as an object lesson to increase the knowledge of society. This has proven true of all human beings who have survived because of a declared miracle. If a God or Goddess has suspended the natural laws, I would expect the Supreme Being to have a reason. I would expect to see threads in the tapestry of life that formed a clear picture. Although these so-called miracles have been examined, and a search made to find a reason or a consistent pattern, all have failed to find one embedded in the studied matrix — the tapestry of life. This can only lead one to the conclusion that there is no Supreme Being guiding the natural laws of the universe or interfering with them. A lack of a consistent guiding force is interpreted by me as documentation that we are living in an imperfect world without directions.

Volcanoes are like cards and dice — they are inanimate objects. Volcanoes do not know that when they explode they can kill living things. The one on the Island of Martinique was not unique; it did not know that two human beings survived its explosion or that it killed about 30,000 people. The payoff has no connection with the natural scientific law of probability. Just because the payoff can be manipulated by an intelligent life form that can say that someone beat the odds or the percentages and a miracle has occurred, does not and cannot change the fact that the computable mathematical odds have no memory. The odds do not know or recognize that a life form is ascribing a payoff to them. Probability remains a universal law that exists even if an intelligent life form is not there to calculate the odds and declare it a miracle.

It is necessary for the reader to understand that how you view these simple mathematical problems will determine not only how you believe your environment is formed, but will control how you act in it.

CHAPTER 11

ESSAY: HABITAT

In this world that we inhabit, there lives a breed of caterpillar which, if you pick it up and set it on the rim of a cup, will, even if it is within inches of its favorite food supply, march around and around that rim, following its scent until all its strength is dissipated; then after collapsing from exhaustion, that caterpillar will fall off the rim of the cup and die of hunger. This type of caterpillar has been programmed to blindly follow the chemical scent laid down by its species, and is unable on the rim of a cup to recognize that it is following its own scent. The scent trail is not meant to be used to distinguish an individual caterpillar's own scent trail. This would be out of context to its original purpose. Nature has no way of correcting for an individual mistake, an individual death. It cannot anticipate that a caterpillar is going to be placed outside its natural habitat — on the rim of a cup. True, if rims of cups were prevalent in its natural surroundings, given enough time and deaths, it could correct for this environment, but never from isolated, non-connected incidents that are outside the adapted to habitat. Please do not feel sorry for such a single dead caterpillar, as it is programmed by nature and is acting under an adaptable gene; a gene that will permit its species to better survive in its environment. If you wish to express your emotions, feel sorry instead for the species that place caterpillars on the rim of cups, as some of them claim that a Perfect, a Just, an Unflawed, an Infallible Designer is responsible for their existence. It is these flawed individuals, following scent trails to their destruction on different cup rims, that we are going to observe.

Because I do not believe in a Grand Designer, I must designate "Nature" as the cause of imperfection. However, limitations in language exist, so I cannot even use the phrase "benign neglect" to describe the relationship between nature and us. Those words are too strong as they imply that the universe is somehow aware of our existence, that it recognizes us. This is an unfounded assumption. Nature is totally unaware of our existence, and so when I accuse it of "benign neglect," it is with the understanding that it cannot deliberatively correct what it has no knowledge of, other than by blind, random chance.

Although we and other species of animals were produced by that blind, random chance, we human beings have an advantage that other species lack — which is to channel nature into a destiny that can correct some of the imperfections that we can observe around us. We are not like the caterpillar, as we have the choice to suicidally throw ourselves off the rim that we adopt or were born on when we realize that we can only seek nourishment while we still have the strength to search for it.

To stay on a rim because we are told that the scent we are following was laid down by a Deity or a political system that knows the destination of all species, is to place yourself with the caterpillar that has no choice. In the struggle for perfection, it helps to understand that in trying to control a situation, it does no good to beseech Gods or Goddesses or Nature for powers that do not exist. If your opponents do not realize this, it is to your advantage.

Those who see a Deity controlling a volcano will try to please this Deity by different forms of worship. Unknowingly, they are doomed to failure even when they can observe some favorable results from their religious practices. It matters not how many young virgins are sacrificed by throwing them live into a volcano, it matters not how many still beating hearts are yanked out of the freshly cut open breasts of young men and women, it still remains a useless practice. The testimony that one hundred percent of these people believe in this volcano Deity has no influence on the eruption of a volcano. Even the worshipers of volcano Gods are covered with the volcanic dust in an eruption. And if you escape being killed in an eruption and believe that your Supreme Being saved you, then you are in the same category as those who believe they are controlling a volcano by sacrificing virgins and pulling out the beating hearts of human beings. You might feel superior to the believers in a Volcano God and call them backward savages, but your reasoning is the same and just as invalid.

To account for the good things that happen when worshiping an idol, or why a volcano will sometimes stop erupting when you sacrifice human beings and animals to it, a new God had to be invented that controlled these results for evil purposes. To explain why a person was cured when worshiping an idol, or why sometimes a volcano will quit erupting when human beings or animals were sacrificed, does not explain how goodness can flow from evil, especially when all powers were, according to the Jewish, Christian and Moslem religions, supposed to flow from a single Supreme Being. It can be pointed out that volcano worshipers will be susceptible to other provably false beliefs. Once you adopt a false belief, it is almost predictable that you will tend to believe that human beings can bend spoons with their minds and move compasses the same way; they will readily believe in UFO's, in extraterrestrial kidnappings and visitations, in reincarnation, in voodooism, in psychic surgery, in Bermuda Triangles, in ghosts and demons and angels that have wings; and they will also believe in unicorns and elves, in astrology, and that pyramid power will sharpen a razor blade. These beliefs are all compatible with a belief in a God controlling natural events, breaking scientific observable laws of the universe, and interfering with human affairs.

As the water of time washes over the religious and political feet of clay, we will turn to new religions and new politics, because the old religions and politics, when exposed, cannot fulfill the craving that we seem to need to hide the truth of what the world of reality is; especially when we see that the feet of clay are melting before our eyes. The thin veneer of religion and political beliefs cannot hide forever the structure of reality that underlie life.

NARRATIVE: CONSPIRACY

What you are about to read is a supposition of what must have happened while I was innocently engaged in trying to determine why I was following a scent that others had blindly followed before me, especially when I could look down from the rim that I was on, and see the corpses of every faith and persuasion commingled with their tattered banners in a common pile of decay. This supposition is needed to explain why those whom I was aligned against were limited in some of their knowledge when they were setting up the necessary plans to frame me for bank robbery, and to explain where and how this false knowledge was obtained.

Communication must have been a limiting element in their plans; so we begin with a supposition in their communications.

"Hello, Johnson? This is Ricker. I am switching over to scramble on the prearranged frequency. Please do the same. Over."

"Affirmative, Ricker. Your voice is recognized. Give the code name, and proceed."

"The code name is Revenge; and we up here in Sonoma County want you to make a final decision on whether we should take the final steps on our plan or call it off. I am trying to limit the people involved in this, but if we do not carry this out soon, we might have to abandon it because it is getting out of our ability to manage."

"All right, Ricker. I understand. You know how I thought all along that we should have confined this operation down here where we had more control; this running around the countryside risking our group's exposure is insane, but I take orders too; and those above me see this, besides other considerations, as a training mission. So, if you have some catch up data for me, I will make the final decision for you to proceed with your mission or abandon it for now."

"I have a couple of things that could be relevant to whether we should go ahead in this matter. First, he is still camping on the beach and not doing a damn thing except acting like somebody on vacation. Our previous speculation that he is here to meet someone could be faulty. A few people did come over the weekend, but as far as we could tell, there was no contact between them. We have an observation point where we can watch his movements and not be seen, so we miss little of what is going on down below us. A few days ago he walked about a half of a mile down the beach to fish for crabs, so I personally went down and checked out his station wagon while agent Williams covered me with his "Walkie-Talkie." When I opened his glove compartment, I could see a .22 caliber pistol and his contact lenses, but because of our previous speculation on his operational methods, I did not take the chance of moving anything. I used gloves and checked for hair traps before opening the car door and the glove compartment. We noticed through our binoculars that he has not shaven in a couple of weeks, so we alerted our man to also stop shaving. Although our man has only a couple of days growth, we can use make-up to simulate the growth if we decide to go ahead with the project. We will, of course, arm him with a .22 caliber pistol, but he will not need contact lenses as he has good eyesight. To implicate him and show that he was in the area, we removed a license plate from an automobile parked near where subject Revenge is camped. So, when we obtain the station wagon resembling his, due here today, we will be ready to proceed. Agent Dove has located from a description and photographs that we have sent him, the matching station wagon we wanted. It is being sent up in a moving van that you can drive right into while the van is in motion. On entrapment day, we are going to make sure that the license plate and the station wagon are seen, then all our man has to do is drive down the road and into the moving van to disappear from the roadway and avoid the road blocks."

"If Subject Revenge cooperates, then our station wagon will be found with the evidence showing that it was used in the robbery; if not, then the moving van, which will be outfitted with an acetylene torch, will be used to dump the cut up station wagon into an old stone quarry that we have located in an out of the way place. We get the moving van back when everything is clear. Agent Dove has assured us that the moving van and the station wagon are untraceable if something goes wrong."

"We will, out of necessity, need to bring another man from outside our group to drive the moving van, as we do not want our people involved if there is the least chance of something going amiss. One of our local recruits here in Santa Rosa has given us the best and safest place to carry out our assignment. This location has been hit five times before, so we know their routine and counter measures that will be taken after the alarm is given. The bank employees have been told to put up no resistance, and because they have had previous experience in being robbed, they should not panic. Another plus for us is we will have at least one of our men there, after the robbery, to warn us if some unforeseen occurrences happen. I can assure you that this operation can be set up within a day or two if you give the final clearance."

"Just a couple of questions, Ricker. What is the pay-off for the driver of the moving van going to cost us?"

"Our Las Vegas contact man has sent us a driver. He will get a straight three thousand dollars and will have no knowledge of who he is actually working for. He will think he is working for the organization in Las Vegas; that this is just a test to prove his loyalty to them. If he is caught, he and our man in the motel will not have information that will lead to us. The two of them believe that we are part of their organization."

"All right; now, do you have the experimental drug that you are going to give him if he does not cooperate with us."

"Yes, I have it in an aspirin container, but I still have doubts about giving it to him. You know, from our past experiments, how drugs react differently on different individuals. Besides, I don't think we have sufficient experience with this one. Remember what happened to the LSD experiments."

"I know; you objected before, but the trance the drug will put him into will be the only way we can control him and the situation without endangering ourselves. This way we get our revenge no matter which way he goes. When the drug is stopped, then he will return to normal. Just remember, that the people he is responsible for eliminating were technically ours. We do not know how he exposed them; so it is our duty to find out so it will not happen to our personnel. I will stress this: Unless something comes up that could place one of us in jeopardy, then you have final approval to go ahead with the plan Revenge."

Although I will use it, fate is not the precise word to be used in describing why I was the one who became webbed by my spidery enemies. The word "fate" has connotations that give credence to superstition; it implies that we cannot deviate from a prearranged and preset course, and that would give the word religious overtones. Throughout this book, I use the word "fate" to mean an ending that nothing has control over other than the actions of the people involved and the law of chance that we cannot control. I wish you to know that I knew that the edifice I became enmeshed in was not constructed for the implicit reason of snaring me. If the fly caught in a web had not been born, that does not mean that the web would not have been spun. What I was trying to do was construct the web from my encounter with being the fly caught in it.

In our daily communications with other people, we must assume that people will interact and change when in contact with reality. Just as an island in the center of a hurricane will change its features no matter which way the hurricane is moving, it will still be recognized as an island if it survives the storm. As human beings, we all have something left that someone can recognize as human, no matter how much we are buffeted by life's storms; but we are changed by our encounters. I was changed by my encounter with my enemies; my enemies were surely changed too.

Every artificial ingredient, whether social or concrete, introduced into our environment by human beings, creates new ecological niches to be filled and dominated. Neither now, nor in the past has the human race ever fitted into all its exploitable niches, *perfectly*. This is because we were, and still are adapting to our environment while we continually add new niches to be filled. Everything artificially introduced into the environment, influences natural selection. It does not abrogate natural selection, just adds different dimensions to it.

It has been noted: when governments are formed and are able to stabilize themselves, they create niches. We call them government bureaus. These structures, operating in every facet of our organized world, can be seen to take on a form and life independent of, and with different needs from, those who formed them. The first law of a bureaucracy is to survive; the second is to multiply — and one way to multiply is to divide. Anything that increases the survival rate or perpetuates the form is good. Anything that consolidates, decreases, or eliminates it is viewed as bad. Even the smallest bureaucracy will go to inordinate lengths to insure its survival, to insure its niches. Who-so-ever brought me to the attention of the group that I was pitted against, had given them false information that evidently led them to believe that I was a threat to their survival. This explains the harsh methods used to try to gain information about how I became that threat. They had to protect their ecological niches, their bureaucracy.

Many people have been raised to believe that governments are formed to arbitrate disputes among the different views present in all societies. This is the ideal state, but not the historical state of the past or the present.

When the arbitrator has an interest in the decisions, the decisions will not be just. When the decision does not interfere with the laws of bureaucracy, the bureaucracy will generally rule on the side that has the power. If, however, the bureaucracy is threatened, it will be found to have a life of its own. Because many people were blinded by the times they lived in, the laws that bureaucrats operated under were not taken into account when the Russian Revolution occurred. Once the Soviet bureaucracy was observed and stripped of its hidden coloration, then one could observe that the same rules applied to all forms of government.

Of course, the spider does not pick the fly that comes into its web, but my choosing was deliberately done by the makers of the web that I became tangled in. In a bureaucracy where secrecy is maintained, they spin webs to catch flies that they have created, then do not understand why their results do not mirror that created world. To spy is useless if you are indoctrinated with a preconceived idea by a government bureau, then sent out to find verification of the preconceived. All bureaucracies dissemi-nate propaganda, but as time passes they are unable to distinguish between their propaganda and the truth, so they base their actions on the propaganda they created. The Communist takeover of China is a classical large scale example of this. To this day the United States Government, which gathered the information and so knew better, does not understand that it was their false propaganda that the Communists had no support in China (disseminated to fool the American People) that they were reacting to when setting their policies toward China. The Russian and Chinese Communist states are not immune to this law; many of their failures can also be traced to the false propaganda that they act on. The interpretation of this nonsense is further enhanced when the interpreters ignore what is in opposition to their preconception. How much truer this is in a small secret bureaucracy where there is a limited movement of information. It was easy, when examining my intrusion into their ecological niche, for them to fall into a trap of acting on information that was not valid.

What would they have learned from me if they had gained control over me and were able to blackmail me into helping them? Absolutely nothing that was not already used in their everyday investigative techniques. One basic of investigation is that human beings are creatures of fixed habits. These habits are like objects in space: once the habit is launched, it stays in a fixed orbit and does not deviate from it unless acted on by an external force. If you take the time to study the habits of people, then you can be sure that if they deviate from those habits, there is a compelling reason for it. Now if you can secretly introduce extraneous material that causes people to break a habit, then you can deduce from this that your material was a compelling reason, when ordinarily it should not be. The introduction of the correct material and its correct interpretation, will lead to a conclusion as to whether a person is indulging in a clandestine operation outside their original group. Once this is established, it is easy to find out to whom they are reporting.

There is no sweet victory over an inept opponent. To enhance our fame, we must enhance our enemy's strength. To become a super hero, we must vanquish a super enemy. I fell prey to this by giving attributes to my enemies that they were not worthy of, and I presume, from their actions, that they did the same in regard to me. They had set up a large, intricate web to catch a fly whose size was blown out of proportion, but instead they caught a small gnat — me; and then only on a single strand of their web that had accidentally become attached to another web.

ESSAY: EXPLANATORY THOUGHTS

Natural laws of survival, which developed for the protection of all species, will frequently come into conflict when we thinking animals use them out of context in human constructed environments that are not compatible to their origination. Imprinting is a language used by nature to pass on information to the offspring of animals. It has been widely studied, so we know that improper imprinting can lead to bizarre complications. We can observe the ludicrous from an example of misprinting that recently occurred in a whooping crane held in captivity. So that whooping cranes will have a better chance to survive, their eggs are sometimes removed and hatched in a different environment. The female whooping crane in this narration was imprinted, when she was hatched away from her species, with the belief that she was a human being. This came about because when hatched, most birds immediately imprint or identify as a parent the nearest moving object close to the size of a mature adult of its species. When it came time to mate, the fixation that she was human, left her unable to mate with her species; her instinct to mate being directed toward her imprinted zoo keeper. This brings us face to face with the ludicrous: a group of human beings trying to correct their first mistake by having the imprinted male zoo keeper perform the male courtship dance of the cranes; thereby tempting the female whooping crane to lift her tail feathers so she could be artificially inseminated.

In this created situation it was a human being that was wrongly imprinted on the whooping crane. In nature, it will almost always be the same species that will be imprinted. This procedure protects newly hatched offspring from endangering their life by going up to a different species — let us say a fox — after imprinting. In nature, if the fox is there at the nest when the offspring hatch, it will not matter what false images are imprinted, because the bird has little chance of growing up and passing on a false imprint that it is a fox if it is immediately eaten by one. And if the false imprint is not a direct threat, for example if the bird is imprinted and adopted by a similar shaped but different bird species, then it still holds that it will have little chance to mate and produce a false image, because it cannot reproduce by mating with a different species. If it is adopted by a different bird species, our fledglings entire life will be complicated; its genes will have encoded a program for a specified action to be performed when it receives a stimulus either from one of its species or from the environment, and these actions will not make sense to its adoptive species, nor will its adoptive species actions make sense to it.

Because it takes maturity to mate, it must follow that imprinting of the species comes before imprinting of a sexual partner; and in the natural surroundings, the sexual imprint will usually be of the same species that was determined by the first imprint. In our whooping crane's situation, nature went on imprinting a mate over the first false imprint, because nature has not evolved a way of knowing when a first imprint is erroneous. It has, however, a blind and unknowing way of correcting such a mistake. Nature eliminates these false imprints by not allowing the holders of these imprints to be able to reproduce. A swan imprinted with a belief that it is a duck, still remains physically a swan no matter how strong the false imprint is. A false belief will not overturn a natural fact. A swan remains a swan regardless of what belief it has that it is something else. When we use civilization to interfere with nature's way of correcting mistakes of imprinting, we will sometimes create, by reproduction of that false imprinting, human beings unable to adapt to their societies; human beings with psychological problems that make them unfit to be called a civilized person; problems that can even lead to incarceration in a prison or mental hospital. One can perceive that the world is overflowing with human swans who believe that they were created ducks; and so are unable to conceive and give birth to a civilization that only swans free from false imprinting can achieve.

By artificially isolating primates at birth and creating false environments for them, we have observed that sex is a learned behavior; it needs suitable imprinting or the isolated subject will not be able to mature; without maturity, primates will usually not be able to mate normally. Imprinting is partly responsible for whom we pick as our sexual partners; and like our whooping crane, when she chose the zoo keeper, we have a limited choice. However, we as human beings have the ability through language to enhance and embellish that limited arrangement of our gene implanted mating instruction, by substituting an envisioned state called "love" for the reality of our animal sexuality. That beauty, like love, is also one of those envisioned states of mind can become apparent if we view the world from a different perspective. Let us say that if in the scheme of things the (to our minds) ugly warthog had become the only dominant thinking animal on earth, then because of imprinting, its conception of personal beauty would be another warthog, and we would be thought of by them as a truly ugly animal. Still, like us they would believe many things in nature, such as sunsets and rainbows, are things of beauty. If we accept this, then we can see why the Science Fiction's caricature of scaly reptile aliens who lust after large breasted earth women, are as plausible as men lusting after warthogs.

Chemistry can also artificially produce false environments. Chemists can make a synthetic sex attractor for moths that can be sprayed over a prescribed area to confuse the moth in its search for a mate. After spraying, you will see the moths trying to mate with anything the sex attractor alights on; whether it is a leaf, a twig, or another species of insect. This sex drive, incorporated into the moth's genes, cannot take into account that there will arise a species that will interfere with its natural environment, and by that, misdirect its reproduction onto objects that cannot reproduce its species. We human beings have also, by creating false environments, misdirected many other human beings into depositing their sperm, allegorically, on leaves and twigs.

When at birth, a monkey is deprived of its mother and, as a result, its whole life is destroyed in that experiment, then, that monkey cannot be held responsible for the outcome of its deprivation. The environment that is created by the scientific experiment, is responsible for all its hostile actions. The monkey has no way of controlling its reactions to that created experience. If, because of the experiment, the monkey commits antisocial acts when it grows up, society has a right to restrain it, but not to punish it. The same is true in human terms when we must live in a created environment. Even with the understanding that each person reacts differently to the environment, we still have an excuse for our actions. We all react differently, but we also have no control over that, either, because how we react is an inheritance from our genes. Even for identical twins, the environment is different; they have different friends, experiences, and so forth.

If you believe we were created by a Supreme Being and can make a free choice to not act negatively toward a society no matter how grievously the environment treats us, then you are blinded by your prejudices. However, you also have an excuse for this belief. The religious person that has this view, did not arrive at this view freely, either. That outlook was supplied by the same type of human created environment that shaped the monkey's reaction to its created environment.

We can see that human beings who have been imprinted with

erroneous information at birth and through life, can interfere with the gene's messages and so pass this misinformation on not only to offspring, but to persons outside the gene's transmission patterns. Genes were developed outside a collective; they are for directing the individual's actions. When the question arises, an individual's genes will always pick the person over the collective, because it has no idea of what a collective is. A collective will survive without an individual, but a person once dead, is no more. Some of us may choose to sacrifice ourselves for the common good, but only fools will knowingly sacrifice their life to a false deity.

We arrive at some of our foolish beliefs because nature, like machinery, is not perfect. If early in life, young children are taught to believe in Easter Bunnies and Supreme Beings, then they unhesitatingly accept those beliefs as equals; they do not have the ability to reject false information. So when people want to widely disperse their beliefs, they try to gain access to young children; they know that once the children accept their beliefs, then most of them will not only hold them for their lifetime, but will become zealous missionaries for their further dissemination. Because children and adults reason differently, no matter how ridiculous the cause you espouse, you can always indoctrinate children's minds with it; and especially, early in life, they will openly and without questioning receive the teaching of anyone on whom they were imprinted. They accept what they are told in the same manner as a person under hypnosis. Children are not able to get rid of false notions until they reach a definable development, which we call the adolescent stage, where they acquire the ability to reason, and have the opportunity to override some of the false information they imbibed. The problem? All falsely acquired information is not equally verifiable. Children, unless they are retarded, will eventually, through experience, reject the concept of an Easter Bunny, because they can verify with facts obtained in their environment, that these images have no substance except in the mind; but only with great mental effort can children reject the parents' religion. They are hampered by having to search out facts that are outside the environment that they grow up in; facts unbiased by the beliefs of their taught religion.

An ability to reason does not imply that those arrived at decisions will be infallible, but to a few it does permit the overriding of information that was formally, before language, imprinted or programmed for life. To others, it just allows them to trade one false belief for another equally false belief. New and old philosophies should continually be questioned because you never can be sure that your new acceptance is the truth; it might just be another false belief you submit to because of a lack of true information.

Because human beings were responsible for the errant whooping crane's behavior through their interference and creation of an artificial situation, are they not also responsible when civilization creates false environments for human beings, and this in turn creates deviant behavior because this artificially created society tends to imprint the wrong message into the deviant's mind? By creating an artificial environment and destroying a natural habitat, are we not responsible when we knowingly or even unknowingly do this to human beings; are we not responsible for caring for those who cannot survive without help in the newly created habitat? If I understand how I am formed into a monster by a created culture, am I not responsible for my actions under those circumstances and conditions, and is it not my duty to try to change those conditions and warn others of these uncivilized traps?

CHAPTER 12

NARRATIVE & ESSAY: PRISONS & SOCIETIES

After my evaluation at the San Quentin Guidance Center in 1955, I was informed that I was going to be sent to Folsom Prison, which was, and still is, California's notorious maximum security prison for convicts. (Inmates were sent to the other prisons, and the connotation of inmate was that they still could be helped.) Most of the convicts sent to Folsom Prison were considered beyond rehabilitation by the prison staff. Many of them were the older, hard-core, recidivistic prisoners who bragged about and were proud of the title convict. A first timer being sent to Folsom Prison, unless doing straight time for murder, was an unusual event. Some of my fellow convicts were naturally mystified about what horrendous crimes I, as a first time offender, had committed to be sent there.

Folsom Prison was where I first tested the use of cryptic coloration as camouflage. I merged with my surroundings by embellishing my criminal acts to such an extent that I was accepted by my fellow convicts and admitted into a dominant clique. (These cliques are known to outsiders as prison gangs.) Being accepted was crucial, not only for survival, but to gain insight into a group in society that I poorly understood, even though technically and mentally I was one of them. By joining the dominant clique, I found out that I had obligations to act a part that had rules as rigid as those the cowboy heroes have in western movies. "Do your own time" was the most important lesson to be absorbed by the new prisoner. All the other rules of conduct branched off from this central rule. (These are convict rules, and are not the ones imposed by the prison administration.) "No informing" was another convict rule, and there was no exception to this rule. Then there was the rule most violated by the new prisoner: Never, and I mean never, in front of other convicts or prison staff, imply by voice or gesture that a fellow prisoner was not sexually a man. Sexual pride is the most highly bruised feature of a male prisoner. Prisoners will go to absurd lengths, many of which can be destructive, even deadly, to their bodies, rather than be labeled as someone that submits and bows down to authority, which they consider a feminine characteristic.

Criminal acts are not homogeneous; this is reflected in the different views held by convicts to acts committed by other inmates. Sex crimes, especially against children, are viewed by the thief and robber as despicable acts; those who commit these acts are considered outcasts by the other prisoners. If, however, you talk to the child molesters, you will find they are mortified to be incarcerated with thieves and robbers, whom they consider immoral. This duel standard is also widespread outside prisons. If you ask the robbers or child molesters: "Why do you break the law?" The answer in prison will be according to who is asking the question. All answers to prison psychologists, parole board members, and prison officials are suspect. The prisoner's main goal is to be released from prison, so they will lie to keep anything from getting into their records that will prevent that release. They also know what the people holding them want to hear, and so that will usually be what they hear. Most convicts are so paranoid that they will not even answer correctly to a fellow convict unless you take the time to cultivate their friendship and profess similar views. If by chance they answer truthfully, it does not mean the answer is correct. The majority do not understand why they act as they do. If they did, many would not be where they were; to truly know yourself allows you to be a different person.

After observing and talking to many prisoners, all I can do is to give you my philosophy on why I think we behave as we do. I attempt this under the guise that I believe that if human beings have a criminal mind, then I believe, because of my criminal acts, that I possess one too. Over the years, many underlying causes have been mentioned for criminal behavior. Poverty, ignorance and plain stupidity have been cited, but then what is the explanation of why the rich, the educated, and the intelligent commit crimes? To try to find a common thread that ties all criminal acts together, you must go to the simplest answer: We are all imperfect animals, still in transition; we have been bred for a different environment where our imperfections do not allow some of us to adapt to current cultures. Human beings were not bred for village life, let alone for living in towns and cities, and we surely were not bred for farming. We are hunter-gatherers, and there has been no time for the basic genetic change (the first settlements only appeared about 25,000 years ago) needed to produce an animal that could fit perfectly into today's cultures. It might take a million years of selection for us to adapt to this culture, but the contradiction is that this culture will not remain stable to give us time to adjust to it. The success of the human race is its ability to adapt to different environments, but there is no rigidity in our adaptation, so everyone does not fit completely into a new culture. *Homo sapiens* have never stratified into a single all-encompassing unit. While we have spread over the face of the earth and have adopted a diversity of cultures, of climates, of foods, and of housing, still, looking back, we can see that no culture has eliminated our animal behavior. Not one of the great religions or the minor ones has been able to eliminate it either. You can chant over an animal for its entire life, but at death and all through life, its actions will be the actions of an animal.

Because *Homo sapiens* have no preeminence over the other animals, then we, as selfish human beings, are all capable of committing criminal acts when circumstances put us into the position where our selfish interests tell us that there are survival benefits in committing them. We may also commit a crime under a *delusion* that it benefits us. We are unable sometimes to perceive reality because we are confused by our genes telling us that under the conditions of a natural habitat, "this" would be the proper response, but if we are living in a created culture, that response might be harmful to our interest.

From observation, we find that only some environments create the conditions that produce certain criminal actions. If it is true that the environment is at fault, then by changing it, we should be able to eliminate some criminal behavior. As an example, it is technically feasible to set up an environment with computers and debit-credit cards to keep track of ninety-nine percent of all transactions where money is involved, thereby eliminating the use of money in these actions. If debit-credit cards were issued at birth to everyone (even to purchase a newspaper, you would need it), then cash could be eliminated in the marketplace. The benefit: it would stop all crime where money is directly handled. Armed robberies, burglaries, narcotics, kidnappings, all crimes where money changes hands could be eliminated by the simple expediency of mandating requirements that all buying and selling must be done with a credit-debit card. The flaw: The loss of your personal freedom, because within moments of a transaction, your location and all your private purchases with the credit-debit card would be known; there would be no place to hide in this culture because you would need the card to rent all accommodations. It is also possible to issue a credit-debit and identification card that could include restrictions on them to control your life. If convicted of drunk driving, then your card could be set up so you were not allowed to buy alcohol with it.

To liberate us from crime and to control some of our bad habits, everyone would have to sacrifice some basic freedoms for this to happen, but in exchange for these lost freedoms, you could close down many of your prisons and jails and eliminate the need for thousands of judges, lawyers, police officers, and prison guards. Understand: The robbers who cannot rob because there is nothing to rob, are not changed by this environment. Mentally they would be the same persons. It would just be that there would not be that niche of robbery that they could exploit. Given a choice, I am sure that many people would choose for it all to remain the same; they prefer the robber, the thief, or the extortioner, than to have their government aware of their every movement. People do not trust government, and history tends to prove that this is a correct belief. Still, the benefits of controlling crime are so advantageous with this method, that I must predict it — or something similar — will eventually be accepted and used.

From the above, we should understand that in a different setting, a different culture, a different system of government, the mentally ill and the judged criminal would function differently. If this were not so, then the created environment would have no effect on an animal, but from observation we can see that it does.

However, if a criminal act is committed in all human environments, natural and unnatural, then we must look at our genes. They are there to ensure reproduction and the survival of the species. We must then decide if a gene is a vestige of a time when it was used in an entirely different habitat, a natural one, to insure survival of the human race. If it is, what allowances must we give to those who have succumbed to that gene and committed a cultural crime under a delusion that it was correct behavior for the circumstance involved?

Let us look at a form of theft in nature: A lion stealing the kill from a pack of wild dogs. The wild dogs have just exhausted themselves in the chase; under the rules of some societies, they have performed the labor of the chase, so, they are entitled to the kill. In nature there is no rule that those who do the killing, get first choice at the kill. Nature's rule here is that the strong take from the weak, the able from the less able. You should comprehend that "the same" wild dogs will steal the kill of other animals when they have a chance; therefore they are also thieves when the opportunity of a weaker opponent is present. Where there is no language to circumvent the strongest, nature uses this method to ensure that the fittest survive to reproduce. This law is not only observed in competition between and among species, but is in effect within species. In this situation, the lion is the obvious thief, but in a civilized environment, the wild dogs are sometimes viewed as trespassers and thieves by those that claim the land and grazing herd as private property; thereby making the wild dogs poachers and not entitled (on the previous divided and limited land) to hunt or even steal from those personally weaker than they are.

By using verbiage, human beings are blind to what motivates a person to commit the criminal act of theft. When a predator in its natural surroundings steals the kill from another predator, we know that that behavior has survival benefits; we call it survival of the fittest. When the human predator does it for the same reason, we collectively call it a crime. When stealing is done communally, we call it war and praise it highly, but we condemn it when a person reverts to war against the system; this we call madness. There surely walk among us today, many people who would not be here if their ancestors had not been clever enough or strong enough to steal enough food to survive that additional day that made the difference between survival and extinction.

The accumulation and inheritance of property are the invention of collective human beings. Whereas holding land territorially is nature's way of improving a species' ability to survive by allowing it to be held by the strongest. Private property also gives, like territorial land, an enormous edge to the owners and their offspring in the survival race, but it abrogates the right of the fittest to contest the offspring or the elderly owners to the disputed land. Property owners, by starting their children with inheritable property, can pass to them, survivability that is not superimposed by their genes, that is outside nature's perimeter. We even pass on survivability to those who might not have survived without property. The results: the rich are able to will their own ecosystem. The descendants of the poor arrive at the starting line of the race only to find out that the descendants of the rich have already started down the course of life; when you ask that the rules be changed to make everyone equal at the starting line, you are told that the rules are made by those who have already won their race, that it is a relay race where you are allowed to pass on your gain to your designated inheritors. From this, it would seem that we have, in some civilizations, abolished the law of survival of the fittest with the invention of land as personal property. A closer observation will reveal that it has just moved into different dimensions.

Where formerly, in nature, only concrete things were passed down through the genes (such as adaptive coloration or strength) and were the determining guide to survival, with language came a new feature. What you believed or did not believe was a new, added element of whether you survived to pass on your genes to the human gene pool. With language came laws promulgated by some governments saying that a natural act of the strong individual taking from the weak is a crime because they — as a collective of *Homo sapiens* — say it is. These governments cannot see that they are just a collective of the weak becoming strong enough to take from the strong individual and the weak collective, and then giving it the sanction of law by their collective strength.

In our human history, we have seen some cultures make some criminal behavior legal and some legal behavior (like owning slaves) illegal, all according to the wishes of the strong ruling collective. Still, a collection of people does not in its numerical superiority give infallibility to a law; it is just usually a majority opinion. Not to steal, only benefit those who have property; and so to keep the loyalties of those who own no property, you must convince and give hope to those without it, that they or their descendants will eventually possess property. This is due to the fact that the property holders are not numerous enough to be a majority in most societies; thus they need the support of those *without* property to hold on to their accumulated wealth.

There are always individuals in a society for whom the advantage of stealing to survive outweighs the punishment. If your family is starving, and the only way to get food is to steal it, then should you steal it? If you believe the verbiage of the government or a religion and do not steal, then you have introduced natural selection outside nature's genes into the equation; which can be just as deadly as a malfunction in the genes that will not allow the body to absorb nourishment. You are being actually killed by words instead of a gene malfunction. You are sacrificing yourself to benefit someone with excess property. In natural selection you do not willingly do this. But as you can see, someone can, by manipulating your environment, succeed in having you perform an act not beneficial to your well being, and do it in such a manner that you will not realize it is harmful to you or your future offspring.

I could never be one of those persons who would lie down on the sidewalks of India and die of hunger without a whimper while there is food for sale in nearby stalls, nor could I be a mother or father watching their children die under the same circumstances. Look at the lowly worm impaled on a hook: see how it wiggles and squirms and struggles to get off the hook. That worm has a closer kinship to me than those who expire or let their children die without a muffled curse. I would use a club, a rock, or use my bare hands to take that food I needed. There are circumstances where it is better to go to jail to prove you are a human being, than to die without a struggle; thereby proving to nature that you do not deserve to pass on your genes.

You say that you are programmed by your religion not to fight, not to steal, not to protest the inequities of life. Yes, I can feel sorry for you, but I can never become you. You have allowed yourself to be brainwashed into believing that inanimate objects, like money and property, are more important than a human life — your life. You are agreeing with them: that in the measure of things, you rank below property rights.

All laws passed by society should be judged by the individuals in that society; they should be adhered to and obeyed only if they do not interfere with your inalienable rights. If you find in your conscience that a law is harmful to you or your culture, then you should not obey or cooperate in its prosecution. Remember: The highest duty you can owe to yourself and nature is to protect, with all your might, one's own life. You, and you alone, are the one to decide when your human form will cease to exist before its natural allotted time.

A close scrutiny of societies reveals that the land on which the herds of grass eaters graze, has been completely apportioned out to the meat eaters, who claim the land and herds as private property. The excluded, we call them the poor, are considered another form of grass eaters, someone to be exploited. To abrogate the natural hunting and gathering rights (inherited through natural laws), collectivism was born. Collectivisms, or governments, whichever label you wish to use, are used to make a group of people stronger than a strong dominant person. Grass eaters, the poor, do not believe that they can be guilty of eating the grass, nor do they believe that anyone has the authority to deny them the right to graze or to gather their substances from the land just because someone claims it as an exclusive inheritance from the past.

Societies arbitrarily divide the land into subdivisions, then try to sort out and interpret these arbitrary divisions (that we created in the first place) by asking how we arrived at them, how they developed, and if they have laws that they follow? This can be seen in the lines drawn in Africa by the different colonizing European countries along lines that had little regard for Africa's existing ethnic, political, and ecological patterns; they were entirely dictatorial. Some tribes were divided into two or more different nations where they were a majority in one nation and a minority in a nation next door. When the colonizing European nations were forced to give up their colonies, there was fighting over these irrationally drawn lines. All minorities are at risk if their language, religion, or political beliefs differ from the majority. The solution — one would think — would be for all the African Nations to come together and divide the land into new nations that are more compatible. The problem: inequality of tribal lines would also bring to the forefront the inequality of national resources. Where one tribe might be a majority and have an abundance of natural resources in the boundaries drawn by the colonizers, it might become a poor nation in national resources if new lines were drawn; because the minority that had merged or formed into a new nation had been living on the land that had most of the national resources.

If you arbitrarily divide two troops of monkeys by running a transit line and placing stakes in the ground to mark that line, then make a map and name one troop the east troop and the other the west troop, you will find that the uninformed simians will ignore that line. We then try to explain it as nationalism or imperialism when either troop crosses over and fights near that artificially made boundary for expansion territory. We cannot see that when two troops of primates fight for expansion territory, the only way they have to solve their animal problem is by the strongest defeating the weaker. They have no artificial way to solve the problem of too many primates contending for a limited territory. Human beings also use this method; but unlike other animals, we are not inextricably bound to use strength alone, as we can control the problem by artificially limiting our population.

Nature does not know that we have drawn lines on the surface of the planet; and by doing this, have denied other human beings their rights to live off the land. Property deeds are human inventions; they are distortions of natural property rights. In reality, history shows that even the threat of death will not deter the breaking of human laws when they contradict those survival traits that we inherit through our genes. Just because some people born before us, have divided the land into private ownership, does not mean we are not entitled to compensation for giving up this right to graze and gather from the land when (by chance alone) we are born into a family without property. We are not bound by past decisions that were made before we were born. The present owners of property have to get my permission to that past agreement, and it will have to be renewed after every generation, because I cannot deny the next generation *their* just compensation.

The reality confronting us now is that the increase in population, caused by land division and subsequently farming, has led to the fact that the land can no longer support the increased population in a truly natural state. (Under ideal conditions, modern hunter-gatherers need about 1 sq. mile per person, so the United States would only be able to support about 3,500,000 human beings, instead of the 64 per sq. mile (1980) that it now supports.) When food supplies increase, those who eat that food increase, but the land does not expand. Because property owners, by claiming all of the land, have interfered with natural selection, the present property owners must pay taxes to support those without property, or the property will be redistributed. In nature you will sometimes see the males or females sacrifice themselves for their offspring, and individuals will sometimes sacrifice themselves for the group, but never will you see the grass eaters, knowingly, sacrifice their bodies so that the meat eaters will benefit.

A rise in the population benefits those who possess property; the more people, the more valuable the land. Welfare is not due to property owners' generosity, which they try to propagandize into the heads of the poor, but to keep those without land quiet and docile. It is a tax that property holders pay to keep the mobs from declaring that all land is owned by the people. Those without land have always outnumbered those who possess land. Welfare is just another niche in our society that should be exploited by the excluded. It is a bribe paid by property owners; it is owed to you simply because you were born into the world as a separate entity. You have as much right to contend for the limited resources as other individuals; and a strong collection of persons, do not have the right to deny you those substances or give your share to someone else because they are collectively stronger than you are individually. Nobody faults somebody using jungle lore to survive in a jungle, but when a person uses their welfare lore to survive in the slums, the taxpayers do not wish to see the relationship, even though it is the same. The game is still to survive and pass on your genes as a survivor.

Of course, criminals are in prison for crimes other than stealing, and one that can be considered the most serious by those who live outside the walls of institutions, is the killing of a prison guard or a law enforcement officer. When it is a male police officer killed in the performance of his duties, the newspapers will scream in bold print:

HE WAS A BRAVE POLICEMAN, WITHOUT SIN, WITHOUT BLEMISHES, WITHOUT FAULTS. WHY WAS HIS LIFE TAKEN BY THIS MONSTER?

They ask the question, but never answer it. Like many groups of human beings, there are some good and fair police officers; and we will concur that this hypothetical headline was correct; that this police officer did not abuse his powers by taking bribes, that he was humane when arresting someone, that he was not prejudiced toward a person's nationality, skin color, or religion; that he was a paragon of virtue. We will concede all this because it usually will have no bearing on why the officer is killed. We will even stipulate that the killer was a monster, a human made monster, a culturally made monster.

Understand: We all live in a closed ecological system where we cannot harm someone mentally or physically without someone paying for the damage. If you concede that there is a closed system, then there are no innocent police officers. When good law enforcement officers or prison guards die, they die for the sins of the corrupt officers and guards. Every act of aggression against another human being, no matter how minute, is recorded in a human brain. Every prejudiced act, every beating in the back room of a police station, every beating by a prison goon squad, every street beating by the police, every humiliation is recorded. Retained in the mind, they are broadcast and rebroadcast and disseminated, and from a single recording it can expand to the knowledge of millions. And when the first human recorder ceases to exist, it does not die, but continues to make more monsters, a new generation of monsters. The persons suffering the original abuses usually cannot get even with the individuals who performed those humiliations, so they bide their time to seek revenge on the system. Eventually someone, somewhere, sometime will pay for every beating, every humiliation, every prejudiced act, and sometimes that will be the killing of a police officer, an innocent police officer, a police officer without sin.

Yes, I can hear your cries of anguish when you scream: "That is not fair!" But I say in rebuttal that only a world conceived and built and maintained by a Supreme Being would be fair. If everything was born perfect in nature, we would not have natural selection. A God created world would be a static world; and it would be a contradiction to believe that a God would not create a perfect world. A natural world could not have evolved in a static universe. Societies and cultures are built and maintained by human beings, and so will not be perfect, or just, or fair. The surrounding universe can never be these things because it cannot reason. The rules we follow are not made by an unbiased nature, but by biased *Homo sapiens* who also judge their rules and laws. Only they can change the equation and attempt to make it a fair society.

Because of this, there is no innocent person in a culture; so no person can be judged guilty by other human beings unless they speak out about all human judged crimes committed against other human beings; crimes not only in the present, but crimes that occurred in the past, even the distant past. Societies are ecologically intertwined; so if you have an erroneous belief, and that belief does harm to another human being, then you are responsible for that harm, even if you were not present to inflict it; even if it occurred in the distant past.

In our recorded history, there arose several philosophers who claimed that there was only one God for the meat eaters and the grass eaters; consequently we keep trying to reconcile that belief with reality. I, for one, say that it cannot be done. Religions, just like language, culture, or nationality are viewed by me as just geographical inheritances. We are simply deluding ourselves if we think that most of us, have the free will to choose any one of the above regional inheritances. Once we are imprinted and propagandized with our language, with our culture, and with the one true religion, it is almost impossible to erase it from the subconscious. No church allows rebuttal time to the opposition religions, let alone to an atheist. They fear the atheist, just as they fear the worshiping of stone or wooden idols, and rightly so. To let the atheist into the church for rebuttal would mean the end of the church. Religions cannot stand against the truth; they can only flourish in dark church basements, unhindered by reality.

When we use nature's imprinting that resides in the genes, and substitute language engineered imprinting that causes conflicts within human beings, we are responsible for acts committed under these circumstances. Gene imprinting is concerned with the survival of the species in a concrete world, not an abstract world of beliefs. You can reconcile a true belief to the genes, but not the genes to a false belief. To believe that we have complete control of our thoughts and actions, is nonsense. There is no feedback in nature; so it does not know that we think that we are able to survive without blind instructions from our genes. We are still protected by them as if we had not acquired reasoning. Nature does not know that we have zoos and prisons; therefore she gives us, in our prisons and zoos, the same instructions as if we were free in nature. The same distortions that zoos create on caged animals are seen in our prisons, which should not be a surprise as we are just like those in a zoo, another species of caged animals. The only differents is that in some cultures, zoo animals by law, have better living conditions than caged human beings enjoy in some prisons.

Because I understand that the jailers gain their right of being strong by collectivizing, I did not object to being imprisoned by the state for theft. What I objected to is that they claimed that they had a moral right to imprison me. The lion that steals the kill does so because it is stronger. There is no morality involved. If you are able to collectively overcome the lion's strength and cage it for stealing, there is still no morality involved; you are just the stronger by the power of your collectivism.

Those who have land today in the United States, have it because our forefathers criminally and forcibly by brute strength conquered and sacked the new world. There was no morality involved; they did it because they were stronger collectively than the smaller collectives they overcame by that force. That is our inheritance. I have, playing with the same rules that have not changed, the same option as they had. If I can organize a stronger collective, I can steal back the same land with impunity, and there is still no morality involved. But if I try to steal it before I have the strength, then they still make the rules and I go to their prison and pay their penalty, not because they are morally superior to me, but because they are collectively stronger than I am.

If you believe that other prisoners and I are the product of a pact with some Superior Evil Being, and that Being is responsible for our actions, then you have a belief like some of the early socialists who believed that crimes were caused by the capitalist system and would disappear when the socialists assumed control of the government. Both are guilty of substituting a false belief for facts observable, instead of relying on the evidence of Observational Darwinism that can be gleaned from the observed world. You have no way of correcting what you deny exists; consequently, all false beliefs will leave you impotent.

We can readily observe that like all other life, we have to eat to live; that all life is afflicted with this malady. The digestive system is an undeniable bond that binds us to the past; it shows that we cannot be separated by words from that past; that we must continually digest other life to sustain our life. If you give it some thought, this is our salvation. Only in struggle can there be growth, can there be a striving toward perfection, but a perfection that can never be reached. We are fortunate that nature cannot decide that "this is perfection" or you and I would not be here today; you trying to decipher some meaning into a life that has no chance for perfection, and I trying to convey some words into a form that can stand against the flood of abuse that I can see gathering.

CHAPTER 13

ESSAY: RELATED THOUGHTS

Stride: to take a very long step. With the limited knowledge of his days, the poet, Omar Khayyam (who died in the year 1122) observed and questioned the imperfect explanations of those who taught how life was created. With today's knowledge and science, we have many more reasons to question the supernatural explanations of our origin.

The language of mathematics and chemistry is universal. The volume of a cube or the molecular structure of pure water is global knowledge that does not change with religious or political beliefs. However, there is no universal religious agreement on how our earth was formed or how *Homo sapiens* appeared on it. Consequently, when presented with the facts of evolution, I accepted them as a valid explanation of our beginning, and realized that evolution, because it is based on an all-comprehending science, would eventually be adopted by all cultures as another universal fact.

To qualify for the title, a Supreme Being needs to be omnipotent. It must possess a force of unlimited and absolute power, and cannot be limited in any way. It has to be always present in all places in the past and future, be possessed of universal knowledge and have infinite awareness, understanding, and insight. It must have unlimited creative powers, and be solely responsible for the actions of anything It creates; and there can only be one Supreme Being. Duality or shared power is a complete contradiction. An observation: Human-created Gods or Goddesses cannot meet all these requirements without conflicting with known facts.

When we interpret the knowledge that we can obtain from observing and studying this world, we cannot find evidence of a Supreme Being controlling or interfering with the natural laws of the universe or in the affairs of individuals or groups of human beings. Because a Supreme Being must be all creative, it follows that It must be the *only* creative force. Religious believers do not want to understand that if a God created human beings, It also created the germs and viruses that can kill us. If It created the earth, It also created the mechanism for volcanoes, earthquakes, hurricanes, floods, and all the other natural disasters that can kill without cause, without reason, without controls placed on them.

When we believe in a Supreme Being, where we falter in our depiction, is when we assign It the faults that human beings have. I cannot comprehend a jealous God, a cruel God, a vengeful God, and to believe that a God or Goddess can be bored is truly to assign human attributes to them. Clearly, a belief in a Supreme Being cannot be reconciled with a belief that *Homo sapiens* has been granted free will; this would be incompatible, be contradictory. If there were a Supreme Being, It would have been responsible for your creation and know of your actions and reactions from birth to death before you took them. You could not deviate from those actions, because they, too, would have been taken into account by a Supreme Being before your birth. All argument that a Supreme Being gave us free will would mean that It limited Its power to see into the future. And surely, Gods or Goddesses cannot play games of chance. I cannot visualize a God that would tell me we are going to play a card game because It was bored by the creation business, but in order for me to have a chance to win, It would temporarily blank out all information It had about the cards dealt me. This would be silly; still, that belief is the one you must have to believe in free will. This is always the outcome when we try to give human reasoning and emotions to our made-up Supreme Beings. It still holds true, as it did in Omar Khayyam's days, that there cannot be a shaking potter at the wheel of life; if the vessel is flawed, then the potter's hands shook; flawed human beings prove that there was no master potter at the wheel.

Life is never fair for everyone. If it were, then it would have been pointed to as a sign that we are being ruled by a Creator that is partial. A Creator, by Its absolute nature, would tend to be partial to Its creations, and because we cannot discern bias in nature (earthquakes shake down the house of the just and unjust alike), then we can assume that there is no grand design, no preference, no partiality. You can observe that many good people are not rewarded and many evil people are rewarded, but there is no exact trend as good people do get rewarded and evil people do get punished.

Examine the questions that the birth of a child with Spina Bifida (open spine) brings up if that child suffers horribly for a few months and then dies an agonizing death. My questions would be: Did this life have equality; was it given free will, or was this child given life, yes, was it created by a God — your God — solely to punish the parents? If the parents were being punished for some misdeeds, then would both of them have to be guilty, or does only one need to be guilty to have sufficient grounds for your God to punish? From the questions above, all you can get from Christians is that their God is a loving God, a caring God, and we cannot know His intentions, His reasons. To allow a child to be born and suffer just to punish their ancestor's misdeeds, presents me with a Supreme Being that I cannot comprehend or believe in.

Because we are here and have the facts that were not known at the time the main religious books were written (how the universe could have been created and how life could have evolved), we now know that the universe was formed without a Supreme Being. One can presume that if human beings were in true communication with a Supreme Being, then they would be infallible in all utterances or writings they claim from these communiques. If the Koran, the Christian Bible, or other religious books were written under divine influence, they would be free of all errors; all direct quotations would be true for all times. When religious books are full of error, then we must assume they were created by imperfect human beings, because if a God wanted his word to prevail, it would be perfect and without fault. Even an infinitesimal mistake in the writing or printing will make it just another delusion produced by an imperfect human mind. Because human beings are a mirror image of what they write, which, in turn, reflects when it was written and the knowledge that was known at the time, then it will follow that all human writing will be flawed. To explain those mistakes could a God then, perhaps, lie? No! Because of Its power to know the future, a Supreme Being would know in advance every person's reactions to a lie, so what would be the gain?

By analyzing a paraphrased version of the Muslim's holy book, the Koran, we can see that like the Christian Bible it is also flawed in its presentation of reality; that it conforms more to the thoughts of a human than a Supreme Being. This can be seen when we examine the paradise promised by the Koran:

> By running streams of water, all believers will be given stately mansions in a garden of Eden ... It will be a place of eternal happiness where they shall dwell for ever ... They shall feast on abundant fruit and sip nectar from golden goblets ... Dressed in robes of silk and rich brocade and adorned with silver and gold bracelets, they will lie down on soft, jewelled couches ... They will not feel the blistering heat nor the penetrating cold ... They shall be served by boys graced with eternal youth who will serve them

food on silver and gold dishes and drink in silver and gold goblets ... Every male believer when he reached the everlasting garden will be given two chaste, black-eyed, virgins.

According to the Koran, these voluptuous maidens, these houris, "will be infinitely attractive and continuously young and virginal," and would be created by special dispensation by Allah for all male believers. When the Koran was written, a man raised in the desert under the harsh condition of those times (about 620c.e.) could envision this as a true description of a paradise. At that time, some of the wealthy did have clothing of silk and rich brocades, did have servants, did eat off silver and gold plates to impress the poor with their wealth, their status. In a paradise, however, wealth is incongruous. Who will be awed if everyone has the same assets, if every male has a mansion and two houris? We know that silver and gold is valued on earth because of its scarcity, but it has no value in a paradise where a God only has to say "Be" and everything can be solid gold or silver, or if It wished, produce diamonds as large as baseballs to hang around the neck. In a world of "Be" and it is, who would be impressed, who would be envious? Love, hate, envy, anger, jealousy, and all the emotions we experience cannot make sense in a fictionalized paradise, because they can have no meaning except to the living in this world. They arose in a world of natural selection for solving a specific problem that is not needed in a paradise conceived in the minds of men and women. When Allah can say "Be" and your clothing is there, then there is no need to grow cotton for cloth, no need to transport it, to have machinery to weave and dye it, or merchants to sell it; in fact, there would be no need for clothes to protect from the cold or heat of the day or night, because there would be no heat or cold, no night or day. Allah's heaven can have no goals, no sacrifices are required, no work, no future growth can be accomplished; heaven's boredom can have no end.

Many concepts that we accept as necessary are unwarranted and unneeded in a created heaven. These needs would have to be artificially implanted. Day and night, which can be broken down into periods of minutes and seconds, are based on a spinning earth revolving around *our* sun. In a paradise, day and night and time would have to be introduced by an arbitrary decision of a Supreme Being. Most of us, to make a living on this earth, have to work. In paradise, leisure without contrasting work is meaningless; it could not be a volunteer response to a need for rest.

The Koran's mental image of a houri is like the conception of a plastic inflatable doll. You inflate it, have sex with it, then put the deflated body back in its box until once again a need — created and implanted by your God — calls you to choose which one of your two plastic inflatable dolls you are going to have sex with. And when you do, behold, the hymen has miraculously reappeared; your houri is once again a virgin. In this paradise, even your need to ejaculate into these houris would have to be programmed into you by your God. You would have to be assigned the emotion to love those eternally young and virginal inflatable dolls. On earth, this emotion, this pleasure, evolved naturally to ensure that we produced more of our kind. Even the frequency would have to be artificial. Twice a day, twice an hour, or every five minutes, whatever is selected by your God can have no basis outside an artificial paradise.

This idea, this concept of an eternally young, eternally virginal female that has no purpose other than to please the sexual appetite of a man is what exposes it, what betrays it, what condemns it as nothing more than a sexual fantasy made-up by a sexist man.

The Koran also said that in this paradise: "There shall be no vain talk, no impure, intemperate speech." This would be true. What is there to talk about, to discuss, to argue about, to disagree about? All these billions of true believers each in their mansion with two houris, each eating off silver and gold plates, each dressed the same, with no labor to perform. No exploring, no romancing, no wars or famines or exploding volcanoes or earthquakes, just everyone doing the same thing for eternity. No bragging, no envy, no hate, no love, no emotions except the pleasure of an eternity of useless orgasmic climaxes.

How does this Allah treat His other created creatures that are not Muslims? Does He choose sides among them? Does He create some so they can be killed for an example? In April 627c.e., after a siege of 25 days, the Jews living near Medina surrendered to the forces of the Prophet Muhammad. Trenches were dug during the night near the main market of Medina. In the morning, the Jews were led out in small batches, their hands tied down behind them, and made to kneel down beside them; then, their heads were cut off and their bodies pushed into the excavated trenches. Between seven and eight hundred men were put to death. Most of the women and children were taken to Nejed and sold as slaves. Allah's reaction: He claimed He put fear into their hearts "so some you slew and others you took captive." He also took responsibility for making Muhammad troops "possessors of the Jew's lands, their homes, and their goods." And declared "victory in war comes only from Allah." I cannot conceive of a Supreme Being who would classify or rate His creations as superior or inferior; only human beings have this concept.

This Allah in the Koran did not see anything wrong with slavery; and through silence did not protest the castrating of male slaves and making them into eunuchs; He even acknowledged them and gave His permission for them to be used in the Moslem harems. This Koran God even interfered in human lives by telling how the spoils of war shall be distributed. Also, Allah was emphatic in declaring "No nation We have destroyed shall ever rise again." If this is God's eternal truth, forever, then what can we make of the destruction of Israel, and now its rebirth?

And we must ask, "Can the Koran's view of women be attributable to a perfect Designer, or does this false view come from an imperfect human being?" A paraphrased version of the Koran reads:

> *Men have control over women because Allah has made them subordinate.... Because men spend their resources to maintain them, women are your personal property.... They are your fields; go into your fields and plow them as you please. If they defy you, admonish them, whip them, and send them to another bed.*

Though not her fault, a captured woman changed status in the eyes of Allah; she became booty; she was made a slave and lost some inalienable rights; she was given a lower status than other females. Unlike the restriction of no more than four wives, the Koran granted permission to Muslims to possess as many female slaves as they wished and could afford for their pleasure.

Muhammad, the prophet, did not know that human beings as hunter-gatherers roamed the earth 50,000 years ago or that their first settlements only appeared about 15,000 years ago. He could not have understood the concept that the instincts and qualities, which were selected in *Homo sapiens* through millions of years of evolution, did not have the time for a fundamental genetic change to take place so we could adapt to our present environments. Nor would he understand that before language, there were necessary restrictions on who could be dominant; only time could give an individual the knowledge needed to protect the troop from danger; so the young were excluded. Only time could give the individual the time to develop physical strength needed for the defense of the troop. The female primates that we are descendant from did not have this prerequisite for leadership; they did not develop the physical strength to be able to challenge the large males, so they were excluded. We are conditioned by that past to accept the harsh rules made necessary for survival under those past conditions, and so we unwittingly accept without protest measures that are outmoded by time. We still deny women an equal right to rule by accepting governments that are based on responses that we developed when we were passing through an early stage of our development. Today's human actions are reflections of the actions and reactions of the troop to dangers that no longer exist. Our environment has changed, and men and women do not need today to physically fight for the protection of the troop, do not need to use physical strength, alone;

but because natural selection has not had time to condition us, the response, from most of us, is still to an environment that has long ago disappeared.

I view the Koran as conceived by a sexist man for a sexist culture, constructed by a man with little understanding of women and their needs; by a man without the knowledge of the true concepts of the universe. The writer of the Koran, the prophet Muhammad, could not foresee a culture where women could become the only support of the family, where women had status beyond their connection with males. He could never understand or integrate into his senses the culture on the island of Kanhaeaque, off the West Coast of Africa, where there is a sexual role reversal that contradicts his. Every day, the men spend hours preening themselves. They anoint their bodies with fragrant and expensive oils; they adorn their bodies with jewelry and dress in beautiful fabrics. They do this to attract the women; they do it so the women will like them. Why? Because on this island, men are treated as inferiors; a woman's life is better than a man's; the women are the ones who choose the man; they alone can leave a man for any reason they wish, but a man cannot divorce a woman. An elderly woman can marry a younger man, but an older man can never marry a younger woman. In this culture, women are the family heads, are the village leaders and have the duty of providing for the family. They consider themselves "the greatest in every way," and that "men can do nothing without women." Their religion: They believe in a woman God. They believe their Goddess sent four women to earth, from which all the clans and people have descended. They believe women came to the earth first; that men were sent here later. That is why only women can talk to God; why only women can be priests. The results: men are embittered in this culture. The reason: because women have all this power, and they have none. They complain that it is not right that women should do as they please.

Those blinded by their religions cannot see that these cultures are flawed and so could not be the creation of a Supreme Being. All paradises created by sexist men or women will be flawed; and by dissecting them, their foundations can be made clear.

The Christian heaven, as expressed in the Bible, suffers the same problems as the Koran's paradise. Both have Supreme Beings that are continually testing the faithful. This does not ring true; a human might try to devise a test, but a God is precluded from this; a God would have to know in advance the outcome. It is impossible to visualize a heaven where for eternity the saved would spend their time in a continuous worshiping of their God. I cannot believe in a God so insecure that It has a need to be worshiped by something that It created.

The truth is obvious: Human beings came first, then out of their ignorance and a need to explain how life evolved, they created Gods and Goddesses that resemble themselves. We have never observed a life form that has not followed a linear path with an attached antecedent. That is why all descriptions of our created Gods or Goddesses are equally valid, as they must depend on a description that has no apparent linear descent.

Outside religion, it can be seen that life created by nature does not have to be perfect, because nature requires imperfection to operate. Life would be static without imperfection, and the impartiality of nature can be observed in the well-known and well documented phrase: "The rains fall on the just and unjust, alike." In the aftermath of a disaster, we hear the voice that had prayed to a God and reaped the rewards of survival, but the nine hundred and ninety-nine, who also had a God's name on their lips, we do not hear, because their lips are silenced forever. I cannot conceive of a God who would punish the innocent; but I can accept nature doing it; because life could not have evolved without death of the innocent. Nature cannot judge, cannot control, cannot protect the innocent, the weak, the powerless; only human beings have that ability. But until they put away their childish beliefs and accept that burden, we must, we will, remain uncivilized.

CHAPTER 14

NARRATIVE: THE TREATMENT

Soon after awakening and being examined by the Vacaville's Medical Staff, I was moved out of the strip cell and placed in a cell which had an iron bed attached to the wall as the only furniture. I found out from that experience that the human body is adapted for periods of going hungry, for periods of going thirsty, and even for periods of being lonely, but has not yet adapted to being caged and made to sleep naked on a concrete floor. This torture was surely designed for the benefit of the animal keepers; to this day it remains and is used in prisons and psychiatric hospitals for the same reason they use it in zoos — it reduces clean-up time, decreases breakage, and is more convenient for the sentries on duty. My new bed was made from a sheet of steel plate that had one inch holes drilled through it for bed springs and a one inch cotton mattress for comfort. I truly cry for those who cannot understand that comfort is relative; that happiness can be a thin cotton mattress laid on a bare sheet of steel plate.

In my new prison cell, time lingered on until it was interrupted one day, by the intrusion of a life form dressed in hospital green. Thus, scene two opened with me being placed into a wheelchair by an inmate, then, escorted by a guard, pushed through the hallways of the California Medical Facility at Vacaville. This institution was, and still is, mainly for the treatment of long-term medical problems arising in the prison population of California and as a guidance center for diagnosing, classifying, and then placing newly convicted inmates into an appropriate prison. They also accepted, under contract from the Federal Government, dangerous persons waiting for federal trial who had a prolonged medical problem that needed treatment in a secure environment.

Built within the hospital walls — while separated only by a denial clause on paper — is the Vacaville prison. Because the hospital depends on prison labor to do all work customarily taken care of in a hospital, there is a hidden structure, set up by the inmate workers, which has some control over work assignments and information.

While being pushed down the hallway, I was surprised to hear a voice, in a low conspiratorial tone, issuing from behind me. "Listen, I don't know if you are pretending to be crazy to beat that charge against you or if you have really left us; if you are faking it, then you can understand what I am saying, but if you are not pretending, then it does not matter. In a few minutes, you are going to be confronted by your mother and aunt and some doctors, who will be there to observe your reactions. Even when the doctors leave, you will be watched and your conversations monitored. One of the "nut" doctors has expressed doubt about you being crazy, so watch out; and lots of luck if you are trying to beat the system."

The guard that had been escorting us down the hallway and through the many locked doorways of the institution, had been distracted by some questions from another inmate and so fell behind us. After he caught up with us, the rest of the journey was accomplished in silence.

To deny one's mother is not a gratifying thing to do; even to this day, my mother does not know what stakes I was playing for. I hope she can forgive me; because in her devotion and loyalty, she was, and still remains a story book mother. Whatever her children did, she did not deny them. Surely a mother's love can be viewed as bread for the survival of the species.

The journey ended when the inmate behind me pushed my wheelchair into a large visiting room that could be monitored visually and audibly. Waiting were my mother, my aunt, and a couple of men who, I assumed from their clothing, were doctors. That warning, from an unknown prisoner, had probably saved me from exposure as a fraud; the sudden confrontation could have lured me into recognizing my mother's presence. The next quarter hour was spent with my mother, my aunt, and the doctors pleading for me to acknowledge them, and me in a deep hypnotic trance showing no emotion to the stimulus that they injected into the proceedings. They then tried the tactic of everyone leaving the room except my mother, to see if I would respond to her pleading when she was alone with me. This also failed because I knew that I was being monitored by a one-way mirror and by hidden microphones recording everything that was said in that room.

In that confrontation, which was scene two, I passed the test; but in scene three, I never was able to understand, for sure, just whom I was acting for. This bizarre act began by me being brought out of my cell, walked down a hallway, and brought into a room with a couch and chairs arranged in a visiting room pattern. I was seated on the couch by the prison inmate that had escorted me there. These inmates were there to take care of the needs of the mental patients, who were locked up in a row of cells that extended down the hallway from the room I was led into.

When I was brought into the room, another inmate, already in the room, began asking, "What is he doing out here? Do you have the doctor's permission to have him out of his cell? You know it's against the rules; if you get caught, I don't want to be implicated."

My immediate thought was that it was another trap because it had the dialogue of rehearsed fabrication in its delivery. By previously reading books on interrogation, I had prepared myself to understand entrapment techniques; these two were using a form of the good guy and the bad guy technique from these books. I believed that if I was correct in my assumptions, then the next words would leave the inmate who had brought me out of my cell and me, alone.

"Don't worry so much about rules and regulations or you will reincarnate in your next birth with blue skin and a badge where your heart should be. I am just curious and want to test him myself. You go and check cells for a few minutes; if I am caught, you can say you didn't know I had him out."

A large mirror, facing me, alerted my senses that I might be under observation again from a one-way mirror; so I put myself under self-hypnosis and waited for him to reveal what oblique line of questioning he was going to pursue.

The next few minutes were devoted to him explaining to me, in a low conspiratorial tone, that he knew I was faking, so I should confide in him because he could help me. After several minutes, when he could get no reaction from me, he proceeded to get angry at me, and finally came out with, "Listen, you stupid bastard. You might take in these half-wit doctors with your act, but you are not going to con me." To get me to react, he began to use a few painful wrestling's holds on my arm. Not one emotion as large as a mosquito's egg, escaped from my body.

"Well, now, we are going to see how good you really are," was his response to my display of nothing. His next act was to take a cigarette that he was smoking, and apply it to the back of my hand, between my thumb and forefinger. I did not even bother to try to pull my hand away from his, as in my mind, I had changed the cigarette into a piece of ice, and so I felt no discomfort. Allowing the cigarette to burn for about fifteen seconds, he then withdrew it and proceeded to give me a compliment. "I still think you are faking; but I will say this, you are the best that I have seen; and believe me, I have seen quite a few of them over the last three years who have tried to fool these doctors. But, I assure you, they have never fooled me. I will also tell you this, all the doctors involved in your treatment now agree that you are not trying to deceive them; you are now home free. And another thing, those who admitted to me that they were pretending were not exposed by me; in fact, I gave them help; so listen carefully: soon, you are going to need my help; you are going to need it, desperately," were his final words as he returned me to my cell.

To this day, I still have doubts about whether he was acting under the directions of the doctors, who might have been watching behind that one-way mirror, or if it was just a question of pride. It is possible that he did not like to be out-pointed in a made-up game that he was playing to enliven the years of boredom that all inmates are heir to. He was right, because if I knew that I could have trusted him, he could have been of immense help in saving me from what was about to befall me.

For the next few days, they continued to give me my medication by injections. Although not in complete control of my faculties, I was still able to remember the goal I had set of trying to convince my keepers that I was a living chapter out of their abnormal behavior books. They had various successes in altering my moods, but they could not get to where all psychologists and psychiatrists wish to, which was to know what I was thinking. As long as those who try to alter the mind, remain ignorant of how to achieve this, then that will be how long we will be able to keep our freedom.

Uncircumscribed time continued to tread the hallway outside my prison cell, where I spent most of my time in sleeping, and the awaking time in reviewing and ingraining on my mind what had occurred to bring me to Vacaville. Then, one day, subtle footsteps awoke me; but not in time to prevent that needle of darkness from penetrating deeply into my arm; and the words of assurance that reached me before I went into that unknown sleep, did little to allay my fear.

Listen to me my friends, and hear me well my foes, you who will gloat and give me no comfort, I had completely miscalculated. I had waited too long for events that were not to be, for actions that were not in the script. I was taken unconscious to an operational room and given electroconvulsive therapy, an electric mind disrupter, commonly known as shock treatment. This is a name that calls forth a benumbing anxiety, to those who undergo it; and for those who undergo its gruesome proceedings more than once, that convulsive terror is increased every time it is used. Under a knock-out sedative and muscular relaxant, they proceeded to send electric current between negative and positive electrodes. My brain cells, situated between those poles, absorbed the shock waves and sent me into convulsions. Because of the knock-out drugs, I had no memory of the first one, but they were not so kind about relieving me of the mental torture that preceded the other electroconvulsive treatments.

In a return visit to Vacaville, for another medical problem, an inmate, in one of our bull-sessions, told me that he remembered me quite well because of my remarkable display of stoicism when I was about to undergo electro-therapy. He informed me that he had never observed this calmness and composure in other patients, so he was interested in why I reacted as I did. I could not tell him the truth, which was that I was not aware of how a mentally ill person reacted under these circumstances. I had assumed, falsely I found out later, that a truly mentally ill person would show no alarm or emotion, so I had acted accordingly under self-hypnosis. But the fear and panic that had welled up inside me was, and still is, the most frightening experience that has ever happened to me. Even under deep self-hypnosis, it required all my will power to keep from giving myself away. Instead of walking in and calmly laying down on the table, I came close to saying, "All right! You win; I have been faking, and this shock treatment is unnecessary." But then, I knew that my enemies would win.

Every living person is at the end of an evolutionary chain. A chain that reaches back to the beginning of life without one break in that chain. We are not now, nor have we ever been programmed by nature to lose. "It is not whether you win or lose, but how you play the game" is total nonsense to our genetic code. This built in desire not to lose was too deeply ingrained in me for me to give up; but even with the help of evolution, it was close; as close as the two sides of a butterfly's wing.

I do not know if this electroconvulsive treatment is blunted for the truly mentally ill, but I can imagine the terror inspired in a true paranoid. Imagine watching your fellow patients walking into a room and then seeing them come out lifeless as a corpse, and then, wheeled away to an unknown fate. This must be seen by them as the culmination of their worst dreams; a nightmare where judgment is given after the punishment is received.

As for myself, there was no sweet awaking to a clear state of consciousness as I experienced when I first awoke on that concrete floor in Vacaville. After each shock treatment, I awoke with a complete loss of identity. I found out later that my mind was forced to start recording on a temporarily erased tape. When I regained consciousness, I found myself lying on a mattress thrown on the floor of a small cell; just an iron bed permanently attached to the concrete wall was my sole companion. For a time, the iron bed could understand and express its emotions as well as I could, but was not capable of making the irregular, drunken movement that I was making in trying to rise to my feet. My clumsy, uncoordinated actions drew the attention of an attendant, who came to my cell door and spoke to me in some unknown tongue; consequently, he was not able to answer my confused utterances of where I was, who I was or what was happening. His mouth kept answering with meaningless words that I could not translate into a coherent meaning. It took a few hours for my mind to recognize that these words had a meaning and could be strung into sentences that I could understand.

I can remember most of the details of taking the subsequent treatments, and knew that I had regained part of my memory back between them, because I was able to use self-hypnosis on myself and knew the reason I was using it. How many I had or how long it took to regain my memory and how much I regained of it between treatments is not recorded on the reformatted tapes. Whether it was input, faulty equipment, or something erased by the electric current, I cannot say. The official records read: "This schizophrenic patient, a Federal case, has had 10 ECT's (electroconvulsive treatments) and after the third one he became talkative but had amnesia for the preceding two months, at least."

My last awaking from shock treatment was a repetition of the first, but I was better able to judge the time that it took me to return to normal (if one ever did) after the last administration of pulsating electric current was forced through my head. I used the excuse of the shock treatment to come out of the faked catatonic stupor, then used the treatment as an excuse of why I could not remember how I arrived at their medical facilities or why I was there. They kept telling me that the loss of memory was a temporary thing; but I could not see how they could prove that my memory had returned if I did not admit that it had returned.

Within a few weeks of my last treatment, I was not only playing chess, but winning at it, and except for the periods when I was drugged and those periods between shock treatments, I remembered what had happened before I had arrived at the prison in Vacaville.

The penalty I paid, for being accused of walking outside society's crosswalks, was the disintegration of my mind's retrieval system. To this day, I have not recovered it. Growing up when radio quiz shows were a nightly diversion, I had prided myself on the trivial information I had stored that allowed my mind to answer question after question put to the contestants on those shows. Oh how my ego was inflated when I was able to go through a complete radio quiz show without missing a single question. All that was gone. The information was still there, but I was unable to retrieve it instantaneously when I needed it. I can still go through a simple true or false test, but where I have to recall names, dates, or places, I am hopelessly lost. I spent six hours one day trying to remember my sister's married name; which will give you an idea of the damage to my transmission lines. When you have no choice of the price you must pay, you cannot waste energy by pounding on a wailing wall that does not reflect back sound. So my struggle continued; it was diminished somewhat, but they were to find out that even a dull blade can be used to stab with.

ESSAY: INTEGRATING THOUGHTS

We all live our life in a narrowed and circumscribed environment where many of us are hopelessly uninformed, so we will never be able to accept a new culture contrary to the one we inherit. These human beings cannot be faulted for holding the false beliefs that their culture has imposed on them. The older we become, the less likely we are to discard our imposed animal heritages. When a culture is projected out to its extreme caricature, it is easy to project a view of helplessness in our relationship with the individuals within it. It can be stated that because of evolutionary constraints, unless they can see a direct threat to their well being, the majority will not protest the mistreatment or misfortune of other persons that they perceive as not related to them. This is an inheritance from our primate culture, where the individual, the family, and the troop were the only reality to defend. Our genes did not allow us to perceive, let alone feel sorry for what was happening to some other creature outside the troop of primates that we were born into.

Homo sapiens developed priorities in their relationships because of that inheritance. First comes the individual needs, then the family needs, and finally the needs of the human troop. These relationships were imposed by evolution; they did not come from an outside source. It was an animal loyalty when we were still constrained by the need to belonging to the troop. You need new concepts and abstractions to explain our actions when we go beyond the troop; you need language to impose new loyalties for such concepts as nationality or world government. Nationality and "one world" are culture additions that to fully accept, you must first relinquish your animal priorities.

Looking at the relationship between primates and their loyalties toward the troop, it shows that as history unfolded, human loyalties went from tribal, to the city state, to the state, to the nation, and recently have progressed to global in scope; and we can speculate that our loyalties will eventually be universal. Those whose loyalties remain tribal, those who are confined in their narrow, limited world to seeing the world in national terms, are doomed to die out and be replaced with human beings that have a universal outlook. I know that it is too late for nationalist to change their ways, because they are but a reflection of their environment. Thus my goal is to try to describe a different environment for the next generation that is compatible with a universal standard of government.

Do not infer that I am against ethnic groups having their own national land and government. I believe every ethnic minority should be allowed to govern themselves and be able to practice and pass on their culture without interference by a majority trying to incorporate them by force or by monetary persuasion into the majority culture. The only condition that I would impose on an ethnic group, is that when they live within borders, they do not use their animal expansion culture (overpopulation) to invade their neighbors or export their excess people, so that they can continue to produce more people than their environment can provide for. It is my opinion though, that many ethnic minorities will have to adopt a universal loyalty to the whole earth if they are to survive.

In all animals there has been planted the will to survive until they reproduce. After that, nature is no longer interested in those that cannot reproduce. Natural selection is only interested in reproduction abilities, not in a gene that might help stave off death after the reproduction age is over. As we age, we all will start to fall apart mentally and physically; it seems that our cells are preset and can only renew themselves within that preset and determined time. This rejection can best be seen in the life of the Pacific Salmon. After going to sea, those who survive are programmed to return to the waters where they were hatched. Then, still acting on instructions from their genes, the female lays her eggs and the male fertilizes them, and then they die; they are each discarded by nature. Although not as abrupt, the policy is the same for all species, as, according to nature, we have accomplished our propose when we reproduce.

This is caused by natural selection not being able to program retroactively. We might be able to extend the life span of *Homo sapiens* by allowing only those who have reached the age of one hundred years, to have children. By that time, however, those women would not be able to reproduce, and the men who still produced sperm would not be able to reproduce viable children. Of course, there are different methods of human selection that can be used to overcome this (induced by nature) result. To increase our age span, we could, for instance, keep records and permit only those who had descendants that lived to be a hundred years old to reproduce. But nature does not have this option, while we, with the introduction of language, do have it.

Before human beings appeared, all traits (good or bad) had to be passed on either before the end of the female bearing cycle, or before the sperm producer was too old to produce viable offspring. With language, those who could no longer reproduce and were discarded by nature, became a benefit because they could pass on knowledge outside the genes.

Yes, the human elderly became an asset to their children and grandchildren because language gives us an advantage over animals without it. When our reproduction capabilities are reduced by aging, then what counts is the ability to defend our offspring and through wealth, knowledge, political and social position, or other favorable accumulations or inheritances, to try to give our direct descendants an advantage over other offspring in competition with them. Only when we are willing to pick what is best for the whole world, over our animal choice of what is best for our direct descendants, will we start down the road to making the word "civilization" meaningful.

Until you admit that you came from animal stock and that you are the inheritor of all things that that implies, you will be trapped in a dream world. If you believe that you were created above the animals, then you will always be preoccupied by seeking solutions to civilization's problems by beseeching a nonentity for the answer. When you come to realize that those problems are due to your reaction to a created and perverted environment, then you have a chance of solving them. To not correct some observable faults in the environment because you believe that you are pleasing some Higher Being, avoiding some form of punishment, or are going to receive a reward in another world, relieves you of the responsibility of deciding what is correct behavior. You must rely on someone else for an interpretation of what is right and what is wrong. Many human beings are so constructed that they will never accept blame for the uncontrolled forces that affect their lives. They must always see another group of human beings behind those uncontrollable forces.

Because religions are all equally invalid, I have come to believe in complete religious freedom. But I go beyond what established religions are willing to allow; I believe a person should, if they are so inclined, have the right to bow-down and worship stone or wooden Idols. The condemnation of this type of worship by established religions had, and still has a valid reason behind it. They could see that the same results could be had by worshiping an Idol as by worshiping their Supreme Being. Because there is no Supreme Being, the results will always be the same no matter how or what you worshiped; to explain this consistency, the Christian Religion had to invent the Devil. If you worship an Idol, you can claim, just as legitimately as any other worshiper, that you survived an earthquake, a flood, lightening, a hurricane, a volcano eruption, or a disaster on the sea, on the land, or in the air. Miracles happen randomly in every nation in the world; they occur to you whether you are an atheist, pagan, deist, agnostic, free thinker, unbeliever, infidel, or if you are deeply religious. There is absolutely no correlation between what a person worships and believes and their chance of surviving a natural or human created disaster.

It has been observed that justice and injustice are distributed to the good and the evil person in a random way. No pattern can be observed, nor will it ever be observed, because there is no Supreme Being to eliminate the randomness in nature.

(Trying to be honest, I will warn you that the next chapter will raise questions that might tend to indicate that I am a schizophrenic, that I have a split personality; but do not make your judgement too soon. Remember, all the evidence has not been introduced and the path will continue after you have read the next chapter.)

CHAPTER 15

REVELATIONS: THE WORD ACCORDING TO THOU

THE BEGINNING: For the thought to be there, the "Source" must be there also; was the first insight I gained. Then came the mental perceptions.

THE THOUGHTS: There was a void, then came the universe; for how can you know empty space if you have not seen the stars. There was darkness, then came the light; for how can you perceive that you were in darkness if you know not the light? There was life, and then came death; for how can you perish if you did not exist? There was hunger for truth, and then came knowledge; for how can you learn the truth if you seek not to appease this emptiness in you? There was truth, and then came falsehood; for how can you taste the bitterness of life if you know not the sweetness in it? There was silence, and then came the cry for help; for how can you come to the aid of the forlorn without hearing them? There was freedom, and then came the chains; for how can you know that you are a slave without knowing freedom first?

THE INSTRUCTION: My thirty-fifth birthday was near, when I heard a voice telling me to "go seek solitude" as I had been chosen as a Messenger.

THE VISION: Ye appeared before me holding a scale with large gems weighing down one side of it. One by one, Thou silently removed the gems from the scale and did strike them against a large rock, which caused many small gem fragments to chip off. These small gem fragments were placed into a pouch and handed to me. The larger parts of the gems, Thou openly placed back on Thy scale. Suddenly! It became dark; and a robed figure, his face covered with a mask, came in the night and led Thee away. Unobserved by the masked figure, Thou dropped on the ground in front of me the large gem fragments from Thy scale. These I picked up and, to protect them, hid them in a nearby cave, knowing not why. Then the figure in the mask came back and felt the bag that Ye had given me; thinking perhaps that I might have hidden the gems that had dropped from the scale, the masked figure tried in vain to judge whether they were in my pouch; but I chased him away and saw the masked figure no more.

THE REAPPEARANCE: Then, to interpret what I had seen; Thou was standing before me, once again. "The gems are gems of knowledge; the small chips are obtainable, universally. The larger parts are for My Messengers and for all that seek the truth. No person may steal these; and when they are brought into the light, they will be recognized as Mine by their size, color, and clarity. The masked individual is a warning to beware of those who would profit falsely by saying they have unrevealed knowledge to give to the world. You will know these by their false ways, as they cannot recognize My Words, because they have not seen My Ways, have not seen My Gems. Have I not said that there is nothing hidden that will not be divulged to those who look for the truth, openly."

THE VISIONS CONTINUED: Be warned of those who come to you and say:
"Hear us; we are Christians; we made a Compact that gave us the Voice."
"Hear us; we are the Children of Israel; we made a Covenant that gave us the Book."
"Hear us; we are Islamic; we made an Agreement that gave us the Prophet"
"Hear us; we are Buddhists; we made a Bargain that gave us the Interpreter."
"Hear us; we are the followers of Confucius; we made a Treaty that gave us the Words of Wisdom."
I say unto them, "You have not kept the faith entrusted to you; so all your contracts are broken. They are broken because you shed blood in My name, did make "Gold" your God, did cage and torture other human beings, did not follow the path that I laid down for you, and worshiped those whose feet made footprints on this earth. I gave you dominion over the lesser animals, and these you did slaughter and decimate their numbers and species, all in the name of human needs. You also received from Me, large forests and streams of clear water. And the trees you did cut down,

thereby, turning the land into barren deserts, and the streams you did pollute, all in the name of progress. You did go forth and multiply as I told you, but I also gave you the ability to reason, so you would not multiply like the unthinking animal. You did reject and break and distort My Messengers words; not once, nor twice, but generation after generation."

GUIDANCE: "If on a winter trip to the mountains you encounter a lost person freezing to death in a blizzard whose only protection from the elements is a blanket full of holes, you do not offer silver coins to cover those holes, neither do you offer gold coins or large expensive gems, nor do you take a brand new blanket and cut it into small pieces and offer them as patches to keep out the cold. And so it is with Me; I am sending you, My Messenger, to completely replace the worn and tattered blanket with a brand new one, and do not displease me by cutting it up to patch the old blanket as it is beyond repair. You do not sow grain in a field of thistle without first plowing, neither do you allow the newborn orphan lamb to be suckled by a wolf wrapped in a sheepskin; and so I am telling you that I am sending, you, My Messenger, to overthrow the old corrupt systems. I am sending you not to move mountains, but to level them. I am sending you to trample down fences; for one should not fence and post what I gave to all humanity. My instructions: you should not waste your time look-ing for the thirsty at a well, but go out into the desert looking for all those who need someone to show them how to dig a well first; for those are the ones who thirst for My Words."

THE WORLD INFORMED: "I made a farm out of the wilderness and gave it to others to cultivate, but retained the title to the land. I then left and went to a place far away. After a while, I sent one of My Messengers to make clear My title. But those I left in charge said that they knew me not and chased away My Messenger. I sent others to try to reason with the usurpers. Some of these they ill-treated, some they imprisoned on false charges, and others they had killed. The usurpers could not even agree among themselves what crops they should plant to receive the most profit from; some wished to receive gold for their labor, which was in contradiction with My Ways. So they decided to divide the farm into two farms; then they divided it again and again, until they each had only a small plot of ground to cultivate. To make it look larger to the beholders, they each partook of rocky ground, ground not fit for cultivation, and added it to their small acreage. They then went about proclaiming to the world that it was part of My Original Grant. Have I not said that a tribe divided in its goals is a tribe that will not prevail. I am sending you to tell them that I am displeased, mightily displeased. To those who have denied Me what is righteously Mine, solace will be denied. Systems have passed away before yours came into being. Look at your history and see the consequences of those who did deny the Messenger, did distort the message. Once again the true words are brought to you. From thy fruits, so shall you know them; so hear me, O world: you have tried pruning the bad fruit away, but each new crop produces its own bad fruit, and from the bad seed of this fruit, more of its kindred is produced. So I say the time has come to tear up your corrupt orchards and plant new trees. Trees free from disease. Look at your homeless children, relentlessly roaming the streets of the world. This is your reward for generations of unkept promises. Did you think you would not be called on to pay for your misdeeds while you inhabited this earth? Have I not said that what you sow, so shall you reap?"

THY INSTRUCTIONS CONTINUED: "If you hear someone say that they can interpret My Words, have a short cut to know Me and My Ways, or have the keys to My Kingdom, then I say to you, they know not the way, have not the keys, and do not interpret for Me. For do I not know your every thought and need; so what need you of a paid interpreter? There is no deviation in the true path; so what need you of a paid guide? Only you have a key to know Me; and it is in your heart; so what need you of a paid locksmith to reach Me?"

FURTHER INSTRUCTIONS: "If you hear them say: 'The kingdom is in heaven,' then the birds will be there before you. If you hear them say: 'The kingdom is in the sea,' then the fish will be there before you. If you hear them say: 'The kingdom is beneath the ground,' then the worms will be there before you. Have I not said that the Kingdom is within each of you?"

THE VISION CONTINUED: I saw Thee standing in front of a large congregation that could not see Thy projected image. To me, Thou spoke: "All the thousands gathered together here to worship are outbalanced on My Scales by one person doing a good deed today. For have I not said that you shall know them by what they do, not by what they say. Do not pray as they do, for they love to pray standing or kneeling in places of worship and on street corners and over the airwaves that they may be seen and heard by others. They are rewarded by their collection plates. Do not pray for others because they need no one to intercede for them. If I note the fallen sparrow in the wilderness, do you think that I do not know your every need. Speak to me from the heart because I will know before you ask. Do not waste your allotted time in praying, but do good deeds in the time wasted by those who pray. Do not bow down and worship or pray to anyone or anything on this earth that has walked on its surface, flown in its air, burrowed in its ground, or swam in its waters. Do not try to make an image of Me; for if you cannot visualize unlimited space, then what makes you believe that you can visualize Me?"

KNOWLEDGE: "And when the foolish come to you and say they saw Me dressed in a robe made from ornate fabrics, resting on a golden throne inlaid with precious stones, eating off golden plates under lighted candlesticks cast in gold and silver, ask them: What need I of clothing; what need I of resting; what need I of nourishment; what need I of light to see by?"

THE INFORMATION: "You were told to give to the government what belongs to it, and to Me what is Mine, but I find that you have rendered up to them what is Mine. Why is this? You give allegiance to some governments even though they cannot provide substances to all who wish to labor. They imprison the humanity in each of you; give death instead of life; yet you bow down to them. Overthrow them by ignoring their unequal laws, by crowding their prisons to overflowing, by bringing their courtrooms to a standstill, for you need them not. If I am the light of the world, then who will pick the darkness over the light? Oh! You depraved generations; you pay for your misdeeds, but seeing not and hearing not, you continually choose the path to oblivion. I had the money lenders thrown out of My house, and now I find that you have mortgaged My house to them. Oh! You shameful ones; hear Me; I am sending My Messenger to offend those who did this. Oh! Foolish ones; why do you not speak out against those who oppress? Are you afraid to offend your adopted master—"Gold?" Have I not said that the rich will not be able to see Me, to know Me, to accept My Ways? All their glitter will not allow them to know Me; so what need you to store their gold for them? Have I not said that where your treasure is, there is where your allegiance will be? Oh! Guilty ones; why do you build these rich structures in My name when your fellow human beings are homeless; why do you fill them with all that wealth when men and women and children go hungry and begging in front of them? Why do you continue to build these places of worship, fill them with earthly treasures, and announce that it is done in My name? When I said that you should not store up treasures on earth, did you think you were exempt because you did it in My name? Listen! For

I say that if you do an unjust act in My name, then you are unfit to know Me."

THE WARNING: "And for these unjust things which you behold being done before you, take warning as the day approaches when there shall not be one false stone used in a human edifice that will not be thrown down and ground into dust. You did build My house on sand. Were you not told to build on bed rock? Were you not given the corner stone? Why then did you disobey My Wishes? You cannot return to My Grace until you divest yourselves of your earthly burdens, which are your churches, temples, synagogues, cathedrals, mosques, monasteries, convents, and all houses of worship. You cannot return to My Ways until all treasures that you own in My name are sold and used to better the lot of the believers and unbelievers alike. You cannot return to the fold until you abolish all rank for those who choose to follow My Ways. Do not support places of worship or the priest in the collection plates, but go out and find the needy and give directly to them. For who among you cannot discern the ones in need from those dressed in expensive business suits? When this is all overthrown, then you will see who were following in My footsteps and who were only there because they had a need to impress other human beings with their importance. They needed the titles, the rich costumes, the servants, the applause of those they considered underlings; and so when this way of life has been dispersed, you will see that it was all vanity, and not My Way that they were following."

THE DOCTRINE: I observed Thee watching a multitude of human beings getting baptized, and heard Thou say to me, "It does not matter if they were baptized in the highest waterfall in the world or were dunked into the deepest part of the ocean if they do not do My Will. They baptize the children to save them; instead they should be baptized by the children because they are closer to My Ways than the baptizers. For have I not said that you should believe as a small child? What profit is there for these foolish baptizers if they sell everyone in this world a candle but cannot neither light the darkness for themselves nor the candles they have sold. For I say that all the stars in the universe, combined, cannot give the light that I give to those who truly know Me. If you gain all the knowledge in this world and know Me not, then you will be poorly served by your knowledge."

THE LAW: "And for those who say that My kingdom is reserved only for right-handed people or left-handed people; reserved only for men or women or children; reserved only for those with black or yellow or white skin; reserved only for this one or that one; I say that they are false prophets, and know Me not. For have I not said that My Kingdom is for all who have room in their hearts for Me? But be forewarned that there is not room enough in your heart for both riches and Me; one replaces the other, like day replaces night."

HOPE: "And for the homeless, who wander over the face of the earth, I am going to send you, My Messenger, to offer them a home; for those who have felt the lash and chain, to offer them relief; for those who have given up on the system, to give them hope; for those who have been cheated, to obtain what is rightly theirs."

THE UNDERSTANDING: I heard a voice ask Thee "In retribution for killing another human being, the state executed a human being today, and many religious people rejoiced. Is this right?" I heard Thee reply, "You say they did it in the name of the state? But how is this, for you are the state; so they did it in your name; for how can you discount and separate the grains of sand from the beach? I say the executed person's crime is least, because while this human being killed like a wild animal, they, the state murdered with premeditation and malice. If you say that you did not approve, but spoke or acted not, then by your inaction, you too are guilty of murder; for did they not do it in your name, too? Have I not said that you shall not kill a captive in chains?"

THE CURE: I saw Thee watching a congregation celebrating the recovery of some of the faithful from a sickness. Then bending down and picking up a stone from the ground, You held it aloft and spoke to me: "This day they were cured because they believed in Me, but hear Me well, for I say unto you that if they had believed in this stone, as they did in Me, so would they also have been cured. The cure is within all who believe. If a person does good and believes, no matter what their belief, who shall deny them."

RENDER: "If a person denies My existence, but speaks thusly: 'I have come to help those in need!' Walk along with them for a short time, and if you see that they try to help the unserved, go all the way with them, for there are many devious ways to gain entrance into My sight. Have I not said that there are many rooms in my house; who among you shall say which rooms do not belong; for only I, the Architect, truly know. In this world there are those who deny Me, but obey My Laws; and there are those who do not deny Me, but do not follow My Laws. Who shall be served? Truly, the ones who deny Me, because they only deny Me in words, but know

Me in their hearts. Have I not said that you shall know them by their deeds? If someone is good only because they fear the punishment if they are caught doing wrong, then I say that this person is just as guilty as those who do wrong. Also beware of those who say that they are one of My Sheep, not because they fear My Wrath, but because they fear the rejection of others."

THY WORDS: "Humanity, born naked into an ever deepening, unbounded sea of remorse, struggles its short span of years away in meaningless enterprises; only to find out, too late, that if humanity does not accomplish anything, then the role it plays means as much in the tapestry of life as a stone rolling downhill. Dislodged from the side of a mountain, a stone will reach the end of the slope and come to rest at the base; and so do human beings at the end of their stage appearance. If it can be said that your life can be compared to the journey of a stone rolling down a hill; if it can be said that if the stone had not rolled or if you had not been born, it matters not; if the stone's journey can be judged with as much importance as your journey down the slope's of life, then that becomes a description of a wasted life. Do not wait until the blind can see Me, the deaf can hear Me, and the crippled can run along beside Me. By then it is too late. If you leave no one to mourn your passing, beware. And if you cannot discern a footprint of those who passed through before you, then look back and see if you are leaving a print for others to follow. What good is it if you spend your entire life in labor if you do not create something for others to follow. Do you think you were given life just to consume? Have I not said that you do not live by bread alone?"

THE CONCERNED: "Be warned, that the time is near when the slogan makers will believe their created falsehoods; cities will be emptied and proclaimed evil; the guards will become the prisoners and their chains become a heavy burden. So be prepared with the truth that you might survive these times."

FURTHER WARNINGS: "These things you shall not do: Do not cheat or take from the poor, whatever your needs. It is ordained that every child born unto this earth shall receive and inherit one share of the available wealth. If some people have more than their share, it means that others will not receive theirs; so try not to be one of those with more than your rightful share. Who shall say that this is my share, this is your share, and there is nothing left for the newborn because we have divided it up before they were conceived? Those cheated of their rightful share have My Blessing to seek their share; no more or no less. Just remember, everything we receive on earth is but a loan. No country should be rich enough to buy another and no country poor enough to be bought; should this not pertain to the estate of human beings, even more so. All human beings are born pure; the earth is what corrupts. So whoever is forced by hunger and cold to sin, then they will be forgiven. The impoverished shall not fight other deprived people, lest the rich become more wealthy. So do not attend the wars made by the rich. Better you should spend the rest of your life in Caesar's prisons than to deny My Way. If your bodies do not overflow the prisons and jails in these times, then you are not on the right path. But if the impoverished rise up against their oppressors, then I say to you that I will side with the poor nations against the rich, the prisoners against the jailers, and will always be against the holders of deeds to my land."

ADMONISHMENT: "Do not preach unto man, woman, or child, but show them the way by living and doing what is correct. If one asks you the way, then, and only then, can you point out the way. But first you must trod the path alone before you attempt to show another the way. If you know the way so well that you can find the path in darkness, surely they will flock to you to hear how you found the path."

COUNSEL: "Do not believe anyone who tells you that you will be punished, everlasting, for your misdeeds. What mother or father would do that to their children? Am I not your Mother and Father? Do I not know what you will do before you are conceived; so why would I permit you to be born on this earth, then punish you for what I knew you were going to do before you appeared on earth? Your only punishment will be that you will never have the comfort of knowing Me; and when you pass on, you will return to the elements and never again will they combine to become you. It is from the great sleep of disintegration that nature eventually produces, from the fallen structures, new life, new recombinations. The only hell is that formed by evil people on earth; and that will eventually be diminished."

CAUTION: "Do not condone or participate in the torture of another human being; for this is a crime with no forgiveness. Do not sit on a jury or judge anyone; for whom among you have not sinned in your heart. Do not censor the writings of others; so that you in turn will be free to write My Words. Do not hide yourself in a monastery or a convent; for evil will not disappear because you renounce the world. Do not mourn the dead, because all that was good or bad has left the body and is dispersed among the living.

Do not participate in a funeral service, because the good individuals have seen Me in their lifetime, and so prayer will not avail the evil ones to know Me after the darkness has descended on them. Do not place the dead in a tomb or vault or mausoleum or use a tombstone to mark their burial place; either cremate them or place them naked into the earth or naked into the sea."

THE FINAL DAY: On the last day of my vision, I heard Him lament: "O! Unbeliever, I hear you pray for your life to be spared. Do you think I cannot give everyone everlasting life if that was my intention? I hear you pray to gain over your enemies. Do you think I cannot remove the violence from their hearts if I wanted to do that? I hear you pray for deliverance from evil. Do you think that I cannot pluck from among you all the evil in the world if that was my wish? I hear you pray to be shown the way. Do you think I cannot put the true path before everyone if I wanted to do it? I hear your prayers of thanks. Do you think that I cannot grant all things to all humanity if I wanted it that way? I hear you pray to Me. Do you think I am a vain Master that asks you to fall down and worship Me? Do you think that I cannot have the world bow down and worship Me if I wanted it so? If I know your every thought, why do you beseech me with empty prayer? Did I not grant you choice; if I grant prayers, where is your choice? Do you think that I assign this one to be rich, this one to be poor? No! Chance governs all. It was I who gave you uncertainty, gave you chance, gave you the lottery of life. These gave you the wise and the foolish, but only you can decide which is which. There is only one way to worship Me: by doing My Will. Where the path leadeth, only I know; so bless Me not for the goodness in life and curse Me not for the evil; for you were not given the knowledge to know what shores your waves will reach, nor know what grain of sand will be disturbed by the winds of change."

REMEMBER: "There were groups in the beginning that had all things in common, so it would please Me if you would return to those days. Recollect that tears shed for the dead of passed transgressions are never lost; they, when they fall, will sprout flowers that will bloom with a light that dispels the darkness. Be reminded, no greater love for human life can be expressed than for someone to give up their life for another; for they give their life for Me."

THE FINAL WORDS: "When they ask, 'Who are you to speak these words?' Say, I am His Messenger. They have come before me, they will come after me; they will come until all the work is done and the stars shut down. And if they read this and say, 'This is surely the work of a human being.' Say this to them, If this be so, why worry, as it will come to naught if these are the words of a human storyteller. But if it conveys eternal truth, then it will flourish and never be overthrown."

CHAPTER 16

NARRATIVE: EXPLANATION

The Word According to Thou was retrieved, in January of 1979, from my court-appointed attorney's files. The manuscript, written in ink and in my handwriting, had laid dormant for sixteen years while it waited patiently, with its pages folded as if in prayer, for a trial to take place. The manuscript was originally found in 1961 when the FBI, looking for evidence to connect me to the bank robbery that had occurred in Cotati, California the day before, had searched my station wagon in the Santa Rosa Police Station's parking lot. It had briefly appeared once again in 1962, when Mr. Robert N. Zarick, my second appointed attorney, had brought it to the Sacramento County Jail and questioned me about its source. He had received it from Mr. Ted Isles, my first appointed counsel. Mr. Zarick wanted to know if it was in my handwriting, if it was an original manuscript or copied from another source, and if I had a memory of writing or copying it, did I know when, where, and why?

When I was brought to the Sacramento County Jail from the California Medical Facility at Vacaville, in July of 1961, the United States Federal Judge, the Honorable Sherrill Halbert, had appointed a young attorney, by the name of Ted Isles, to be my court-appointed counsel. The appointed attorneys practicing in the Federal Courts did not, at the time of my arraignment, receive compensation for defending indigent persons, but only for the expenses incurred in the defense of a client. Consequently, the defendants were often not properly defended, as the appointed counsel would generally attempt to get their appointed clients to plead guilty. This was so they would not have to be bothered to assemble a case for the defense when they felt that their valuable time could be better utilized by making money from clients who had the money to pay for justice.

You will see from the following that there was great confusion about when I was arrested, who arrested me, and under what legal conditions was the arrest carried out. You will also be confronted with and read some excerpts from the "Defendant's Supplemental Memorandum of Law." This twenty-five page memorandum was filed, on my behalf, by my appointed counsel, Mr. Ted W. Isles, on September 21, 1961, in the Federal Court of Sacramento, California.

"DEFENDANT'S ILLEGAL COMMITMENT TO THE CALIFORNIA MEDICAL FACILITY."

"On July 26, 1961, the defendant was brought before the Court and defense counsel was assigned. Counsel first appeared on July 27, 1961, and made a Motion to Quash the Commissioner's warrant of April 22, 1961. The Court denied that Motion on the ground that the issue thereby projected was moot in view of the defendant's having been brought before the Court the preceding day "under indictment" (i.e., under arrest by virtue of the bench warrant issued on the indictment date, April 28, 1961)."

"This Court has now reached the stage of the proceedings where the question of the legality of the defendant's arrest under the Commissioner's warrant of April 22, 1961, is no longer moot. It is inextricably connected with the merits of defendant's Motion to dismiss the indictment."

"The Fourth Amendment to the United States Constitution provides that no warrant of arrest shall issue except upon probable cause supported by oath of affirmation. Despite this mandate, the Commissioner's warrant of April 22, 1961, was issued two days before the execution on April 24, 1961, of agent Stamp's Complaint and affidavit of probable cause. The issuance of the Commissioner's warrant was therefore in violation of the Fourth Amendment; and the defendant's arrest under that invalid warrant at the County Hospital in Santa Rosa on April 23, 1961, was consequently illegal."

"The defendant was committed on April 26, 1961, to the California Medical Facility by virtue of the Order of this Court made on that date, two days prior to the indictment and issuance of the bench warrant on April 28, 1961, but 18 U.S.C.A. 4244 provides for such commitment of mentally disturbed persons only "after arrest." On the day this Court made its Order of Commitment, April 26, 1961, the defendant had not been legally arrested; this Court's natural reliance on the propriety of the issuance of the Commissioner's warrant on April 22, 1961, was in this instance misplaced, with tragic consequences for the defendant."

"Surely, 18 U.S.C.A. 4244 only contemplates commitment to a medical facility after a valid arrest. In the eyes of the law, an unconstitutional arrest should be no better than no arrest at all. To hold that this Court could commit the defendant to the California Medical Facility under an illegal arrest would be no different than saying that the Court could direct the Marshal to go out onto the street, clap his hands on the shoulder of any innocent passer-by, and forthwith transport that unsuspecting citizen to the confines of the Vacaville institution. The Court's Commitment Order of April 26, 1961, could not in itself supply the valid seizure which the prior illegal arrest had omitted. Any contrary implication would indeed be foreboding. The indictment two days later on April 28, 1961, likewise in itself could not serve as an actual or constructive seizure of the defendant's person by legal authority. And the bench warrant issued pursuant to it the same day (April 28, 1961) was not used to arrest the defendant until nearly three months later when the defendant was arrested on July 25, 1961, under that bench warrant at the California Medical Facility. By no lawful authority, therefore, was the defendant committed to the California Medical Facility; not one minute of the defendant's three months confinement at Vacaville had the sanction of law ..."

"Not only, as heretofore shown, did the Vacaville staff not have lawful custody of the defendant but also the "authorization for such treatment, given by the Superintendent" exceeded the scope of treatment authorized by this Court's Order of Commitment, which in itself was illegal. This Court directed that the defendant be committed to Vacaville "for a psychiatric examination" only, and "that the Court be notified of the completion of said examination." The Superintendent of the California Medical Facility, therefore, clearly exceeded the scope of his "authority" when he directed that shock treatment — something far afield from "a psychiatric examination" — be administered ..."

These Motions, consisting of twenty-five pages in the one above, and another twenty pages filed earlier, were filled with documented case histories of previous rulings that had to be answered by the Assistant U.S. Attorney, Robert E. Woodward. Here is his full response to the defendant's Motions:

"It appears that the sole issue before the Court is the capacity of the defendant herein to assist in his defenses and it further appears there is no divergence of opinion that he does not have such requisite capacity. The government is now, and always has been, ready and willing to cooperate in this regard. The Government has no desire to proceed against a defendant who is mentally incompetent."

"It is the belief of the undersigned that the various motions made on behalf of the defendant are scurrilous and insulting to the Court and the Government." "For these reasons it is respectfully prayed that the Court read all of the documents presented on behalf of the defendant and if the

Court is in accord with the contention of the undersigned that such matters are scurrilous, that the Court consider this prayer as a motion on behalf of the plaintiff to strike from the records such of the motions, affidavits and memoranda in support thereof as may appear to the Court to be scurrilous and offensive."

The author wants you to notice that nowhere is it pointed out where in law Mr. Ted Isles' briefs of about forty-five pages, go astray. It just ignores the law completely and just gives the Assistant U.S. Attorney's personal beliefs and opinions. You would think that the Federal Judge would call the Assistant U.S. Attorney before him and tell him that he is practicing before a Court of Law where his opinion and beliefs should be supported by citing the law in arguing against the defendant's motions. This did not happen; instead, on November 2, 1961, the United States District Judge, Sherrill Halbert, issued this Memorandum and Order:

"Defendant has filed in this case, several motions in his defense to an indictment for violation of Title 18 U.S.C. 2133(a) and 2133(d). Included are two motions for the suppression of evidence, a motion to dismiss the indictment, and motions under rules 15(a), 17(b) and 41(d) of the Criminal Rules."

"This Court has carefully considered the basis of each of these motions, and has found each to be without merit. Accordingly, each and all of the defendant's motions are denied."

"Defendant's attorney, Ted W. Isles, Esq., is hereby relieved of all responsibilities and obligations as the court-appointed counsel for the defendant."

NARRATIVE: UNDERSTANDING

Not being too dogmatic about it, I can only surmise why my court-appointed counsel was relieved by the court of all responsibilities and obligations in my defense. I believe it was in some way connected with Mr. Ted Isles' misunderstanding of the law as it is practiced in our courtrooms. (This was his first appointed criminal case.) He was naive in not understanding that in his training to become a lawyer, he had absorbed and come to believe in some of those grandiose ideas that his law professors were blindly repeating to him. Such splendid and illustrious ideas as, "Justice is blind. All human beings are treated equal under the law. The courts were set up to be an impartial arbitrator. You should seek the truth, no matter where it leads to."

Because of that training in idealism — that he accepted as fact — Mr. Isles did not understand that in the world outside his classrooms there was a large gap between teaching the grandeur of an idea, and the everyday practice of that idea in a courtroom. I admit that I am not spared or immune from these exhortations. Because I analyze my culture, does not mean that I can separate myself from it, and because I do not believe in your fabricated Supreme Beings, does not mean that I do not believe in life, liberty, and the pursuit of happiness. On the contrary, such words as *With Liberty and Justice for All* reverberates in my brain and make me feel elevated; and such songs as *The Battle Hymn of the Republic* have words and music that can only be described as awe-inspiring to me; they make me feel sublime. These words, however, speak of a world of fantasy. I know that there is no God out there reversing the wrongs of the world, tramping out evil, and avenging the weak. These are just words that obscure and blur reality. Despite knowing this, I still feel uplifted by the words and the tunes, but I would not use the words as a basis for acting or not acting in situations where my life was involved. Because I know that words and music can be used to manipulate human beings, this understanding sets me free as I can enjoy my emotions without succumbing to that manipulation.

By observing them, you can see that courts of law are set up to protect the vested interests of those who set them up. No one, nowadays, other than those blinded by their self-interest, expects the Communist's courts to protect the workers against the bureaucracy; they only protect the workers when it is incidental to or coincides with protecting the system. And I am not naive enough to believe that the capitalist's courts will protect the poor unless the desired effects match a corresponding need of those in power. The vast majority of judges will not be neutral; mainly because they are not chosen in a vacuum. To become an appointed judge, you must agree with those who have the power to make you a judge, and it is hard to fake this agreement in ideas. So when you are chosen and enter the judgeship, your actions will coincide with those who appoint you. (This is the same in the Communist systems, too.) Because Federal Judges are appointed for life, we are told that they do not have to please the politicians, so this is the reason Federal Judges will be neutral and impartial. But it is already too late, because by the time they are appointed, their ideas agree with those who appoint them. The poor and those without power do not appoint judges. In the federal system, the Attorney General, the Assistant Attorney Generals, the Federal Prosecutors, and the Federal Judges are appointed and selected, and their duties are to winnow out those attorneys that do not meet or agree with their views.

Those with small minds are able to filter into the system because they go right through the strainer and into a recognized position as a future colleague; but someone like Mr. Ted Isles is caught in the strainer and viewed with suspicion. He refused to play their game of "Plead this impoverished client guilty, then we (the Court) will see what we can do when you have a paying client." Of course, I do not believe that they are so crude that they have to use words to convey their meaning. The system is more subtle and infinitely more subliminal than that.

Mr. Ted Isles, being new to the Federal Criminal Court System, had not informed the Federal Judge that he believed that as a court-appointed counsel, he should defend his client with all the will and knowledge that he would use if the client was paying him. He believed in the same justice for the poor that the rich received for their money. An aberration such as that seldom escaped the halls of learning in those days, but I was lucky enough to overcome the odds when Mr. Ted Isles was appointed to defend me.

Mr. Isles had filed several briefs in my case, bringing up different issues that the Assistant Attorney General and the Federal Judge did not think were relative or pertinent to the matter of having me plead guilty. They wanted to get on with the outward trappings of justice and not have their valuable time wasted by a poor and obviously guilty bank robber. Because of this, there came the day when Mr. Isles was summarily dismissed and relieved of the responsibility of participating in any way in my defense. In a letter written to me, he used the words "I was stunned when the judge relieved me of your defense." He then went on to explain that there was nothing he could do about it. To my aunt, he gave reasons that led me to believe that he was dismissed because he would not plead me guilty against my wishes. I had informed him that I wanted a jury trial if I was found competent to stand trial. Also his law office, where he was a junior member, was putting pressure on him for wasting his valuable time by researching and writing up the different motions that he filed in my behalf. Because he did not have the clerical help, he also had to do the typing of the briefs before he could file them with the Court. I am sure that Mr. Isles was informed — in an indirect way of course — that if he wished to keep his employment at that law firm, then they did not wish him to intervene further in the case, even if he proceeded on his free time.

In the letter saying that he was stunned by the court's action, Mr. Isles informed me of the appointment of Mr. Robert N. Zarick as my new court-appointed attorney. Although Mr. Isles praised Mr. Zarick and stated that the court had provided me with an extremely capable attorney who had had some notable successes in criminal law, I, of course, put the darkest connotations on his appointment.

You should know that I had not acquainted Mr. Isles with the situation that I was involved in because at that time I had no way of knowing who was in the conspiracy or how much power it had to influence others. At no time did I confide in him that I was faking mental illness; nor could I tell him that I thought that I was being framed by a group that I believed had access to government resources and ties with the FBI and CIA. I knew that the only way I could come close to convincing him that a conspiracy existed was to prove that I was being framed for bank robbery because of my activities in the underground of a far-left political party. That would mean exposing the people who had worked under me and myself to charges of conspiracy to murder, and that I was not willing to do. So, you can see why my fears were enhanced. I thought that the courts might be involved in this inept plot, which could mean Mr. Zarick might also be a part of the intrigue against me.

Although I was wary, in the next two years of our relationship, I was only once (I thought) able to perceive the wavering on the part of Mr. Zarick to having the Court drop all charges against me. He always asked me what I wished to do in regard to my defense and never brought up the possibility of my pleading guilty. Still, only in 1979, about sixteen years after our relationship expired, was I truly able to believe in his full integrity and that he had not been picked by my enemies to throw me out of the scales of justice so that I could not be weighed.

When I decided to write this book, I was apprehensive about trying to retrieve my attorney's files. I was not sure that if when I started to look into my old files, whether it would start some rusted gears into motion and, somewhere, someone would be alerted to that noise. Yes, I was afraid of "Them" awaking to my rummaging through those files. You cannot know the relief I felt when I contacted, over the telephone, Judge Robert N. Zarick about photocopying my files and found out that he did not even remember my case. After a little prodding, he remembered it and gave me permission to have the complete files sent to me, as he said that he could not think of anyone else that would have an interest in them but me.

But back in 1962, I was in no position to trust anyone, so I told Mr. Zarick that the manuscript *The Word According to Thou* was in my handwriting, but I did not know when or where I wrote it or even if I had written it. I am sure that Mr. Zarick was thinking about introducing it as evidence, if I went to trial, to prove I was under a delusion of talking to God. This would automatically make me mentally ill under the criterion set by the "World Wide, International, Supreme, Royal Order of Psychosis Determiners." Lucky man, thou Moses, to be born before the validity of the messenger could be determined, because I am sure you would not have liked the free institutional care you would have received if you were born in my century. In my created world, the validity of the message — and not the source of its origin — would be the determining consideration in its acceptance.

I still speculate about a jury's response to that manuscript. Its introduction would have been an interesting defense tactic, but it would have been a deception perpetrated, unknowingly, on the Federal Judge, the jury, the U.S. Assistant Attorney, and my attorney Mr. Zarick.

I must insert here that another article was found with the manuscript that had some bearing on the thoughts of those who knew about it. The article was a robe similar to those worn by the priests in monasteries. It confirmed the belief of some that I had robbed the Bank and intended to use the stolen bank money to set up a religion. From that fact, the finding of the robe, followed false reasoning; it shows how facts and coincidences can be misinterpreted when you do not know the reason behind a person's actions. Yes, that robe was made for me in Los Angeles by a person who made costumes. The purpose was to verify my continual thoughts on the best way to hide underground if my Socialist Party was forced through circumstances to do so. This was not paranoid, because we have seen where entire leftist forces have been eliminated because they were not prepared with plans to go underground. Like Sir Arthur Conan Doyle's *The Case of the Purloined Letter*, I was interested to see if we went underground, if we could hide in the open by using a monastic disguise. I wanted to see the reactions of people to seeing someone dressed like that; especially the police's reactions to such a disguise. Although sidetracked, it was still a valid experiment, as you do not want to use an unproven tactic when your life might depend on the outcome.

Now to the truth of that pseudo manuscript that was deliberately written, by the author, in a mystical terminology. What you have read is an unfinished manuscript that was written by me on that beach at Bodega Bay (mainly to pass the time away) while I was trying to make up my mind about what I was going to do about what had happened back in Los Angeles. The writing was an attempt to see if I could write a more concise religious document with fewer ambiguities when applied to this factual world of substances. Although the manuscript was incomplete (I wrote it in a week), I would have expanded it and introduced many more categories if I had not been interrupted. I was trying to eliminate some of the obvious conflicts that existed in the religious books, which pictured God as someone that had human emotions. Although I had later thought up several scenarios on how it might be used, I had not made, at the time it was written and found, a final plan. Only after it was shown to me at the county jail and I observed the reaction of my attorney to it, did I start to speculate that if found under different circumstances, it might be mistaken for a true religious manuscript. I can safely assume that many readers might not believe that they can be deceived by a manuscript like mine because they would have noticed that a competent linguist could date when the manuscript *The Word According to Thou* was written. The author came to understand this; and with the later accumulation of information, I theorized that it would be best to find a manuscript like this, in an unknown language and then interpret it. So, if I had planted it, this is how it would have probably been found. Fraud! Deceit! Trickery! Yes, all this entered my mind; it would become all those because at no time did I think that I was in communication with a Supreme Being. But, for a time, I did convince myself that I had virtuous reasons for perpetrating such a fraud.

In 1961, I had this distorted concept that you should not suddenly withdraw the support of religion from people who have grown up and been indoctrinated with beliefs that contradict observed reality. I was of the opinion, or delusion if you prefer, that if you took away the support that the believers had, they could not function; so you would end up with a society of cripples. I was going to attempt to fashion a better crutch that would bring them closer to reality.

Some of you readers will insert about here, "What conceit to believe that you could start a new religion or reform an older one." However, since there is no Supreme Being, then all religions were started by human beings.

To explain why I believe anyone can introduce a new religion or revise an old one, we must examine the founder of the Mormon Church, Joseph Smith, and his declaration that in the 1800s he had found some inscriptional golden tablets covered with hieroglyphics. Joseph Smith claimed an angel, who led him to those gold tablets, had buried them in 421c.e. when he became the last survivor of a lost Jewish Tribe. With the help of his "Holy Angel," he claimed he had translated *The Book of Mormon* from some "Reformed Egyptian Encryption" on those golden tablets. In 1835, Joseph Smith, from papyrus scrolls found with some mummies that he had bought, translated *The Book of Abraham*. The papyrus scrolls were later identified as common funerary scrolls buried with the dead.

In 1843, Joseph Smith was given the "Kinderhook Plates"; six, bell shaped brass plates covered with "hieroglyphics" that nine men had intentionally fabricated to trap him into translating the fake hieroglyphics on them. His angel did not warn him that the Kinderhook plates were a joke played on him, so Joseph Smith translated them, and fell into their trap. Attempting fraudulently to claim that you have an angel to help you translate the history of the new world leaves you with an insurmountable task if this is not true. We can see that Joseph Smith did not overcome this handicap. The time he describes, from 2000b.c.e. to 421c.e., does not match the history that archaeologists have uncovered. He had the inhabitants using iron and steel weapons in a stone age culture. He had them sailing to a land that had never been inhabited, but we now know that it was inhabited by Indians that had come over the Bering Strait's land bridge thousands of years before the reported sailings. You can recite mistake after mistake, but this has nothing to do with the belief of the religion. They believe because they were taught to believe. If you are taught that *The Book of Mormon* is the correct history and the Mormon schools say it is true, then how are you going to prove that it is not the correct history. The believers are taught: "When the Prophet speaks, the thinking has been done." This is a universal way of quieting the questioning. Listen to the voice of the Russian Communist Party: "When Karl Marx or Lenin speaks, the thinking has been done." Is there a difference in the two thoughts? Of course not; Communists are not immune to being irrational; they also defend absurdities. Once it becomes a belief, then only by a personal search by the individual can it be overturned. Even if you could produce evidence that Joseph Smith had plagiarized *The Book of Mormon*, it has nothing to do with the beliefs that the Mormons accepted and are indoctrinated with. A belief is held regardless of facts that can be produced to prove that a belief is based on false premises, on false facts, or on fraud committed against gullible people. It took me a long time to understand that it is not a question of whether a religion is true, but that people truly believe it to be so, and no amount of evidence that you can produce will convince a believer that it is not so.

There are other people that can be proven to have committed fraud to start a religion. Look at the female founder of the Seventh-Day Adventist Church, Ellen White, who claimed to be a prophet, a messenger of God; a God that personally gave her visions of the unalterable truth; who claimed her writings could not be of human invention. And what is the judgment of some of its scholars within that Church: It is that for seventy years she deliberately plagiarized the material she claimed was divinely inspired from other authors. They found that she paraphrased and even copied some passages, word for word from many books, then lied when confronted with the duplications. Today, most of the members still believe in Ellen White, and if the Church allowed the truth to be preached, and the suppression of the information of their scholars was revealed to them, it still would not change that majority's beliefs. They would simply believe that their God gave the material first to other inspired writers, then their God had Ellen White gather, copy, distill, and accumulate in one place, all this previously inspired material into the bosom of the one true church — the Seventh-Day Adventist Church. The truth will not change the believers. Once the wrong pattern is branded deeply on their cortex, imperfect *Homo sapiens* are not able to judge correctly.

I will admit that the Mormon Church produces through their teachings a group of people who, even when they leave the church because they no longer believe in it, are a superior grade of human beings. I have personally never met a Mormon who I did not like; and there were several that I met in my Socialist Party who I admired; but I know that they are only human beings who will behave and act in their selfish interest, just as we all do when faced with a choice where there can be only one winner. But because I know there is no Supreme Being, I then know that the writings that Joseph Smith claimed he found, were a fraud. Which means that the church was founded by a human being who had human motives. And just because the belief produces a proportionally large amount of good human beings, does not make it a true belief, because it does not take into account good people produced by other beliefs that contradict and are in exact opposition to the Mormon beliefs.

It is readily apparent that the main difference between an atheist and a believer in the one true religion, is a single religion. The believer in the one true church knows that all other religions are in error, except their church, their religion; the atheist does not exclude even that one.

Because I had an adequate amount of time to think and deliberate on the matter in the different institutions where I was incarcerated, I came to realize how wrong it would be to trade one set of chains around the mind for another set that was lighter but still limited the mind. I came to the conclusion that one cannot deal with ambiguities in the modern world of reality with different ambiguities. There are basic questions and answers that can only be asked and answered correctly by an atheist, by someone who will not be hampered by delusions that a religious person must acquire to accept a belief in a Supreme Being. Human animals should stand erect and stride toward the future without using a crutch, because we cannot become civilized until we rid ourselves of all supports. I was going to try to fashion a better crutch. Adding a better one was not the answer to the question. Instead my goal should have been the rehabilitation of human beings so they have no need for a crutch.

Even though this explanation above is true, you must still take into account that these words are the words of a diagnosed schizophrenic. So, you should ask yourself if there might be other explanations that can be just as plausible? A few could-be's are: could you believe that I was on that beach plotting to rob that bank in Cotati and wrote the pseudo manuscript for an alibi of insanity if I was caught; or perhaps, you could believe that I was truly insane and believed that I was talking to a personal God? Could-be's are incessant in the mind of a schizophrenic.

The above shows that you can draw several conclusions and speculate on a mirage of endings from perceptible facts. Perceive my state of mind, my moods, and my thoughts just before the bank robbery occurred. You, reader, to deduce which ending is compatible with my state of mind.

CHAPTER 17

NARRATIVE: THE JOURNEY

Although it was a physically exhausting two thousand mile odyssey from the jail in Sacramento, California to the Federal Medical Facility in Springfield, Missouri, it was an interesting experience. During the trip, I and two other prisoners, who were being transported back East for trial, were handcuffed and shackled with leg irons in the rear seat of an automobile. To add a bit of historical realism to the trip, there were two United States Marshals riding shotgun. My view was that it was a decided break in the flow of events. I was started on this journey, in April of 1962, by being found by Doctor Bromberg to have a mental condition that prevented me from putting up a defense if forced to defend myself in a court of law.

It is noted here that if in a state of delusion, a male mental patient who was being transported across country tried to escape because he believed he was being taken someplace to be murdered, then he could have been shot dead by the escorting U.S. Marshals, and no disciplinary action would have been taken against them. To the U.S. Marshals and the U.S. Government, mental illness is an excuse to be decided in a court of law, and not by them. Deciding not to let my supposed delusions interfere with my future well being, I volunteered, to myself, not to try to escape; and so I arrived safely at the Federal Prison in Springfield, Missouri.

This Federal Prison was set up like the California Medical Facility at Vacaville, with a hospital and prison separated on paper, but run under the rules and regulations of a prison. The guards did not differentiate between patients and prisoners or between those convicted of a crime and those waiting for their trial. The guards, like the U.S. Marshals, did not ask for your classification if they observed you trying to escape. They would shoot first, figuring they would have plenty of time to make sure the right notations appeared on the stone marker denoting your departure from their facility.

On arriving at Springfield, I was subjected to a barrage of intelligence and psychological testing. These tests were administered not to find out if I was mentally deranged (that determination had been made by Doctor Bromberg, one of their colleagues, and they were not going to contradict a finding of a colleague), but were given because some unknown, former bureaucrat had ordered that everyone entering the Springfield Medical Facility had to have these tests. These probes, which cost the government thousands of man-hours, were filed away — I later found out — without being interpreted or read by my appointed ward doctor or the other doctors in the Springfield Institution.

If you know anything about these tests, you will know that psychologists have spent a small lifetime in trying to introduce a new test for the sole purpose of the prestige that derives from that accomplishment. Still, all the tests that I have taken appear to presuppose that the persons taking the examinations are mentally ill, and so do not know what they want it to show, or they are sane and want the inquiry to show that they are sane. No provision is made for a sane person wanting to show that he or she is mentally ill; thus, all these tests can be circumvented and defeated if you know beforehand what you want the person who will interpret it to find out from the test. Wanting to show my hostile criticism for one of their tests, I set a goal of showing through sarcasm that I did not care what their interpretation or diagnosis was. Sample: What are your favorite colors? Answer: Red, white, and blue. Sample: What day is it? Answer: Today. Sample: What enemies do you have? Answer: People who do psychological testing. Page after page of my best wit, lost. Lost because my humor was filed away without anyone even seeing it until the doctors found that they were in a trap that I did not even know that I was setting up. Fate, the unbiased god, even gives the unbelievers their moment of luck. They were to pay dearly for going on the assumption that I must be mentally ill or I would not be in their institution. Instead of checking my mental status, they made an erroneous assumption, put it on record, and then were unable to change the records when they found themselves involved in a game of strategy where I was making up the rules as I went along. As a diagnosed schizophrenic, their books told them that I should not function in a competent manner when under stress. So later, they had to either deny their books, or change their diagnosis; a truly painful decision for bureaucratic psychiatrists and psychologists to make.

My fight for survival came about when I discovered that the examining doctors could keep me confined at the Springfield Medical Facility until they determined that I was well enough to stand trial. A few unconvicted inmates that I met were only accused of minor federal crimes; if they had been convicted of committing them, they would have served only a short sentence. But some of them found that they had been imprisoned several years beyond the time they would have served if convicted, and were still waiting for a trial; I was informed that some had even died while waiting to go back to court for their trial.

I talked with my fellow inmates; I listened to them; I argued with them, and then I listened some more. What I heard, I did not like. Nobody was released until the medical staff said that they were ready to leave. Many had come before the local Federal Judge, under a Writ of Habeas Corpus, to try to convince the Court that they were able to stand trial; but the Federal Judge is bound by law to accept the findings of the expert testimony given by the Springfield Medical Staff that the person before them is insane and unable to stand trial. After a passage of time, it became routine for the hospital to send along a report that they would testify that the petitioner was still mentally ill; therefore the Federal Judge, as an alternative to wasting everyone's time, would deny the writ. I did learn through prison rumors, that the Federal Judges had a suspicion of what was going on at the medical facility, and were sympathetic toward the patients, but they could only follow the law.

The fact was that nobody had ever left the Springfield Mental Hospital without the staff's recommendation that they were fit to stand trial. I also found out, and later had it confirmed by an intern, that if they found out you had a connection or sympathy toward the political left, then your chances of getting out for a quick trial were slight; but then you must know that the staff considered a belief in socialism as a sign that you were suffering from a mental illness. Their views were just the opposite of the Russian doctors who believed that a belief in capitalism was a sign of mental disturbance. Yes, Virginia, there are political prisoners incarcerated in the United States Mental Hospital and Prison at Springfield. All this time — I am willing to bet — you were thinking it was an excessive Russian abuse. Sleep well Virginia, as you now have the knowledge that those Russians are not completely ahead of us in this race to punish those who have different political views.

A warning: take heed, you on the left, only embark on these murky waters if you have no choice. As for the right, do not rejoice; because unequal treatment of the political left, can also mean equal mistreatment under the same law when it falls into the hands of your opponents. My choice was either serving twenty-five years for a crime I did not commit, or the rest of my life in a mental institution; therefore I had no choice but to embark on this road that had no signs to warn of the dangers involved.

Discouraged, I started visiting the law library to see if I could find out if somebody had preceded me and broken a few branches to mark the trail through the brush. In that period, while waiting for the hospital staff to commit their views to paper, I always acted in a sane, capable, and rational manner to influence their diagnosis, although I had little hope from observing my fellow ward patients, many who were, except for their clothing, quite indistinguishable from the guards and prison staff, but who were still being held.

I do not want you to think that everybody was in good mental health. There were wards where there were acutely ill persons who could not function at all in the limited protective environment of an open ward. Mostly they were convicted prisoners who had broken down under the prison system. There were a few, however, that were found sane at the time they committed the crime, sane at their trial, but completely nonfunctional on arrival at the Federal Medical Center. The reason: some psychiatrist had convinced a judge and jury that the man was simulating mental illness; so he was brought to this mental institution to spend the rest of his life in a strip cell. The "Catch 22" goes something like this: If he is pretending, he will file a motion to declare the trial vacated because he claims he was insane at the time of the trial. However, this writ proves that he is not insane or he would not be capable of filing the motion. The insane person is not capable of filing a motion; therefore that person proves by his inactions that he is truly insane at the time of his trial; but he is condemned to serve his time because there is no provision made to file a motion in his behalf. He was convicted wrongly because a trial should not have taken place as he was unable to defend his actions; and so by law should not have had to stand trial.

In my case, before I could do anything, I had to wait until the psychiatric staff made their determination. The day finally came when I was called before my ward psychiatrist and informed that I was unable to defend myself in a court of law, at that time, because I was mentally ill. He told me that by law, they would review my case at least once every six months; then report to the Federal Court in California my progress or lack of it. Their diagnosis was that I was a schizophrenic, undifferentiated paranoid with a sociopath personality; and there was little hope that I would be well for some time, if ever, as a schizophrenic rarely recovered. Because of my conversations with other patients, I was expecting the report to show something similar, so I did not protest the findings. I just shrugged my shoulders and asked the doctor if that was all he wanted to see me about. A perplexed look appeared on his face, and I could see he was expecting me, like his other patients, to argue with him about the findings. He began to get fidgety in the chair that he was sitting in, and finally came right out and asked me if I thought the report was correct and if I wished to try to change the staff's mind about the report's findings. I told him, "No, it is your report and you will have to live with it," which I could see further mystified him. I knew that he would just put all my words and actions down to my diagnosed illness, so I could conceal my little joke at his expense under the umbrella of that diagnosed illness, without him even being aware of what I was talking about.

My quick perusal of the law books had brought me to the opinion that the law is nothing but a quagmire of independent rulings, which brought me some hope. I found that you can cite many court cases that favor one side and your adversary can cite even more cases that show the exact opposite. This pleased me as I saw that I would be able to maneuver without someone knowing the direction of my attack. Not that the staff was expecting one; that was another advantage that I had. They did not even know that they were in a contest, and I was not about to alert them until....

Showing them the familiar plans of a square building, they were not the least bit worried when I asked for permission to spend time in the law library; they were confident that they could corner me in the well known corners of this familiar architecture. They had seen the same plans produced time after time in the courtroom, only to be stamped condemned as structurally unsound, by the courts. So when I asked, there was no hesitation by the hospital staff, in giving me permission to go to the law library.

One of the rights a prisoner has, is filing a Writ of Habeas Corpus. It is a document that you are allowed to seal in an envelope and send out of prison without anyone reading or censoring it. Because believe me, it would not have been sent if they did not believe it was the same old, familiar plan of a square building. Instead, mine was designed as a round building so that they had no corners to hide their mistakes in. As a precaution, two separate copies were prepared.

The extra copy would have been smuggled out of the institution if they decided not to play by the rules of law. You should understand that paranoia is a survival tool in the world that I was living in. Soon after sending in my writ, I was brought before a disciplinary board when, after a search, the extra copy was found. The search occurred after the original copy had reached the Court. The prison disciplinary board explained that I had no need of smuggling out a writ as they would have sent it out no matter what the outcome was. I informed them that they should then consider it an act of a paranoid mind, and if they punished me for being a paranoid, they would be punishing me for being mentally ill. I hinted that I would take a decision to punish me as a direct challenge to my well being and react by taking the matter to the review of the courts. I then received, after they discussed it in private, a lecture on the proper respect for the rules and regulations of the institution, then I was informed that I would be let off this time, but was warned not to let it happen again or it would lead to a serious disruption of my privileges within the institution.

ESSAY: ENLIGHTENED THOUGHTS

Reflecting on my incarceration at Springfield, I came to believe that in examining the behavior of some birds, I could explain some of the actions and motivations of the hospital staff. The North American Cowbird and Eurasian Cuckoo are species of birds that lay their eggs in the nest of other birds so those other species of bird will unknowingly hatch and raise them. For maximum results, the Eurasian cuckoo will usually deposit a single egg in several different nests, then remove an egg from that nest so as not to alert the nest builder. Their eggs usually hatch before those of the nest builders, and when they hatch, they push all the other eggs out of the nest. If they hatch later, the larger Cuckoos push out of the nest all the newly hatched chicks belonging to their foster mother. This is to lessen competition for the food brought to the nest by the adoptive parents. The nest builders, in whose nest the cowbird and cuckoo deposits its eggs, are birds trying to use their limited time and energy to build nests and incubate their eggs; they are following a set of gene patterns that does not allow them much leeway in discerning that the eggs have been fraudulently laid in their nest by a different species of bird. This is an evolutionary strategy that the parasites are using, so no fault can be assessed against the species for using it. And because the nest builder does not know that it is raising a different species of bird, neither can it be faulted.

There can be observed a symbiotic formula here that prevents the parasitic birds from eliminating all nest builders in their area; if they did, they would have no place to lay their eggs; consequently they would become extinct. It can be stated that this symbiosis also helps the nest builders that do not have parasitic eggs laid in their nest. Those eggs and hatchlings that are eliminated by being pushed out of the nest, means less competition among that species. Another safeguard is that each cuckoo, because it is imprinted with a single species of bird (its foster mother's species), will only lay its eggs in that species nest; so the bird population will continually fluctuate and be controlled by these symbiotic pressures. They will reach a natural equilibrium under these conditions.

If the nest builder in whose nest the parasite lays its eggs could be told that it is an advantage to the species to not have so much competition, would it accept this and sacrifice its lineage for the good of the species?

Absolutely not! If they knew that they were parasitic eggs and had the choice, I am sure they would not sacrifice their hatchlings to raise another species of bird, even if it gave an advantage to the species. When they can detect the parasitic eggs (the Eurasian Cuckoo is detected about one time in ten), the hosts — rather than sit on the parasitic eggs — make a new nest and lay new eggs. Nature can only save a species by having each individual making the decisions to do what is best for itself; it does not recognize a group as a unit because it can only pass information through the individual. The nest builders are not willing to sacrifice their time and their energy, and take the chance that their future descendants might be eliminated from the gene pool if they are physically eliminated before the next breeding season, just so other birds of their species have a better chance to reproduce due to the lessening of competition.

What is true in the natural surroundings of the animal kingdom will usually be true when the human animal uses similar tactics in the evolutionary race. Being opportunistic, some human beings, I am going to call them "human cowbirds," use language as their eggs in this evolutionary strategy. By using propaganda, they can convince nest builders that there is an advantage to letting someone else lay their eggs in their nest. When human beings use flag waving and patriotic propaganda to convince someone to fight in a war to protect their property rights when there is obviously no advantage for those individuals without property to sacrifice their life, then he or she is being parasitically used by human cowbirds. It is discernibly easy to convince someone that it is glorious to die for your country, for your God, for your species. We even fight wars to convince other people that we have a right to deposit our eggs in their nest, even when they recognize that they are parasitic eggs. The British and Chinese Opium Wars in the 1840's and 1860's are examples. Here, the use of opium was destroying the fabric of the Chinese Culture, so the government outlawed its importation. But the British were horrified by this act; they thought they had a fundamental and moral right to sell opium even if it did harm to the Chinese; and so they went to war and won, both times, the right to lay their parasitic eggs, even though the Chinese recognized them as such. Another example, in recent times, is the United States trying to impose their parasitic eggs — a government that the United States wanted — on the Vietnamese people.

It is difficult to escape being taken advantage of by human cowbirds; they can resort to the use of the most flagrant type of propaganda to achieve their goal; propaganda that plays on sentiments already organized into our genes for our protection. The reality is that the human cowbirds are unaware that they are using the propaganda for their selfish interest, because they are also doing a natural thing — trying to obtain an advantage over other selfish human beings. Although difficult, our educational system does not preclude your learning that you are a victim of the human cowbirds; and once you learn that you are being used by a human parasite, you should also know that you do have the choice of kicking out the laid eggs of the cowbird, or of even building a new nest and guarding it so someone else cannot lay their eggs in it.

Is it ethical for a human cowbird to gain such an advantage by using this evolutionary strategy of having other human beings sacrifice their time and even their life so that the human cowbird can gain an advantage? Anything we view as odd behavior in nature or in a structured culture is a human value judgement. This holds especially true when we view other species and cultures. It is only when we duplicate the results in our culture (results that naturally evolved parasites produce), and then view it as something as alien when discovered being used by our culture, that we can be faulted. You should know that I can view it as harmful to be used by a human cowbird, but still not condemn the cowbird as performing in an alien way. It is not a sin to be a cowbird or to resist being used by one. We human beings can condemn them by a human value judgement, but it is not binding on the cowbird; it is not performing a crime but a natural act performed to benefit its genes; even if it means that other genes will not be passed on to the next generation because of its actions. It is an act of selfishness, true; but without selfishness by our ancestors, we would not be here to question whether right or wrong behavior is a value judgement. I can condemn the communist, capitalist, and fascist forms of cowbird behavior because they can be taught that acting that way, although not a sin, can eventually be damaging to their offspring when everybody recognizes their eggs as parasitic and refuses to let them deposit them in their nest. Because they have reason, human Cowbirds can be taught to build a nest, lay their eggs in it, and support their nestlings, thereby joining the human race again. But they will be forced to do it by limiting their egg production to what the environment will support. This we as human beings can do, but the dumb animals cannot; so for them the fight for survival must continue in its present form.

CHAPTER 18

ESSAY: OBSERVATIONS

I spent much of my time, before and after I began writing this book, contemplating why almost all human beings I came into contact with acted in such a destructive manner toward other human beings; why was there this massive all-inclusive prejudice that almost everyone I met exhibited toward other individuals that were not of their persuasion? I was continually contemplating and comparing past observations with a daily observation of the present. I had this need, this compulsion, to learn from the past; to form a coherent historical path that would continue its course, its direction ascertained by the study of previous paths that had led us astray. If I were to find the common threads in the tapestry that would lead to the all-encompassing web, to the unifying links, yes, to the "Grand Unifying Engine" that I surmised was continually running in the background, I believed that it would emerge from a Darwinian study of history. Then, by applying what I learned to the future, I felt that I would be able to see if it would give a more realistic picture of why old roads led only to strife that produced massacres, pogroms, and holocausts. Perhaps, I might even be able to point out a way of creating a path that would diverge from and bypass these old familiar roads; yes, to find a path that would lead to a civilized behavior that would mesh with reality.

After studying many entrances and exits to roadways, I will try to describe some of the side paths that I could discern. You will see that some of them were not unused and obscure paths, but deep rutted roads that left me wondering why those who traveled them needed to delude other travelers by describing them as of little consequence or as paths that led to dead ends. Some of the other paths that I came on were so faint that I could only guess how far they extended. As time and space limitations must be considered, the future will have to work out the length that can be traveled on these paths and eventually judge their value, to those who follow them.

A unified theory was needed to explain all the acts of barbarisms perpetrated by human beings on other human beings from the beginning of recorded history to the present. It was needed to explain why all institutions set up by us to overcome or solve a problem, eventually, not only failed, but developed a hierarchy that became just as corrupt as those they replaced. And it was surely needed to explain why human beings massacred with blind hatred those who they claim, are different because of their religion, nationality, skin color, or political beliefs.

So we must ask: Can we learn anything from the 1946-47 Hindu and Moslem riots during the partition of India — riots that took hundreds of thousands of lives? What happened to the peaceful Hindu believers who were so deeply religious and so revered life (so we were taught in American schools) that they would not knowingly harm any form of life? What knowledge is gained by explaining and integrating the 45 million people killed during World War II? Six million of those were innocent Jewish civilians killed in the concentration camps and gas chambers of the Holocaust. Also, let us not forget that we must look for a reason that 100,000 Chinese civilians were killed by the Japanese in Nanking in 1937. Then, how are we to explain the mass carnage of 1914-1918 that saw about 10 million people killed on the battlefields alone? We must also integrate the massacre and genocide of 1 million Christian Armenians by nationalistic Turkish Moslems before and during World War I. As we go back further into history, we need to know why there was this fanatical massacre of the North, South, and Central American Indian tribes by Christian people who proclaimed that their God was a caring God, a loving God, a merciful God, a God of peace. Every nation, every religion, every political creed has committed gross acts of murder, has slaughtered the guilty and the innocent alike. Not one is exempt from the list.

We must ask also, about the natural disasters: Where can they and how do they fit and integrate into the larger mosaic? In 1976 in China, 800,000 people were killed in an earthquake; in 1970 a cyclone in Bangladesh killed 300,000 people; in 1931 a flood killed 3.7 million Chinese; in 1300c.e. the Bubonic Plague killed as much as half of the population in Europe. In a unified theory, these natural occurrences must be taken into account. We must ask if all death is alike, if death serves a need, if death benefits the living?

In the next branch, down the path, I will show you that the World War II Holocaust was no displaced or cracked mosaic; the Holocaust was not unique, it was not a historical occurrence that was new or radically different; it had roots. The earlier holocausts were smaller only because the population was smaller. The reasons, we are told, were different, but an independent outside observer, after eliminating the rhetoric of self-serving gain, would not be able to see the difference.

We will start our search by looking at some of the history described in the Old Testament of the Christian Bible to see if the actions of human beings described in it are different from the actions of other human beings in the present. We must ask: Has there been enough time for natural selection and human selection to intervene in the affairs of human beings to change their actions when they encounter similar situations described in the Old Testament?

Because I do not claim the expertise, I will rely on scholars who have studied the Bible and have established by competent evidence that the Old Testament is just a fragmentary version of the history of the Jewish tribes passed down vocally through many generations and finally written down. Also in the Old Testament are many distortions of natural events that were changed into supernatural occurrences and inserted into this Jewish history book after the fact. With that limitation, I wish to use the Bible to show there has been no change in the adaptation of the mind to immoral acts against other human beings.

To start with, we are going to examine some actions and words of Moses; the historical Moses who, according to the Christian Bible, led the Israelites out of Egypt under the direct command of his Jewish God. The historical Moses who was alleged to have brought the Ten Commandants down from the mountain not once, but twice. The historical person who, as we start our examination at *Numbers 31* in the Old Testament, is leading the Jewish Tribes to the promised land. A land occupied by other tribes who were culturally different; they not only worshipped other Gods, but spoke different dialects. This Moses, according to the Old Testament, was a human being in daily communication with his Jewish God. Because of this, he did not have to pass his orders down through a third party or use parables. Moses received his orders *directly* through "mouth to mouth" communications with his God. If you believe the Christian Bible is the word of God, then, there can be no mistake or ambiguity in its interpretation. This Jewish God is commanding the Israelites, through Moses, to go to war with the Midianites because they have insulted Him by enticing some Jews to worship some Midian Gods. He has already punished the Israelites by indiscriminately killing 24,000 of His chosen people with a plague, but still He was not satisfied with that. To satisfy the petty grievances of his God — yes, they were petty — Moses proceeds to gather an army of 12,000 men to follow out those orders.

Because God was on their side — like nature, a Supreme Being is always on the winning side — they defeated the Midianites and proceeded to slaughter the five kings of Midian and all the captive adult men, which included the old, the sick, and the wounded. They then proceeded to burn all the villages, the towns, the cities, and the castles that they had captured. They brought back to their camp, on the plains of Moab, the spoils of war, which consisted of 675,000 sheep, 72,000 oxen, 61,000 donkeys and about 77,000 women and children, plus gold chains, bracelets, rings, earrings and tablets, which each soldier had seized for his personal benefit.

After the army had returned, Moses gathered his soldiers and gave them further orders that he had received *directly* from the mouth of his God. Those orders were: "Kill all the male children (about 32,000 of them), kill all mothers and all women and young girls that have known man by lying with him (about 13,000 of these), and divide the female virgins (about 32,000) amongst yourself and the people of Israel, with 64 virgins to be given to the priests in charge of the Tabernacle."

To carry out his orders, Moses is about to be confronted with a logistical problem; one that will confront other human beings down through the centuries, especially in the 1930s and '40s. That problem is how to massacre with as little disruption as possible 45,000 human beings. Massacres, when they are planned, must be organized, and that calls for a bureaucrat to do the organization. An Adolf Eichmann is needed, someone to carry out the orders of his superiors. Here the Superior's orders come *directly* from "mouth to mouth" conversations that Moses has with his God, so Moses will organize the troops. Then there are rituals to be performed, before and after the slaughter. There are grave questions to be answered: For instance, the question of which women and young girls are virgins? For this you must spread the legs of the young women to see if the hymen is intact; and woe to a virgin that had ridden astride a donkey. Fragile hymens have been known to be prematurely ruptured from this cause. What would have happened if some young women claimed that they were virgins until, on the long march to the camp, Jewish soldiers on guard duty raped them? The question — which would immediately arise if the guards denied it — is can you take the word of a person who believes in a different God, especially against someone who believes in the true faith? In their defense, the soldiers could point out that some people, usually foreigners, have been known to lie to save their worthless lives. The consensus would have been that it was despicable of these women to accuse their heroes, who had fought bravely against a common enemy, of rape. But even if it were not the consensus, the Adolf Eichmanns of the world understand the situation, and would tell them,

"Verily, you cannot make a mistake because you are acting under the commands of your God, the true God, so how can you rule wrong? Your God has ordered you to kill all women that have known men; so drag off those who claim rape and kill them with the rest of the non-virgin Midian women."

The organizers, the Adolf Eichmanns, know that time is short and should not be interrupted by entanglements in side issues. There were mass graves to be dug. The gas furnaces that could handle thousands of bodies at one time had not been invented; that would come later. Someone was needed to remove the hidden gold ornaments from the women; it was well known that there were hiding places that must be searched; a gold ring, a gold chain, a gold broach, all can be hidden between a woman's legs; they could even swallow them; thus forcing a search through a cut open stomach, which is not an agreeable task. Because clothing was expensive and they had slaves to dress, the garments of the slaughtered needed to be saved. Dentistry was not widespread in those days, so there was no need to knock out the teeth that had gold fillings as they had to do at Auschwitz and other death camps; so that cut down on the work load. Then the slaughter of the captives had to be organized. This was and still remains a messy business when you do not have the efficiency of the gas chambers. When you stick a sword into a body or cut a throat, the blood tends to spurt out on the person wielding the weapon. Of course you can take young boy babies, swing their heads against a convenient rock, then throw them into the mass grave; that makes the work load easier and less messy; but when they get too big, then someone must decide who will be assigned the dirty work, who the easy work. Every soldier wants to do the examination of the virgins and search for hidden gold; there would be many volunteers to spread the women's legs, but the work load must be equalized, so to make these decisions, Adolf Eichmanns are chosen.

After the slaughter is completed, there comes the ritual of absolving the participants of the blame, for the bloodbath. The Jews believed that it is unclean to carry or touch a dead body and that the blood of the slaughtered had to be removed from their clothing, their weapons, and their bodies; so there was a ritual to be followed if one was to go into God's Temple or return to the main camp and not offend their God. But worry not, because how to ceremonially purify yourself is all written down. Your God has had His word written down so you know how to absolve and purify yourself before you enter His Temple. Even though He was responsible for the blood letting, the killing of innocent men, women and children, surely one would not want to enrage, to offend such a powerful, such a vengeful God by appearing in His temple without benefit of the ritual of absolving yourself for following out His orders.

Yes, I can hear you; hear your screams of outrage: "This is obscene, this is blasphemy, this is designed to incite, to offend, to cause hostility." True, I do not, as the Old Testament does, make innocuous the words within it. I do not hide behind high sounding phraseology. These are the true acts behind the words. I wrote this to show that these are the human beings behind the facade; hiding behind their religion, behind capitalism, behind communism, behind fascism, behind every belief that has been invented to excuse and hide animal behavior. Yes, this is the animal in us; and after all the bath taking, the cutting and shaving of our hair from our face, our head, our legs, and under our arms, the dousing of our skins with perfumes, after shave lotions, and the use of under-arm deodorants, the painting and cutting back of our claws, the hiding of our natural shapes under layers of clothing, still, all this camouflage does not entirely hide that we are animals and will continue to act like them. This is the way we were, and this is the way we are, and the way we will act when faced with the situation where we have to choose between "them and us." Only the Gods we ask to purify us, to forgive our animal deeds, will change. Some of the old ones will remain and, as time passes, we will add some new ones just as abstract as those they replace. All ignore the factual reality that we slaughter because it benefits the animals that live; for the survivors, it lessens the competition for the limited resources.

"Do not lose faith with us," were the words from the Holocaust victims. "Someone must live, must survive to tell what happened," were the fervent pleas from the death camps; "if we are to rest in peace, you must describe the road that brought us here to the death camps and completely remove it or you will have broken faith with us."

Many Jews came out of the Holocaust believing that their God had failed them; but you cannot understand the Holocaust by declaring that your God deserted you. Assumed guilt solves nothing. If you do not know or cannot describe how the road to catastrophe was built, then 45 million people (6 million of these were Jews), died in vain. What can you do if you come to believe that your God could not prevent the Holocaust or, even more insane, that He was responsible for it and using it to punish the Jewish people? That would put the Jewish people in the center of the universe; that would lead them to believe that the other 39 million deaths during World War II, were not equal. If Hitler was God's earthly agent for the punishment of the European Jews, then, why should we blame Hitler for the Holocaust? How could Hitler be responsible for killing millions of people when he was just carrying out the wishes of a just, merciful, loving, caring, omnipotent, Jewish-Christian God? If you come to believe that a God was responsible or abstained from intervening in the Holocaust, then there is nothing to learn from the past, there is no room for human intervention.

If religious people had known beforehand that there were no Gods to intercede for them, then they could have looked elsewhere for a solution. All religions are handicapped when they go looking for solutions that depend on their personal God to intervene with a miracle. Understand: The road to the Holocaust was not built for the Jewish people, alone. It was built to eliminate from the world its surplus populations. The road has always been there; it is being maintained by human beings in power who can designate who will be eliminated. Because human beings have usurped natural selection, the strong and powerful within the governments are able to say, "This person is surplus, this religion is surplus, this political party is surplus, this nation is surplus." And if you claim that they are usurping the power of a Supreme Being, then you must depend on your God to remove you from their list. To believe in a God when your opponents do not or in a different God than the majority, will leave you helpless because of your ignorance.

Many came out of the Holocaust believing that civilization failed them. A close look will show that civilization did not fail them, because there was no civilization; laws did not fail here, because there were no laws. It was just a false perception that we had overthrown the natural law that the strong take from the weak; that the strongest could take the life of other human beings without a valid reason. For those survivors of the Holocaust who still believed in a Supreme Being, the idea that except for the proportions, the Holocaust was to nature just another simian border war with casualties, was something their minds could not accept. It was incomprehensible to them that all their sacrifices were meaningless to nature; that only living human beings could judge the morality of those sacrifices.

"Do unto others as you would have them do unto you" can be seen as a Darwinian observation. Look at the Polish people and their treatment of the Jews before and after Hitler's invasion of the country. The dominant Catholic religion in Poland produced few people who showed ethical or moral qualms when the economic crisis of the 1930s was blamed on the Jews. The majority saw nothing wrong when boycotts and pogroms against the Jewish people killed hundreds and wounded thousands. It is estimated that in 1935, 1 million Jews (one third of the Jewish population) were unemployed and living in squalid poverty. Still, there was heard, "How dare that a Jew has work when there are good Polish Catholics without work." Like the Germans, the Polish people looked on the Jews as inferior; the majority saw nothing wrong with taking away the citizenship of Polish Jews. After the invasion, when the extermination began against the Jews, there was no sympathetic population to hide in; the Polish people had, with the consent of the Catholic Church, been anti-Semitic for hundreds of years, so the majority gladly cooperated in the genocide. But once again I must stress, that if the Jews had never been dispersed and there were no Jews in Poland in the 1930s, there would still have been a need to exterminate the excess population that was on the land that the Germans wanted to annex for their surplus population.

When the Germans crossed the Polish frontier, they immediately murdered about 10,000 Polish priests, teachers, technicians, and political leaders and sent thousand to concentration's camps. The Polish people were horrified by this treatment; they could not understand why the Germans thought of them as an inferior race. Did they not, like the Germans, agree with the policy of genocide of the Jewish people; were they not cooperating with the policy of the extermination of those inferior Jewish people? They knew that the Polish people had a right and a duty to judge the Jew, but, "Where did the Germans receive the right to judge them?" they kept asking. They could not comprehend that the Germans received it by the same right that the Polish people judged the Jewish population: under the natural law that those in power make the law; and that all the prayers and beseeching to a nonexistent God would not change that, could not stop the powerful from carrying out the extermination of millions. They never came to understand that their prayers were useless against a human death machine; that their only hope was a stronger army that would defeat the German Axis and save them from complete annihilation.

Truly, the allies did not win because they were more religious, because they represented good over evil, because they represented the truth. If they had, how could we explain the Russians winning the war, explain a God on the side of the Russian concentration camps where the Communists were also murdering and torturing human beings? If we believe that a God controls these things, this is the absurdity that it leads to. No! This can all be rejected; they won because collectively they were stronger militarily than the Germans.

The Reich's Citizenship law of September 15, 1935 and the law for the Protection of German Blood and German Honor, passed on the same day, made German Jews second class citizens. Although, 100,000 Jews served in the German Army in World War I — 12,000 of which, fell on the battlefield — their citizenship was also taken from them. On September 1, 1939, Adolf Hitler signed a decree that permitted doctors to kill homosexuals, to murder the mentally ill, the retarded, the chronically ill, and habitual criminals. It is estimated that 275,000 German citizens were murdered under this decree.

How did they judge, what criterion was used, what definition was used to determine a habitual criminal's actions from their *own* acts of murder, from their *own* theft of property from millions of innocent persons? Why did they find it necessary to sign decrees and pass laws to legitimize their barbaric acts when there was no law to be observed? Certainly an act is not sanctified because it is done by a group of human beings. If a group has a natural right to commit an immoral act (an act judged by human beings as immoral), then that act committed by an individual is also right. All those affected by these decrees — the Jews, the Gypsies, the Jehovahs Witnesses, the homosexuals, the mentally ill, the chronically ill, the Communists, the socialists — had the right in this Germany to lie, to steal, to cheat, to spy, to betray their country, and even to kill to protect their self-interest. They owed no allegiance to the German government, to German laws, to German culture; there were no innocent Germans because there was no way to ascertain the innocent from the guilty.

Human beings should understand that their denial of natural selection did not, could not, and does not exempt them from the competition. The Holocaust was not an aberration. Adolf Eichmann, a normal bureaucrat following his superior's orders, was not inhuman, but sad to say, all too human. We cannot blame ignorance because the head of the death camps and the death squads were mostly university educated and could be described as ordinary people. Surely, Adolf Eichmann was a selfish person expressing the thoughts of his superiors. Selfish individuals, when they form collectives, will always produce selfish institutions. All religious and political institutions seek their self-interest over other individuals and institutions; our best deeds and our darkest deeds are for the same reason. We all do what we think is best for ourselves, what is best for our town, city, county, state, or nation; what is best for our family, our religion, our political beliefs.

I picked the Midian situation to show that what they did on the plains of Moab and what the German Fascist Party and the Russian Communist Party did, were similar except for the reasons given. The German Fascists were acting under the misconstrued idea that they could ascertain a difference between human beings; they could (for the betterment of the human race) use the same tactics they use in animal breeding — kill off what they considered inferior stock and then breed to their specifications what they considered worthy stock. The Russian Communist Party was acting under the misconstrued idea that if there is no God, then there are no rules that have to be followed. Only the Jewish tribes have an excuse. They truly believed they were acting under the orders of their God. It was not their fault that there was no science, no natural selection theory that they could compare; so how could they know that the orders were not being received by Moses *directly* from "mouth to mouth" communications with a God.

The reasons given might be different, but the results were the same: the killing of surplus men, women, and children so that the living can benefit by having less competition for the limited resources. We do not know the contents of the Midian's Bible because it was destroyed with them; but, I am sure that if they had won, their God would have approved of the slaughter of the Jews, and there would have been rituals to clean the guilt from their minds after the massacre. With God on their side, the Jews did win, and then proceeded to capture the rest of the land that Moses said their Jewish God had promised them. And, probably because of the experience at Moab, they proceeded to slaughter all the men, women, and children in the later victories, not even the virgins were spared.

How could the Jews kill all these innocent captive women and children; did they not have the Ten Commandments at that time? Yes, they did, but you must understand that these Commandments were like their religion — they were tribal; they only applied within the Jewish tribes. They could not kill with impunity within the tribes, they could not covet a neighbor's wife or property within the tribes; all the laws and Commandments were tribal. Their excuse was that their Jewish God had given them the land of a non-Jewish neighbor and told them to dispossess the inhabitants and drive them out of the land and slaughter them or they would become a thorn in their side and be vexed by them when they became numerous again. Their Jewish God also warned them that He would be on the Midian's side the next time and have the Jews all slaughtered if they allowed the Midianites to live. So they were destroying under the coercion of the false belief that they were allowed by their God to treat other tribes who did not believe in their God, differently. This gave them their excuse (all cultures seem to need one) for the mass slaughter that took place.

All survival laws are inherited from nature. These laws permeate all human societies, past and present, and are observable in their operations. Do I believe that Moses was communicating with a God, which gave him those orders described in the Old Testament? Do I believe Hitler's excuse that the Jewish people were an inferior race and they deserved to die in the gas chambers? Do I believe that Stalin killed all those human beings because they were all counter-revolutionaries? No! I don't! That leaves the question of why they did what they did. If all these acts are the same underneath the facade (which I believe is true), then they were following a survival law that permits human life, because of its mental development under natural selection, to define who will be selected by usurping natural selection and instituting human selection. Survival of the fittest is carried out by people who get to name the fittest by measuring the defeated, by measuring the prisoners, by measuring human beings by arbitrary method; but which has the same results of survival of the fittest, because after the facts, the natural and the arbitrary, only the living can be the measure of the selection. The living, by surviving, becomes the fittest, because nature has no way of determining one death from another. Nature deals with death in a concrete method. It uses death as fertilizer to recycle the chemical elements into new life. To nature, death is the same regardless of the reasons given by the living.

The taking of another human life was the action of an animal when it was used in nature as an act of eliminating competition for the limited resources. Human beings have extended this action to include the elimination of competition in abstract ideas. A unified link can be seen in the law of Natural Selection that ensures that an individual animal tends to do whatever gives it the best chance for propagating its genes, even to the killing of other *Homo sapiens*. Civilization, to me, is knowing about this law, but not practicing it or participating in it; because although it benefits the individual, in the long run it does not benefit the world. We have reached the point where we can no longer, with impunity, mass murder other human beings without ourselves being mass murdered. What has always been wrong with this natural law is that you must win every time against the other religion, against the other political creeds, or you are the one who will die before your time. If you let someone persuade you that it benefits you or your society to let them kill you, then you deserve to die because you are not attuned with nature that stresses life.

Did the slaughter of those Midians on the plains of Moab help the living? Yes, just the same as death from natural disasters, from accidents, or from diseases help the living. Let us speculate on a Pandora's box being opened on those plains of Moab that contained three ingredients that would have allowed all descendants from one couple to survive until the 1980s. Let us just take those two Midians and analyze the future Midian families that would have been produced from just two of those 32,000 boys and 32,000 girls that were brought to the plains of Moab. We will take the year that it probably happened — about 1250B.C.E. — and extrapolate how many descendants would have been living today. We are going to use the figure of 1 percent per year growth which will double the population every 70 years. (This is not excessive, because Jordan's rate of growth in 1985, was 4.1 percent, which would double the population every 17 years.) By the year 10C.E. the progenies from a single Midian couple would be 524,288 people; by the year 920C.E that couple would have produced 4.29 billion living descendants; almost equaling the present population on earth of 4.76 billion. Today, 1988, the population from that couple alone would be about 140 trillion people if the Jews had allowed just a single couple to live. Multiply this by 32,000 couples and you reach a population of about 4,500,000,000,000,000,000 (4-1/2 quin-tillon).

This is an absurdity; not the figures, because the mathematics are correct and you can prove it by allowing a single celled organism to have enough nourishment and space to double 47 times; the absurdity is that we cannot support that many human beings on a finite earth. In order for this to have happened, what dreadful and obscene specter would that Pandora's box have had to contain to give us that population nightmare? Two of them would be peace and medical knowledge. Yes, no more wars and the development of medicine to keep a person alive until he or she can reproduce their genes. They are obtainable goals with our present knowl-edge. Still in the box, however, is the third one: the knowledge of how to feed, clothe, and house that many people. That knowledge can never be obtainable; there is a barrier, a space and resource limitation that all the science in the world cannot solve; and no political subdivision can solve it by an equal (under democratic socialism) or unequal (under capitalism, feudalism and fascism) division of the limited resources. So human beings have a choice: control the population by birth control and abortion or do away with modern medicine, do away with peaceful settlements of disputes and allow local wars to continue, or let millions of people starve to death.

There are beliefs that we all must hold to retain a diversity of beliefs. If you do not accept those beliefs, then what happened on those plains of Moab is your last, your final, yes, your ultimate destiny. The world must remember that to nature, the road to those plains of Moab continued until it reached the Holocaust of World War II; it was an extension with many side branches that always returned to the main road.

The road's object was not to exterminate the Midians; nature could not distinguish between them and the exterminators. All sacrifices in nature are equal; the harsh reality is that the German soldier giving his life for his country, giving his life for Hitler, had the same value in abstract nature as did our dead soldiers; only the individual judgement of a human being can give it a separate meaning, only a living human being can say they were not equal. Why should you be kicked out of the nest before your time? Once you are out of the nest, there is nothing to appeal to. Only the living can ask for justice. We human beings have preempted nature; we have taken over its duties. Only selfish human beings can choose, can separate, can distinguish between individuals; so the strong will say who the surpluses are, say who will live, who will die. An abstract description of an abstraction (Nature) can have no interest in the dead. Only the living can take note of them; only the living can ask "Why?" Nature is utterly indifferent to our standard of justice or injustice; only the living can take note of it and ask why this justice or injustice. Nature cannot take into account our suffering, only the living can do that; and if we forget, there will be no record to learn from. Nature cannot perform the miracles of enlarging the earth's surface to support an unlimited population. It has no way to prepare or plan for a future because it cannot anticipate the future; that is reserved for human beings. When human beings must use wars, diseases, famines, or a human-instituted holocaust to eliminate its surplus population, then we must assume that it is a cold world without Divine presence; from this it follows that if there is a solution, then only human beings can find it.

CHAPTER 19

NARRATIVE: MISDIRECTION

Not to learn from the past is a demonstrable handicap. Locked into a well-trampled path, it seemed that all previous Writs of Habeas Corpus that had been filed by prisoners in the mental wards of the Federal Medical Center in Springfield, Missouri had claimed that the petitioners were sane and capable of defending their interest in a court of law; thus, they were being held illegally in that institution. Because the courts could only accept the admission of expert testimony, and the medical center's psychiatric staff did not agree, admit or concede with the petitioners that they were sane and capable of defending their self-interest in a court of law, the court could not compel the government to go to trial; therefore, the writs were routinely denied and the petitioners not allowed to appear in court.

In my Writ of Habeas Corpus, I admitted — purely as a tactic — that the neuropsychiatric staff's diagnosis was correct; that I was undeniably a true schizophrenic, and my ward doctor, the medical staff, and the literature that I had read, all agreed that there was no cure for a schizophrenic and only a small chance for remission soon, even with the correct treatment. (The literature that I had access to was compiled by the prisoners and patients at Springfield because they needed to cite published material to prove to a court that they were not mentally ill.)

I then went on to point out to the Court: that despite the appendage of the words "Medical Center" to the name of the institution where I was incarcerated, for all definable purposes I was being held in a prison and these words only superficially obscured that fact. The facts were that over ninety-nine percent of the population confined at the Springfield Medical Center were convicted prisoners, that it was a prison hospital directed by prison guards and staff that were under the supervision of the United States Department of Justice Bureau of Prisons, and that the institution was managed under prison rules and regulations. I pointed out to the Court that the doctors on the hospital staff had not only succumbed to becoming an arm of the prison staff but had become powerless to act independent of it. Their titles of psychiatrist and psychologist were just synonyms for highly paid prison guards. A conflict that arose between treatment and rules and regulations was decided by security first, so all treatment had to be designed with this obstruction in mind. The medical staff had to obey all prison rules and regulations and put them before the welfare of their patients. A security prison officer was in charge and could overrule a doctor if there was a conflict of interest; all treatment of the mentally ill took second place to security. As there was no distinctions among the categories of inmates, all convicted prisoners or mental patients waiting for trial, were punished equally for breaking the prison rules and regulations.

I gave information in my writ that many other prisoners and I were not being treated for our diagnosed mental illness; and if treated, our chances to respond favorably to that treatment in a prison setting were almost nil. I informed the Court that instead of treatment, I found myself being punished just like the convicted prisoners; but unlike them, I had not been convicted of a crime. This brought up the Constitutional question of whether I should be considered innocent until proven guilty, or does diagnosed mental illness change my status under the Constitution from a person to a nonperson? Do I lose the protection of the United States Constitution if I become mentally ill; and does this allow the justice department the right to punish me before a conviction for a crime?

I did not question their right to hold me; I questioned their right to hold me in a prison. I informed the judge in my writ that if the government wished to hold me, then they should place me where I had the best chance to go into remission so that I could go to trial and be proven guilty or innocent. I pointed out that the Federal Government had established for the treatment of the mentally ill an institution, St. Elizabeth Hospital, that did not have a prison setting; therefore I should be sent to that institution.

Realizing that the Federal Judge — because of being so geographically close — probably knew him personally or was at least familiar with his worldwide reputation, in my writ I cited the writings of Dr. Karl Menninger. (His reputation was not only in the treatment, but by changing the patient's environment in the hospital, the remission of many mental afflictions other doctors had problems treating.) Dr. Menninger's writings agreed with my assumptions; which were that under the conditions of a prison setting, you could not expect an optimum amount of remission.

From the limited amount of records that I had access to, it seemed that prisoners waiting for trial were at one time treated at St. Elizabeth Hospital. They eventually refused to handle the prisoners because they objected to the security that they had to impose on all the patients or treat the person waiting for trial in a different and segregated manner, which they felt was not conducive to treatment. What I inferred from the records and from unreliable prison rumors, was that, at that time, they did not want to turn St. Elizabeth into a prison or even to have one half of it become a prison. (From recent newspaper accounts, relating to the confinement of David Hinkley, we can now assume that part of it has become a prison.)

I informed the Court that I knew that St. Elizabeth Hospital did not wish to undertake the treatment of patients under indictment for criminal actions, but where did they gain the right to exclude me from the most humane treatment obtainable; especially if I were going to be institution-alized for years or even the rest of my life without the correct treatment. And if there were hope for remission in an environment more conducive to that remission, then it should be the burden of the Federal Government to furnish that treatment if available, because my only hope to resolve my legal status would be for treatment under conditions that would improve my chances for remission and eventual trial.

As St. Elizabeth Hospital was under a different government bureau than the Medical Center at Springfield, as a tactic I tried to embroil them and the Court into a jurisdictional dispute. (When you have two govern-ment bureaus involved in a jurisdictional battle, you can, inadvertently, force one of them to fight on your side.) And yes, I did understand what St. Elizabeth was probably trying to avoid; at the same time, I knew that if the unconvicted patients were sent there, that eventually security would dominate there also, just as it did at Springfield; then the doctors and nurses would find that they were subservient to that security. But I truly did not wish to be sent there. I felt if I entangled the St. Elizabeth Hospital staff in my case, that they would be enticed into fighting my coming there, and that would help in my fight to be sent back to Sacramento, where my object was to have them drop that false charge of bank robbery against me.

It was in the late fall of 1962 that the warden and hospital staff at Springfield had their first hint that there was an incipient challenge to their authority. They had been delivered a copy of my Writ of Habeas Corpus along with an order to produce me in Federal Court and answer all the allegations that I had incorporated into my writ. In all the years that this institution had held mentally ill patients waiting for trial, this was the first time that this had happened to them. Nobody had ever claimed before that they entirely agreed with the medical staff's diagnosis that they were indeed mentally ill. Only, when I was congratulated in the hospital elevator by an intern, did I become aware that my writ was received favorably by the Court. It seemed that I had knocked down the facade of the medical building and behold, something was behind it; the hospital staff was amazed to discover that someone had not only built a prison behind it but had an organized prison staff running it.

The next day, without a comment or a discussion of their merits, I received from the hands of the warden the notice that my writ was accepted by the Court. In it, I was informed that to protect my interests — because I had been judged mentally incompetent — an attorney would be appointed by the Court to contact me and discuss the legal implications of my writ.

So that they do not acquire sloppy work habits in prison, all federal prisoners are required to work. My work assignment was to operate an antiquated hospital elevator for a couple of hours, each day. As it was the main access to my floor, it became a conduit for information and allowed me to get acquainted with the different personalities who made up the medical and prison staff. The medical staff's diagnosing me as mentally ill did not preclude me from acquiring information by observing the observers in an environment where they felt safe and comfortable. I was especially delighted in observing their reactions to the introduction of new factors and information into that environment. They became my temporary ant farm; uncontrollable, true, but then neither does a naturalist in the wild control. Still it is interesting to watch and observe people. What I was doing was an anthropological study of the institution and its inhabitants and part time inhabitants.

It was in my work assignment elevator that a couple of interns sought me out to inform me that they agreed with much of what I had to say about the inequities of the treatment received at the medical center; they were especially against the dominance of security that was imposed on them. But the way that these interns approached me was frightening in its implications. They informed me, but only when they were alone with me in the elevator, that they were unable to corroborate openly in court my assertions, even when they were true; nor were they allowed to signify their displeasure with the system or their internship would be in jeopardy. When they first approached me in this conspiratorial way, I could not believe these were grown men who were so apprehensive about their future in medicine that they let themselves be intimidated by their superiors. The frightening implications were that these were to be our psychiatrists and psychologists of the future; they were going out into the world to diagnose and treat the mentally ill when they were not able to diagnose or cure their personal fears.

I want you to know that I do not claim that I was completely taken by surprise by the interns' actions; from books and observations about the behavior of subordinates toward their superiors in bureaucratic systems, I had deduced that this kind of behavior would apply here; this was just confirmation of the theory that I had built up from my previous conclusions on the subject. I also theorized that if you examine bureaucratic systems, you will find that they revert to the lowest level of competency. That if you continually remove that vestige of competency that enters a system, then you become powerless to correct an incompetent system from within it.

Those foolish enough to remain in the system with the view of correcting it from inside, would find out, when they rose to a position of influence, that they had continually compromised their beliefs to such an extent that they would no longer wish to endanger the system that they headed. That was the information gap, the trap hidden for years that was ready to drop the foolish into a fraudulent defense of the system. They would become "nulls" and be unable to say when they crossed the demarcation line.

However, my battle was with the present "nulls." I did not expect the permanent medical staff to acknowledge that my accusations were worthy of their consideration; and was not surprised when I found myself correct in this assumption. Besides the interns, only my ward doctor mentioned my writ, and he took it as a personal challenge and informed me that this writ proved his contention that I was mentally ill. Just thinking that I was a special person and should receive special privileges not accorded the other patients, was evidence of that illness, and he would testify that I was getting adequate treatment and all my accusations were just part of my illness. He then warned me that I had better understand the way things were run around here as I would be here for some time. Delusions of Grandeur with a continuing schizophrenic process, was his diagnosis. His hostile and childish tirade underscored my belief that he could be manipulated into an untenable position that was at odds with the rest of the medical staff.

His hostility toward me could be anticipated as it is a common occurrence and reaction by those who occupy positions of authority without having the genes required to be dominant. A piece of paper saying that by your schooling you have a right to be considered a dominant person in your field will never replace those genes. My ward doctor was practicing in an environment where he had to be obeyed or he could punish with severe force. His usual dealings were with captive patients who had to depend on his good will to find them cured or in remission. (The psychiatric department's main business was the diagnosing and treating of convicted federal prisoners, and until those prisoners could be judged cured or in remission by their ward doctors, they could not be released on parole.)

From the first, my ward doctor could not understand why I did not accept him as a superior being; he went to great length to explain to me that I had to please him if I wished to get out of Springfield. He could sense my disdain for him, which I was deliberately manifesting. His threat to keep me at Springfield began when I first arrived and did not confide to him my thoughts about being sent back to Sacramento. I kept repeating, and never did deviate from it, that I did not care which way he ruled as I was not concerned and did not want to get involved in the obvious little game of "we are neutral" that he and the hospital staff were playing. I further informed him that what he thought or what he did would not interfere with what I intended to do; and that because he was not neutral or independent, but just an extension of the justice department, he was not going to be privy to my future actions or my thoughts. I thought of him not as a doctor trying to help me, but as a highly paid prison guard and informant for the justice department with a degree in medicine.

Because I had read some of the same books that my doctor had, I knew his thoughts about my little speech without having to ask him. "A classic example of a paranoid" would be his response. Even before speaking, I knew in advance that my speech would be interpreted as paranoid, and I deliberately made it so to provoke him. Of course, I knew that he wanted to be stroked; the other prisoners had to do it to please him; that was his extra pay for the humiliation of knowing that he and his profession were a grotesque sham when they were working in a prison setting. To cure a prison psychosis, you must remove the prisoner from the prison environment, and this the prison psychiatrist and psychologist cannot do.

By then, I knew that no matter how I acted, no matter what I said, the doctors were going to act on the assumption that I was mentally ill; all my actions and words would only be interpreted from that point of view. A hard look at the Special Progress Report put out to answer my writ in court will verify this.

...indications of some grandiose thoughts; ... indications of thinking he is omnipotent; considers himself a special person; ... continues to be expansive in his thoughts about himself; ... is superficially friendly to those he comes in contact with ...

Although taken out of context, these views were unanimously held among the doctors, but most of the information required to arrive at these opinions was acquired through my ward doctor's evaluation.

Only by dissecting one of their statements are we able to understand how they arrived at all the opinions that they expressed in this report. What they were saying when they said that I was "superficially friendly" was that they could see that I was friendly with the staff that I came into contact with, but I did not trust or confide in them. This was true, but how many deep friendships had they developed with their patients? It takes two to make a friendship and there has to be some mutual benefit or attraction to the participants. Their acting as an arm of the justice department would forbid such a friendship; the prison setting would forbid such a friendship; the mandatory and enforced treatment would forbid such a friendship. Adversaries can only have a superficial friendship. They entirely ignored the fact: that even in a transitory environment — that I was caught up in — I had made a few close, trusting friendships, with my fellow ward patients. The hospital staff did not know this. They were entirely deprived of observation on on my conduct outside their limited view. When I was in their limited view, I was conscious of their observations and projecting a falsely designed image for their consumption. In other words, I was controlling their information through my ward doctor. So their assumptions could not have been made on valid observations, but purely on books that said that schizophrenics do not make deep friendships, and because I had been diagnosed as a schizophrenic, we run into just another situation of which came first, in their diagnosis, the chicken or the egg?

I did not think that my expansive thoughts were grandiose; they were not embellished out of context; they were being used to accomplish an attainable goal — my removal from their confinement to a Federal Courtroom in Sacramento. By my actions alone, I had successfully manipulated and maneuvered the United States Justice Department into going into Federal Court and answering questions that I felt they did not want to answer, or to immediately find me competent to stand trial. The minute my writ was answered, I suspected which they would choose and prepared myself for it. I felt sure that the Justice Department would not want to take the meager chance of having their jurisdiction at the Medical Center curtailed or even abolished. They knew and understood the implications; if I was successful in court, there would come a deluge of writs to wash over them and undermine their foundations.

They had no intention of saying where they received the power to send the unconvicted to a prison to suffer the same punishment as those convicted in a court of law. I had noticed that vagueness in the laws and statutes were an asset for governments; they did not want to have them defined, so they would never voluntarily come into a courtroom seeking such a clarification. Nor did they want to answer whether I had a right to be treated in a hospital where I had the optimum chance of recovery or remission.

So it was no surprise to me when on December 19, 1962 a Special Progress Report was issued, after I appeared before a committee of four staff doctors, which ended like this:

Psychological studies at this time bear out our opinion that he is an intelligent man and in possession of facts and the rational ability to understand the proceeding against him...

But this had been true all along; at no time, at my stay at the Springfield Medical Center, had I faked mental illness as I had at Vacaville or in my appearances before Dr. Bromberg. They had just concurred in the findings of Dr. Bromberg without independently verifying them.

Only after they had brought in an outside psychologist and he found me competent, did their diagnosis match the facts. And he was only brought in because my ward doctor still held the belief that I was incompetent to stand trial, so the hospital staff wanted to have a neutral report to show the Federal Judge. They did not want him to think they were removing an insane person from his jurisdiction and from the protection of the Federal Court by finding me sane when I was not. (Federal Judges are jealous of their jurisdiction; they have harsh penalties for those who do not heed their court orders or who try to circumvent them.)

I am sure that documents still exist to show that some intelligent person from the U.S. Justice Department in Washington, D.C. had intervened to close this loophole, because locally, I do not believe they had the knowledge or the power to decide such a question. Whoever it was wanted to have outside evidence in the event I went into court to dispute their latest findings that I was sane. Certainly, this person did not know what I wanted, he was just anticipating what would happen if I tried to prevent them from taking me back to Sacramento by going to court and claiming that I was still mentally ill and this was just a strategy to remove me from the court's protection.

Misdirection, a tool of a magician, is helpful in the kind of encounters I was having; that is why I depended on no one, trusted no one, and informed no one of my intentions, and so was judged and labeled a paranoid. While my ward doctor was working with labels, I was working with reality and could not afford the luxury of worrying about becoming entangled in his gummed labels.

You might think that somebody from the Washington D.C. Justice Department was a figment of my imagination unless you understand the bureaucratic systems and the mentality required for advancement within it. Civil Servants do not make decisions without going through conventional channels. They abhor making decisions on their own. Successful bureaucrats will always defer to their superiors and seek permission of those above them for an act that might be misinterpreted; if there is a departure from the rules, they will insist that the reason given should be received in written form. It is inconceivable that locally they had the power to decide how to proceed in my case when it obviously affected the complete Justice Department. So, the intervention of someone from the administration of the Justice Department with decision-making powers must be the explanation of why they decided to make my case moot by finding me sane, thus allowing them to send me out of the jurisdiction of the local Federal Court.

If examined outside the mental hospital setting with no hint of a previous mental condition, I would have passed all tests given to me, and then, none of my actions would have been misinterpreted; but once you have been diagnosed as mentally ill, you are able to fool the doctors because every normal act is viewed and interpreted by them as the actions of a mentally ill person. This gave me the ability to even fool the outside psychologist they brought in, if I had wished to.

One reason they brought in the neutral psychologist was to persuade my ward doctor to change his mind. Ward doctors at Springfield had the authority to be the sole judge of their patients' competency. His superiors would not overrule him without proof that his findings were incorrect; they could not blatantly overrule him without damaging the system's rules. These rules are inextricably entwined with the way the system survived with the use of "nulls." My ward doctor's superiors, however, must have had their orders to get me out of the jurisdiction of the Federal Judge so that they would not have to answer that writ. Evidently, with the outside psychologist's report, they persuaded him that a miracle had occurred and that I was in remission; but as a conciliatory gesture to my ward doctor's dignity, the following was incorporated into the final report:

In these tests there is evidence of a continuing schizophrenic process but under good remission at this time ...

The "at this time" was my ward doctor's way of putting out a disclaimer. They had inadvertently used in those three words, phrasing that was beneficial to my plans as I intended to act incompetent when I reached Sacramento.

When ejected from the Springfield Medical Facility, I was sure that I would not be allowed to return; and if I was still found unable to stand trial when I reached a Sacramento courtroom, their option would probably be to drop the charges because there was no place to confine me without me filing another writ and bringing the case back before a Federal Judge. Because of my lack of information, I underestimated them; to my amazement I was to find out that they had another card to play that I was not expecting.

When I left Springfield, I felt sad; because there were many unanswered questions that even now remain unanswered. To this day, I am haunted by the memories of those patients caught up in an insane system that I had the opportunity of overturning for the few that were waiting for trial; or at least getting them removed to a true hospital setting. (There was no way to help the convicted patients as they were unable to use the tactics I employed.) All I would have had to do was convince the outside psychologist that I was mentally ill; then they would have had to take me to court and answer my questions. I might have had a true victory instead of a small personal victory. I have berated myself these many years, but my mind keeps protecting me by telling me that it would have been folly to go against them, to threaten them. I was living in a prison environment where prisoners have been killed over a single pack of cigarettes. To be approached by someone who had the power to free you, gave that someone unlimited power as there is nothing he or she cannot ask. You could also be placed in one of their basement cells (yes, they had them); and a note to the Federal Judge that the patient is in a comatose state (yes, they had the drugs to put you in one) was all that was needed. You see, I knew my enemies, I knew them only too well; so it was not in ignorance but through that knowledge that I acted. That put to rest their contention that I thought that I was omnipotent. A person who believes he is omnipotent is not afraid of anybody or anything; and I was afraid of their power and what they could do to me if they felt that I was a threat to them.

So, I was banished from the Medical Center in Springfield. I was found to be a chain-rattler — one who produces discordant musical notes with their chains. It is the reason I was not welcome at Springfield and why I knew that they would not send me back there. They knew that chain-rattlers like to orchestrate others into the harsh and discordant sounds made by rattling chains; and like the mythical horns at Jericho, they can bring down walls, prison walls, their prison walls, and that they did not want to happen.

CHAPTER 20

ESSAY: POLITICAL THOUGHTS

Searching for the truth, I have come to believe that all systems of government should be examined empirically. There is now sufficient data to compare the present contending forms and ascertain whether we need them, and whether an accumulation of *Homo sapiens* that gathers together and forms a government, in someway inherits extraordinary powers from that amalgamation. If governments are found to be structurally equal, then despite their rhetoric, they hold power not because they are historically right or God's chosen people, but because they are stronger than those that want to replace them. It is a natural law that the strongest dominate, and until human beings could reason, there could be no morality involved in the power structure of the animal kingdom. If governments remain strong by having either the consent of the people or by controlling the opposition by force, they can, because they dominate, say how goods and resources are to be manufactured and distributed, and arbitrarily pick persons to produce and receive those goods. The results: unless we can and do introduce human morality, we will always be swayed by those who resort to playing to our basic animal needs, by those who do not recognize that ethical and moral standards are human inventions, by those who claim there is no need for human created ethics and morality.

The cosmos cannot detect or distinguish among the moral or immoral actions of individuals or a community of individuals. To counter immoral philosophies, human beings must be able to show that human ethical and moral codes can be shown to be beneficial without needing the trappings of an imagined Supreme Being. They need to show that human codes of conduct can be used as an extension of natural selection, can be used to take advantage of it and control the randomness of natural selection, to control the variations, to subjugate it to human needs.

In common with all life forms, we can see that men and women are continually engaged in the survival of the fittest. We, *Homo sapiens*, are able to use and adopt different creeds, religions, and political acts as weapons that will give us an edge in this struggle. Do not interpret a state's adoption of morality and human rights as a policy constructed only on idealism with no other foundation. Adopting morality and human rights is not idealism, but a concrete act of self-preservation. It is an adaptation for survival; it is just as essential to adopt a morality based on materialism, as was the need to adopt the spear or the bow and arrow if your opponent had acquired them. Ethics give to those who adopt them, an advantage in the struggle to survive over those without them.

A socialist economy is not synonymous with the automatic elimination of gender, ethic, cultural, or religious discrimination. Ethnic and cultural persecution prevails and invades all forms of society; it is not attached to a particular brand of production or distribution, not attached to fascisms, capitalism, socialism, communism, or a particular religion. When we left the primate troop — by evolutionary means — to form other cultures, we brought with us (in our genes) the process of discrimination against all animals that are outside the troop and are contending for the same turf. The human mind is regulated by the adaptation of the view that other groups of people (other ethnic and cultural groups) are a threat to them. There is the "rub," because with language, they do not have to be an actual threat; they just have to be psychologically viewed as a threat to be discriminated against, lied about, humiliated, tortured and even killed. By the way we treat minorities, we can perceive the amount of psychological threat that they represent in the minds of those who hold the power.

No matter how perfect a government's ideology is on paper, it still must prove in practice what it predicts on paper. Marxists were mistaken when they proclaimed religious morality as a trapping of religion; claimed it was part of and firmly connected and rooted to the past, firmly connected and rooted to feudalism, firmly connected and rooted to the middle class, and so would be unessential and unneeded when the workers achieved power. Marxists cynically proclaimed that atheism gave them the right to ignore religious morality when fighting capitalism, feudalism, or fascism. If this is true, then how are they going to introduce morality into their relationship with other individuals, with other Communist or Socialist governments? From what source is their morality going to come? What would be its ancestry, its roots?

They created this problem because they attributed exclusively to religion and the past a morality that did not belong exclusively to religion and the past. If as an atheist you believe that morality does not and cannot come from a nonexisting Supreme Being, then it has to come from human beings in response to their environment or it would have no roots. Because there is no God, morality must be a human invention; it must be constructed from the human experience and must include natural and human selection in its makeup. If it is true that the adoption of morality does, under natural and human selection, give a higher survival rate to individuals and their offspring, then it becomes a standard that would benefit all cultures and governments that adopt it. This argument introduces natural morality into the political world without needing the false explanation of a Supreme Being to account for it; this gives an atheist government a concrete foundation for human rights.

Over time and through evolution, natural selection adapts us and all other life, to the environment. Simply expressed, natural selection is a mechanism for passing on a favorable genetic mutation of a gene to our offspring. Allowing for the fact that more than one random, beneficial alteration could be going on at the same time, evolution requires the holder of a beneficial gene to produce more offspring than those without that gene so that after many generations, the beneficial gene spreads throughout the species. For billions of years evolution, proceeding on its uninterrupted course, adapted organisms to the changing environment without the need of organisms to know or understand the process of evolution. That has now changed. Recently, we have gained the ability to change the environment so quickly, that nature does not have the time to adjust us and the other life forms, to it. This forces some individuals, in order to survive, to manipulate and change the environment to suit the organism.

To produce a good biological theory, you have to see through the clutter produced by evolution and try to describe the basic mechanism (the Grand Unifying Engine) lying beneath. Nature cannot give a purpose to life, but human beings by their human selection can select for a purpose. Instead of waiting for natural selection to adopt a useful trait that surfaced and was beneficial to *Homo sapiens*, human selection was able by choice to accelerate that adoption, (possibly by millions of years) and thereby form the characteristics of human beings.

Most primate's mating structures (only twelve percent of all primate species are monogamous) tend to hamper a new physical trait or ability from becoming dominant within the primate troop. However, if a human male in a monogamous family unit can choose a female that has some particular physical feature or ability that he is attracted to, and his descendants in a family unit could also through human selection pick that particular feature, they would thereby create a dominant line of descent for that feature. But in a polygamous primate troop, a single line of descent for a particular physical trait or ability could not be obtained because the dominant male primates tend to mate indiscriminately with all females that come into heat; so some physical traits and abilities that gave human beings their uniqueness and separated us from other primates, would tend to permeate and be diluted through the entire troop. A polygamous group would tend to remain stuck in their environment, because they would have to depend on natural selection, which usually requires isolation from the main group, for it to quickly pass on a desirable trait. This is also true if the female can pick her partner, because she also can choose traits and abilities that can be beneficial to change. When a father can distinguish, or even believe that he can distinguish his children, then those children also have a better chance to pass on his genes because of the concentrative help he can give his descendants if his loyalties are not dissipated among the troop. When the most successful males and females get to choose and pick their mates, the more chances there are for useful traits to be passed on and survive, and the faster they can adapt to a changing environment.

If human beings organize their affairs so they harmonize with the environment and so do not cause premature death, then on an average, they will leave more offspring than those who destroy their surrounding environment. Language has given us the ability to describe some actions that, if followed, will, just like a favorable, random genetic alteration, increase the offspring of those who ascribe to those actions. The proof is the survival and the increase of those who follow those actions, and the decrease of those who do not.

Selfishness is a trait of all human beings, and because they form governments, it can be observed in all forms of government. Selfish behavior is natural, it is animal, and it will always lead to uncivilized behavior unless we can find a way to control it. We are unable to deny that competition is not one of nature's way of eliminating the weak, the helpless, but this is animal behavior and not civilized behavior, which we as human beings are striving for. All through history, we see that human beings cannot, will not, correct what they disclaim connection or responsibility for. The capitalists can never correct the contradictions in their system until they admit that there are contradictions. But is this not also the laws that govern all governments, even communistic, socialistic, feudalistic, or fascistic forms?

The capitalists are a minority in their system and, so far, the Communist parties a minority in their's; the two of them, have to resort to persuading the majority through different forms of propaganda that they know how to achieve a better life for the people. The capitalists use money to exclude the majority; the Communists use ideological purity to exclude the majority. They serve the same purposes — to deny access to power. Most of the people under socialism, capitalism, feudalism, and fascism believe the propaganda dispersed by their governments; and to be realistic, you cannot fault them for it, because in natural selection, to hold a belief held by most of the inhabitants in that culture can be beneficial to the human beings that hold them. If the culture always remained the same, there would be no problem, but dialectical materialism (which gives us: thesis, antithesis, and from this a new synthesis) precludes us from gaining an advantage if we do not change our allegiance to the new synthesis.

Lamentable by John Wiseman

As the far left, we appeared on all the world's stages.
We were hailed as the New Synthesis Players.
The say you cannot change the course of history, but we did.
And when we arrived home, to honor us,
They handed us the script to a new play

In it, every line was so faithful, so true.
We agreed they exactly expressed our present view.
As the lines were so familiar, I looked up the role credits.
Then I knew!
In the new Script:

We had become the opposition to all change.
We had become the Philistines.
We had become the defenders of the status quo.

All governments that do not change their beliefs when presented with new facts, will like the government they replaced, become the new discards of history.

The need for a government only becomes obvious when there is a shortage of goods to be divided and distributed. Individuals cannot be impartial when there is only one loaf of bread to distribute between two or more people, especially when they are the individuals affected by the division. To lay claim to the future, all governments in power assert that they will eventually provide an adequate amount of food, clothing, and housing for everyone. Until they do, there will be a need for a government to resolve the individual conflicts that arise when there is a shortage of produced goods to be distributed.

Simple mathematics show that the larger the population in a defined area, the faster the natural resources and land are depleted, and so the greater the competition for the produced goods. There are only two ways to increase the standard of living for a defined area: either increase the goods to be divided or lower the population. However, if you have a limited amount of natural resources for that area, then you have only one choice — to lower the population. The problem is that the earth is finite for all governments. Socialist governments are not immune to this mathematical law. No government can create resources out of nothing; they can only distribute those goods produced from their fixed and limited resources. You cannot, by changing the name of private property to communal property, change or increase the natural resources or the size of your country. All you can do is to make a more equal distribution of the limited resources.

Individuals cannot be impartial without a constitution to guide them. The problem: selfishness continues even with a constitution, because an interpretation of a constitution will be made by people who will favor the selfish interest of the government that gave them the power to judge. To overcome this difficulty, later you might come to accept my belief that a truly neutral government might be formed by using the observable principle of uncertainty that seems to rule the universe; a system of government run by lottery, run on pure chance.

When the "Dictatorship of the Proletariat" was instituted in Russia after the revolution, it was an admitted atheist government whose stated goal was the elimination of the class struggle. The elimination of groups, classes, and other divisions in society, however, do not stop the underlying cause of the human struggle, which is each individual struggling for a share of the carcass. The composition of all classes or divisions, is always the individual trying through a class or division of society to obtain as much of the carcass as it is possible to obtain at the expense of other individuals in other divisions of society. All unequal distribution has produced people willing to break the law to try to get what they believe is their equal share. Because communism still discriminates with its distribution system, they find that they cannot stop the crime produced by that unequal distribution. After the 1917 Revolution, the Communist Party in Russia accepted bourgeoisie criminal laws in their totalities. They did this without reviewing criminal laws in relation to the undeniable fact that human beings are a species of animal living in an environment that was imposed on them; an environment that many are not able to accommodate because of their animal genes. There are people who, when they are denied their equal share, will, if they have the traits, get it at the expense of those who denied them their share. When criminals can see that some governments believe that morality comes from a God, and that this Supreme Being can allow them to deny to others outside their tribal grouping, an equal share of production, then the criminals can see no reason to be moral.

An early, widespread Marxist's belief was that the party intellectuals would hold power until they were able to consolidate it and hand it over to the workers; the workers would then be able to rule without exploiting other human beings. That was their original goal and intent, but because the intellectual Marxist-Leninists had no models to work with, they constructed on paper a world that turned out to have little resemblance to the noble ideas and goals expressed in "Socialism." They did notice that under capitalism that human beings exhibited selfishness, but thought that communism would change that. Although Karl Marx had examples of early capitalism to observe and study, and he did this excessively well, he did not try to extrapolate what would happen when a Communist government replaced a capitalist government. We do not have that handicap as we have some examples to study.

By delving into history, it can be seen that Karl Marx was correct in the concept that because of competition, individual capitalistic nations would be unable, under the intrinsic law of self-interest, to come together to settle their differences, and that this would create contradictions which would bring on wars and revolutions. He failed to understand that because competition is a natural law, it would also apply to communism. They also had to compete in this world for the limited natural resources. Lenin and Stalin abstracted the spiritual belief from Karl Marx that under communism there would no longer be strife; that people would lose their selfishness because communism would produce an abundance of consumer goods. They based their belief on the presumption that the same rules that led them to power would not prevail in their future, and so believed that "Communism" would be the last form of government. Lenin and Stalin allowed no review of the physical world when it came into dispute with the spiritual world of Karl Marx; the spiritual became dogma; it became church; it did not allow for the future to be outside the teachings of Karl Marx or, later, the interpretations of Lenin. It did not allow for the thesis, antithesis and the new synthesis that they claimed had predicted their coming to power, to continue. The Communists claimed that this natural, scientific law of dialectical materialism only operated against feudalism, against capitalism, or against fascism. This would then have to give the observed law of "dialectical materialism" a judgment that can test, study, find out, and then decide and determine whether it will act for or against a created human institution. A belief like that is a religious belief, an article of faith. All observations contradicting it would have to be ignored; and the people who called attention to a contradiction would have to be charged with blasphemy; yes, be charged with "Slander Against the State." Which is an unsubstantial mental concept that coexists in the minds of those in power. So, the charge of slander introduces pure religion into the affairs of the faithful Communist party members.

The Marxists claimed that strife would end with their successful revolution, that there would be no more contradiction. We can see that competition remained; selfish individuals against other selfish individuals, selfish Communist nations, not only against capitalist and fascist states, but against other selfish Communist countries. We can observe that the Communist nations are fragmenting the same way the capitalist countries did when they tried to divide the world amongst a small minority of nations. The Communists still do not understand that natural law is guileless; it cannot interpret, cannot assign, cannot distinguish among contesting beliefs, among contesting governments; natural laws cannot withdraw from the arena because a government claims exemption from them; they have no form that can be recognized, be contacted, be addressed.

You can deduce that when people have a false belief, they limit the niches they can enter and compete in. Because they are ignorant of a natural law does not mean they avoid its impact. We can readily see that we change our view with age, we change it with the accumulation of property, and we change it with the taking of power. A person with property has a different view of property than those who do not have it. The same is true of becoming a ruler. Your views are changed by it; you will not give up that power without a struggle. The Marxist-Leninists did not take into account that the intellectuals that led the revolution would change their viewpoint when they became the government. Their new vistas were seen through the eyes of a ruling class; their new and different perceptions were not the same view the workers have. Those who take power from a corrupt ruling class will, like their predecessors (especially, if they do not understand it) become corrupt because they are following the same natural laws that the rulers of the past followed. We become what we become. A prison inmate who becomes a prison guard after a revolution will abuse that power just like the guards they replaced. The taking of power corrupts all unless it is limited by law. The change from the title of king, president, commissar, or the other titles has no effect, and does not change the ruling body receiving first choice at the table. The Communists were not exempt from taking advantage of the weak even though they declared that communism was a different form of government and, therefore, exempt.

Today we find the Russian Communist government still shouting, quite irrationally, that they were the first, so they are correct; preaching dogmatic rules, preaching infallibility in a Godless world. When the Communists declared that it is inevitable that communism will rule the world, they set up a religious belief that something controls our lives, that there is a goal in life that has already been determined, that we have arrived at a predicted form of government that will have no contradiction.

Some Russian Communists believe there are some mythical words in the writings of Karl Marx or Lenin that condone their actions, their behavior. We hear them shouting that thou shall not worship another Communist state or you will be excommunicated from the "True Communist Party"; shouting that there is no other road than the road we show you, and then claiming that they are different from previous ruling classes. The trouble with taking the writings of Karl Marx and Lenin as gospel for all times is that in this world, all writings will produce errors when written by imperfect human beings. When you try to make a statement fit into a mold and can see with all the twisting and bending that it still does not fit into the mold because it is shaped differently by time, then you are caught in the same trap that the believers of religion fell into. They found that they were trying to reconcile supposed infallible words in their religious writings with reality. Time will contradict you if what you say is not correct, if it is not the truth.

Communism is not immune to the pitfalls inherited by all governments. Without moral guidelines, you will need the bayonet to control those you govern. An atheistic belief does not suggest or indicate an automatic approval of Socialism or Communism. The Communist Party in Russia usurped and perverted the sublime and religious experience of atheism into a holocaust of murder. They are not above the judgment of the people; they are not above the judgment of an atheist; they are not above the judgment of history. They did what the believers in National Socialism did with the Holocaust; what the Catholic Church did with the Inquisition; what Ayatullah Khomeini did in the name of Islamic Justice. It shows us that if those in control of a government do not have limits placed on their actions, then the long struggle for justice and morality must continue.

It was the Russian Communist position, arbitrarily taken, that free speech and a free press were only needed in a system of government where there were different classes contending for power. We were told the lie that we did not need these freedoms in Communist countries because the Communist press would express the true needs of the workers; because anyone who expressed doubt about an act of the party was an enemy of the workers; because a Communist party was infallible when acting under Marxist ideologies. Free speech and a free press were won on the battlefield by the sacrifice of millions of human lives; they were not something given freely by religious institutions or by a capitalistic, fascistic, or feudalistic government. A political system that hopes to succeed, needs freedom of speech and the press to make an informed decision; not because it is a basic or natural law, not even because it is the right thing to do, and not even because it is the civilized thing to do. These can all be put aside. It is needed because it handicaps those who do not have it. It is in the selfish interest of the person to have them; it is in the selfish interest of a government to have them. I will admit that freedom of the press and free speech cannot be guaranteed to always produce the truth, but if you lack them, then you cannot distinguish between what is true or false; you are denied the future because you do not know the true past. Political and religious systems are not exempt from human and natural selection; all denied information can be harmful; distorted or lack of information can prove fatal. When you try to foretell the future, you will be handicapped by a false belief; only time will give relevancy to one's beliefs; time is the final arbitrator.

Marxists must understand that the class struggle is a compilation of individual struggles that mask the personal struggle under the banner of a class or state; that individual groups (which are human creations) are not assigned by nature a monopoly on morality or exclusive possession of *Freedom*, *Liberty*, and *Equality*. The removal of all class distinctions will reveal that the individual struggle against other persons still will persist; and will persist until all decisions are made in a fair and reasonable manner.

Viewing a herd of animals as a social group, it can be asserted that it contains and represents an original "Social Contract." The social contract is an evolutionary mechanism that arose out of natural selection that can explain if and when we owe allegiance to the group. The social contract in a herd of animals is only binding when everyone has an equal chance to retreat into the protection of the center of the group. If a part of the social group is able to gather together and make rules saying that some of the herd is more equal than others, that some have a right to remain in the center of the herd longer than others, and can condemn some to remain on the outside of the herd, then that breaks the social contract. It is only valid when it gives everyone equal protection, else those not treated equally, the excluded, are better off not joining or forming a herd.

The "State" is an illusion, a false perception. All social contracts are between an individual and other individuals who we collectively call the "State." Governments are just another human creation that nature has no knowledge of. Only, when those collections of individuals (the State) are willing to give the same freedoms and division of goods — that they enjoy — to those people outside the ruling group, do we owe allegiance to them.

The immorality of the state is also reflected in immoral acts committed by individuals. If the ruling class is willing to take my life by executing me because they think that I am a threat to them, then I have the same right as they do to take a life that I think is a threat to me. If the state believes that it has the right to steal the land and wealth from those nations it conquers because they are stronger, then I also have the right to steal from those weaker than I am.

A "Constitution" is always needed to give some protection to the individual against those in power. Even if it only gives limited protection, it can be cited as a directional sign to civilization. Still, remember that a Constitution supported by 99 percent of the people does not validate its laws. It can make the state stronger if that many people believe in its law, and so it can punish the minority with impunity, but it still does not define the truth. The constitution, a contract between the individual and the state, must from time to time be reviewed to work correctly. A contract made before a person was born, cannot be binding on the youth of today; it is not something that you inherit when you become an adult. It has to be signed and affirmed by every new generation. That social contract must specify that the moment a person is born, he or she is entitled to some inalienable right that cannot be denied them just because someone was born into this world before they were.

History tells us that the words *Freedom* and *Equality* mean different things to different people according to the power and property they hold. So, I believe that interested party wishing to contest an existing government should put a complete constitution in writing, before a revolution. These future constitutions should, when feasible, explain every single law in minute detail, and instead of using such broad words as *Freedom*, *Liberty* and *Equality*, they should explain in detail those freedoms. It should also explain the rights of those whom they replace, and assure the defeated the same right as all other citizens, even the freedom to express opposition to those in power through free speech and a free press.

A truly classless society would not have individuals competing for the distribution of the produced goods needed for life or competing for desired work, desired schooling, or desired positions in their government. We can see that the Communist states do not meet this standard. There is preferential treatment for party members. If you eliminate all classes in society, then you must eliminate the government class; then you must revert to the chaotic — each person seeking his or her share of the pie. When we have a disagreement we must have someone to intervene and settle the differences or we automatically revert to the strong dominating the weak without laws to protect the weak. We revert backwards to a natural animal law, it is true, but we cannot arrive at civilized behavior unless we do succeed in passing through this stage and arriving at a constitutional type government. This calls for setting up a class in society, a government class to settle these disputes. If we could design an ecosystem where there is such an abundance of produced goods that there would be no competition for them, and the government would be neutral in its decisions, then that could be a solution to the problems of government. But this is the false promise that all governments are making, and we know that these promises cannot be met in a finite world.

When viewing the past, we can see that each of the successful divisions in society that survived has achieved a binder, a cohesive force that held individuals together and allowed them to survive an attack, sometimes even from a superior force that did not have the glue to bind them as close. At times, this binder, this glue, was language, skin color, or religion, and at other times economic theory or nationality, and sometimes it was a coalition of one or more of these cohesive forces. Major historical events can be viewed as a parade of smaller divisions becoming larger and stronger, with the weaker forces being eliminated or conquered and absorbed.

In the last few hundred years, through imperialism, large nations have tried to divide the world into empires, but this all unraveled because imperialism did not find the binder, the glue, the cohesive force to hold the empires together. The colonial nations were told that they were unable to rule their countries because they did not have the capabilities required to run a modern society. We are now faced with communism trying to unite the world with "Imperialistic Communism," but they are also finding out that they have not found the binder the glue, the cohesive force. They used "Dialectical Materialism" to examine capitalism, but neglected to use it on their system of government. They became static in a world they had diagnosed as working under the laws of dialectical materialism, which envisioned all previous cultures in constant motion, in resolving constant contradictions that arise and are settled in a new synthesis. They did not understand that imperialism failed the capitalist because human beings are selfish; and because of censorship, the Communists still do not, still cannot (because of the lack of information) see that "Communist Imperialism" will also fail for the same reason. Because they keep themselves ignorant does not mean that they are exempt from natural principles.

Nature is not fair (we are all endowed differently), so we must look for a civilized way to offer every person an equal opportunity to work, to play, to eat. Because individuals form governments, and all individuals are prejudiced in their own behalf, and because we all have inherited the genes that make us selfish, we have to look for a form of government where the governed can try to make the government neutral by restrictions. A government depending on the good will of the individuals within it not being biased, is not realistic.

Elections can create a government class in society, but cannot eliminate their biases; so the solution is a form of "Lottery Government" to write new laws and settle the disputes that arise in society. This kind of government would tend not to write oppressive laws affecting those not in power if — after a short period — the writers of those laws would be governed by those oppressive laws when they were not in power. The only government that I can foresee that would have a cohesive force, a common glue, a true binder that would hold in check an individual's greed for power and possessions, would be one that I would call "Democratic Lottery Socialism." All government positions would be filled by a lottery; all work would be assigned by lottery, which means that if physically able, all persons would be eligible to become the president of their country or a garbage collector according to chance. I am capable of envisaging a lottery government where all odious labor is assigned through it; and with the coming of the robot to do the odious work, it will be necessary to use the lottery to distribute the work that only a human being is capable of doing. This government, with a constitution limiting the time a person could be in the government, should prove to be above the animal passions of individuals. It could prove to be a government neutral to all factions, a government that does not allow the majority to benefit at the expense of the minority because that majority has a false belief, nor the minority to benefit because of their false beliefs.

CHAPTER 21

NARRATIVE: THE COURT

After being cast out of the Springfield Medical Center, I was driven by two United States Marshals to the Kansas City Jail where I was to be incarcerated for several days. I was delayed there because I had to wait for a law official who was traveling west on an airplane, to become available to escort me back to Sacramento, California.

While in the Kansas City Jail, I was introduced to life in a setting that would not be believed by the public, even if it were presented in a documentary film. I had a winning streak in a poker game and was informed that I could get paid in candy, cigarettes, dope, liquor, or if I wished, I could have the use of a young and willing boy for sexual purposes. I personally saw the jailer hand in several pints of cheap whiskey and watched inmates get high on several different substances, so I knew that I was not being conned by my fellow prisoners. And having done time in San Quentin and Folsom Prison, I was familiar with the availability of young homosexuals in those institutions, so was not surprised at that offer. I must admit that the head inmate was modest and discreet as he always hung a blanket over his jail cell when he was renting out his boy, but I was surprised by the openness of it all. I was even informed: if you had the price, you could be taken up to the women's wing, for a few hours of relaxation. You were supposed to be taken there to clean up and do the heavy work assignments, but you were guaranteed a willing bed partner for the price. Unhappily for my neglected sex life, I did not win nearly enough money to personally check out this advancement in penology; so I could not verify if it was true or if my fellow prisoners were putting me on. By way of contrast, the Sacramento County Jail was so strict that a good word or a smile was considered contraband; the rumor was that you could be sent to solitary confinement if caught using either. If I remember correctly, I converted my winnings into fifty cartons of cigarettes, twenty boxes of candy, and to relax with, two pints of bourbon. To uphold this false image that bank robbers are successful criminals, and because I had to leave in a couple of days anyway and could not take my winnings with me, before I left for the Kansas City Airport, I distributed all I had among some prisoners that were without funds. (After all, I was playing the part of a bank robber, which gives great prestige in the pecking order of thieves.) I am sure that many times, mythology is enhanced from similar mistaken and misinterpreted actions.

The above is included in this book to show that after leaving Springfield I still was adaptable and could immediately fit into and thrive on the improbable situations that I encountered; and the preconceived notions that were present in my mind about jails and guards and their prisoners were no handicap to my ability to adapt to those new situations. I was amazed to find out that not only my fellow prisoners, but even my jailers treated me with deference. They seemed to be fascinated by one person being transported around the country by two US Marshals, who played up their roles by telling what a dangerous person they were escorting; they also informed my temporary keepers to be sure to place me in a maximum security wing as I was a dangerous person and might try to escape. The fun part of this was that it was a farce. If they had handed me my airplane ticket, I would have gone directly to the airport, boarded the airplane, and on arrival, checked into their Sacramento County Jail without an escort going along to make sure that I did.

That I arrived in Sacramento with a piece of paper saying that I was sane enough to stand trial, did not mean that they were going to set a date for my trial. First I had to be re-examined by Dr. Bromberg. When confronted by him, I went immediately into my former successful schizophrenic act to convince him that I was still unable to stand trial.

On the 28th day of February 1963, Dr. Bromberg sent a report of his examination of me to the Assistant United States Attorney, Robert E. Woodward, Esq. In the report, and much to my amazement and despite the fact that I was still acting mentally ill, he reported to the Court that I was "now" legally sane, knew right from wrong, and could confer with my counsel in my defense.

Because of this report, on March 5, 1963 I appeared once again before the Honorable Sherrill Halbert, Federal Judge for the Northern District Court of the United States, Northern Division, in which the following dialog was transcribed:

The Court: You may proceed.

Mr. Woodward: Your Honor, in this matter this is sort of a continuation in order to endeavor to determine whether or not Mr. Kennedy is capable of going to trial. We have requested Mr. Bromberg to appear. He has recently examined Mr. Kennedy and we would like to bring the Court up to date on the doctor's findings.

The Court: Very well.

DIRECT EXAMINATION

Mr. Woodward:

Q. Doctor, will you state your name, please?

A. Walter Bromberg.

Q. And will you tell us very briefly your background in medical training?

A. I graduated from the State University College of Medicine in New York City in 1926, and interned in a residence in neurology in New York City until 1930. At that time I was assistant physician in the Manhattan State Hospital and at the Bellevue Psychiatric Hospital until 1941. Following that I entered the Navy and served until after the war. I have been practicing in Reno, Nevada, and Sacramento since 1946.

Q. And do you specialize in any particular medical field?

A. Yes; I am a neuropsychiatrist, specializing in nervous and mental diseases.

Q. Doctor, I believe you have examined professionally Jack Wise Kennedy on three occasions.

A. Yes I have.

Q. And the gentleman that you examined is the man seated with Mr. Zarick at the counsel table?

A. Yes.

Q. Will you tell us when you first examined him?

A. I saw him first on July 31,1961, in the County Jail.

Q. And at that time would you tell us what your opinion of the condition of Mr. Kennedy was?

A. At that time I reported to the United States Attorney that this man was technically sane but medically ill, and that he suffered from a depression, and that he was not in a medical state to be able to help in his trial.

Q. Then you had occasion to examine him a second time?

A. Yes, sir. I saw him again on February 2,1962, in the county jail.

Q. What was your opinion of his condition on that occasion?

A. At that time I felt there was a little improvement, but not much, but still in a mental state which I call depression, which would not allow him to stand trial or confer with his counsel.

Q. And I believe recently you had a third occasion to examine him?

A. Yes, sir; I saw him again on February 28th of 1963, again at the county jail. At that time he showed a little improvement. I felt that he was legally sane, but still medically ill; but that he was well enough to confer with counsel in his defense and stand trial.

Q. Now, Doctor, I believe that there is some indication in Mr. Kennedy's past record, at least since the time you examined him, about a complaint of amnesia. Did you find that complaint with Mr. Kennedy?

A. Yes, he still had amnesia for the offense and some of the circumstances following it.

Q. Were you of the opinion, though, that he would be able to assist counsel in his defense to the charge of bank robbery, which is the charge before this Court?

A. I think he can assist to the extent of his memory and knowledge. His memory is impaired by virtue of his amnesia.

Q. But other than for the period of amnesia you feel that he could presently assist his counsel in his defense of the bank robbery charge?

A. I do.

Mr. Woodward: You may cross-examine.

CROSS-EXAMINATION

Mr. Zarick:

Q. Doctor, in your examination of Mr. Kennedy were you able to determine the period of his amnesia?

A. No; he did relate a few facts about his early life. While he was unwilling to go into much of his life — not cooperative, that is to say — but the amnesia was pretty general for about three or four years preceding this date — three years from now backward. He does remember the hospital episode and his treatment in various institutions he has been in.

Q. I note in your report of July 31, 1961, Doctor, you state that he has no memory of any event from Christmas 1961 to the present. That is July 31, 1961.

A. Yes.

Q. That would cover the entire factual situation — in effect he had no recollection at all of the robbery or the circumstances surrounding it?

A. That would cover that period, yes.

Q. Did you examine this letter from Dr. Houck of the Department of Correction, dated January 16, 1963?

A. I did.

Q. And in that letter, Doctor, Dr. Houck was of the opinion that Mr. Kennedy was insane at the time the crime was committed.

A. Yes.

Q. And that Dr. Houck examined him approximately a week afterwards.

A. More or less, yes.

Q. And that certain shock treatments were then administered to Mr. Kennedy?

A. Yes. That is correct.

Q. Is it reasonable to assume, or would you say it is medically probable, Doctor, that having in mind Dr. Houck's report, Mr. Kennedy would be unable to recall any of the incidents concerning the robbery itself?

A. He is unable to recall them now. He may in the future, but I think your question was can he recall them now?

Q. Yes.

A. I think he cannot.

Q. Doctor, can you tell us what effect, if any, the shock treatments would have on Mr. Kennedy?

A. Well, the shock treatments besides improving the patient would give him an amnesia for recent events, a week or two before the shock itself, which gradually fills in in a matter of two months. This is a very common finding.

Q. Then as I understand, it is medically probable that although Mr. Kennedy can assist his counsel, he had no method with which to do it, because he has no recollection of any of the events?

A. That is correct.

Q. Could the shock treatments have contributed to this amnesia?

A. In my opinion no, because the shock treatment amnesia is only for a short period before the treatment — we see it every day — a week or two, and doesn't invade the whole life earlier.

Q. Doctor, one further question: Mr. Kennedy in his present physical state and mental state, would he be a proper person to be admitted to a state hospital from a civil standpoint and not criminal insanity?

A. In my opinion, yes.

Q. And how long, under a course of treatment, do you think it would take for Mr. Kennedy before he would be discharged from a state hospital?

A. I think he needs both medical and psychiatric treatment and I would have to guess, it would be at least a year, perhaps two years, before he would improve from his depression enough.

Q. And under a state hearing you feel he would be a proper person to be admitted to a state hospital?

A. Yes, I do.

The Court: Doctor, what you are saying then is that he is mentally ill, but legally sane?

A. Yes, your Honor; that is exactly it.

REDIRECT EXAMINATION

Mr. Woodward:

Q. Doctor, with respect to the amnesia, is it possible that Mr. Kennedy could be feigning that?

A. Well, he was depressed and the depression does give some amnesia. There is always a slight unconscious element of gain; so it is possible that some of it might have been exaggerated, not feigned, but how much I can't say.

Q. Is it sometimes possible that where a person is apprehended for having committed a crime they have the feeling that everything is falling down around them and they could suffer some sort of shock or whatever the proper medical term is?

A. Well, depressionists do have patchy and hazy memory. Any emotional shock may fill out that amnesia so it is complete. That is what I think happened. It is possible, I have seen that.

RECROSS-EXAMINATION

Mr. Zarick:

Q. As I understand it, Doctor, you are telling us that as a symptom of this ganser syndrome that you have described in your report, he could have developed a complete mental block?

A. A ganser syndrome itself is a mental block. That is our way of saying it, yes.

Q. And from the fact that he did have shock treatments this must have been fairly severe at the time.

A. Yes, ganser syndrome is part of the depression which is a definite mental illness.

Q. And part of it would be amnesia as one of the symptoms of this syndrome?

A. That's correct.

Q. And it is not likely, is it, Doctor, that this amnesia would have been feigned or exaggerated to a large extent that such drastic treatment was given the patient?

A. Well, I won't make a comment about exaggeration because there is no black or white in this business, nothing comes out like a text book, but there is always a little possible exaggeration in every depression. He was depressed enough to be called mentally sick and the shock treatments were properly given, I think. I think the amnesia is valid. That is about as far as I can go here now.

Q. In fact, Doctor Houck was of the opinion that he was mentally insane at the time.

A. Yes, he says that.

NARRATIVE: EVALUATION

The system aligned against me had extensive limitations; it was seriously flawed. The system had no way of always keeping track of me when I was incarcerated in the county jail; yet, they had to use expert testimony on whether I was sane or insane. The facts were that they simply did not have the time, money, or facilities to keep track of me or any other individual suspected of faking mental illness. That would have required a trained psychiatrist or psychologist to keep a suspected person under observation twenty-four hours a day for the weeks or months necessary to detect that fraud. Dr. Bromberg was certainly not at fault, because he had to deduce from what he observed in an interview room where I had complete control over what he observed. He had no way to compel me to be honest at the interviews or to check if what he observed were my same actions outside that interview room. Dr. Bromberg, although brilliant and competent and a person who had extensive experience in diagnosing the mentally ill, was not fooled completely by my act. His testimony led me to believe that he was trying to protect the incompetent actions of the medical staff at Vacaville; and because he was, and had been playing the game of "Protect the System" for many years, he was handicapped in his actions. He did not want to imply that the staff at Vacaville had made a mistake in giving me shock treatments. There was also the possibility that he knew that the Court did not wish this case to go to trial because of unanswered questions that might arise from those "Motions" filed by my first attorney, Mr. Ted Isles. Although these motions had been denied by the Court, they could resurface if I went to trial, was found guilty, and then appealed that verdict.

"...would he [Jack Kennedy] be a proper person to be admitted to a state hospital from a civil standpoint and not criminal insanity?" Elicited this quick response from Dr. Bromberg: "In my opinion, yes." You can infer that this was not a spur of the moment question and answer session, but a planned response; everything had been agreed to beforehand. It is true that this was a deal being made in my favor, but it only came about because the Court also wanted to see my case disposed of; and notice that the Assistant District Attorney also did not question the advisability of me being sent to a civil mental hospital; he also knew that that question would be brought up and answered in the affirmative. His orders from Washington D.C. were to take the case to Court and prosecute me, but for the system to work correctly, it would require that he anticipate how the local Court wanted to handle the case; so, he was acting accordingly. Government systems are designed to work this way; and from reading the transcripts, you can see that all was well with the system.

ESSAY: THOUGHTS ON INDUSTRIALIZATION

Looking back, I now know that I (like many economic students) had without proof, absorbed a false, adolescent belief that Third World countries needed to become fully industrialized to overcome their poverty; that the socialistic ruling class would not sacrifice the worker's health and safety for the sake of competing with capitalism for world markets; that socialism would produce without the need to destroy the environment.

Few people can read about the English Industrial Revolution without being disturbed by the helplessness of the people to remedy the horrible conditions they were forced to work and live under. Not only the actual workers in the factories, coal mines, weaving mills, iron works, etc., but everyone living in the towns, cities and countryside was subject to the pollution of their air, water, and land. Although Karl Marx and others adequately described these conditions, Karl Marx dealt more with wage exploitation than with the exploitation and destruction of the ecology by capitalism.

Except for child labor and unreasonable working hours, all the harsh working conditions and excessive destruction of the environment described by Karl Marx and others under capitalism, can be observed happening to the socialist workers in present day (1989) Poland. In 1985, four areas of the country were described as "ecological disaster areas." These regions were so contaminated with industrial and municipal pollution that it was suggested that the 11 million people (30 percent of Poland's population) living there should be evacuated. As the Vistula River passes through the heart of Poland and empties into the Baltic Sea, most of the 813 communities (plus 10,000 industrial polluters) dump their raw sewage and harmful waste products (tons of nitrogen, mercury, cadmium, lead, copper, zinc, phenol, and chlorinated hydrocarbons) directly into it. The Vistula River is just a large, open sewer line, where along 81 percent of the river's length, the water is too dirty even for industrial use. In 1981, the Baltic Sea — where for years, seven nations, including Poland, have been discharging their industrial and municipal pollutants into it — was described as a gigantic toilet bowl. In 1988, 100,000 sq. kilometers of the Baltic Sea floor, were found to be biologically dead. In 1980, the Polish fish catch from the polluted waters, was 640,000 metric tons; in 1986 only 28,000 tons were caught; and most of those were either stunted, horribly deformed, or sick with cancerous sores on their bodies.

The Polish people (like the workers at the beginning of the Industrial Revolution) are forced to live in these polluted areas because there is no place to move to. In 1987, 180,000 units will be completed in Poland to house 270,000 newly married couples, which leaves 70,000 married couples without a place to move into. In Warsaw, if you get on the list today, there is a wait of over 50 years for an apartment.

The economic problems in Poland today (1989) cannot be blamed on the Jews, because the Jews in Poland have been almost completely exterminated, so there are too few of them to make a viable claim that it is their fault. The left cannot blame it on the Catholic Church owning and controlling large amounts of land, because all that land is now under the control of the Communist government. That capitalism is the reason for the economic problems, is no longer tenable, because capitalism has not controlled Poland for over forty years. When you eliminate all political opposition, and have only one political party, you have no one to blame for your economic failure but that one party (the Polish Communist Party, in this instance). You cannot blame the capitalist press or their propaganda for your troubles, because by censoring and controlling all news media, you cannot even admit there is a problem, let alone blame someone else for it.

Poland's debt in 1981, was $26 billion; today (1989) it is over $40 billion. They did not borrow more money; they only had the hard currency to pay part of the interest, so the owed interest was added on to the debt. For the sake of paying the foreign and domestic debt — so irresponsibly contracted by the socialist ruling class — worker's wages, social expenditures, and the ecology are sacrificed. The health of the people means nothing to the Central Committee in Warsaw; their main concern is to earn foreign currency. An example: In Glogow, Poland's copper ore is mined and melted down at several large facilities, where, in the process of extracting the copper from ore, it releases toxins, thus polluting the surrounding areas. Because Poland is in competition with capitalist producers (who pay lower wages and extract the metal from ore that has a higher content of copper), it receives only pennies on the world market for its copper, thus forcing it to produce copper without adding on the cost of keeping the environment from being polluted. Several years ago, whole regions around Glogow were ordered to be abandoned because of the highly contaminated soil. Yet everywhere in the disaster areas, contaminated fields continue to be farmed; 20 percent of the food tested was classified as hazardous to public health; 70 percent of the drinking water tested in 1984 was unfit to drink; the contaminated air (that kills, deforms, and makes the workers and their children sick) from the industrial areas is dispersed by the prevailing winds, all over Poland.

If examined, some of the main polluting culprits might be charged to antiquated plants and production methods, not using waste treatment on human sewage, the combustion engine, and using coal without paying the full cost of adding on modern methods of pollution control. But the main fault is that socialistic nations do not recognize the fact that to compete in the world market of exports and imports, and earn hard currency, the socialist (and capitalist) ruling class must sacrifice the health and safety of their workers to achieve lower, competitive prices on the world's markets. The socialist governments are the exploiters of the economy when they use the hard currency earned by exporting the limited wealth of the country to import luxury goods for the small amount of elite workers and the socialist ruling class. An example: Poland produces an adequate amount of ham, bacon, and Polish sausage to feed the demands of their people. Why then is there a shortage of pork? The capitalists blame it on socialism, but the true reason is that Poland has a limited amount of goods that it has to export to pay its debt or to pay for imported goods that they do not have but need to run an industrialized nation. They are not informed by their economist (mainly because their are blinded by their own beliefs) that the shortage of pork is caused by the Polish government importing petroleum products to run, among other things, their private automobiles; they are not told that because they are limited by their resources they cannot afford to have private automobiles that use the combustion engine. Mr. Lech Walesa and all the other private persons in Poland who own automobiles (2.8 million in 1980), are the reason why there is so much pollution, and such a shortage of food and consumer goods. If everyone is equal in a socialistic country, do the government and elite workers have a right to own and drive, and thus pollute the environment of the workers who cannot afford to buy an automobile? In a socialist country, until everyone is adequately fed, clothed, and housed, hard currency should not be used to import luxury goods for either the elite workers or the socialist ruling class.

After examining Poland's natural resources, there can only be one conclusion: if Poland returned to capitalism, it would not help the economy or reduce its pollution. Of course the capitalist because of their belief that the poverty in Poland is the result of imposed communism would not oppose the return of capitalistic markets to Poland and Eastern Europe. However, the return to capitalism in Eastern Europe would expose them to the fact that most of the countries that had socialism imposed on them are in debt because they have not lived within their means. These are the same countries that could not make it under capitalism in the 1920s and '30s.

The fact is that Poland is a burden to Russia and would be a burden to the United States if they returned to capitalism. The West, through loans, is already draining Poland of all its hard currency, so what would be the gain to capitalism? Would the West or Japan buy or invest in the antiquated Lenin foundry in Nowa Huta that uses two and a half times as much energy as a modern foundry, and annually emits 400,000 tons of carbon monoxide and 50,000 tons of sulfur dioxide? Why would capitalistic investors put money into upgrading production facilities that would be in direct competition with their other investments in countries that have much lower wages and production costs? And socialist should understand that if Poland adopts Democratic Socialism, the same problems exist. The poverty of Poland is not caused by the chosen government but by the limited resources that can only support a limited population. All the chosen government can do is distribute the limited resources in an equal manner under Democratic Socialism or an unequal manner under capitalism. Under Democratic Socialism they should be given the fact that they can have an adequate supply of ham, bacon, and Polish sausage or have gasoline to run the cars of the elite workers and bureaucratic. They cannot have both.

If examined, the facts will show that Poland cannot afford either ecologically or monetarily to be fully industrialized; it cannot, without destroying the environment, support the present population. The death of 6 million people during World War II, temporarily helped, but the emigration of 500,000 Poles since 1981, had very little influence on stopping the destruction of the environment. Until Poland realizes that socialism, like capitalism, cannot solve the problem of too many people by industrialization: and until like China, they pass strict laws that only permit one child per family, then their standard of living and destruction and pollution of the environment will get worse, not better.

CHAPTER 22

ESSAY: ECONOMIC THOUGHTS

Economics are boring, so why should you be interested in them? Why should you subject yourself to boredom? Because daily, throughout the world, human beings are dragged off to prison without cause, where they are mentally and physically tortured. All around the world, humans are being killed with bullets and bombs and mortars, they are being beaten to death with clubs, hacked to pieces with machetes, and kicked to death with steel-toed shoes. Much of this is caused by someone feeling threatened by another person's economic beliefs. Understanding economics may not save you from being falsely accused, jailed, or tortured, or even save your life. However, it might give you a foundation for not jailing or killing other *Homo sapiens* for their economic beliefs if you ever have the power to do so. Most importantly, it will keep you from needlessly sacrificing your life for a false economic theory.

From patterns I see in scattered, random dots obtained from a study of economic and history books, I will try to draw a partial, but true, economic portrait of competing governments. Beneath their rhetoric and self-serving propaganda, governments unwittingly perform the same service: to produce and distribute a limited amount of goods so that individuals, who always seek what is best for themselves, will not resort to the chaos of the animal kingdom — the strongest taking what they want from the weaker. Governments are set up to confirm that *unequal* property rights can be assigned by laws; and to inform strong individuals that they cannot dispute (even if their evaluation is valid) those assigned property rights without fear of punishment from those who presently hold power. "Too simple," you might declare, but history has shown that if you look for a theory in nature to prove a point, you can usually discard the most complicated and use an uncluttered, simplistic explanation. Nature does not try to confuse, to complicate, or to hide; these are observed only in human beings trying to explain the inequality of life that they observe happening around themselves and others.

As a Socialist, do I believe in the Marxist's concept that Communist governments will eventually wither away and disappear because people will be so changed by their Communist environment that they will no longer need an arbitrator? The answer is emphatically "No!" I believe that governments will always be needed to keep people from plundering the environment at the expense of other individuals, to keep them from viewing other human beings as exploitable merchandise. Without government, we will return to the need of individual animals contesting every killed carcass. (Read here, continually contesting every piece of land; ownership could never be solved except by brute force; land would become a burden; why plant a crop or build a house if every strong human being, singularly or in a group, who came along could contest it?) There is an observable ratio that reads: the greater the population per unit of land, the more law a government requires to keep strong individuals from seeking what is best for their well-being at the expense of weaker human beings. (I want you to know I am aware of the inconsistencies in all governments that have a belief that when individuals unite into a government they can legally do what would be considered criminal acts if an individual did them.)

A close study of capitalism and communism will show that like other systems, they still believe and teach absurd theories and ideas of eighteenth century economics that do not dove-tail with today's world. When you examine a working economic system and can see that someone's constructed theories do not work the way the books describe them, then those books should be revised and the absurd theories removed. Neither capitalism nor communism does this. They only point out each other's absurdities, but do not correct their own.

A qualifier: Because of self-imposed limitations on structure, I will raise, question, and lightly touch upon just a few beliefs that Marxist-Leninists have accepted on faith alone. As a Socialist, I cannot blindly accept that Marxist-Leninist's Scripture is above examination; that there are no mistakes within it; that even to question a line in it or suggest that it contains contradiction, makes me an enemy of Socialism.

Science assumes that all forces in the universe have no objective, no purpose, no goal; they can have no end in mind; they cannot recognize or attache themselves to a cause or to a class; that only the human mind can project a purpose on the forces of the universe. We are now going to look at some statements of Karl Marx and scrutinize a belief of his (Surplus Values) that if proven correct would dispute some of these assumptions.

Karl Marx's premise is: "Part of the labor contained in a commodity is paid labor and part is unpaid labor. The 'Surplus Value,' or that part of the total value of the commodity in which the surplus labor or unpaid labor of the working man is realized, I call profit." He then goes on to say: "It is nonsense to suppose that profits, not in individual cases, but that constant and usual profits of different trades, spring from surcharging the price of the commodities, or selling them at a price over and above their value. To explain, therefore, the general nature of profits, you must start from the theorem that, on an average, commodities are sold at their real value, and that profits are derived from selling them at their value, that is, in proportion to the quantity of labor realized in them. If you cannot explain profits on this supposition, you cannot explain it at all."

Simplified, he is saying that it is a delusion that the capitalists realize their profits from a surcharge on commodities.

Let us look at a factory (set up on Karl Marx's principle) that produces 1 million steel monkey wrenches a month. For simplification we will say that 80 percent of the production is paid labor and the other 20 percent is Karl Marx's surplus values or unpaid labor. After a month, the capitalist owners could have sold 800,000 of the produced monkey wenches at $6.25 each ($5 million) — the total cost of production and overhead (including interest on loans, taxes, etc.) divided into the 800,000 monkey wenches — and had the other 200,000 as surplus values or unpaid labor. To receive their profits, the 200,000 wenches are sold ($6.25 X 200,000 = $1,250,000), which brings the price they receive for the 1 million wenches to $6,250,000.

Now if they had evenly distributed all the cost and sold the entire amount of production of 1 million monkey wenches at $5 each ($5 million) — which makes up the entire cost of doing business — then there would be no profits, no Karl Marx's "Surplus Values," no unpaid labor. However, if they added a 25 percent surcharge and then sold the wenches for $6.25, both bookkeeping methods would receive the same price ($6,250,000) for the wenches. The two methods would be selling the wenches for $1,250,000 above their production cost. I intend to argue that no matter how an arbitrary bookkeeping method tries to allocate the cost of labor to the commodity, the selling price must reflect the full value of all cost (that includes all taxes, labor cost, interest on loans, etc.) divided *equally* into each item produced in order to arrive at and set a competitive price.

That Karl Marx was wrong can be verified by using the scientific method of contrasting two experiments; because other than the introduction of one single new bit of information in one experiment, they are the same. This can lead to the truth.

If you have a factory in Mexico and a factory in the United States and each assemble identical television sets with the same business cost and assembly time (about 10 hours per TV set), but the single difference is the wages paid the workers who assemble the sets — say $1 an hour in Mexico and $5 an hour in the United States — then you can be sure that wages are the results of the difference you can perceive in the production cost of those television sets. If their shipping costs were the same, and they sold these television sets in the United States at identical prices — at the exact cost of the United States assembled sets — then those assembled in Mexico would make a profit and those assembled in the United States would not. This is caused by profits being a surcharge; the television sets produced in Mexico are selling in the United States with an added surcharge of $4 per hour on each hour that it takes to assemble the TV sets (10 hours), which amounts to $40 per TV set above their total production cost. The price of each TV sold reflects the full labor cost, but the United States' assembled sets must add a surcharge and sell at a higher price to produce a profit as there is no way to obtain them from "Surplus Values." According to Karl Marx, this is a delusion; but I say his perception is the false one; mine is reality, a fact that can be proved over and over again in a scientific experiment.

To examine the relationship between wages, profits, and prices, we will examine two imaginary factories that are producing the same commodity. Except for the cost of wages, each has the same business cost: $5 per item. Factory A is unionized; each item produced has a $6 an hour wage cost, which makes the full cost $11 per item. Factory X is not unionized; each item has a $5 an hour wage cost, which makes a full cost of $10 per item. Each adds a 10 percent profit (surcharge), which brings A's cost to a wholesaler to $12.10 per item and X's cost to $11 per item. It is immediately obvious that A cannot compete in the marketplace. The only way that A can compete is my eliminating its surcharge (profits), then they can each sell their item for $11. If they received no profits from their investment, A's investors would, of course, be unhappy. But in a competitive market, X can cut their profits to 5 percent and sell their item for $10.50. Now, if A attempts to be competitive by lowering their price, they will lose money on each item they produce. Knowing they cannot compete with X, A's stockholders decide to close the factory. Faced with the prospect of losing their jobs, factory A's employees decide to buy the factory. Because the workers own the factory, they do not have to pay union wages, so they agree to cut their wages to match factory X's. Factory A also has another advantage: in a competitive market, they, as shareholders, have the option of lowering or even eliminating all profits and living off their wages. (Remember: all labor cost, taxes, and interest on loans are included in the cost of doing business for each factory. Profits are added on top of these costs.) It is true that factory X can also eliminate all profits to compete, but now we have X's stockholders that would not be making a profit on their investment. What we have here is a confirmation that profits are surcharges; that lower wages will reduce the cost of an item in a competitive market, but does not by itself raise profits as long as there is competition in the market; that businesses owned by outside stockholders (who are buying the right to impose a surcharge on some other person's labor) cannot compete against businesses owned by the workers.

The truthful and unbiased economists with the right software and a small computer would immediately see the true economic picture. They would also find that one of Karl Marx's main tenets — that workers in a capitalist society cannot, because of profits (surplus values), buy back the goods they produce, and, because of an accumulative effect, this in turn will eventually lead to a collapse in the capitalist system — is meaningless rhetoric. My argument does not in itself disprove the belief that capitalism has embedded within its matrix the seeds of its own destruction, it just states that profits cannot be judged to be that collapsing agent if after reassessing profits as surcharges, it is found that it is *not necessary* for workers to buy back all they produce.

One of the faults of Karl Marx's methodology was that it was too restrictive. His economic model was only used to examine and try to explain a business that produced a commodity. His method cannot analyze today's military-industrial complex, where they pay wages, produce a commodity (tanks, airplanes, guns, ammunitions), make a profit, but the workers do not have to use their wages to buy what they produce. Neither can it integrate or explain the wages paid to government employees, where they do not produce a commodity to buy back, or a service industry that pay wages, make profits, but also does not produce a commodity. All these employees can and do use their wages to buy commodities produced by other workers, whose wages alone cannot buy back all they produce.

Remember: The surcharge is placed on a person's labor, not on the items produced. Otherwise, how can you produce a profit from a person that produces no product? The item produced is just a handy-way to store that surcharge until it can be transferred into another person's hands. Until it is transferred, the full cost and the surcharge on an item are stored in the inventory.

To explain some economic conditions, it helps to understand that we are paid and buy in "Conditional Labor Hours." What workers are paid for a labor hour reflects how many and at what price they can buy some other person's labor hours. A Worker that works 40 hours and is paid $16 an hour, can purchase an equivalent amount of labor hours, or they can buy 80 hours of $8 an hour labor, or 10 hours of an attorney's time at $64 an hour. Money is just a convenient bookkeeping method of keeping tract of how many "Conditional Labor Hours" are owed you.

Karl Marx did not discover that selling and production are two different things; they are apples and oranges. The wholesaler has no control over how the manufacturer's bookkeeper arrives at a competitive price; they buy a monkey wrench with the total cost to the manufacturer and profits already included in that price, and cannot by looking at the wrench, distinguish what part of the price is cost and what part is the surcharge, or even ascertain, if the profits were added, how large they are. When retailers buy from a wholesaler, their cost of an item already has paid out all cost and surcharges (profits, taxes, transport charges) levied by all previous handlers of that item; and these surcharges, plus the retailer's cost and profits, are reflected in the final retail sales price. It is true that all these added surcharges must be paid for by additional labor hours from the buyer, but the price to produce an item remains the same. Karl Marx did not understand that the labor hours in a produced commodity, remain constant, but the "Conditional Labor Hours" required to buy that item varies with who buys it and where it is purchased; this is what causes much of the inequity in the marketplace.

How did "Surplus Values" receive their world-wide validity; what gave the concept creditability, and why the mysticism that surrounded it? To understand its impact and its acceptance, you have to return to a period before the forming of the 1871 Paris Commune. Living and writing in obscurity, Karl Marx had analyzed the French Revolution of 1848-1851, and had, like Shakespeare, concluded that "All the world is a stage," but his players were not individuals, his players were governments that represented a unique class; each type had a predetermined part to play that allowed only a strikingly small change in the part they played on stage.

Feudalism, capitalism, and socialism had a part to play defined by how they produced and distributed their commodities. What was observed as revolutionary chaos by others was just the fault of the viewer, Marx claimed; in this chaos he was able to detect scientific rules that each group had to follow, which showed that all those on stage were just following a prepared, predetermined script. He went on to predict that feudalism would be replaced by capitalism; suddenly, on the world stage, it was happening as he predicted: feudalism began to disintegrate and be replaced with capitalism. He further foretold that down the economic

road, the workers would unite under socialism and overthrow the capitalist; and just as he predicted, there they were at the barricades of the 1871
Paris' Communes; shortly after, Karl Marx was discovered; his previous
writings, that had been ignored, became fashionable.

In those earlier writings, Karl Marx had taken the French Revolutionary period of 1848-1851 and step by step — after it happened — explained
each player's movements. Those who represented feudalism, those who
represented capitalism, and those who represented socialism, all played
their parts exactly to the tune of Karl Marx. When one side gained an
advantage, that was explained, when that side lost that advantage, that was
also explained in scientific, economic terms. There was no deviation from
his earlier written script. He claimed that he did it scientifically, and later
he was to declare that his book *Capital* explained exactly how and why
capitalism would replace feudalism; then how capitalism would be
replaced by socialism, which in its turn would turn into an advanced and
final form of socialism, which he called "Communism." With the revolution of 1917 in Russia, everything he wrote was *seemingly* confirmed,
was *seemingly* verified, was *seemingly* validated, and everything he had
written about was accepted as gospel. Did not his writings explain
everything that had previously happened on stage? No one had used the
past and present to so accurately describe the future like Karl Marx's book
Capital seemingly did.

Hypnosis is just suggestion. Under hypnosis, you can be told there is
someone standing in front of you, and see that person when no one is there;
or you can be told a person standing in front of you just disappeared, and
you will be unable to see that person. We are imperfect and easily
hypnotized; in a class room we are always vulnerable to suggestion; when
some economic professors tell us that "Surplus Values" are there, we
believe; just as they probably believed when some previous authoritative
sources told them that they are there. It can be pointed out that thousands
of economic students have noticed that something did not mesh with
reality; but most of them must have thought it was they who could not see,
that they were at fault. It is also true that many Marxist scholars have over
the years pointed out some of the fallacies incorporated in Karl Marx's
writings, but they have usually been ignored for the same reason we
ignore all criticism of our religious beliefs.

If you overthrow the original premise of a theory, then everything
connected to that original premise is suspect. You need to read Karl Marx
to realize how much "Surplus Values" is intertwined; how much it is the
cornerstone; how much it is the engine; how much it is the science of
Marxism. Here we see the science in Marxist ideologies disappearing, and
in its place, the appearing of a religion. The science is replaced with

another illusion created by a human being, replaced with just another fable, a religious fable.

By understanding surcharges as profits, you can now understand the role of unions in the labor process. Socialist can postulate all they want to about the relationship between labor and capital, and whether there is or is not a zero-sum character of capital-labor conflict, but unless the speculation is based on a true relationship that exist in the environment, the answers they receive will not correlate with the truth.

Left orthodoxy defines "history" as the narrative of the class struggle. Question: What happened to the inherited revolutionary potential of the working class that was so widely theorized? Answer: It was extinguished by the success and rise of unions into a category of elite workers. Instead of capitalism producing workers in the factories that would become the van-guards of the revolution, it created a class that was (for its own benefit) against socialism. It is a separate class that has privileges that are not granted the majority of workers; a class of elite industrial workers that use and need capitalism to retain its power. Elite labor can in a sustained way advance its material interest entirely within capitalism; it can (when conditions are right) force the capitalist to give its members higher wages; not at the expense of capitalism, but at the expense of non-union workers. With the rise of unions, the inherent revolutionary potential of the working class in capitalistic states — that Marx theorized — can be discarded. If the unions in socialist countries assume power, to retain their status and benefits, the elite workers will prefer a free market economy where they can strike and receive more than other workers who do not have the power to shut down the state.

It is incompatible with unionized workers' interest to have them unionize farm and service workers. Larger wages for none union workers, means higher prices that a union factory worker has to pay. It is not in the elite workers' interest to achieve higher wages for other workers that are producing a service or product that they must buy. Capital and the elite labor force are not irreconcilably antagonistic toward each other; in fact they become allies in keeping down wages.

Most of the old and new left have accepted the belief that the industrial working class is the central force for revolutionary change in advanced capitalistic countries. With the correct information (profits are surcharges) you can analyze and come to some conclusions about labor unions and their relationship with capitalism and socialism, and can rid yourself of the false view that labor unions are always a progressive force under capitalism. Because capitalistic unions are set-up to gain benefits for a select group of workers, this will restrict them from forming into groups that will go beyond their original goals of higher wages, benefits, and working conditions for their workers. Unions were formed by workers to receive a larger share of the produced goods for their union members, but it also created (without intending to) a class of people that are in competition with non-union and other labor unions for a share of the same economic pie. If everyone is unionized in a capitalistic or socialistic society, who would decide which workers receive a pay raise that is larger than the average? Only when you view profits in its true form, can you observe labor unions in their true form. Then you can explain why early unions, although formed by radicals, never became socialistically oriented; why they came to view socialism and communism as alien to their purposes; why they became a harsh critic of socialism.

The majority of people in Eastern Europe where communism was imposed on them, have for years resisted this imposition by not cooperating either mentally or physically with the imposed government. (In reality it was not communism; it was a dictatorship of a group of professional intellectuals that created an elite bureaucracy to distribute the limited resources, always making sure that the created bureaucracy received their share first.) Even in Russia this duplicity was recognized and has created massive apathy, careless work habits, and emotional cripples that drown their despair in alcoholism. If they had the chance to vote, I am sure that many in Eastern Europe would vote to return to capitalism. Soon, however, they would find out that (like in the 1930s and '40s when they had capitalism) only a minority of people would improve their standard of living. If they decided to vote in Democratic Socialism, still this would not solve their poverty. However, through free debate, they might be able to learn that the true cause of their poverty is their limited resources that can only support a limited population.

Interviewing capitalistic and socialistic workers, you will find that there is little difference in their views; they both want higher wages for their labor, but want lower prices for what they buy. Neither system explains to them that because workers are both producers and consumers, these two desires are mutually exclusive. When socialist workers feel that the system is taking advantage of them, and this alienates them so that they produce shoddy goods and take two hours to produce an item that they could without effort produce in one hour, it would not injure them economically if they were only workers and not also consumers. At the end of the week, workers would still get paid for 40 hours of labor whether they goof off and take two hours to produce an inferior item or produce it in one hour. But socialistic systems, like the capitalistic systems, determine the price to charge for an item by adding on the full amount of labor in the item before adding on the surcharge or profit. Thus (assuming they have the same hourly rate) when workers use their wages to purchase an item that other workers in another factory, also took an extra hour to produce, they gain nothing. In fact, they both lose economically; because if everyone is goofing off and producing shoddy goods, they will have to use two hours of their 40 hours to buy the item, instead of one hour of labor. Their standard of living is decreased by 50 percent because wages only buy half of what they could if everyone is giving a good day's work for their labor. Neither capitalistic nor socialistic labor can make correct decisions until they understand that if they slack off and do not give a fair day's work, they are not beating the system, not beating a capitalistic or socialistic market system, but are exploiting their fellow workers. Exploitation by workers would enter if workers in factory B produced (by an honest day's labor) the same item in one hour that they previously took two hours to produce. Now workers in factory A can buy the item from factory B for one hour of their labor, while factory B's workers must still use two hours of their time to buy factory A's produced item. (At no time, in this mental exercise, do I condone work rules that would lead to the unfair and unhealthy speedup of labor. I believe that all work rules should be arrived at democratically with the full participation and cooperation of all workers in each factory and farm co-op controlling and deciding on what is an excessive workload for their members.)

Studying the union movement in the United States, we can see that the false belief of surplus values was carried over and influenced the formation of them; it is obvious that unions truly believed that the capitalist received their profits from surplus values. Every time they received a raise in pay and benefits, they believed they were getting a larger share of the profits.

To explain what happened to the unions' dream of equality in the marketplace, we need to understand that just because someone is willing to sacrifice everything for a cause, does not mean their beliefs are correct. I have come to believe that you can fight for justice, for dignity, for all human rights, and still be utterly wrong in your beliefs. Look at the accomplishments of the American Communist Party: for years the membership put their lives in jeopardy; daily, they were organizing, they were on the picket lines and marching in parades of protest, where they were kicked, beaten, harassed, lied about, falsely accused, and sometimes killed. But even following what turned out to be false materialistic gods, their sacrifices were to help produce the eight-hour workday, unemployment insurance, unions, social security, child labor laws, and many civil and social rights. Looking back with dismay, we can recall that all these advancements were at one time considered subversive and un-American by the United States Government.

Many who fought to form the unions thought that the unionization of workers would bring working-class power, would bring economic peace between labor and management; would solve the major problem of the workers not having equality in bargaining. When they were first formed, trade unions were hailed by the union organizers as a good method to arrive at this peace; but observation shows they did not gain equality so they could control prices and wages. The capitalist bookkeepers soon observed that the unions did not interfere with their profits; realized that if they gave a 6 percent raise today, all they had to do was calculate how much this raise would cost them, then raise the price the next day by the needed percentage to keep profits (an added surcharge) where they were yesterday. For the length of the contract, the workers had no way to catch up with that raise in prices.

The union leaders soon found out that this accommodation with management was to their advantage; so since the times were good after World War II, the workers received their annual raises, good working rules, and cost of living raises without a damaging struggle. And because all the companies had to adhere to all the same rule changes and cost of living raises, no established company was worried about competition. Even nonunion companies gave those raises and rule changes to their employees to keep them from unionizing. Higher wages and added benefits allowed capitalism to expand without hurting profits.

Because there is constant motion and change in all economic systems to adapt to new situations, it is no longer valid that union wages are raised automatically in the United States. Understand: There was no competition inside or outside the United States after World War II that had to be taken into account. In that period, everything produced could be sold for a profit (a surcharge) over its cost. Now the United States is faced with a global economy where high wages in the United States must compete with much lower wages in places like Singapore, Hong Kong, Taiwan, and Mexico. And in Japan, to meet global competition, some companies will even accept lower profits or no profits at all in some market places to keep their workers working. All new facts must be taken into account when analyzing the economy today; this is why the old economic assumptions are becoming so outdated — they do not allow for either capitalism or communism to adapt to new situations. They do not allow for thesis, antithesis, and a new synthesis to modify future economic systems.

As I explained, the capitalist profits are not hurt when unions strike and receive higher wages, because they set their profit margin after the strike is over by an added surcharge. So if wages and other costs increase and cause inflation, the capitalists lose nothing because they just reset their profit above all inflated cost. The American unions therefore end up not fighting the capitalist, but fighting other workers for a bigger share of the distributed pie. The economic pie to be divided, does not expand when union workers receive a raise; it always remains 100 percent of the assigned labor cost; so their larger share cannot come from profits, because they are a surcharge added on after the raise is taken into account. The higher the wages are above the average, then the bigger the percentage of the pie is distributed to those workers. Until unions realize that profits are surcharges, wage earners will always be fighting each other for an unfair percentage of the pie; a larger share for one person, means that someone else must get less.

To explain more thoroughly, let us examine two factories producing two different commodities. Workers receive $16 an hour take home pay in one factory, and $8 an hour take home pay in the other factory. That they are not playing on a level economic playing field can be seen if they each bought a $400 VCR that cost $8 per hour to produce. The worker receiving $16 an hour only has to work 25 hours to pay for it; the other worker has to work 50 hours for the same product. For comparison, in a foreign country where someone is paid 25 cents an hour, it would take 1,600 hours of labor to buy that same set. At the other extreme, a president of a large company might be paid $500 an hour, so that person would only have to work 48 minutes to pay for the same VCR. (In economics, it is important to know that the $500 an hour executive's pay does not come out of profits, but is calculated into the cost of production, so the larger their wages are, the more they receive of the economic pie.) If you remove the capitalist's profits (the surcharge) from the VCR, it would require fewer labor hours to buy it, but it still would not eliminate the 2 to 1 inequity in the labor hours required to buy it. The salient fact here is that the labor hours required to produce a product (a constant) does not match the "Conditional Labor Hours" required to buy a product. That varies according to who buys it; and later you will see that where it is bought, also brings about an unfair economic advantage to some countries.

One reason all workers are not unionized is because union workers have an advantage over other workers in bargaining; so if everyone belonged to a union, they would lose that advantage. Unions are another method being used by individuals to get an unequal share of the produced goods by joining a pressure group. Historically, I still admire union members for fighting and sacrificing their lives to achieve the civil rights labor enjoys today. I can still see a need for them, now and the future, to keep those rights, but until unions represent all labor and become international, they must be viewed as a group that is limited in its scope to achieve bargaining parity within the capitalist system.

We know that in Russia the workers and farmers all belong to a trade union, but they are not allowed to strike for higher wages. The reason: If they all strike and demand higher pay, then all it would do if they received it, would be to cause inflation; because like the capitalist factory owners, the Communist party would reset prices after the raise. From this we can see that free unions when they are strictly used to try to get a larger part of the distribution pie, are incompatible with socialism and communism; it is a futile gesture. All it would do if some unions were more successful than others, would be to distribute the wealth unequally as the capitalist's unions do. I still feel, however, that free unions are needed in Communist countries as a check and balance to unequal government policies.

Do not be mislead by my argument; as a Socialist, I do not believe that all workers should receive the same wages. For instance: I believe that a coal miner or any other type of laborer that is working in a dangerous, dirty occupation, should receive more than a worker in a clean, warm office environment.

If correctly examined, we might find that the capitalistic economic system is similar to the Communist system — they are both revolving systems where profits and many taxes are surcharges; they are both just distribution systems — a way to distribute wealth equally or unequally to different classes of people.

In the capitalist system, the managerial class has replaced most of the builders of large corporations who previously ran them. The same managerial class can be observed in Russia. The difference is that they take a smaller percentage of the pie than the capitalist managerial class because of the smaller salaries in relation to what their workers receive. That is because the managerial worker's wages in each political system are included in the production cost, so they each receive a larger share of the economic pie than does the production workers. The Communists should understand that surcharged profits are no more harmful to the distribution system than their added surcharges are. What is harmful is that profits are used to exploit the natural resources for some individuals (capitalists), whereas taxes and Socialist surcharges should (theoretically at least) be used to distribute the natural resources more evenly.

American unions must realize they cannot increase their share of the wealth without harming others; all American workers are interlaced into the economy and in competition with all other workers outside the United States, where, to compete with them, they must either lower their wages or raise the wages of the foreign workers. Like the multinational companies, unions must also become international; they must understand that they are so completely intertwined with all the workers in the world, that they cannot compete against lower wages unless they adopt a plan to control the surplus population — the main cause of the low wages.

CHAPTER 23

NARRATIVE: REUNITED

On my arrival at the Sacramento County Jail from the Medical Facility in Springfield, I put on my act for Dr. Bromberg, with little success this time, then went through that court inquiry where I was still judged incompetent to stand trial. The government prosecutor then was in the position of not having too many options on how to proceed with the disposition of my case. According to my attorney, he was being pressured, from the Attorney General's Office in Washington D.C., not to drop the charges against me. Although I never saw the documentation, I can assume that the word was also passed to the Assistant District Attorney in Sacramento that under no circumstances was I to be returned to the Federal Medical Center in Springfield, Missouri.

A couple of weeks after the court inquiry, my appointed lawyer, Robert N. Zarick, brought me their temporary solution, which was for me to voluntarily sign papers committing myself to the DeWitt Mental Hospital near Auburn, California. This was with the understanding that I would be treated like the other volunteer patients. I accepted this offer mainly because this complied with some of the questions that I had brought up in Federal Court in Kansas City.

The prosecuting attorney had been informed in advance that DeWitt Hospital would not take me as a patient if the federal authorities insisted that I be kept on a locked ward and treated differently from the other volunteer patients. They also warned him that volunteer patients had the right to sign out of the hospital whenever they wished, and I also had that right, but they would take the responsibility to notify the authorities if I asked to be discharged or if they were going to discharge me because my mental illness was in remission. Nevertheless, I personally had to give my word to my lawyer, who then relayed it to the Federal Court and to the Federal Assistant District Attorney, that I would not try to escape if I had a chance to, or to sign myself out of the hospital without notifying them.

Unbelievable? Yes, it is. But it is not fiction. They obviously believed that I was a bank robber; they knew that I was a former inmate of San Quentin and Folsom Prison and had just been found unable to stand trial for the third time (in other words they considered me mentally ill), and yet, here they were taking my word that I would not walk away from the hospital; which I could have done within a short time after entering it.

I can say that when I arrived at DeWitt Hospital, those in charge of the hospital lived up to their agreement as I was able to have full ground privileges within thirty days of my arrival; and within sixty days, for all practical purposes, I was in complete charge of the recreational and therapy workshop and managed all the materials for those who wished to do handicrafts. This was my work assignment. Although an outside volunteer was technically, on paper, the head of the shop, she deferred to me in the scheduling and the running of it as she only came in a couple of times a week for a few hours. I also participated with and without volunteer help in running bingo and birthday parties on open wards, and was given the keys to the therapy workshop so I could obtain the different prizes and games, hand out handicraft materials, and teach leather craft to my fellow patients when the volunteer workers were absent.

I confess that I abused this privilege of having a key by using it to disassemble a lock and make a master key for the entire hospital. I then made several sets by sending the key out and having it duplicated. These master keys were sequestered around the grounds in the event of an emergency. You must remember that at that time, I was still not sure of the powers allied against me, and if I found myself locked behind a locked ward and felt that I was in danger, I wanted to be prepared to go through seemingly locked doors.

From some of the questions that Dr. Bromberg had asked me at my last interview with him, I received the impression that he was annoyed at the medical staff back in Springfield finding me able to stand trial so soon. Only eight months had elapsed since he predicted to my attorney and the court that I might be hospitalized for years and my arrival back in the Sacramento County Jail. Although he went along with the Springfield staff finding me able to stand trial, I believed from his testimony at the court inquiry that he secretly agreed with the court finding me unable to stand trial. I believe he was being pressured by the district attorney to find me competent to stand trial against his better judgment and against the courts wishes to see the case dismissed. Once again, this time under oath and in the courtroom, he had predicted that I would need at least one or two more years of treatment before I would be able to stand trial.

Everybody seems to have a weakness of some kind, and in my position I needed leverage to move society; or more appropriately to move those in Washington D.C. who did not want the charges dismissed. So, before Doctor Bromberg had left the courtroom, I felt that I could use his reputation for that leverage. My plan and strategy when I arrived at DeWitt Hospital was the same one that I followed at Springfield, which was that I was always going to act in a sane and competent manner. I believed that when they sent me back in a couple of months saying that I was in remission, that Dr. Bromberg would think that his competency was in question and again find me unable to stand trial. I was still going on the assumption that if they had no place to send me, then they would have to drop the charges against me.

The clever traps we construct in our minds work so well until we build them and attempt to use them. The predicament I put the doctors in at DeWitt Hospital, was that I showed no mental abnormalities in front of them or the nurses and trained orderlies, that I knew the answers to their questions that showed me mentally normal, and I was perfectly able to get along with the staff, fellow patients, and outside volunteers. I was able to assume command of the work that they asked me to do, and had self-confidence in myself and was able to exhibit this to the people around me, and by my actions, did not allow them to hang a label on me. Yet, they had these reports in front of them from Springfield, Vacaville, and Dr. Bromberg, which they had to take into account. They could not reconcile these reports with my actions. (It was not like the prison in Springfield where the doctors could not observe me. At the DeWitt Hospital the patients were continually under observation when on the wards from a trained staff and all odd behavior had to be entered into the patient's chart.) All they could do was keep asking me what I had done to acquire these labels; I kept telling them nothing, as I was perfectly sane and always had been; and the only reason I had signed myself in was that I preferred living in a hospital to living in the county jail. When questioned about my Habeas Corpus writ where I claimed that I was insane, I told them I did this to get myself out of Springfield as I did not want to be in a prison either. Of course, I did not tell them that I was faking a loss of memory; I told them when they asked that I thought the memory loss was caused by the shock treatments given me at Vacaville.

I did consider myself "relatively" sane and in no need of treatment. I found myself able to survive in the hostile environment I was thrust into, and believed that that should be the adequacy to be judged by. If a person is truly mentally ill, he or she will not survive and get well in situations of extraordinary stress. Although disappointed a few times by my lack of progress and a few setbacks, I believed that I was bettering my position and coping with each new event as it occurred. If I had taken no action, I would have lost the battle, completely, two years past, but instead I could see the possibility of winning out in the uneven contest that I was engaged in.

DeWitt Hospital, like all mental hospitals, having no conception of an expanding insight by their patients, put me on tranquilizers on my arrival. When I arrived there, tranquilizers were being hailed as the new and final solution to all mental illnesses. Because I have this thing about not having control of my mental faculties and could see the calming effect and dullness produced in the patients around me who took their medication, I proceeded to palm and flush down the hospital's drainage system all medicine ordered for me. In the wards where they had to give hundreds of different doses of medication, it was an impossibility for the nurses to check each patient to see if they were swallowing their tranquilizers or other medicine ordered for them. You should understand that a competent doctor, nurse, or trained orderly can enter a ward and tell who took their medication; they are the ones sitting in front of a television set with a vacant stare; and if you walk up and turn the station in the middle of a program, you will not hear one word from them as no impressions are being recorded. Before you fall into a trap of words, I must tell you that even though they know that the medicine is not being taken, if the patients behave and create no problems, they have to ignore it for several reasons. First, the medical staff does not have the time to hassle about ten percent of their patients every day, as it would take up all their time, and besides most of the patients had the power to sign out of the hospital if they wished. Second, most patients were there because of an inability to make decisions on their own, so a refusal to take medicine was seen as a positive sign that they were willing to make a decision about their treatment. This would not be true for those true paranoid personalities committed against their will who could become violent without medication. They were treated on different wards and the medicine was forced on them.

The DeWitt Mental Hospital, which encompasses five and a half months in this narration, was originally built during World War II for the Army as a medical hospital. It was a group of single story buildings with long corridors connecting each ward. These buildings were surrounded by large lawns with beautiful shade trees scattered throughout the grounds. Because it was designed like an Army barrack and they had (because of the war) used inferior construction materials, it was immediately abandoned when the war was over, and sold to the State of California, with all its inherited weakness, to be used as a mental hospital.

For some of the self-committed patients, it was a barricade to hide behind while they tried to marshal their mental forces before going back into battle with society. For some of the self-committed alcoholics or drug users, it was a place to dry out before returning to their drinking or drug taking. And for some mentally ill patients, it was their permanent home where they would linger on, in their little world to which they escaped, until death relieved them of their mental and physical pains.

At DeWitt Hospital, I found once again that I was an abnormality in the surroundings I found myself in; I became aware that others around me questioned my intrusion into the DeWitt Mental Hospital. The other patients, the hospital staff, and the outside volunteers kept asking me, "What are you doing here?" Even some of the mentally retarded seemed to have absorbed vibrations from some unknown senses; they continually kept approaching me to intervene on their behalf in minor disputes they were having with their custodians, and kept calling me, "doctor"; believing that I was one of the treaters and not one of the treated.

Still, I can truthfully say that there were many advantages at DeWitt Hospital if you were not mentally depressed by observing so many retarded and mentally ill human beings not being able to cope with the outside world, especially if you compare it to a jail or prison. There was the park-like atmosphere, the hidden sanctuaries where the patients could have their sex, the inability of the staff to keep you under observation when you were not required to be on your ward, and the open visiting on the lawn where anything could be passed to you or taken to the outside world without the knowledge of the professional watchers. Then there was the complete use of the outside telephone without being afraid of someone listening to the conversations, the complete mailing privileges without censorship, and a canteen where you were able to have your money to spend as you wished. All this, after spending time in the Sacramento County Jail, was like being elevated from prisoner to warden on the first day of a revolution.

For about two months, the earth had rotated through its calculated path without an unexplained deviation, when an unusual last name came up in a conversation with Janet — an engaging young patient with many unresolved problems — who had recently been granted the privilege of leaving her ward without an escort. What had attracted my attention to this uncommon last name was that it was the same surname as Lili's.

Shortly after I asked her, Janet returned with the information that the first name was also the same as Lili's. Occasionally, through the passing years, thoughts had intruded about what dreams Lili was heir to; what mortar had she removed from between the stones since our separation. I had hoped that all wounds received after we were forcibly separated were of the flesh, because damage to the body can heal, leaving just a scar as a reminder, but wounds to the intellect will rarely heal. Words are the most deadly weapons; and unlike a loaded gun or a sharpened knife, words do not need to be aimed at a specific target to do harm. A single word, a misinterpreted glance, an innocent gathering out of a person's hearing, can all break open a mental wound.

The master keys I had made for the hospital doors did not allow me to get past those nurses and orderlies on duty on the locked wards, nor was I allowed on those wards with materials to make handicraft items or with bingo games as most of the patients were in no condition to enjoy anything but drug induced solitude. I solved the problem of getting information by blackmailing a female orderly whom I had accidentally caught a few weeks before, having sex with a fellow patient in a linen closet. Because one of her duties was cleaning up the hospital file room, this act of informal extortion gave me access to Lili's files. This woman orderly had no way of knowing that I was bluffing; that it was against my code to inform on anyone that was not harming another human being. From the files, I confirmed that it was truly Lili on that locked ward, and that she had committed herself so that she could receive treatment for a drug dependency. The records showed that this was her third try at breaking a heroin habit; two previous tries at Lexington, Kentucky, were evidently without long-lasting success.

Although I was occupied in a serious game, not of my choosing, I had to see if I could roll a boulder into position to temporarily divert the cold waters of reality from engulfing my Lili. Given the time, I knew that I would have to replace that temporary boulder with a permanent dam. The question was time; how much time did I have to correct the erroneous treatment of the past?

To manipulate people in your immediate environment for personal gain can give you the false feeling that you can control that environment. I hoped that I was not fooling myself by this false perception as I suspected that this kind of delusion could lead to playing games that I could not win.

At my request, Janet pointed out Lili's window to me, but all I could see from the outside was a shadow being cast on the surface of the heavily frosted windowpane; a window that hid and enclosed Lili in her nine by seven feet structured world. After Janet had left, I stood there in solitude and allowed my mind to project on that shadow, a remembrance of the one I loved; a remembrance that had not faded under the harsh sunlight of the passing days, weeks, months, years.

I found out that it was just a matter of days before Lili would be allowed ground privileges; and found out that I was not entirely immune from the mundane worries that former lovers have about their image. Would she remember our love, our youthful love? Had she wondered why

I had not come looking for her when her father and mother had taken her away? Did she think that I believed her father when he threatened to have me killed if I got in touch with her?

Time! Time! Where had it all gone to? I the youth, I the social leveler, I the dreamer of better worlds had succumbed to the passing of time and showed the scars of that encounter. Eight years had elapsed since that spring day when we first met, and the environment had been caustic to me, physically and mentally. Lili had also changed. Reading her files, gave me a hint of a malignancy that had grown unchecked while we were separated. I felt that malignancy, that growth, might be cured by radiation; a radiation produced by being loved. Given the time, I could give that love, that radiation; but once again, I had to ask myself, "Did I have that time?"

Wanting my presence to be a surprise, I arranged with Janet to bring Lili to the meeting rock, because when you first came off a locked ward, you had to be escorted by someone who had complete ground privileges. That person had to sign you on and off the locked ward and was responsible for your conduct while you were away from the ward.

Tall, unmowed grass, dried to its summer tan, surrounded the large flat rock that was hidden just over the rise from the hospital. Patients referred to the rock as the "meeting rock" and used it as an easily locatable object to guide other patients to its base; starting them on the road to a life of insidious plotting against the hospital staff, the establishment, the all encompassing "them."

The sun was almost directly overhead so the two women cast no shadow as they came over the rise. Slowly, I arose to greet them when they approached within twenty feet. As she pointed to me, Janet's soft voice came drifting on the warm air currents, "This is the surprise I promised you. Someone who thinks he knows you." For a moment a puzzled look appeared on my Lili's face; which was replaced with one of recognition; then by one that immediately removed the intervening years of separation as she hurdled her body through those eight years of separation into the present, into now, into my arms. We found ourselves intertwined in each other's arms; just hugging and kissing and crying and laughing and carrying on like a couple of acid freaks at a rock concert. Past and future were meaningless to us as we were living only for that suspended time of here and now. Janet had departed saying something about us having an hour before Lili had to be back on the ward, but it did not matter because we could only see each other; all others were intruders. Time is a measurement for those not in love; we were on lover's time which stretched to infinity; so we could not comprehend such a humdrum thing as being back on a ward at a stipulated time. We left that up to Janet. She would have to come back and tell us that the world was shutting down for the day. Questions and answers were left to future meetings as we could not waste lover's time on the past. The guilt would come soon enough, but we had this day to turn into new memories. The joy and exhilaration of just being in reach of her was overwhelmingly beautiful; and to see and touch her, each was a separate pleasure in itself. For the first half hour, all we could do was look at each other; then we would bust out laughing; then we would start to cry, then we would kiss each other's sweet, salty tears away; then comfort one another by cradling each other and rocking ourselves back and forth in a motion that dissolved the troubled world away. Growing hungry for each other's body, we made love, lying on the sunburnt grass behind the large meeting rock.

CHAPTER 24

ESSAY: ECONOMIC AND POLITICAL THOUGHTS

When Karl Marx wrote his polemics, he had a definite urban bias; he somehow lost sight of the farmer's importance in economics. By not analyzing or incorporating them into his theses, he could not explain that what is good for the rural sector can be bad for the urban sector and vice versa. If he thought of farmers at all, he probably viewed them as just peasants and having little influence on the world's economic stage. Observation will show that in some agricultural countries, the farm workers can be the predominant players and the main guiding force in a country's economy. So an assessment should be made to explain small, primarily agrarian societies and to analyze whether it makes better economic sense for some small agricultural countries not to mechanize their farms or to become fully industrialized.

American farmers are caught up in their own propaganda about the advantages they believe they can perceive in a free market system. They think they are producing in a market system where competition regulates the market and eliminates the less competitive. In the United States, the factory owners set their profit margins (their surcharges) after they know their production cost, but this is not so for the American farmers. They *do have* this economic law where farm prices go up when there is a shortage and comes down when there is a surplus; the farmers do plant, when there is a shortage, a crop in short supply. They do not have the advantage in a free market of pricing what they produce above their production cost as the automobile industry does. Because they are in competition with millions of individual farmers around the world, the more they produce, the lower the prices fall on the world market. Most American farmers will not organize into crop unions that designate how much to plant, and then sell at a price over the production cost. To them, crop unions would be a form of socialism, which they will not admit is one of the ways to guarantee they do not overproduce and bankrupt themselves. The results: to meet world wide competition, the United States factory farms and individual farmers must be subsidized (a socialistic method) by the taxpayers.

In Russia, they also subsidize farm prices by selling at below production cost. This gives (as in the United States) the urban factory workers lower food prices. We are continually being told that the Russians are unable to grow food to feed their people because the farmers do not have the incentive that the capitalist farmers have. This is only partly true. As Communist, the cooperative farms are not allowed to create or exploit a large migrant farm population as in the United States. As they must support and provide for their farm workers annually not seasonally, this does inhibit their ability to produce more with less farm workers. A glance at a world map will quickly give you the main reason they cannot produce the food: they do not have the climate to grow it. The best United States farmers could not succeed where a large portion of the land has a climate that allows you to harvest a good crop once every 4 years. The Russians have made the mistake of wasting large amounts of labor trying to defeat the elements, trying to prove they can with less agricultural land per person, feed, house, and clothe more human beings than the capitalists can with the same resources. But to pray for good weather so your crops will grow and can be harvested when there is no God, is just the same as believing that because you are a Communist, you can grow crops where even the capitalist farmers cannot because you believe in and worship Marxist ideologies. They are both useless practices. Even with the death of 20 million Russians in World War II, they do not understand that it is their population they need to control. It is foolish to open for cultivation land not fit for cultivation, a result of believing their self-made propaganda that they represent something different.

Look at the success of the Communist agricultural system in China: a nation a little bigger than the United States, with only half the farm land, and yet they support five times the population. When the United States is forced to support 10 times its present population, we will see that it, too, will have no surpluses. Even with this success, the Communist Chinese have beliefs absorbed from Marxism that they must excise from their minds before it is too late. One of them is: that to compete in this world, they must — by emulating countries, such as the United States — industrialize their country and mechanize their farms. Before they do this, they should come to the United States and study the facts, study an Amish family farm — where they use animal labor — and a mechanized one. They will find out that the mechanized farms cannot compete economically or ecologically with a farmer using draft animals and human beings as their source of power.

To solve the food shortage in some Third-World counties, the governments have imported tractors, combines, and trucks. Their object is to grow crops for export, and to feed their starving people. Under the tutelage of foreign agrarians, these countries have been told that by planting improved varieties of crops, by using imported fertilizers and pesticides, and by mechanizing their agriculture, they can increase their production of food, and thus expand the amount of their exports. What is missing in the equation is that plowing with a tractor instead of a draft animal does not increase the crop; harvesting with a mechanized combine instead of with a draft animal combine does not increase the crop; and transporting with a truck instead of a draft animal does not increase the crop. All this machinery does, is to allow farmers to plant, pick, and transport the crop quicker with less human labor.

The main problem: the entire crop harvested by the machinery (or its equivalent in natural resources) must be exported to pay the cost and, if bought on credit, the interest on that cost, of the imported machinery, the spare parts, replacement tires and batteries and, the largest cost, the fuel to run the machinery. The imported fertilizers, pesticides, and improved varieties of wheat, corn, and rice do increase the crops, but that increase, too, must be exported to pay for the mechanization of the farm. Instead of a gain in food, there is a decrease. Food exported without a benefit, makes the country poorer, not richer; there is less food, not more. The land, which at one time supported the farm workers, now supports the imported machinery. Realistically, the local farmer using the same land and draft animals, can, instead of supporting the machinery, produce wealth that can be consumed locally or exported for a gain instead of a loss.

We are taught by the agronomist to believe that it takes fewer labor hours to produce a crop with machinery than with animals and human labor. But prevalent wages and locale can drastically change the hours replaced by the machinery. For instance, in country Alpha, a $100,000 imported combine in a 25 cents an hour labor market, replaces about 400,000 working hours divided over the life of the combine. In the United States at about $3 an hour for farm laborers, it replaces only about 33,000 hours over the life time of the machinery. If imported fuel is used in country Alpha at $2 a gallon, and the same fuel cost $1 a gallon in the United States, then 3 gallons replace one agricultural labor hour in the United States, but in country Alpha, 3 gallons replaces 24 agricultural hours. We must also add up the replacement time for spare parts, replacement tires, batteries, repair time, and interest if the machinery is bought on credit. When this is all added up, you find that some agricultural crops can be produce in country Alpha with fewer labor hours using animal and human labor than by using machinery.

In a small agricultural country, the importance of imports and exports should be understood. There is no free lunch hidden here; every loaf imported must be paid for by an equivalent loaf of bread exported. When a rich person imports a $20,000 automobile, into the Republic of Haiti's, most people think of paper money being traded for the automobile. This is caused by us having in our cultures a distorted view of wealth. Paper money is not wealth! It is a substitute for barter; it is a simplified bookkeeping method; it is a symbol used to keep track of the debt and credits of a society, and it also symbolizes how much of the pie we receive. It is an agreed on abstraction for wealth, but it is not wealth. Wealth is the land and the sea and the natural resources that can be produced from them, which is always limited. That imported automobile must be paid for with concrete goods; it represents $20,000 worth of agricultural goods or $20,000 worth of bauxite or copper ore that must be exported to pay for this luxury. This leaves the country with that much less to distribute locally. If sold locally, $20,000 worth of agricultural exports would require 80,000 hours of 25 cents an hour labor to buy it. However, if the that automobile was bought in the United States — at an average production worker's wages of $8 an hour — it would require only about 2,500 hours of work. This inequity has nothing to do with capitalistic profits or socialistic surcharges, but is caused by the difference in wages being paid for an hour of labor in different countries.

If a small agricultural country wishes to modernize one of its cities by importing buses to modernize its transportation system, and imports them from a country that pays substantially higher wages, then that bus system cannot make a profit. You cannot pay for the buses with $2 a day wages that cost $60 a day to produce in the country they were imported from. Except for your local worker's wages, all other costs: fuel, spare parts, batteries, tires and so forth, if imported, would have the same inequitable cost ratio. The buses would have to be subsidized and paid for by the government, because the low fares that would have to be charged would not pay the upkeep and the operation cost, let alone pay for the buses. And like the $20,000 imported automobile, those buses also must be paid for by exporting the country's wealth. These economics hold true when a small agricultural country puts in a modern telephone or electrical generation system and must import the equipment. They also would not make a profit; so, all imported materials would have to be subsidized and paid for by the government. The same disparity can be seen when a factory is set up to produce only for the local market. All the required machinery and material that is imported, to make the item, must be subsidized by the government. What is gleaned here is that a local or foreign capitalist will not invest in any enterprise that cannot make a profit, so in order to modernize their services or set up a factory for local consumption in a small agricultural country, a Socialist government is needed to provide and support these services that cannot make a profit.

Growing staple crops for local consumption in small agricultural countries in the Caribbean and Central America does not interest large outside capital. Still, just because they do not want to invest in non-profit enterprises, does not mean that there are not niches that can be exploited by local and foreign capitalists in these smaller countries. The most profitable ones (besides mineral extractions) are those with low-priced land and wages to grow crops (bananas, coffee, cocoa, cotton, sugar, etc.) for export to countries that (in comparison) have high land values and high wages. When you produce bananas on $10 an acre land and pay 25 cents an hour wages, then you can add a large surcharge (profit) when you sell to a market that can afford to pay a high price for the imported goods. In essence, the capital investment in land and advanced wages, returns a higher profit than can be earned (on the same amount of investment) by producing crops in the United States for local consumption or for export to a country with low land values and wages. The United States and other capitalist governments view any system of government that does not allow for this type of exploitation as a threat to its continuation; that is why they interfere in the internal affairs of small countries that wish to remove themselves from capitalistic domination. Until all countries control and reduce their populations so there is no need to control, to exploit, or to invade other countries to support their excess populations, then this exploitation of small countries by large countries will continue.

To try to redress the grievances of the agriculture workers in some Third-World countries, I approve of "land reform" where large estates are broken-up and distributed to the workers and their families, who as nameless peasants were forced to work the land without the hope of ever owning it. This is with the understanding that in some forms of agriculture, it makes better sense to hold the land in Co-ops; especially if it needs large amounts of machinery to cultivate it.

I approve of this, even knowing that "land reform" is not going to solve the land problem for more than a couple of generations unless there is a fundamental change in the thinking of those who receive the redistributed land.

The Problem: Mathematical division is inflexible. A peasant who receives and needs 5 acres to make a living, and has five children, can only leave each 1 acre. Allowing for the spouse to also bring an acre of land into a marriage, that leave the next generation with two acres to farm with. If each grand child also produces 5 children, then each family (who need 5 acres to survive) must make a living on only 4/5 of an acre.

In a co-op that begins with 25 peasant families, and where each had 5 children, there would be 125 person to support in the first generation after the redistribution, and 725 persons in the second generation.

The solution: limit the family to one or two children, or pass a law that only the first born is entitled to the farm land or allowed to remain in a Co-op. Assigning the land to the first born, of course, only solves the problem for the rural population; the majority of surplus farmers must, as always, seek a living in the city.

Using the concepts discussed above, you can take a small agricultural country such as Nicaragua (population 2.8 million) and gather some pertinent facts that relate to its economy. For one thing the labor hours are restricted by the population. Twelve hours per day, seven days a week, per working person, is the most that you can expect. But all labor hours in a country are not equal, those expended on work that does not produce a product must be subtracted from the hours available to the economy. The labor hours of everyone in the army, the government, and in some service industries must be subtracted if they produce nothing. In 1982 exports were about $370 million and imports $775 million, which created a deficit of $405 million. You will find out that there is no way that Nicaragua with its low economic base can pay that $405 million deficit. Those who gave them the credit will eventually have to write it off as a bad loan.

Do not be deceived by those who lend capital to Third World countries. Third World countries should understand that they cannot modernize and improve their standard of living by going into debt to capitalist or socialist countries. Eventually the interest on that debt will drain the country of its ability to raise its standard of living. The repayment of the debt will go to raise the standard of living of the ruling class that supplied the capital. This type of exploitation, successfully used by the United States and other advanced states, can be named: Imperialism Two. You do not have to conquer a Third World nation, nor pay an occupying army; yet, you can exploit that nation to its limit. The irony: The lenders use their propaganda to tell these Third World nations that their supplied capital is a magnificent benefit to them.

Of that $370 million that Nicaragua exported in 1982, $317 million were produced from agriculture and from fishing. The labor hours of roughly 354,000 people in agriculture and fishing, and 6,000 in mining are supporting about 2 million people who are not producing the wealth for the economy. The irony: those 360,000 people (mainly farm workers) must be exploited by a capitalistic, fascistic, feudalistic, or socialistic government in order to support about 2 million surplus people. The main social and economic inequality in Nicaragua is between those producing workers and the non-producing city dwellers.

In 1971 the population in Nicaragua was approximately 1.8 million people; by 1981 it was 2.8 million people. Although the population increased by about 1 million people, the natural resources and the available land did not increase, nor the number of people required to produce the exported wealth from the land. (The increase was 1 million children, which did not alter the number of people required to farm the land.) You have seen the dead-end produced by mechanizing the farm; so that would not solve Nicaragua's economic problems. You have seen how an hour of labor in a poor country does not buy an hour of work in a rich country; a dollar's worth of razor blades in the United States might cost 10 minutes's labor, the same product imported into Nicaragua might cost four hours of work. This inequity could be overcome if Nicaragua was able to sell the labor in its products for an equal amount of labor hours in the products it imports. But notice: the same inequity exists if Nicaragua buys from a Communist country that has higher wages. Then, the Communist nation they buy from would be the exploiter.

Because of competition, Nicaragua will usually receive world market prices for its exports, but because labor cost to produce a product, remains low, even receiving meager world prices, the exported product still sells way above the small wage production cost. Notice: It does not matter whether the government is capitalistic or socialistic, or you call the attachments surcharges or profits, because the increase over actual labor cost must go into supporting those (mainly in the cities) who produce nothing, but by their consumption, are responsible for the large deficit. To compound the problem, the city dwellers and the rural inhabitants are continually increasing, and those living on the land, have no choice but to send their surplus population into the cities.

If the 360,000 workers who produce the wealth in Nicaragua, had only to support themselves, and they kept their population stable, they would all be wealthy. The flaw: it is impossible to accomplish this unless neighboring countries also set up the same policy; else your overpopulated neighbors would invade the country that solved their overpopulation problem.

As explained before, governments are needed to distribute the limited amount of wealth. The less equal the distribution, the larger the repressive forces needed to carry out that unequal distribution. When the unequal distribution of the natural resources becomes so obvious that most of the people in a country wish to change it, then in order for the government to survive, it often resorts to severe measures (including torture and murder) to prevent a more equable distribution. A "Dictator" can be described as a disperser of shortages, a person who must use unyielding police or military forces to accomplish an unequal distribution of resources of a country, a person who rules a country where the smaller the amount of natural resources to be divided per person, the harsher the methods needed to carry out an unjust division. If these are true descriptions, then a dictatorship has roots, is economically viable, is necessary as long as there is a shortage to be distributed. It follows from this that the General Augusta T. Pinoche's of the world are not anomalous, are not abnormal, but are consistent with what would be naturally expected and needed for unequal distribution; and so these dictators can, with the control of the army and police, continue an unbalanced apportionment until they are overthrown by a stronger group. However, from my study of history, it seems that a dictator on the right or left is always needed when there is a shortage of goods to be distributed; that democracies do not survive when it is necessary to allocate unequally the limited resources of a country.

We have recently been enlightened that "Liberation Theology" has invaded some Catholic countries in the Western Hemisphere; that some Catholic priests and nuns are beginning to side with the poor against the rich, with the landless against those who control the land, with the rebels against the present rulers, and even in some instances with the Communist against the capitalist. Although changing side is encouraging, and I applaud them for it, these priests and nuns must understand that even if the poor and landless take power, they cannot solve their problems unless they change their Catholic beliefs. If they live in a Catholic country that does not believe in family planning, they cannot solve the problem of too many people. Even if the Catholic Church supports a democratic form of government, if it clings to its worn and outmoded philosophical baggage of no birth controls or abortions, it must accept responsibility for an undemocratic form of government. The historical reason that dictators are needed in poor Catholic countries is because the Catholic Church demands the birth of millions and millions of people that the environment cannot feed, house, or cloth. Unless these priests and nuns change their beliefs, then the sacrifices and martyrdom of some of them, will only change the oppression from the right to the left. The results: Genocide will still be needed to control the population.

Until the population problem is recognized, the Catholic Church will continually insist on solving their problems by selling poor people candles to light, instead of allowing them to use the pennies to buy bread for their children. For now, the soul (their chief priority) is more important to the church than the housing feeding and clothing of the people. Once our religious, political and nationalistic history is written to the mind, most of us are willing to kill, murder, torture, and imprison other human beings rather than accept the idea that all our teachings were accepted on beliefs, not on observable facts.

The introduction of one child per family is the only thing that can solve Nicaragua's population problem, and hence, its economic problems. But, the government in power should understand that in a Catholic country, the church's indoctrination on abortion and contraception *does harmonize* with the information given by our genes, genes that we have inherited by natural selection. When a Catholic mother and father have eight children, they believe they are following the church's doctrine. Although they might not believe in natural selection, they are following the dictates of the information planted in their genes, that tell them that the more offspring they produce, the better the chances for their genes to be passed on. They are being ruled in essence by the building blocks that they deny exist. The government that can educate their people that population control is the solution to their poverty, is the one that will inherit the future.

"Production is Wealth," is the familiar "Ignorance is Strength" argument. Every gallon of oil produced and used or exported, makes the producer nation poorer, not richer. True, the faster you extract natural resources the more human beings you can support at a higher standard of living. But it is also true that you will exhaust your wealth sooner. No one is exempt from this law. Population expands when production expands. Every rise in production, gives an increase in population until it meets a barrier, a concrete barrier. Capitalistic surpluses allow for this increase in the population, and if it is true that a capitalist government will in some circumstances produce more in a shorter time than a Communist nation, all they would be doing is making the country poorer at a faster rate; they are just using up their natural resources faster. More efficient production just produces more population to meet that greater production. This is the reality that all governments will eventually learn.

This was written to show we can understand economics by scientific observation; all economic theories can be tested and do not have to remain abstractions. The Russian and other Communist systems, to understand their true economics, should compare the ideals expressed in the writings of Marx, Engels, and Lenin with not only the study of the true economics of capitalism, but their own exploitation of the workers; but for this they will need freedom of speech and press which they mostly do not have. I do not despair, however, as time will increase their population and they will use up their resources and will eventually be forced to re-evaluate their economic beliefs. The Communists will find out that they are not immune to economic laws just because they say they are.

CHAPTER 25

NARRATIVE: HOOKED

Lili and I were parted in the spring of 1954 when she was almost seventeen and I had just turned twenty-eight. Being older and having had more experience, I could see by the way she communicated and acted toward me that she viewed me not only as a lover, but as a warm father figure that she could confide in. Even though she was an only child, she told me that her parents, in the infrequent times they had hugged her, acted as if they were holding an icicle instead of a young girl with needs. As she entered into puberty, her favorite dream, that occurred over and over until it became an obsession, was that she was being warmly held in either her mother's or father's arms; and when she awoke from this, she told me that the yearning remained, and there was this emptiness, this loneliness, this hollow feeling that something was missing, that something was being denied her. She told me that she always felt that it was her fault that her parents did not respond to her needs.

When they brought Lili home, they moved her back to the same culture that she had rejected; to a culture that could not satisfy the needs of her genes, the needs of a healthy young adolescent girl. The parents now had to also contend with the lure of the street, an experience not easily blunted, once you have it. The street offers intangible dreams: excitement, love, romance, doing what you want to do, answering to nobody for your actions. Parents can never compete against the illusions created by young minds. Lili's parents could only offer her materialistic toys and a chance to go to school and receive an abstract education. Schools, however, have become as lost as discarded toys in an attic; they have lost their purpose. Instead of teaching a student to think, they have become institutions that indoctrinate a set of precepts that the higher the education, the higher on the culture ladder you can climb, that education has a destination, which is to gain wealth, status, and prestige.

We were not bred for classrooms; the mind did not evolve to dwell on economic, political, religious or other philosophical abstractions. It takes a special mind to connect these abstractions with being relative to your life. Education by sitting at a desk and learning abstractions, is a recent invention of human beings, and because we have not adapted to it, it must be, in most instances, instituted by force, by pressure of adults. Our education evolved in the forest, the plains, the mountains, and was for concrete reasons. Everything we learned had a purpose, which was to survive in the environment we lived in so we could pass on our genes. We had to learn only what was needed in the limited environment we found ourselves in. When we were successful in hunting, fishing, or gathering berries and roots, it produced food that we could see; it was a natural education that we accepted. Now, when we sit in a classroom for hours at a time and learn to spell the name of the animals we can hunt, the fish we can catch, and how to count the berries and roots picked, it is not the same thing to our senses. To most children, going daily to school becomes boring, it becomes work, it loses its meaning unless you become the few who can form a relationship with a teacher or a mentor who cares, a teacher or a mentor who wants you to think; who gives you the love and warmth that you do not have at home. One who can show you that learning is a continuum that will last your lifetime, and that you should not learn because you are bribed or threatened or because you are told that schooling means success in the culture you live in, but you should learn for your personal benefit. You should learn because it can make you free; it can make you your own master, even if you live as a slave in a slave culture.

After being brought home, Lili's activities were restricted to attending school, where she was delivered and picked up after school by one of the mothers in a car-pool. Whenever she went out, she had to be accompanied by a grown-up. She was also not permitted to renew her friendship with the girl she had run away with to San Francisco; each mother had blamed the other for being a bad influence. Eventually Lili's parents found out that by restricting their daughter's movements, they restricted their's, also. Their endless preoccupation with their isolated little world of country club lunches and parties, and vacationing at the right resorts were interfered with, so after a few months, when this became a burden on them, they began to allow Lili a few privileges.

When living with me in San Francisco, Lili had made friends with a couple who lived near us. It was unusual but they had a telephone, and Lili (who had an ability that I did not have) remembered their telephone number and address. When things had quieted down, she surreptitiously contacted them. When asked, they told Lili they did not know what happened to me, as they had not seen me in months. She then informed them that she was coming up to San Francisco to try to find me and intended to stay and look for work. She said that she had enough money to last a couple of months (She had a bank account of about fifteen hundred dollars which she planned to take with her.), but did not want to live alone. Although living in a three room apartment and cramped for space, they told her to come on up as she could "crash" on their couch until she could get settled. She probably ran away again and arrived in San Francisco about the summer of 1955 when she was almost eighteen years old. (After we were united at DeWitt Hospital, Lili told me in bits and pieces what had happened after we were parted; because of this, the continuity might be unintentionally blurred and dates and times might not be accurate, but her life portrayed here is factual, and whether they occurred six months or a year either way should not distract from the fact that they are true.)

The coffee-houses were still operating; by dressing the part, Lili managed to obtain work as a waitress. The people she had moved in with were not on heavy drugs. Uppers and downers with alcohol and smoking a few reefers (joints of marijuana) were the norm. She stayed with these friends for about three months before she moved into a new pad with a couple of girl friends that she met at work. There she and her girl friends began an orgy of partying, where no holiday, no weekend, no birthday celebration, or excuse was needed. Everything was free. Young men and old men, with and without partners, all gravitated to their apartment, bringing with them all types of food to alleviate hunger, all kinds of substances to make them high.

Lili was still eighteen when she was first tempted to try heroin by skin-popping it. Like all individuals, Lili believed that she was different, that she was unique, thought that she could relegate the use of heroin to an occasional skin-pop. Slowly the crowd, the group that she hung around began to vein-it, began to be hooked. To the uninitiated, you should know that the drug scene becomes a replacement for the need to belong; it is an accumulation of many people in the same condition as you, it becomes a cult, it becomes your extended family. Feeling left out of the family, Lili at one party, allowed someone to tie off and inject the heroin into one of her veins. Remember, if you are genetically vulnerable, you have no power to go back in time and control your parent's genes; and if you cannot stop after the first injection of heroin into your vein, you will become hooked.

What is this hold, this hook, this snare that grabs you when you use heroin? It is pure pleasure, the ultimate pleasure. Unless you have tried heroin, the best you can do is to compare it with other pleasures. It is more intoxicating than alcohol; it is better than the sexual climax. There is a rush of ecstasy and a warmth of unimaginable pleasure that surges and spreads over your body and into every nerve fiber. Once experienced, you will never forget the sensation, the incredible euphoric, the ecstatic feeling of omnipotence. For a brief time, the drug was free, but there came a time when Lili could not wait for the next party, could not wait for someone to bring it to her. She had to go out on the street and buy it.

From facts obtained in England, we know that if heroin addicts are supplied the drug at a reasonable price, some of them can live a normal life. In the United States, this option is denied to all addicts. Because the average job will not support a heroin habit, Lili was also denied this option, and so was forced by the United States culture into illegal activities to obtain the drug.

The consequence of being dependent on this drug was that the most important things in Lili's life, the mysteries encompassed in life, the search for the meaning of life, all the human goals that she set, all became assimilated and relegated into a constant, never-ending search for the money for her fix, for her medicine, for her "get-up." There came a time when a complete outfit (a spoon and candle or other heat source to prepare it, and a hypodermic syringe to inject it into her veins) had to be next to her bed or nearby because she could not get out of bed until she had her morning fix. The "get-up" became Lili's life. Wars and revolutions were occurring around the world, but they had no meaning to her. National issues, local issues, politics, famine, overpopulation, abortion, God, country, and the flag did not intrude into her narrow world. Lili's life converged on a single issue: the next fix, keeping well. Her Heaven was to be well and already have the money for her next fix; her Hell, to start getting sick and being forced to scurry around trying to scrape up the "bread" for her next jolt of relief. On earth, the need to live is the whip; the need for food, clothing and shelter is the whip; but the need for the "get-up" becomes the most unrelenting whip that necessity forces on you when you are hooked. And immediately after the fix, Lili's mind could not rest, it continually reminded her that there was the necessity to get together the wherewithal for her next injection. This is the bleak life, the reality that all addicts face.

Let us ponder on the latest experiment going on in research institutions that takes primates and offers them, after they pull a lever a specified amount of time (this instills in them the work ethic?), the choice of food, water, or a shot of cocaine. What happens? They become hooked. Hour after hour, day after day, night after night their life is devoted to pulling that handle. Water is ignored, food is ignored, sleep is ignored as they frenziedly, furiously, intensely and madly pump, pump, pump that handle the required amount of time for their "get-up." They grow weaker and weaker and finely will die unless they are removed from the experiment. Trying not to mislead you, I will inform you that they have tried the same experiments using heroin and it is not as bleak as the cocaine habit. The heroin user will eat, drink, and sleep if they get enough drugs to stay well. But if you set the condition where the pumping is set so high that they only have the choice of enough medicine to stay well, then they also will pick the drug over the food and water.

Are their lives different from Lili's; are their motivations of pleasure different? It does not make sense, to me, to believe that there is some evil incarnate enticing these laboratory animals into performing these acts; making their choice of a drug a decision they are responsible for, making it a test of good or evil, a test that if they fail by taking the drug over food and water, they can be punished by an everlasting hell. To me, the truth is as simple as recognizing that human beings have inherited the same response to drinking harmful chemicals, sniffing dangerous drugs, or injecting foreign substances into their bodies, as the other animals. They have not evolved a way (because these substances were so recently introduced into the environment) of not becoming addicted to them.

Outside the setting of the primate laboratories, there were no free drugs being given. The drug dispenser's payment was not observation of your actions, but was sold for cash or goods. Females have fewer options in the drug culture than men. They usually sell drugs, shoplift, or become prostitutes. A few young males also pay for their habit by prostitution; but because of the smaller market, the percentage is low when compared with women. When they are on heroin, most men and women become uninterested in sex; they receive no gratification from it; receive no pleasure in the act. When women become prostitutes, they live in a world of pretenses where they are forced to pretend to their customers that they are enjoying the sexual act; it becomes just a mechanical act performed to support their habit. Our environments are not perfect; we still produce human trash. Society has warped these persons' minds until they thrive on degrading, debasing, and humiliating those around them. Like those hooked on drugs, you cannot judge those that take advantage of the drug addicts, as they are also produced by the environment. I never asked Lili if she had to resort to prostitution to support her habit. Done freely, or under the compulsion of a habit, there was nothing for me to forgive. Love can transcend all the pettiness of human degradations. I never felt that she owed me an explanation for her actions. I just did not want to dredge up unhappy memories, and I was even happy that her personal guilt was for a time, relieved by her going to confession and being relieved of some of the guilt by her faith.

For a while Lili was able to pay her living expenses by working and pay for her drugs by using her savings. When her savings were spent, by buying three packets of heroin, selling two, and keeping one for her personal use, she was able to temporarily alleviate her drug needs. But there came the time when her habit grew and selling required all her time just to satisfy her drug needs. While still able to work, Lili had made many useful contacts. One of these contacts not only taught her how to shoplift, but supervised her and a stable of three other shoplifters that he controlled. All were young women that he personally trained; all the women he recruited, were addicts. He planned all operations; he choreographed and costumed them and made them believable in the parts they played. She told me that one character she played was an expectant mother. He had built this hollow container, which could be strapped around a body, that resembled the protrusion of an advanced pregnancy. She wore over it a skirt that had a stretchable band at its waist, and this was covered over by a large, loose blouse. The false protrusion had an elastic opening at the top where she could raise the blouse and stretch the skirt and the opening in one motion, then drop large items into the receptacle where the baby was supposed to be. She also was provided with a small collection of small packages in bags printed with the logos of prestigious stores in the vicinity as a cover. He would pick up the women in a van, check to see that they were dressed correctly (Because they shoplifted their clothes, they were always dressed in the latest fashions.), and then take them to the store he had chosen. When through, he brought them home and paid them off with heroin and money according to what they shoplifted, then drove off with the shoplifted merchandise. How he disposed of it, they never knew. As long as they worked for him, they had no need to find a buyer for their stolen goods.

All drug addicts live in an impermanent world; live with impermanent friendships. People were constantly disappearing. Some were caught and went to jail, some moved to different cities or different districts in a city, some died from over-doses, some from disease that ordinary would not kill a healthy person, but they were quickly replaced by the recruitment of new faces, new impermanences. For about nine months, Lili shoplifted for her recruiter, for her needs. Questioning the other women, she learned that he had been operating about two years, and in that time his women had only been arrested a few times. These he had bailed out, and then he gave them money to move to a different city or state. In the drug culture, two years is several lifetimes of permanence. When one person left, he would recruit another. He kept his stable at four women and had them all living in the same apartment.

One day he did not contact them. By the second day, their minds panicked. True, they knew how to shoplift, but none of them knew how to safely dispose of what they had stolen. They had become dependent on him for disposing of everything they stole. No one ever saw him again; he became an enigma in the drug culture as all anybody could do was speculate as to what happened to him. Lili told me that no one knew his background, as he never talked about it. Though he would occasionally party with them, he never was known to have gone to bed with one of his women; he never became intimate with them. He was not celibate though, because Lili knew him when she worked in the coffee houses, and knew that he picked up and slept with some of the young girls and women, but as far as she knew, none of them had been hooked on heroin. When you are on heroin, you usually lose all your desire for sex, and he knew that, because when Lili had brought up the subject one time, he told Lili that he did not feel that it was right to impose his needs on a woman that could not enjoy it. Even some criminals have standards, have ethics; do or do not do things because of beliefs that they have adopted; feel guilty about the things they have to do to survive.

With his disappearance, there was a scramble to find a "fence" for their stolen goods. Finding a pusher was easier, as users have developed the ability to go to a city and within a short time make contact and obtain drugs. Unorganized, one by one the women began to make mistakes and be caught. Lili was the second one to be arrested; she was caught in the false pregnancy outfit, so even though this was her first time, she could not plead that she was an amateur. It was the fall of 1956, and she was nineteen years old, when she had her first bust. Lili had given a phony name and address when she was arrested because she did not want her family to know her predicament, but as time passed, and nobody came to put up her bail, she began to panic because she had been told what going "cold turkey" in a jail cell would mean. And the detectives knew what those turkey tracks on her arms meant; they knew that she was lying to them; they knew that it is physically, mentally, and emotionally painful to quit. They knew that all they had to do was wait. Lili became sick, she became deathly sick; every nerve fiber in her body called out for relief from this sickness. The detectives wait until all you can do is scream for a little relief from the agony, from the pain of withdrawal; then they start the questioning. But they have to catch you at the right moment because if they wait too long, they cannot communicate with a person that has the dry heaves, that is shaking and sweating and vomiting, that has diarrhea and cannot control their bowels, and mess all over themselves.

"Tell us your true name and we will get you some help." You tell them;

the help is not given. "Give us the name of your pusher, your fence, and your accomplices, then we will see that you get some relief." You tell them; the relief is not given. The guilt will come later, but if you are a first timer, you find out that you are engaged in a game you cannot win. When they drain you of all your information, they discard you; send you back to your cell. The humiliation of turning in your friends for a promise of help that will not be granted, will remain as a festering sore that will float to the surface at the most unlikely times, in the most unlikely places. Once it is recorded and ingrained, it is not like a recording tape that you can record over and replace the original recording, it cannot be erased until the cells that the recordings are on, die. And what do they do with the information they receive? They put it in their files. They know that they cannot build a criminal case on the unreliable information received from an addict, so they use it to keep track of who is out there dealing, shoplifting, pimping, receiving stolen goods.

With no other choice, Lili contacted her family, who arranged bail and provided her with an attorney. They then arranged for her to be sent to a private hospital that treated drug addiction. Because Lili had the correct family background, she would have ordinarily received a suspended sentence if she had pled guilty; but when out on bail, she immediately ran away from the private hospital and began taking drugs again. While on the street, she was caught selling drugs to a federal agent. Her mother was told that Lili could be rehabilitated if placed in an institution she could not escape or be released from until she was cured. So, the attorney that her mother had hired arranged for her to plead guilty in one courtroom to shoplifting and guilty in a federal courtroom to selling. Being a first timer, and judged a drug addict, qualified Lili for being sentenced to a year in the federal institution at Lexington, Kentucky where they treated drug addicts.

Lili had always attended a Catholic school where the students were indoctrinated with the beliefs of that faith. Where did all this indoctrination go to? They, such as all beliefs, were in competition with the genes. In her actions, one could see that Lili's genes usually won out, but it was not a complete victory. Little pockets of remembrances remained; the guilt remained. So when she had her fix and was well, she would rush to church and seek absolution for the sins of her genes. The church which instilled the guilt also forgave her transgressions. The irony here is that forgiveness was always granted by a man who did not believe that the genes were at fault; so unknown to him, all he was doing was giving her a short lasting placebo that could not cure her, and only lasted until the urge for the next fix arrived.

When Lili was released in remission from the Lexington drug rehabilitation program, she began a familiar, repetitious pattern common to drug addicts. She came home, then went on the road again, on the street again. She then acquired a large habit that she could not support, and in desperation had contacted the Lexington hospital where she was readmitted to their drug program. Most addicts sent to rehabilitation programs by the courts are recidivists, and so was Lili. Many of those who are voluntarily readmitted, enter with the knowledge that they only wanted to get rid of their large habit, not their habit; they just want to cut back on the drugs needed when they start-up again. Sadly, Lili also was one of them. She told me that she even daydreamed and anticipated going back on the street and experiencing that rush of pleasure from those first few times she used it again. By signing herself out against "medical advice," she was released from Lexington and went on the road again, on the street again. She once again developed a habit that got out of control; and because Lexington would no longer take her back, she applied and was admitted to DeWitt State Hospital, in Auburn California, where I was being treated.

When she was about to inject herself with heroin, Lili always told herself, "This is the last time; this is the last time ever!" This useless monologue is repeated over and over again by heroin addicts. In lucid moments, it is always the last time. Alas! These were not the magical words. The words were always lacking something; it seemed that they were never arranged in the correct combination or the placement was out of kilter. The few that did escape from the habit were not able to recall, and so were not able to tell other addicts what incantations, what conjured images, what magical combination of words allowed them to get rid of the habit. All the good intentions in the world can come to naught when allied against the human genes. No prison, no hospitalization, no punishment can force a cure on an addict. The few people that do escape, tell you that the reason has to be personal and come from deep within, but even when you quit, you always remain addictive prone. You are still an addict; your status will always be an addict temporarily off drugs.

Lili told me that she never felt guilty about shoplifting, about stealing money, about selling drugs, because it made her well. "I rationalized," she told me, "that so long as I got my medicine I did not care what I had to do to get it." And she was correct, because feeling guilty and beating yourself is like running on a Mobius strip: no matter how fast or how far you run, there is no ending. Your religious belief, your political belief, your status in your culture, or being street-wise does not save you from lying, stealing, and cheating if you become hooked and do not have the money to support your habit.

Can we judge people that fall asleep when they are given ether; can we judge people that get well when they are given penicillin; can we judge people because a chemical produces an effect on them? Of course not, they did not make the universe, so how can they be culpable for its fixed formation. If the drug addicts are forced by the culture to remove their mental and physical bodies from the race, it just lessens the congestion, makes the pack smaller, the running easier; they unintentionally produce a gain for the unhooked racers by producing fewer descendants to compete with. (In 1969, heroin killed over 800 addicts in New York City alone. Most of them are young people capable of fathering or producing children.) Only individuals can decide if this is the way they will pass their allotted time; only they can decide if they want to devote their short life to mindlessly pulling that handle over and over again to meet their needs. But the harsh truth, that all societies must understand because human beings are capable of changing it, is that there are people living in environments where the endless pulling of that handle, that hell, is preferred over their present existence.

CHAPTER 26

ESSAY: RESILIENT THOUGHTS

Dedicated Communists believe that their proletarians represent the "final revolution." That in time, because of the unavoidable contradictions in capitalism, the world will turn to communism for an answer to its problems. Thus, capitalism as a viable competitor, will be removed, leaving only "Communism" on center stage to play out the remaining billions of years of economic production. However, it is now apparent that there is no "Communism" that automatically follows "socialism" as the force of production develops sufficiently. Looking at its first 75 years of existence, it is now discernible that communism is not monolithic, nor infallible, and its adherents, like the capitalists, are already arguing and fighting other Communist nations for allies and markets. They are frantically searching (in a limited market) for satellites to insulate their borders from contamination by not only capitalist, but other Communist systems that do not agree with them. Furthermore, to contradict their contention that they are the last revolution, you can envision from information readily obtainable, a curtain being raised on the world's stage for a new type of production. In its cast, a replacement for the Marxist's proletarian can be seen. It is true that this replacement (by its forced composition) will call for a government that would be limited in its form, but within those limits it can incorporate an amount of freedom that can be considered nearly all-inclusive.

Who or what is this proletarian replacement? It is what Karl Marx first observed in its infancy — machinery. Not common, ordinary machinery, but the mechanical devices we call "Robots." Not the crude, stationary robots of today (although these robots are already reproducing themselves), but the ones anticipated in Science Fiction. Within a couple of hundred years, and with some adaptability and a few more advancements from the present technologies, they will become a reality. Eventually the robots will replace not only the Marxist's proletarians, but the capitalist workers, too. They will be used to produce almost all marketable commodities. True, the government formed under robot labor will have the same handicap that governments have today. They will still be limited by the human beings who can be supported by a finite amount of land and resources.

If Karl Marx could have thought through his "Surplus Values" by way of a robot economy, he would have instantly seen that profits were surcharges. If the capitalists controlled and owned these robot factories, then to set their price so they can add a profit (surcharge), they must still set the labor cost above the full cost of the robot (their human replacement). What is important in a robot economy is that robots do not pay income, Social Security, unemployment, disability or property taxes, so they cannot support city, state, or federal governments; nor do they have wages to patronize and support the service industries. The limitation is that except for the wages paid the few human beings needed to oversee production and a few items they can barter or sell to other capitalists, there would be no market to reconvert what is produced back into capital. One can instantly see that there will have to be a reassignment in the distribution systems when the robot arrives, as the "Robot Economy" is not compatible with the distribution systems of today. From this, I contend that the distribution system will have to reflect its production; and as it cannot be sold, it will have to be distributed in some other way. The ownership of the robots and their factories will, out of the need for a market, belong to the people, and that will be reflected in the government chosen.

The lottery and robot economy are in the far future; so while we wait for it (the last government?), we must solve many problems that will not go away. Because of the threat of atomic war and global pollution, if we do not solve them, we may not reach that time in space, and then all will be for naught. The destruction of the world over a meaningless argument about temporary distribution systems, where each system will eventually reach the "Robot Economy," is senseless. Before I release you on my argument, let me speculate on which governments will put up the greatest obstacle to this future. The American and Japanese capitalists, out of need for profits and because of the low international wages that foreign competition has access to, must use the latest innovation in cutting cost of production. When the robot arrives, it will be used in the capitalist factories; whereas the Communist will tend to fight the elimination of their workers by robots. The same outcry and arguments that feudalism used against capitalism and capitalism uses against being replaced by communism, will probably be used by the Communist against the "Robot Economy."

Capitalists are also deluded by their illusions. Under capitalism there is this fervent belief that "Capital" (which they believe is an accumulation of savings from earlier performed and paid work) is needed to accomplish growth; that the loan of this capital is essential to buy or expand a business; that Third-World nations must borrow money at high interest rates from capitalist countries with surplus capital if they are to expand their economies. This belief has as much validity as Karl Marx's "Surplus Values." Except where they need outside material for construction and have no option but to import it, they need no outside capital or outside credit if they have the natural resources to start with. Internal capital or credit is just trust. All governments can get the same results by having money in their vaults or by just saying that they have it. This is caused by "Capital" being an abstraction in the economic systems, just printed symbols on paper that can be loaned out and used to stand for that "Capital." When the United States Federal Reserve System loans its printed money to banks at 8 percent — which can in turn lend it to their borrowers at 12 percent — the question arises, "Is this ordained?"

To find out if this is economic gospel, let us say that a corporation was formed in the United States by all its future employees to build and run a modern, $5 billion factory to produce iron. Now, visualize a master counterfeiter printing $5 billion of counterfeit money, which is so perfect that it could not be identified, and lending it out with interest to build that steel mill. If after the money was paid back (say in five yearly payments at 5 percent interest), $5 billion of currency was destroyed by the counterfeiter, then what would the economic effect be after five years? The money in circulation would be the same because of the destroyed money; the country would have a modern, $5 billion steel mill that was paid for, and the employees would have equal ownership of the mill in a form of "Capitalistic Socialism." Interestingly, the counterfeiter (instead of the bankers) would have $750 million as interest for supplying the capital. What I am pointing out and advocating here is that the Third-World nations can do the same thing to exploit their natural resources without resorting to borrowing the money and paying high interest rates to a foreign bank.

Then, how did this myth of "Capital" come into being if it is not needed? Once again we are fooled by our created illusions, caught watching the magician's hands when the black velvet curtain was released by a stagehand we could not see. Accumulated capital is not sacrosanct, it is not ordained, it is just another concept that can be replaced by an equally valued illusion that performs the same function. It is true that under the above form of capitalism we still must ask who will receive loans from the government to build factories, who will be chosen to manage them? To be neutral, a blind lottery government must come into being. You must surely see that this "Socialistic Capitalism" would doom the capitalist system as we know it; if they can no longer reinvest their money or receive interest on it, they would disappear as a class.

Most capitalists believe that progress is intimately connected with the need of constant population growth; that all problems caused by population increases can be solved through technology. The last is false, but it is true that to forestall the collapse of capitalism, they must increase their population or face collapse from a shrinking market, they must produce in ways that can be harmful to life, they must produce useless articles at the expense of the environment, and they must be able to continually reinvest their capital or their system will not work.

Capitalists have the problem that they can never expand their numbers beyond a certain point. Their mathematical formation requires them to always be limited to a small minority. This is expressed by the simple mathematical term: For each produced and functioning capitalist, there must be a corresponding amount of individual labor and markets to be exploited. The higher the standard of living of a functioning capitalist, the more exploitable labor needed to support one. (I use exploit here to mean: someone outside the government, who adds a surcharge (profit) on another person's labor for personal gain.) A small capitalist might make a living by exploiting just three or four people; a larger one might need the labor of a thousand individuals. A shrinking population, like a Socialist country withdrawing its labor force from capitalistic exploitation, creates a dwindling market, which also limits their numbers. When former colonies become independent and create their own capitalistic or socialistic class to exploit their own labor, that creates more competition. That is what was at stake in Viet Nam and now in Nicaragua. Those conservative "Think Tanks" know that Nicaragua is not a military threat to the United States. What they fear is the lost of the markets, the loss of that exploitable labor, which means the further decline of capitalism.

Capitalists have temporarily found a partial solution for their surplus profits that has allowed them to survive without a major economic collapse since the Great Depression; but ensnarled in a false view of how their economy works, they seem unable to recognize the solution or to even know what has allowed them to avert that catastrophe. What has saved the system is the trillions of dollars in national and consumer debts. These loans allow them to receive billions in interest for money that they have no other outlet for. A salient fact, that can no longer be ignored, is that there is too much accumulated capital in the world. There are not enough safe investments for all that excess capital. Because they have this surplus money, American Banks are being forced to invest in the economy of foreign countries even though they know they are poor investments. But if they had listened to the conservatives who have no understanding of what the national and consumer debts were accomplishing, the capitalist bankers would be faced with the horrible specter of a balanced national budget and no place to put their excess capital. The disaster that it would create if the borrowers stopped borrowing and started to pay it back, is still not understood. Where would they invest those trillions of dollars? There is no solution in a continued larger and larger national debt and more and more consumer debt because the yearly interest will eventually become greater than all the wages and dividends paid out in the United States in that year. The capitalist system has reached a point where — no matter what capitalists do — they face an economic disaster.

ESSAY: PETRI DISH

When you place a single culture in the center of a sterile petri dish, because it has no competition, it will expand outward until it occupies the entire dish. Its life time as a functioning colony will (without interference) be measured by the consumption of its food supply. When you place two or more different cultures in a sterile petri dish, then there will be competition for that limited food and growing space. As each culture expands around its perimeter, it will meet and fight to destroy each of the other cultures. With or without the death of other cultures, the surviving cultures will live as a colony the same amount of time. The food supply is not depleted because of different cultures, but by the totality of the population consuming that limited food. If the cultures are equal in strength and are unable to destroy each other, then the fastest growing one will have the most space. Its life time, however, is still the same as the other cultures. Because it is more numerous and occupies more space, it still will exhaust its food supplies as quickly as the other cultures that have less space and less population. When food supplies (natural resources) run out, they all die.

We know, that when animals are forced by an increased population to expand their territorial perimeter, there will be the same opposition and condition as in a petri dish. The intrusion of *Homo sapiens* into the North America Petri Dish, and their occupying it to the tip of South America in a few thousand years, can demonstrate the ability of human beings to expand when there are no other cultures to impede that expansion. By the time the Europeans arrived, however, that condition no longer existed in parts of the Americas. Expanding populations were beginning to meet other expanding populations on their perimeters.

Being outside observers, we might put labels on the cultures and call one (because of its fast growth) an expansionist culture, and another (because of its color) the blue culture, but understand: these labels can have no meaning to those cultures. Our labels applied internally, however, do have meaning; because all our labels are used by human beings as a subterfuge, a pretext to carry out and give meaning to their actions. Still, all our noble reasons given, all our sacrifices, all our patriotism and flag waving, all that sound and fury — that we use to explain our actions — are accomplishing the same purpose as in those petri dishes. It is to obtain as much space as we can for our culture and, if possible, to kill off the opposing cultures so we can have the entire dish for our expansion. How else can you explain the Spanish repugnance of human sacrifices practiced by the Indians than by contrasting that with the butchery of countless Indians and the systematic rape, destruction, and obliteration of all Aztec culture by Cortez and his successors. How else can you explain what happened to the inhabitants of North, South, and Central America when the European culture arrived on these shores? The conquest of the Americas was carried out in the same mindless way as a culture in a petri dish tries to expand its population. Our use of language to give a reason and an excuse for our acts, simply means we are trying to explain our mindless actions. We do not want the true reason: we do it because our genes tell us that competition means that you must produce more offspring than your competition to claim the environment around you; and if you have to kill to claim that environment for an increased population of your genes, nature cannot judge that.

I am going to try to explain how I view some national petri dishes and make some statements and assumptions about them that will be circumscribed by my earlier beliefs expressed in this book. Only time will verify if these beliefs are the true reality; for this to happen, they must be valid today and valid in the far future. They must account for the constant change that we can observe, and must remain valid when that change occurs.

The Arab and Jewish confrontation of today can be seen as the classic cul-de-sac, the classic blind alley, the classic impasse, the classic petri dish. There were 750,000 Palestine refugees dispersed by the 1948 War into Arab Palestine, Transjordan, Lebanon, Syria, Gaza, Egypt and Iraq. By 1966 there were 1.4 million Palestine refugees. Most of the Palestinians are still in camps where they are supplied with food, clothing, and housing from the United Nations and sympathetic Arab nations. There, under harsh camp condition and fighting a war with Israel, they still have increased their population. Already these dispossessed people are discriminated against, massacred in their refuge's camps, seen as a threat to the overcrowded local populations. The Palestinians are beginning to be viewed by most of the world as the "New Jews."

How do strong human beings gain their attributes? The same way the Jews arrived at their condition of being resourceful, imaginative, intelligent and all the other attributes they inherited. The Jews are that way because the non-Jews have for generations slaughtered the weak, the less intelligent, the less resourceful, and the less imaginative; thereby producing (unwittingly of course) a group with attributes that can be considered superior to those who have tried to eliminate them as a race. The Palestinians will also be selected for these superior attributes — thanks to the adverse conditions of their lives.

With this constant population growth, all the Palestinians' children are being taught (and this is an acknowledged fact) that 80 percent of Israel's land area was land abandoned by the Arab refugees fleeing from the war area, and then confiscated by the Israeli government. They are taught that when they conquer the Jewish State and return triumphal from their exile, they will divide not only all the land and property confiscated by the Jews, but also all the Jewish property. To establish a state today, where another group of people already occupies the land, requires the subordination, expulsion, or annihilation of the indigenous population. This is what Israel tried to do to the Palestinians, and because "do unto others as you would have them do unto you" is applicable here, that will be what the Palestinians will do to them if the Jews lose just one war.

There can be no permanent solution in an agreement, because if there is an agreement by which the dispersed Palestinians are granted a homeland on the West Bank and Gaza, it can only be a temporary solution; all they can do is move their United Nations supported camps from Jordan, Lebanon, and Syria to join the ones on the West Bank and Gaza. The problem: besides the 30,000 Jewish inhabitants, there are nearly 1 million Arabs on the West Bank. Except for what the Jews hold, all the farming land is already occupied by Arabs, all the housing is already occupied by Arabs, all the businesses are already occupied and managed by Arabs, all the political offices are already held by Arabs. And yes, I understand that the West Bank Arabs support the Palestinians now, but when they invade the West Bank's limited petri dish, there will be war between them.

A further liability to solving the Palestinians' problem is that most of the Jewish People still believe that God gave them the land that they are occupying and still fighting for. Because of this delusion that the Jewish people have a God who shows partiality to them and will excuse their conduct, the Moslems surrounding them must worry that they will become the next Midians. We cannot historically condemn the Jews for their animal actions on those plains of Moab; we cannot morally judge them because they acted like animals. All we can say is that this is not civilized behavior. But when they did it, they had no scientific knowledge to judge by; they had no better understanding of what they were doing than the cultures in a petri dish; no better understanding of what they were doing than the lion has that kills for food or to protect its territory. To condemn them would make as much sense as making a moral judgment and condemning a lion or what is going on in a petri dish. But today, the Jewish people have the knowledge, and if they commit genocide against the Palestinians, the Holocaust sacrifices were in vain, the Germans are vindicated in their practices of eliminating what they considered their surplus people. If the State of Israel can pass a law in their country denying the Palestinians citizenship or making them second-class citizens, how can they judge Hitler and the Germans who, because they were more powerful, did the same thing to the German Jews?

The problem is that the growth that was happening in the Palestinians' camps was also happening in Israel. Even, while fighting several wars, the Jews — from emigration and population growth — also increased their population. They now approach the limit that can be supported by the land, and unless they control their population growth soon, there can be no solution except through war. If the Russians decided to let all the Jews who want to migrate to Israel leave, then expansion of the Jewish State would be needed to accommodate them. But the land they would need is already filled and overflowing with *Homo sapiens*. Some Jews are already thinking and expressing the view that for them to survive, "It should be made clear to the Arabs that they cannot be free to maintain the world's highest birthrate in our small and poor country." These Jews see the problem created by overpopulation as only an Arab problem that can be solved by forced birth control on them. The Arabs' view is the exact opposite; they see the uncontrolled Jewish population as the problem.

Yes, we all need room, need Lebensraum. Look at the experiments with mice and rats where they had unlimited food, but were confined in a small space. Chaos! They became cannibals and ate their young. They fought and killed each other; there were no loyalties, no order, no laws. "And what has this to do with us?" the religious believers ask. You might think that it has no effect if you believe that you were created by a Supreme Being; but once again I will inform you, "Your beliefs will not prevent the overcrowding and the animal behavior caused by that overcrowding, it will just prevent you from doing anything about it."

"What relevance has the past to do with us today?" is continually asked by each culture. I believe that if the Jews had taught their past and cried for the loss of the Midian culture, then, perhaps, their future would have been different. They now have to cry at what happened in Europe during the Holocaust and shed tears over those thousands of pogroms that have occurred wherever they have settled since their dispersal by the Romans. And I cry with them, but until they realize why the massacre happened on the plains of Moab, and cry with me for those dead too, then they will not have learned from history.

Because the Moslems, like the Jews, also have a similar religious belief that their religion is the correct one and they will be rewarded by killing non-believers, then who among them will put aside their religious beliefs and be neutral and decide what is best for humanity? Neither belief is compatible when the division is the land; a land that cannot support them together without population control. The Arabs, too, have genes that tell them to increase and occupy the surrounding environment and to kill off, if possible, the surrounding culture. The mathematics of division is a concrete law that does not, and will not coincide with a false belief that a piece of land can be divided endlessly. This is the modern rub, the splinter in our eye that we cannot see; always, the religious and political beliefs will falter when they come against a concrete reality.

As I write this, the world has discovered that a million people will die in Ethiopia within the next year from starvation. This over-populated nation has, like billions of hungry locusts, destroyed the environment. They have denuded the country of forest because of their need of fire wood, and their live stock has devoured all living plant life before it could go to seed. The people have had to eat their planting seed to survive just a few more days. The result of all this is that some of the land has become a moving desert. In this created chaos we find the Christian Churches and its nuns and priests begging for food to feed these starving human beings. This tragedy is all blamed on the drought, and Malthus is completely ignored. "God will provide," is the answer of the involved Christians. "It would have been a moral sin to interfere in procreation and prevent this tragedy from happening," we are told by the Catholic Church and by Phyllis Schlafly and her followers. "Abortion and the prevention of pregnancy are unforgivable sins," so we are denied these methods by God, they claim.

Because they are taking the responsibility for feeding them, I would personally feel better if Phyllis Schlafly, her followers, and the Catholic Church would sell their possession and feed the starving with the proceeds. I would feel better if they would pauperize all those believers and mortgage their children and grandchildren's future for the beliefs that through their sacrifices they can feed, clothe, and house an unlimited number of human beings; that there is no need for human beings to do what nature does, to cull the human population. If they pauperized all the people who agreed with them, I am sure they could save that million from starving to death; and by supporting them for 20 years, instead of death, the starving could reproduce more of their kind. But surely, Phyllis Schlafly and her followers could support the 2 million, and in 20 years more, their support would produce 4 million, and I believe they also could provide for them. Eventually, when all the surplus food in the world is accounted for, is spoken for, the culling will still have to take place. We are dealing here with natural laws, not created illusion. Malthus' laws are implacable, are unyielding, are unmoved by a counter belief. Here, the problem is not feeding the 4 million in 40 years, but the growth of the entire population. The 30 million now in Ethiopia would in twenty years and with the needed food, grow to 60 million, and, finally, in 20 more years, to 120 million. So, you would not have 4 million surplus mouths to feed, but 90 million additional hungry mouths to feed. Remember: This is only one country that we are speaking about.

If those who do not believe in abortions and using contraceptives in family planning, have a theory that we can feed all the starving, why not change our emigration laws and transport them to the United States. Bring in one billion, 2 billion, or 4 billion human beings; if you are correct, numbers should have no meaning. But I will tell you that the Holocaust will begin. Yes, the culling will take place long before the first billion. So, I speak to you, Phyllis Schlafly and all your followers, "You are not Gods or Goddesses, nor do you have the capability of assuming the mantles of one. Even if you and your followers were willing to take on this burden and pauperize all your believers, you could not hope to stay the hand of nature by your beliefs."

Nor do the Marxists have the power to feed those hungry people. You too, just because you have a belief that Marxism can perform miracles, do not have the capabilities to stem the natural law that the land will only support a limited number of human beings.

Other countries have the same problem — growth. Observe Cuba; she is now a debtor nation and supported by Russia. Under capitalism she was a debtor nation, and if she returns to capitalism she will still be a debtor nation that has to be supported if she retains her present population. All communism did for her was give the population a more equal distribution, but it did not increase the land or the natural resources; it did not change the individual from a selfish person into a self-sacrificing individual. Only natural selection and time can do that. That requires individuals to have sufficient time to live in a world where they are not threatened by other individuals for generation after generation; that they live in a world where two people are not at each other's throats for one piece of bread; that they live in a world where they do not have to take the life of another to survive. All this can only be accomplished by lowering the population. It cannot come about by increasing production, because the more you produce, the faster the population will grow to fill and use this increase. All animals do that, and because you have a belief that human beings are rational, it is still just a belief; and as I have pointed out it has nothing to do with observed reality, so it cannot be used to change that observed reality.

Cuba could once again become the winter playground of the rich, but they would pay for this. Their women would once again become prostitutes for *las touristas*, and the men, pimps of their mothers and daughters. It is true that they can make a living for thousands of Cubans by filling the beaches with condominiums; and yes, a million *touristas* producing a million pounds of garbage a day that will pollute the island's water and land will postpone the culling; but the culling will eventually come; prosperity will produce more children who will in their turn produce more children until that prosperity is used up. Prosperity can only postpone, and this postponement only leads later to a greater culling. If I were an adviser to Castro, I would tell him to set a course before he becomes, like other national leaders, senile in his reasoning. Let the population decide; use democratic discussions, use freedom of speech and press in the debate. If the reality is pointed out to them, even the most ardent Catholics will adopt birth controls if everyone is treated as equal under the law; if the posted laws are for everyone; not one law for the party members and a different set of laws for those outside the party structure.

It will become self-evident when the population of China starts to go drastically down, that the smaller the population they reduce down to, the richer the country will become. They can even create a true paradise if — as the population declines — they are willing to reduce their large cities and reforest unneeded land and deed it back to nature. China's present plan is to reduce the population down to 900 million in about a 100 years, but if they reduce to about 100 million or lower they might achieve a true paradise in China.

Mongolia (about twice the size of Texas) with a population of about 1.9 million (Texas has 15.28 million), has been a Communist state since 1921. It had previously controlled its population by having about 40 percent of its adult males living in monasteries as celibate Buddhists. Because the revolution has, by the 1980s, all but wiped out Buddhism, that control has been lost. The benefits of population control, which had become mindlessly attached to a religious belief, were thrown out by the Communists because of their religious beliefs. Although the Mongolians were a successful nomadic culture, the government is now trying to impose a culture that requires large cities and factories and settled agriculture. To accomplish this they need a bigger population; so couples are rewarded with subsidies for large families. True, an economic structure such as this will support a larger population, but is that the goal that all civilizations have been seeking? Is success to be measured in the population per square mile that can be supported? Where did this sterile, bleak culture derive from? Where does the quantity of consumers' good produced and consumed prove that this is the correct culture to adopt?

Dissecting the Russian Communist system alone, we can see that soon, because of birth patterns, the Russians will become a minority in the Union of Soviet Socialist Republics. The study of history shows that the Russians have for years treated and used the other smaller Republics as colonies. As the population grows and the pie becomes smaller, those colonies will start demanding an equal share, and as I have showed you in the capitalist system, that means a lesser share for other Soviet Republics. When this happens you will see the glue of Marxism holding them together loosen. The binder holding them together, at this period, is a false belief, a religious belief in "Surplus Values," a belief that their mortar is composed of a different material than the mortar holding together capitalism. A belief that they are above the fray, the daily battle of existence; a belief that as individuals they can subvert their personal animal needs by joining a group; that they have no need of individual genes, as all information, all morals can be passed down through the group, through the mob, through the government. We have the past for an example, where Roman Gods were overthrown when they were no longer compatible with the human knowledge of that time; and so it will be with the Marxist Religion when human knowledge is no longer compatible with it.

For years, few on the political left wanted to admit that the horrible stories coming out of Russia were true. Only when Khrushchev admitted and confessed to the world that he and his fellow leaders had to participate in these horrible acts on other human beings to survive, could they believe it happened. Their reaction in Russia: they blamed Stalin; they blamed an individual, for leading them astray. Although they had the German concentration camps for examples, they still believed that their concentration camps where they tortured and starved to death millions of human beings were different. They still believe today that they had, and still have a right to do what they did because they represent the future; that they, by their beliefs, become something special in the scheme of things.

The survivors in the Russian concentration camps and mental institutions ask the same questions that were asked in the German and Polish concentration camps: "What paths led us here, and could they have been avoided?" Many German war criminals were tried and executed, but how are we to account for the Russians who were equally guilty before, during, and after World War II? I hope you have not forgotten so soon; did I not explain to you before that the victors made the rules, made the laws. Did I not explain that the victor — no matter what the crime — can say with impunity, "This is right when we do it and wrong when the defeated do it." The victors decide what is right conduct; and if the victors have a religious or political belief, they can say that belief is correct and all others are heresies; they can declare it is a universal law because the victors decide what is universal. Intellectually, you might abhor the torture and killing of a captive, but comes the decision where it is your life or some other impersonal man, woman, or child, then your choice will be your life and their death; just as Khrushchev chose his. Your only hope is to change the path so you are not faced with the choice. If you have to choose, if you have to make "Sophie's Choice" it is already too late.

Eventually the Communist nations will, even without free speech and press, awake from their Marxist Religion, their dream state, their misconception that their Communist system can in some way produce from a concrete whole a division greater than the capitalist can. While we wait, they will be deluded and handicapped by their created illusion that what they produce can be divided by their system into more and larger portions than can the capitalists. But do not let me deceive you, the Christian and Marxist Bibles have much to offer if you wish to sift out the unreality in them. Only, when we get over the delusions in them, can we understand that the "Robot Economy" will eventually replace capitalism and the dictatorship of the proletariat.

Because of my experiences, I had arrived early at the reflective time of life. I still would support a socialistic revolution, but before the revolution must come the laws, the constitution, the rights of the people explained in minute details. Not only the winners but the losers must know beforehand what changes will be made in their lives. No longer will blind fate receive my signature. If the constitution and the laws cannot be written before the revolution, then I will remain on the dock. I refuse to sail on uncharted waters when there is time to make complete charts from information supplied by the notes and from the lips of survivors who have been wrecked on these reefs and have charts showing their location.

The above paragraph was inserted to spring a trap, a literary trap; I wanted to make what I consider an important point about reality and ideal beliefs. I want you to understand that I, like other frail human beings, sometime use words that sound good to the senses, but do not reflect reality. Have you forgotten so soon that I have human frailties? My knowledge of navigation and where the shoals and reefs are, does not protect me from the unexpected hurricane that would drive me onto the beach or onto those plotted reefs. Do you think that I have the means to keep myself clear of the turmoil of a revolution? Do you think that I can choose to be neutral? Do you not think that I would be accused by all sides of being guilty of abandoning my principles, and being attacked by each as an enemy? How could I refuse to be in the parade just because the route taken does not pass by my house? No, I realize that I have no control over a revolution once it is started. My duties require me only to point out the paths previously taken and where they lead to. But comes the "Socialistic Revolution" in the United States, I will, if alive, be on that revolutionary march, and I am sure that you, my readers, will eventually hear my lone drum beat and in time march to it. As an atheist, I also have faith, I also believe; and will continually ask the question, "What have I to fear; because if the tune matches the cadence of the marchers, will it not eventually be adopted as their's?"

CHAPTER 27

ESSAY: CIVIL-DISOBEDIENCE

To be consistent, the masses reflecting must affirm that by the time the chosen obeyed their orders to assemble into corrals, their chances were narrowed; by the time they were loaded into the transports, they could only talk about resistance; by the time the cattle cars arrived at their final destination, there could be no revolt. It became apparent, by those in charge of the concentration camps, that the physically fit should be temporarily spared to do the hard, dirty, and distasteful work needed to run an efficient extermination camp. To survive in an extermination camp, meant to obey the orders to kill your family, meant becoming mindless machinery, whose goal was to dispose of the gathered surpluses.

Eventually, the life of the created "special-detail" depended on the arrival of the next trainload of prisoners. When there were many, the special-details were enlarged, and there was no weeding out; fewer trains meant immediate liquidation. The policy of the "Resistance Movement" could only be concentrated in the hands of the temporary living — those that were allowed to survive to carry out the labor needed to keep the camps running smoothly. Resistance in the concentration camps was not geared for an uprising, but for the survival of those "special-details." For their protection, these prisoners counseled that there should be no anarchic, no individualistic activity that would jeopardize their standing; no personal escape, no personal uprising, no individualistic killing of their tormentors. The consequence of a prisoner killing or trying to escape was, instead of taking the next prison barrack in rotation on their list, those in charge would immediately exterminate that barrack where the prisoner was housed. They were still utilizing their full killing capability to murder the same amount of prisoners, it was just that the next barrack on the rotation list, was allowed to live the required hours needed to exterminate that inserted barrack.

When you find yourself in a concentration camp, you will be surrounded by death and say to yourself, "If I had acted sooner, I might have staved off this day. Now it is too late." While you live, that is your punishment, your purgatory. Your torment will be because you did not act.

From these reflections, it can be seen that the resistance must start before the command to assemble in a ghetto is obeyed; that the struggle must begin even before the law is passed, and must continue when the orders are given. You struggle not imbued by some immature fantasy that you are fighting a God created animal that has gone astray, one that has made a prejudicial mistake in choosing you, one that if they capture you, will shortly realize this and rectify the mistake by ordering your release from detention, but knowing that to be interned means the final solution. So you do not allow yourself to be gathered together with the others of your chosen markings, instead you go to your death grasping weapons that you are using to kill those who come for you. Never again, means you will never again obey those orders to move into a ghetto; that every time the authorities send someone it will be a struggle to the death; new repressive systems that arise, will have no live prisoners to detain, to transport, to murder.

As a final closing scene in a movie or a play, a dramatic ending would be to have a group of Gestapo bursting into an apartment to seize their prey, then show a hand coming out of a huddled, terrorized family to push down on a plunger that sets off an explosion that blows the apartment complex into small pieces of flying debris. Instead of the slow march to the death camps, this can be viewed as an idealistic way to die; except in a few isolated instances, it is not going to happen enough times to deter the enemies of mankind from carrying out their roundup. Because of the way the mind is constructed, it is not capable of giving up hope; it will not believe that *their government* is capable of exterminating t*heir minorities*, capable of the final solution. No minority will believe what happened in Germany will happen to them. So, it is implausible that the chosen minorities will give up all hope and choose to fight to the end, will save the last bullets for themselves.

Keeping this in mind, is there a tactic that can be successfully used to correct the inequities that confront many nationalities without resorting to armed struggle; can there be no resistance without counter violence, without advocating genocide? If the answer is, yes, then I believe it can be found in Henry David Thoreau's civil-disobedience — a form of warfare that Mohandas K. Gandhi used to successfully defeat an imperi-alistic government. If the oppressed are the majority or represent a large minority that can gather enough support to make a difference, then civil-disobedience is called for. An examination of the past, however, will show that it has never been tested to its full potential.

Although I do not believe that civil-disobedience would have suc-ceeded in Germany (because the Jewish population was so small, and had so little support from the majority), I believe that it can be used success-fully to bring some professed democratic governments — that claim to be civilized — to the negotiating table to redress the claims of the oppressed. However, to win, the abused must understand what sacrifices are re-quired, and then, organize in advance a plan similar to the one I am going to advocate for the Palestinians. By necessity, this must remain just a general outline of tactics; they can only be loosely applied in other situations.

In the streets of Ireland, South Africa, South Korea, the West Bank, and Gaza Strip, and all the rest of the world that have discontented rioters fighting for redress of their grievances, we see those rioters on our TV screens throwing sticks, stones, fire bombs, and anything else that can be thrown, and then running away from those who want to arrest them. All I can say is that they obviously do not understand the goals, tenets, and principles of civil-disobedience. Apparently their leaders have fostered a false belief on their followers about how to put pressure on the govern-ment to correct the faults that they are out there, protesting about. They cannot do that by running away and dogging the commitment and sacrifice they must make by allowing themselves to be arrested and detained. I wonder if this is caused by their leaders not wanting to lose control of those they lead; or maybe they worry that if they taught them the correct tactics, the discontented could use it also on their leaders when they came to power and were found to be just as corrupt as those they replaced.

I have pointed out that the Jews and the Palestinians must come together to solve their problems, but I felt that there was little hope for that; as long as the Israelis are not affected by internal or external pressure, they will not negotiate away to the Palestinians the land and resources they won in their wars. Because they cannot exert that pressure militarily, to make themselves coequal in the negotiations, the Palestinians must use a strategy that negates that power.

Thinking like a Palestinian and mentally assigning myself as a tactician to their cause, this is the advice I would give them: My Palestinian brothers and sisters, you have overstayed your welcome in the neighboring Arabic countries. You have become a burden to them; your plight can only worsen with time. Certainly, the Muslims sympathize with your plight, but your presence endangers their population, their people's welfare. You are in competition with the Jordanian, the Syrian, the Egyptian, and the Lebanese people for their limited resources; so you are not exerting pressure on the Israeli government, but on those that believe like you. Being realistic, your Arab neighbors are not going to go to war for you; they are now, and possibly for the next forty or fifty years, outclassed militarily by the Israelis. Time is not on your side; your support is eroding away. Morally, terrorism and counter terrorism are abject failures. Understand: The Palestinian army has not failed because of a lack of courage, not because of a lack of commitment, but because of the lack of the correct moral tactics. You are using your weakest point to attack the Israelis strongest point — their army.

Your solution: massive, economic civil-disobedience. All Palestinians residing inside and outside the borders of Israel must gather into small enclaves and plan the beginning of their return. To accomplish this, you do what the Jews did after World War II — you invade Israel. You invade it not with guns blazing, but in peace; not with a military army, but with an unarmed civilian army comprised of everyone that can walk, crawl, or be carried to the borders of Israel. Because they were denied entry to neighboring Arabic countries, the Jews were handicapped when they came to Palestine. They could only invade from the sea, but you will have access to the entire Israeli border for your invasion.

The British put the Jews they caught coming into Palestine into concentration camps and then tried to expel them back to Europe. So, when you cross the border, you also, will be arrested and interned in a concentration camp. If you are prepared, they will have no place to return you; because all Arab countries must refuse to let you be sent back to exile. "How will we cross the border," you might well ask. "Every single foot is fenced and mined and patrolled, so how can we get through?" It is true that the Israelis have spent billions of dollars to fight a conventional war with their Arab neighbors. They have the best planes, the best tanks, the best missiles, and so forth, so they can defeat an Arab army that attacks them, but all this armament is useless in the type of struggle you will embark on — massive, economic civil-disobedience.

When you organize, you will need a symbol to show your commitment, to show your solidarity, to show that you believe in nonviolent civil disobedience. As a symbol and as a badge of honor, you will have tattooed on the arm of every member of your family an identical tattooed number. The tattoos will be needed to reunite those families separated in the confusion that is bound to happen in your struggle. Those first few thousand mothers and fathers that will be interned in the concentration camps might have their children taken away from them as punishment, but when the number exceeds their capability to handle them, the children will be interned with their parents. However, the main reason for you to tattoo numbers on your arms, is that — in your struggle for redress of your grievances — you are going to deliberately use the tattoos for the psychological protection that they will give you against the Jews behaving in an inhuman manner.

Although crossing the border looks formidable because of the use of double fences with detection sensors, mine fields, and patrolling soldiers, just know that it is only working so successfully because it is set up to handle the few isolated crossings of small teams of infiltrators. It cannot handle tens of thousands of people cutting the fences in thousands of places and crossing at the same time. If possible, you will do your crossing in the daytime, and the cutting of the fences should be done by an unarmed Palestinian army if there is the danger of being shot at when cutting through it. All those crossing will be unarmed and will not run or try to escape from an Israeli patrol; you will allow yourself to be captured and interned in a concentration camp.

Now a warning: there will be Palestinians who will see this as an opportunity for soldiers to hide among the returning refugees, to bring explosives and guns across figuring that a large percentage will get through. Free yourselves of these thoughts, this error of judgment. You will not jeopardize the lives of your men, women, and children. You will not send armed soldiers among them, and thereby, subject the returning refugees to the chance of being shot at as terrorists. You will not give the Israeli soldiers that excuse. At as many crossing points as possible, you should have independent outside news sources photographing and reporting the crossings on each side of the border. This is to let the outside world know that this is a peaceable, nonviolent invasion.

Because this is going to be an economic, civil-disobedience war, all refugees crossing the border will carry no money or wealth; if they do, what will happen will be that those with assets will have them confiscated to pay for the transportation and expenses of the internment of those without property. All Palestinians with property must set up a system to safeguard their wealth before they cross the border. You will not burden yourselves with household items or even with a change of clothing; you will bring no money with you, because you will live off the land. You will become human locusts — a plague on the land.

Those Arabs on the West Bank and Gaza Strip who own property will not be expected to endanger their property by participating in some tactics that I am about to advocate, because all they would accomplish would be to have the Israelis confiscate the land and business and turn it over to

Jewish ownership. If they can find a way to transfer their property into foreign control so it would not be confiscated, then they should join in the following tactics: the day set for the "Crossing" will be the same time when all those on the West Bank and Gaza Strip who are going to participate in this massive, economic civil-disobedience will migrate out of their villages and cities toward Israel. There will be no protesting in the Arab cities or villages, no rock throwing, no bomb throwing, just a peaceable exodus. Mothers and fathers will bring all their children; they will bring their old, their crippled, their sick with them. From here on they will live off the land. They will go into the Jewish fields and feed off the fruits and vegetables produced by their land; in the cities they will go into Jewish food stores and eat and feed themselves off the shelves. They will enter Jewish restaurants and order meals and refuse to pay for them; they will enter Jewish hotels and occupy the rooms and refuse to pay for them; they will go into Jewish clothing stores and put new clothes on themselves and their children and refuse to pay for them.

Those who owned houses and business that were confiscated will go to them and tell the occupants that the property belongs to you, a Palestinian; and you, as the rightful owner, have returned to claim it. When arrested you will plead not guilty and demand a jury trial to determine who owns it, who has a rightful claim. You will inform the Jewish courts that the Jews who survived the Holocaust looked for the return of their property, even though it was occupied by Germans who had received it legally under the color of German confiscation laws; and you request the same rights to the return of your property even though the Jews occupying it now received it legally under the Jewish confiscation laws.

All those crossing the border will try to reach an Israeli city and resort to the same tactics. Yes, you will be arrested, but you will plead not guilty and demand a jury trial. You will not resist being arrested, but when you arrive at the police station, you will not cooperate. If they interview you, you will remain silent. You will only identify yourself by the number tattooed on your arm. Your object is to create chaos, confusion, disorder. The Israelis have the means to control a few thousand people, but when they have to deal with a million prisoners (and that should be your goal), then they will be helpless to control the situation. You will put up no bail and refuse to be released on your own recognizance. You will pay no fine, and when you serve your time, you will immediately go out and get arrested again. You will not allow the Jews to get out of the financial burden of feeding, housing, and clothing the convicted Palestinians by letting them set up United Nations displaced persons' camps inside Israel, the West Bank, or Gaza Strip.

Because they know the truth of what has been happening to the

Palestinians, to show their solidarity, you will find that many secular and religious Jews will join you in those concentration camps. Many of these Jews will realize that to survive as a nation, Israel will be in a precarious position if it lost the support of the United States; they understand that there must be a settlement before there is an economic collapse in the United States. They understand that the Jewish problem in the United States has not been solved for all times, because the economic conditions in the United States have not been solved for all times. Comes an economic depression, and once again the Jews will be one of the minorities, irrationally, blamed for it. When that happens, if there has not been a settlement, it could lead to the annihilation of the Jewish people in the Middle East.

If successful, what will the Palestinians achieve? You can get a Palestinian homeland on the West Bank and Gaza Strip and the removal of all Jewish settlements from them. You can get compensation for all the private property seized by the Israelis and have a secular law giving equal treatment, for the Arabs that remain in Israel. You might even get the permanent Jewish immigration stopped until every Jew and Arab in Israel and Palestine is being fed, clothed, and housed decently. What you will not get and what you do not need, is an army. From such a meager amount of resources — that would be available to them in their allotted homeland — there is no way the Palestinians can support an army and at the same time, their people.

What will the Jews receive in this peace treaty? First: They will still have a homeland; they will survive as a state without having to resort to the same holocaust measures that were used on them. Second: They will have peace on their borders. This does not mean they can disband their army. The Israeli and Palestinian problem of too many people also confronts all the Arab nations that surround them. The only way those Arab states can use Israel for their excess populations is through genocide of the Jewish people, and the only method Israel can use to support its surplus population is to commit genocide against the Arabs.

Because the Jewish and Moslem governments will not be secular, in this struggle for equality, what the two of them desperately need, they will not get, and that is one child per family until the population is reduced to its carrying capacity. This can only be attained under secular governments that are not biased by a religion. "Never again" carries the responsibility of seeing that it does not happen again to the Jewish people, but also that the Jews do not inflict it on another nationality. It is not what is best for the Orthodox Jewish or Muslim religions, but what is best for the Palestinian and Jewish people that should determine the actions of those engaged in this struggle.

The Arabs and Jews should both reflect on the following: The protective herd — an evolutionary method of protection — is useless against an assault by a person flying over it and killing all the bunched-up animals with a machine-gun. Instead of protecting the individuals, the compacting, the gathering of the animals into a herd can become a liability when modern weapons are used against them. All those millions of years of evolution where billions of individual animals were sacrificed by nature to create the herd as a protection device is negated within a few minutes. The Jews in Israel have also created, through sacrifices by millions of individuals under natural selection, a group of people with superior capabilities of surviving in a hostile environment; the sad fact is that it can also be negated by using similar tactics against them.

But the Arabs have nothing to gain here, because if they threaten the extermination of the Jewish population, they also are vulnerable to modern weapons. The Jews know that defeat means their annihilation in the Middle East; and they might (as the last resort) use their atomic weapons (yes, they have them) to destroy not only all the capital cities within reach, but might also destroy the holy cities of Mecca and Medina. If there are just large holes in the desert where Mecca and Medina stood, how will the surviving Mullahs explain this to the Muslim world?

CHAPTER 28

NARRATIVE: RELEASED

Dr. Bromberg had predicted in court that I would need at least one or two years of treatment before I would be able to stand trial. Therefore, on this assumption, he signed the doctor's certificate stating that I needed to be treated in a civil mental institution. So, when I signed myself into DeWitt Hospital, I was treated like the other patients; I was treated as mentally ill.

A good explanation can be found in the study called "On Being Sane in Insane Places." This is an account of some experiments performed by Dr. Rosehan and eight colleagues, five men and three women, with Stanford University as the educational binder. These men and women were admitted to twelve different hospitals with the fraudulent complaint of hearing voices. After admittance, all pseudo-patients informed the staff that their symptoms had disappeared; but! it still required from seven to fifty-two days to be released with the diagnoses of "Schizophrenic in remission." In this hoax not one psychiatrist, nurse, or attendant suspected that the patients were not mentally ill. They were all treated as if they were, which was the crux of the experiment. Later, a hospital, which was well acquainted with the experiment, was told that one or two pseudo-patients would try, in a three month period, to gain admittance to their hospital. Of the approximately 190 patients admitted during that period, twenty-three were alleged to be fraudulent patients by the attending psychiatrists. Interestingly, not one pseudo-patient was sent by the experimenters. One other thought-provoking fact came out: the true patients in these mental hospitals were sometimes able to detect the fraudulent patients and even guess that they were in some way connected to an investigation.

Another case worth commenting on occurred just a few years ago. A new psychiatric worker who treated the mentally retarded, noticed that one adult resident, who had, it was established later, been at the hospital since his birth, showed some signs of reacting differently to some situations than other patients. When tested, to everyone's surprise, he proved to be normal. Still, all his actions were of the typical mentally retarded. When his background was looked into, there came the realization that he was never tested before. Being raised with the mentally retarded, he had adopted their mannerisms; he was able to blend into his environment so well, that he was indistinguishable from the other mentally retarded. When he was growing up in the hospital, he thought that how the mentally retarded acted was the correct way, so having no other reference point, he used the other retarded patients as his role models. Although his records were not complete, it seemed that his mother, who worked at the hospital, had him out of wedlock; she had a doctor working at the hospital (maybe the father) sign the papers saying that he was mentally retarded. Further tests proved that he was of normal intelligence, but severely handicapped because of his being raised in an institutional environment.

Whereas the other patients and the volunteer help that I came into contact with, were quizzically inclined to question my being at DeWitt Hospital, all the doctors, except one, believed that I was mentally ill. If I had wanted to, I could have stayed there indefinitely, but I would have had to put on the trappings of a mental patient. I would have had to do a balancing act where, if I slipped, I could have, as in Vacaville, landed in that room where they send pulsating current through your container of memories.

The question about staying in the hospital arose because my court-appointed attorney, Mr. Zarick, had written me, twice, that the U.S. Assistant Attorney, Mr. Woodward, was trying to get the U.S. Justice Department in Washington D.C. to drop all charges against me as I was incarcerated in a state mental institution. But it seemed that someone back in Washington D.C., did not want to make that decision to release me. I came to the conclusion that it would be too dangerous for me to wait and depend on the Justice Department eventually giving Mr. Woodward permission. I speculated that they had information and files on me that maybe the U.S. Assistant Attorney did not have access to.

Although I did not give the doctors at DeWitt Hospital an excuse to prolong my stay there, it still took four months before they would certify that I was ready for discharge as a "Schizophrenic in remission." Because of the excessively crowded conditions at the hospital, the hospital administration wrote my attorney and the U.S. Assistant Attorney in

Sacramento, California that I was ready for discharge as the hospital staff agreed that I had no further need of hospitalization. They went on to explain that they needed the space I occupied for patients who truly needed to be hospitalized. (Beds were six inches apart in my ward, and the other patients and I, had to crawl over the foot of our beds to get into them at night.) All they received were requests that I be kept at the hospital until I could be taken to court. Finally, John A. Mitchell, Superintendent and Medical Director at DeWitt State Hospital, had to threaten the U.S. Attorney that he would release me from the hospital unless arrangements were made to pick me up by the date that he specified.

Soon after, on October 15, 1963, I was hurriedly removed by two U.S. Marshals and returned to the Sacramento County Jail. When the U.S. Marshals arrived to transport me to Sacramento, they told me, out of deference to my sensibilities I am sure, that they would not put handcuffs on me until we arrived at their automobile, which was outside in the parking lot. When I started to laugh, I could see the worry that appeared in their eyes. I did not have the heart to tell them that I knew they were coming and had debated whether I should catch a bus down to Sacramento and walk into their office and tell them, "Here I am. I wanted to save you the trouble of coming and getting me." Not wanting to make a farce of their escorting me to the county jail, in handcuffs, I said nothing.

It was just a forty-five minute drive to the Sacramento County Jail, where once again I took up residence. When I was called out of my cell a few days later and brought downstairs to the interview room, I was sure that this would be my final confrontation with Dr. Bromberg. I was about to enter that interview room with confidence; had I not deceived him three times before? We never seem to learn to expect the unexpected, and I was no exception. Opening the door to the small room, I was confronted not with Dr. Bromberg, but with an unknown face staring at me from behind the small desk in the room. I knew that a look of shock and amazement appeared on my face before I had a chance to tell it to rearrange those facial features into a bland expression. I should have expected this, because from the questions and demeanor of the U.S. Assistant Attorney in that court hearing in March, I had detected a note of disbelief about them finding me able to stand trial at the mental institutions, but found by Dr. Bromberg to be medically ill and in need of further treatment. To test my true abilities at deception, Mr. Woodward had used his powers to deal me a new psychiatrist. But it was too late, in my two and a half years of contact with fellow patients and the staff of mental hospitals, I had gained too much insight into the working minds of psychiatrists to be afraid of those who professed to have a science, but which I knew only too well to be a sham. Good con men and women will freely admit that they are not able to escape or detect someone else running a good con game.

The surprise of not knowing in advance that there was going to be a different psychiatrist to examine me was to instantly give me the new tactic needed to open that final door that would lead me to sunlight that was not filtered between iron bars. The words "Open Sesame" were what Ali Baba used to open the cave door; the single word "Paranoia" was to be used by me to open that last door barring me from continuing my interrupted journey south. I took the offensive immediately. Instead of answering questions put to me by the new doctor, I began to question him. I asked him, who he was; and if he was a psychiatrist, why had not my attorney informed me that I was going to be examined again? Had I not just come back from DeWitt Hospital where they said that I was ready and able to stand trial? When he asked me, "Who do you think I am," and "what do you believe that I am here for?" I told him that he might be a detective or FBI agent sent from the prosecution's office to try to trick me into giving him information, to make it easier to convict me. When the new psychiatrist pulled out his impressive identification and showed it to me, I knew that the U.S. Assistant Attorney had thrown into the pot his last chip, which was in the shape of a key. From that moment I knew that I held the winning hand. A few more subtle insinuations that I was not satisfied with his identification because law enforcement people would come prepared with false identification, and so he was still a suspect in my mind, were all that I needed. When I told him that I could not fully trust him not to betray the information I gave him, the interview came to a close.

When he concluded his interview and was waiting for the elevator to take him downstairs, I gave him a final salvo of words to blast loose all the doubt he had left about my paranoia. In a pleading and quaking voice, with my hands gripping tightly the iron bars that separated us, I blurted out, "Maybe you are who you say you are, and if you are a psychiatrist, then you just have to find me sane enough to stand trial. I cannot stand much more of this confinement, this not knowing, this uncertainty. I am sane now, but I will go insane if I do not go to trial soon." I then turned and walked away from the bars as I muttered in a low voice, but not low enough so he could not hear or understand my words, "Boy! I must be losing my mind, pleading like this to a policeman." Before I could say more, the door of the elevator appeared and opened on cue; he stepped into it to be whisked away to some office, where he would be confronted with his dismal science when he tried to explain my observed behavior; never knowing or understanding that my mental state could only be explained with my full cooperation, which he did not have.

It came as no surprise, when, within a few days of the last interview, I was released without bail into the custody of my aunt. They had no place to send me; so, my assessment was correct when I made that decision to act normal at DeWitt Hospital instead of playing insane and hoping they would drop the charges after a couple of years of confinement.

A short time after my release without bail, I once again found myself standing in front of the United States Federal Judge, the Honorable Sherrill Halbert. My appointed counsel, Mr. Zarick had already informed me that all charges of bank robbery were to be dropped, and so I knew that there was no need to put on an act. There were two things of interest that took place that day: one was that the U.S. Assistant Attorney had to ask Judge Halbert how to go about dropping the case against me. The other was the remarks of Federal Judge Sherrill Halbert: "It's about time, you dropped the charges. If you had listened to me, this case could have been disposed of a long time ago."

Two years and eight months had flowed from the calendar since I had been stopped that spring day of April 22, 1961. When I had time to review those years, I was surprised when I found that I had not grown bitter over the impediments that had plagued me. What I had learned could only have been learned under those extreme adversities. I eventually would come to miss the struggle, miss the pitting, in the arena, of my mind against theirs. But the knowledge gained of other human beings I met in those institutions, and the helplessness of some of those to do anything to alleviate their suffering, would remain fixed in my mind. It was something to ponder over, something to coordinate into future thoughts, something to try to explain why them and not me. I, myself, drew strength from my enemies defeat, and in some ways I was a far stronger person than when I began my unequal battle against them. How else can you find out that it is useless to try to change society until you change yourself by eliminating all false information and beliefs that you have been indoctrinated with, than by observing the results of false beliefs and information on humanity. No matter how noble and sublime they are, these false beliefs will not enable a person to change into a civilized person. Changes adopted because of a false belief cannot now, or could not in the past, be permanently reconciled with reality.

NARRATIVE: BELIEVERS

After my release, my life did not come to a standstill; I continued to learn from my new environment. Some encounters that I vividly remember took place over a period of a year with a religious group who came regularly to my door.

Their formation and dress code fascinated me; men and women never arrived singularly; the dress code required all the women to wear dresses and the men to always wear a suit and tie when they faithfully made their rounds. Arriving in late model cars, the young, dedicated believers, led by their elders, would fan out like precisely trained troops, and go from door to door. They always smiled, even when you shut the door in their faces or were so rude as to suggest that you had doubts about their church. They would be here, at my house, telling me about the great change it would make in my life if I joined "The True Church." The answers to all the world's problems were in the Bible cradled under their arms, with several bookmarks strategically placed to mark the answers to current problems so they would not lose their valuable time in solving them. The past and future were all explained to those who had faith to believe in their interpretations. Were they not living proof that "He" was on their side? It could be read in their demeanor!

Always with them was an older leader who would answer the questions that the young people were too inexperienced to answer. One of those leaders who came to my door was named John. "If I can save just one person by bringing him into the church, then my life is complete," John told me when I asked why they worked so hard to recruit new members. John also told me that he had never brought into the church a "True Atheist" like me, and so he had discussed with other members how to save me. There came a day when he asked me if there was anything that he could do or say that would bring me into the church. Surprised by the question, I asked him to let me think about it for a couple of weeks. When he came back, I told him that there might be a way to make a believer and a convert out of me, but he and his family had to be prepared to make a great sacrifice. If he could prove to me that he and his family had unlimited faith and he did what I said, I would spend the rest of my life trying to bring others into the fold. What John had to do to convert me was to turn over to me everything he and his family owned, with the prospect that I might give it back by being converted, but I could keep it if I wished to. I assured him that I felt sure that his God would reward him either here or at some other place and time if he gave his wealth to me.

The outcome? Monetarily, I am still a poor atheist and John is still a wealthy member of the "Only True Church." Think about it. If you were a true believer, what would you have done? Here is some information for you to use in making up your mind. I would have kept everything if John had put it into my name. Why? Because John's reward, for bringing me into the church, would have been his knowledge that he brought me into "The Only True Church" which, if his belief is true, is far above the monetary gain that I would have obtained. Would I truly have believed if John had turned everything over to me? Certainly not, just because you have the finesse to con a person out of their property is no reason to accept a false belief.

The result, John's martyrdom would not in itself prove anything. Because then, if a Buddhist made that sacrifice, I would have to accept Buddhism as my belief, or if a Muslim did the sacrificing, I would have to accept the Koran as the only source of religious truth. The beliefs and sacrifices that other individuals make, have no bearing on the truth. The sacrifice of a saint's life for their religion, or the sacrifice of a Russian soldier's life for Stalin, or the sacrifice of a German soldier's life for Hitler cannot be construed to mean that their cause was righteous and would triumph, or was even worthwhile because they gave their lives; nor can they be cited as signifying that one cause is more valid than the other. What John would be trying to do is to buy something that he claims money cannot buy; and I was willing to sell because I believe that this, the earth, is the one and only market for "Immortal Souls." All true churches and all true political beliefs must indoctrinate and brainwash their individual members into believing that their true church or true political belief is unique and different; that their motives are pure and uncontaminated; and only their members have the knowledge of the goal and the precise ritual needed to arrive at that goal.

From observing and talking to the constant parade of religious believers who came to my door, I came to realize that there was no difference among us that could be changed by me pointing out the observed contradiction in their beliefs. It was the same when I was immersed in my beliefs; I did not believe my reactions to my beliefs were different from theirs. I came to realize that the truth cannot be forever denied, so that I did not have to change someone's belief with arguments, because events would by natural and human selection, eliminate all falsehoods.

When the bank robbery charge was dropped, I did not return to Los Angeles or even try to contact the underground of my Party. I had reasoned that someone in the Party who had known about my activities had given misinformation to a far-right group who had framed me. This betrayal bothered me. It bothered me in the extreme, as only the few underground members who knew about my work could have betrayed me. The Socialist Party that I joined was openly against all forms of terror and betrayal, especially those perpetrated under the name of socialism in the Soviet Union. Many members had defected from the American Communist Party because of their revulsion of what was happening there. The party members who I personally met, in the short time that I was a regular member, all condemned the repressive tactics used in the Soviet Union against the opposition. They always expressed to me a belief in a free socialistic society, and professed a belief in morality, in justice, and in the dignity of all human beings, just as I did.

Between my arrest for bank robbery, and my release two and a half years later, my mind dwelt on this betrayal. It was only when I went back to the basic law that all human beings are here because of natural and human selection, and to be a survivor you had to have genes that selected for selfishness, that I could see that this animal trait will always dominate us. I eventually saw that from outside the power structure, human beings can afford to condemn the selfishness of those who held power, but once we acquire that power, most of us will also act in a selfish way. All governments in power believe that they are the chosen; that they have a duty to hold that power even if it means condemning to death the opposition. I realized that if my Party came to power, it would, like all political parties before it, eventually become corrupt; belonging to a political or religious group does not change us from selfish human beings into unselfish ones. Only natural selection, combined with human selection can do that, and only if the pressure of competition is removed can this happen. I realized that it was useless to return to the Party and try to inform its members what was going on in our Party's underground. Only from outside the party structure could I have the time to analyze it. This comes about strictly because when you are working for a political party, you do not have the time needed to analyze, to ponder, or to weigh the true economic picture. When I understood this, I was able to delve into communistic and capitalistic ideologies and learn that I had gone astray because I had blindly accepted beliefs from the Marxist Bible as facts that had been verified.

ESSAY: ON IMPERIALISM AND GENOCIDE

Without rationalizing it, intentional genocide, committed as the result of imperialism or past imperialistic intervention or immigration, is an act of eliminating competition by resorting to an arbitrary human decision rather than letting nature (evolution), over a long period of time, eliminate the less fit. By going outside natural selection to human selection, you can by an arbitrary method of choosing, designate who the less fit are, but with this method you also eliminate some genes that under natural selection might have proven superior and thus, in natural competition, replaced the descendants of those who are now doing the arbitrary selection. If those who commit genocide could hold power forever, this might be a good strategy to follow, but when they lose the power to decide, then there is no place to appeal to if the new ruling group declares you less fit, declares that you are surplus. The reason: there is no method to prove you are superior if there is no criteria to meet, no set standard to live up to, no test to pass that can overcome and overrule an arbitrary decision. Live by the sword, die by the sword, is apt here.

I describe imperialism as gaining direct or indirect control of either or both the political or economic life of a group of human beings by force of arms, indirect coercions, or by monetary means, so that the national resources and the people's labor can be exploited by those either occupying or living outside the boundaries of the entity being subjugated.

By right of conquest, imperialistic invaders claim absolute dominion and sovereignty to employ the forces of the occupied state to enforce and make legal all its arbitrary laws. They can declare that all forms of resistance by the occupied entity are treasonable, that any resort to propaganda, armed struggle, or sabotage is mutiny, and that any assassination of the occupying force, its approved local government, or those who cooperate with them, is terrorism.

You cannot dissect and correctly examine imperialism if you view it as some recent esoteric practice of a few large nations. Even a cursory inspection will show that it has massive roots that can be traced to the formation of the first tribal groups that needed to expand their territory because of growth. It is the same law observed in the animal kingdom that gives the strong the right to exploit and even to kill the weak.

History shows a country's reaction to imperialism and genocide is always from the point of view of whether it is the subjugated or the subjugator. Even today, large, strong countries believe they have the right to exploit weaker countries. Extending imperialism to its logical conclusion, Germany in the 1930s and '40s viewed the weaker, smaller, surrounding countries as imperialistic meat. But the other imperialistic nations (Britain, France, Spain, and others) were alerted to the fact that this could lead to anarchy. These small countries surrounding Germany were not backward, uncivilized, unchristianed nations, which were some of the major imperialistic nations' definitions of whom could be exploitable. Not realizing that they had gained the right to determine those definitions because they were strong enough to enforce them, the dominant, imperialistic nations of the 1930s, believed their definition would last forever. They did not take into account that if they lost their enforceable power, they lost their ability to define what groups of people or countries were eligible to be victimized.

Germany, under Hitler, had as much right ("Right of Might") to set the rules for subjugation of her neighbors as did Britain, France, Spain, and the other imperialistic countries when they colonized and subjugated other lands. After all, these imperialistic empires had also made their arbitrary rules based on strength alone. When the American Colonies were under the rule of British imperialism, they objected to being treated as subjects without the legal right to protest laws (made in Britain without their consent) that were detrimental to them. Understand: The American

Colonies did not object to imperialism per se, just that, as British subjects, they could be viewed as inferior to those who were raised and educated in Britain.

Very few historians dispute the statement: when the young United States conquered the land and people from coast to coast, it had to use imperialism for that expansion. In 1803 they bought from France the Louisiana Territory, thereby doubling the size of the country. In the 1848 treaty, Mexico ceded to the United States their claim to Texas, California, Arizona, New Mexico, Nevada, Utah, and a part of Colorado. In 1867 they purchased Alaska from the Russians. At no time were those residing in these territories consulted or asked their opinion of whether they wanted to be purchased or ceded from one imperialistic country to another. The rest of the United States was also annexed from the native populations by imperialistic force of arms.

The true imperialistic America can be ascertained by examining the brutal war waged against the Philippinos who had declared an independent republic in 1898. It is estimated that at the conclusion of the war in 1906, up to one-seventh of the population (one million Philippinos) were obliterated. Many of the dead were civilian men, women, and children who died of disease and neglect in concentration camps erected and run by American soldiers. The United States atrocities in the Philippines were as cruel and brutal as any conflict in the history of imperialism. Because they were taught otherwise, today, most American citizens do not consider themselves imperialistic; they approve of all the above acquisitions and consider it was their "Manifest Destiny" to do so.

"Manifest Destiny; Spheres of Influence; The Right of Expansion; Balance of Power; The Right of Containment; The Right to Secure Borders; Divine Rights of Kings" are some of the phrases used for a foreign policy of "Imperialism." The United States people, by absorbing the territories, obtained by imperialistic might or purchase, and giving them the same rights the rest of the United States had, believed that they were constructed differently than other imperialistic states.

The extermination of the entire native population of Tasmania can be used to show what happens when an occupied petri dish is invaded by an imperialist strain of human beings. Tasmania (26,178 sq. mi.), a little smaller than the Irish Republic (27,137 sq. mi.), supported a population of about 5,000 hunter-gatherers when discovered in 1642. Mostly white, Christian, English settlers and sealers began their imperialistic invasion in 1800. The first settlers immediately began killing off the men and kidnapping the aboriginal women and children to be used as slaves. It is pure genocide when a government can officially and legally make and post a law (that the native population cannot read) saying that the white population is allowed to kill on sight, any aboriginal man, woman or child that is seen in a settled area. Thirty years after the invasion, all the remaining Tasmanians had been rounded up and removed thirty miles away to Flinders Island, where in November of 1830, they were reduced to seventy-two adult men and three adult women. The "final-solution" to the native population was accomplished when in 1876, the last full-blooded Tasmanian women died. Today, the offspring of those native women who were raped and used as concubines by the white settlers and sealers, represent the only remaining gene pool of the Tasmanians.

The problem: The environment in Tasmania could not support both the hunter-gatherers, who needed a large area to support their population of 5,000, and the arriving settlers, who needed the land to grow crops and graze their livestock on. The cultures are mutually exclusive, because the hunter-gatherers, who did not understand that someone could own the land, would view the planted crops as something to gather and eat, and the livestock as something to kill and eat. Because the invaders could support a larger population (417,000 in 1987) on the same amount of land, the Tasmanians were at a disadvantage. The natives were so widely dispersed, they could not make a common defense against the invaders, so individual tribal groups were massacred, without them even knowing that they were at war. Of course individuals and tribes when alerted, did fight back, but from the beginning, it was a hopeless and uneven battle.

The Tasmanian history books (like most of the North, South, and Central American ones) depict the imperialistic occupation and genocide of the native population as a glorious battle for civilization. The Tasmanian authors do not stress the facts that the invaders had to subdue people that had only some simple stone and wooden tools, people who did not have the boomerang or the bow and arrow to fight back with. They lacked agriculture and livestock, did not produce pottery or have a written language, have nets for fishing, know how to sew, or have the ability to start a fire. And how did the Christian church, the defenders of morality, react to these atrocities? In the late 1820s, they formed a commission and considered proposals to capture the remaining aboriginals for sale as slaves or to poison or use animal traps to kill them off.

In this book, when I accuse a group of people of a particular historical crime, it is with the belief and understanding that if conditions were reversed and those being oppressed had the power, they would act in the same manner. We commit genocide not because of our race, religion, political beliefs, or nationality, but because we are all human beings that react to a limited environment in the same manner. To believe otherwise is in itself racist, because you would have to be saying that there is a biological difference in human beings who are imperialistic or commit genocide. If they have the power, a minority culture will — like the white minority in South Africa — discriminate just as harshly as a majority. And when they win their independence, former colonies will act toward competition for a limited environment in the same manner as their former imperialistic masters; they will resort to the same criminal acts that were perpetrated on them.

When Indonesia, a former colony of the Netherlands, won their independence in 1949, they demanded that West New Guinea become part of Indonesia, even though the people living there had a different ethnic background in language, religion, and culture. Solely on the claim that Western New Guinea and Indonesia were both ruled under the title of Netherland East Indies, it became a colony of Indonesia, and was named West Irian. By being invaded by the surplus people of Indonesian, the same type of slaughter that happened in Tasmania is happening in New Guinea. Former colonies, when they become imperialistic, act in the same detrimental way toward their invaded territory; they still have ethnic problems when they throw off the imperialistic yoke, still commit genocide against other human beings, still invade neighboring countries for Lebensraum.

Imperialism and genocide are a reaction of animals to the environment; there are no differences between those who commit them, except those who commit them have the power and ability to carry them out. If you believe that imperialistic nations are different, that people who commit genocide are different, then you cannot explain what has happened and is happening in the world today; you cannot reconcile the past with what is happening now. You cannot explain why the Jews, who have been grievously mistreated for generations, can do the same thing to the Palestinians. Trying to prove that Germans in the 1930s and '40s, were different from the surrounding states, is an impossibility. Germany was and still is a Christian nation, where 90 percent believe in a Supreme Being, believe in the miracles described in the Bible, believe in Jesus Christ. The German soldiers and people believed that they were fighting for a just cause; they mindlessly gave up their lives, because they believed God was on their side. Even Hitler believed that there was a God, and what he was doing had the approval of that God. The people carrying out the extermination of the prisoners in the concentration camps, did not believe they were doing anything wrong. All through World War II, the Germans attended church, got married in the church, were baptized in the church, prayed in the church, and believed that those they were killing had been legitimately condemned by the state, so they did not feel guilty about it. (Many Christians around the world still believe in the commandment "thou shall not kill," but believe that it is alright for a government to kill human beings if they were condemned by law; even arbitrary imperialistic laws.) The sad part is that all cultures are capable of killing.

True: Discrimination is taught, but its roots are not divorced from the environment. It evolves and is stored in the genes to protect a living organism from other living organism in competition with it for limited food and shelter. If the other organism is obviously different from us, it means beware, be careful, as it might mean danger, it might mean competition for our food and shelter; and this all had to be incorporated into our genes, because for billions of years there was no other language to learn to discriminate between them and us. We know it still survives in animals without language and in us because we still react negatively to anything or anyone that is different from or in competition with us.

When the environment is limited and in contention, all that is needed is something to distinguish between them and us for the killing to begin. In Tasmania, it was in the settlers' genes' interest to believe that blacks were inferior, that they were heathen because their religion was not Christian. It was in their interest to discriminate and commit genocide, and history shows that the settlers' imperialistic genes were correct, because their genes did survive.

If you believe we were made by a God, you cannot explain discrimination and genocide as a natural animal process. Most religious people cannot accept their descent from other animals, that their animal genes make them commit their animal acts; that discrimination and genocide are genetically programmed into our genes; that we are only responding to a stimulus of a limited resource that we are in competition for.

Because it is exhibited by all human beings, imperialistic discrimination and genocide are not just a capitalistic, feudalistic, or fascistic trait. Even today, ethnic turmoil still exists in all socialistic countries that have minorities. Marxism cannot adequately explain what happened in Tasmania; cannot explain imperialistic discrimination and genocide, nor internal discrimination and genocide in a pluralistic society. Nations becoming socialistic, continued to discriminate, to commit genocide against minorities, which proves that who owned the means of production, does not change our animal behavior, because it does not change our genetic inheritances. When there is a shortage of goods in any system, the distributors need to determine who will be discriminated against, blamed and punished for that shortage. If a nation is comprised of only one religious sect, one ethnic group, one level of income, one political party, then it would be hard to discriminate, but still (unless it was done by lottery) an arbitrary way would have to be found if the distribution would determine who would live and who would die.

CHAPTER 29

ESSAY: COMPREHENSIVE THOUGHTS

As Lewis Carroll might have said, "Now is the time to talk about cabbages and kings and speculate on why Pandas have developed five fingers and a thumb; and time should be taken to theorize on why writers have this odd belief that they can change the perceptions of other animals by sorting and rearranging words into sentences."

Although the many freedoms that I enjoy from being born in the United States were conceived mainly by immigrants fleeing from the poverty of their land and the tyranny of their rulers, I have always felt guilty that they were animal, tribal freedoms, and so were not implemented or given to the inhabitants who met them on the shores. Today, the adoption of a culture where the industrialization of work and the compacting of human beings into an urban environment — mistakenly equated to civilization simply because we keep written records — is at the core of my discontent. You cannot put animals in the middle of some machinery and expect them to be civilized because they learn to run it. All you have are tame animals engaged in perverting their natural ability to adapt to strange circumstances. The outcome of human beings adopting this or some other strange culture: they will persist and endure as animals with animal needs and wants.

This arrangement of civilization can philosophically be compared to the once prevalent custom (now, rejoicingly replaced) of binding the feet of female children to prevent their growth. The binding was used by those who could afford it, to produce a status symbol of a useless, idle woman, to show the lower class peasants, who needed their women to work around the house and in the fields, that it took a superior person to provide this leisure for their women. This caused these women, these status symbols, to hobble around on ugly, distorted, pain-riddled stumps of useless flesh, instead of having the use of naturally adaptive, clean-lined appendages, produced by natural selection for walking and running free.

If you think of those bindings as civilization and being used on the human mind, then from this you can infer and understand what happens in society to make individuals become ugly, distorted lumps of useless flesh that fill our prisons and mental hospitals. We condemn these human beings to hobble through life with warped minds, and all the time, we keep informing them that societies — the bindings — are not responsible for these distortions; that the bindings are meant as a benevolent gift, a gift that will free them from the burden of an animal existence and from the burden of depending on natural things.

They give us as models those who can ignore the pain and have personally managed to go great distances with their distortions. These individuals can ignore their pain to such an extent that they can also inflict it on other human beings. They cannot understand why the binding-caused screams of pain coming from their prisons and hospitals are not ignored. They claim that they bind the mind in the name of a grand design that they can detect hidden from view by those bindings. And when the bindings are removed, they point with pride when the misshapen, rotted mass is revealed, and claim that this is the true and ordained way for society to proceed. They claim their bindings improve on nature, and the useless minds that they produce, are things of beauty. How is their view different from the cultures that viewed the hobbling around on useless stumps of flesh, produced by binding the feet, as a thing of beauty and grace?

As we age, we tend to slowly merge into and subside into what seems a static form of existence. But do not be fooled as this is just a temporary form that can be reversed overnight by circumstances that threaten us and our families. We will do it reluctantly, but we are all capable of uniting behind the barricades when our life is threatened. There is a natural political law that reads: If the ruling class feels it might be replaced, the oppression in that country is in direct proportion to that jeopardy. Historically, you will find that this law affects and intrudes into all forms of government. Just because the government in the United States has, except in a few isolated instances, been lenient toward dissent does not imply that it is better than the Communist states; it is just that it was not, and is not now, under the pressure that the Communist governments feel from their populations. When the American government feels threatened by revolution, then, to protect its privileges, you will see the terror that all governments resort to. Ask the American Japanese what happened to their freedoms, guaranteed by the United States Constitution, when the government felt that it was threatened by them. If the United States Supreme Court could say that what we did to the American Japanese by sending them to concentration camps in World War II was legal and in the national interest, then you can abolish all constitutional safeguards by declaring it so. Then it would legitimize what the Germans and Japanese did to humanity in their national interest.

History shows you do not have to be a threat to your government, just accused of being a threat. With the attainment of equal rights in Western and Central Europe, Jews in those European countries prospered, and so the Jewish population from 1800 to 1840 doubled from 1.5 million to 3.6 million. They truly thought that the "Jewish problem" had been solved. But ask the few German and Polish Jews who survived the Holocaust what happened to the freedoms guaranteed under the German and Polish constitutions? In the 1930s the Jewish population was less than 1 percent of the German population; there was no danger of their taking power. Still, the German government, needing a scapegoat to explain the adversities created by too many Germans in a restrictive space, lied and told the German people that the Jews were an economic and political threat to them. Germany was in the middle of a deep economic depression, so most Germans in this Christian country believed this propaganda. It was to their economic advantage to believe them. In all economic situations where there is a shortage of food, clothing, housing or work to obtain these benefits, no minority is ever safe from the majority, and constitutional rights and guarantees won in today's battle, give no assurance that they will not be taken away in tomorrow's crisis.

Even as I write, the news media is informing us about the tragic plight of the American farmers. They emphatically believe in the "American Dream." Believe that by hard work they can rise above the crowd; that the only thing separating them and the poor is that they are willing to work harder; that the poor are in some way defective in their work habits. The Horatio Alger fiction in which success is achieved through self-reliance and hard work is still with us. The farmers cannot see that when you live under uncontrolled, unplanned economic conditions, there is no way to guarantee success to everyone, because failure is needed to eliminate competition. That is what capitalism is — prosperity at the expense of those who fail. The American farmers did not read the history books that told of children, as young as 6 years old, working hard for 12 and 14 hours a day, seven days a week, without being successful, without rising above the herd. Millions of these children went to an early grave, but we are only told about the lucky one or two that were successful. It never entered their minds that the American Dream is a myth; just another way that governments can use folklore to manipulate them. The American farmers cannot deny their beliefs, so to explain their failed economic conditions, they must look for a scapegoat, look for an outside source. Once again, they are finding one in anti-Semitism. The most flagrant lies against the Jews are once again with us. The distressed American farmers are not about to admit that their economic beliefs are at fault for their plight. When the next depression comes, do not delude yourself that capitalism will take the responsibility when this disaster occurs. All minorities should heed this warning: like Germany, the United States Government will set up its concentration camps and find a minority to blame for the economic collapse.

Karl Marx diagnosed the young capitalist system and was able to say, truthfully, "The modern bourgeois society that has sprouted from the ruins of feudal society has not done away with class antagonism. It has established new classes, new conditions of oppression, new forms of struggle in the place of the old." This statement is still used by the Communists to castigate capitalism, but they cannot see that the same statement today also describes communism. Because they do not allow the Communist Bible to be disputed by free speech or a free press, they have no reference to learn from. They cannot correct the mistakes in it; so they are condemned, like the Christians, like the Moslems, and like all religions that have the written word, to defend the written mistakes inherited in them. They donate their short allotted time on earth in a meaningless and mindless struggle; they are foolish atheists, condemned (by their personal biases) to pray over empty grave-sites; yes, they will spend their time on earth in defending something false because they have no way of detecting that it is false.

As some of us age, we enter into a "Seminary World" in which we believe that our personal prayers or our political beliefs are going to affect natural mathematical laws and change the sums derived from those laws. It is the same mental world in which we believe that our prayers can calm a volcano or stop an earthquake or revolution. When we enter this "Seminary World" we also come to believe that all our needs will be provided for by our chosen system of government. If you believe that somewhere in time, a multitude of 5,000 men, besides the women and children, were fed from five loaves of bread and two fishes, then, you have met your own created Transylvania werewolf; and so you will not be able to reject other absurdities until you realize that it is just allegory, just a symbolic representation.

Today, because of that belief, we are told that the perplexity of the starving human beings we see on our television sets, is simply a problem of donations and distribution, and hunger will vanish and be solved. Because you, as Christians, accepted an impossibility, an absurdity before, then your unperfected minds cannot admit that this is also false reasoning.

And if you are an atheist, then you are told to trust in a God of Science to come up with the answers, to come up with a modern miracle to overcome the shortages of the future. In that tomorrow, the concrete mathematical 1+1=2 will be overruled and be replaced by a Science God who can take a concrete loaf of bread, a concrete fish and feed a multitude with it. Hunger will disappear from the earth; a Scientific Capitalist or Communist God will provide an unlimited population with all the food and consumer goods they need; provide them for ever and ever from a limited supply if they believe in the appropriate communistic or capitalistic system of government.

These common beliefs come about under communism because the Marx, Engels, Lenin Bible is like the Christian Bible, flawed when it tries to extrapolate the past and the present into the future. Because he had no God to consult about the future, Karl Marx, the prophet, had to rely mainly on information from the British Museum, which at that time was perhaps the best available. However, you cannot accurately predict the future if you do not have the correct information, and so you start with false premises. Today we have a 100 years of history that was denied to Karl Marx and information that would have changed many of his views. We also have a 66-year-old Communist government in Russia and several recent ones we can compare to capitalism. Karl Marx had a valid excuse for some of his mistakes. He was, like the rest of us, a fallible human being; so some information was either ignored (Thomas Malthus essay on populations), or the information had recently appeared (Evolution), but not enough evidence was obtainable or known for him to make the correct judgment on these theories. He could see the misery produced by early capitalism, but was not objective enough to see that it was changing many of its harsher acts, that it was in transition, that it was not static, but was still bound by natural laws. He could see the proletarian as a producer, but could not envision that the capitalist would also come to need the working class as consumers. If you just give the workers only enough wages to subsist on, then who will buy the mass production of modern societies needed to keep capitalism growing?

Karl Marx could not see that private property arose, not because it was a natural law that had inevitability written on its overthrow by communism, but because it gave an advantage in human and natural selection, gave an advantage to the individual. Private property helped the offspring of those who had it, to survive and produce more offspring than those who had no land or property to pass on to their children, grandchildren, or relatives. This is the same natural law that territorial animals use. Those that hold a territory, will have an evolutionary edge over those that do not have it.

The English nobility recognized early the importance of not only inheriting the land, but keeping it intact by leaving their estate to the first born son. The reason can readily be seen by a hypothetical, equal distribution of an estate of 10,000 acres to a couple who had five children and divided the estate equally among them. The descendants would each inherit 2000 acres. If these five children each survived, married, and had five children, then continued the equal division, the grand children would receive 400 acres. And if each of them survived and had five children, the next division, to the 125 great-grandchildren, would be about 80 acres each, and if continued, the 625 great-great-grandchildren would receive 16 acres. Let us say that the original estate also had 40 people (20 married couples) working that 10,000 acres; and they, too, produced five children each generation, who all survived to reproduce. Then — when the 625 great-great-grandchildren inherited that 16 acres — there would also be 12,250 great-great-grandchildren from those original workers. They also would also have to live off that original 10,000 acres. It is true, you might find the descendants of the original farm workers in the city working in factories, but still about 12,875 people must get their food from that original 10,000 acre estate, which gives about 0.78 acres per person. From this you should understand the problems that Thomas Malthus was trying to explain; this is why he claimed that populations increase by a geometric ratio while the means of subsistence increase only by arithmetic ratio. Being pragmatic, the nobility not only restricted the inheritance to their first born son, but also controlled the sex lives of their workers; that is why their farm workers and servants had to have permission to marry and produce children. Although undemocratic, this solution of limiting the population cannot be unconditionally condemned. No social group can be completely without merit; they cannot exist without some redeeming social feature.

Communist collective farms are faced with the same problems that the English Nobility had, but they, because of their false beliefs, cannot admit that their farm population cannot keep doubling and remain on the farm. Whether the surplus stays on the farm or goes to work outside of it, their share of farm products must still come in essence from the same amount of acreage. Plus, the entire labor force without a farm background is also doubling, and their food must come from the same source — the finite land. Communist theoreticians equated unequal distribution and under production, under capitalism, with the idea that with their distribution system, they would have no limits on their production or population; thought that capitalism was the only thing limiting everyone in the world from having unlimited consumer goods. Marxists must realize that ideological beliefs cannot increase natural resources or create them when they are not there.

Strength, hidden or exposed, has always been paramount in the relationship of societies. This flows from the premise that if we are endowed with selfish traits manifested physically by our actions, then the adoption of a political or religious belief will not change us when, in competition with other individuals or groups of individuals, we must choose between them and us for a restricted amount of goods and services. If one choice is our own death, or the possibility of it, we will usually choose our life, even if it means death to another human being. And if you do adapt and sacrifice yourself for the benefit of others, this would produce just the opposite of a better world. In the end it would produce a more selfish population because you eliminate your unselfish genes from the gene pool. Because competition for the meager resources is what produces this gene, and because you cannot eject the selfish gene from the breeding pool when there is a restricted amount of resources, we are faced with asking the question, "Is there a solution?"

You can exclude what some human beings would designate as "bad traits" from the human population by controlling breeding, but there is the damn cruel irritation that it cannot be done democratically. The end might justify the means in this situation, but only if you can know and guarantee that good end; and this you cannot do. History shows that the means can change the end and actually cause the opposite of the original intent.

During his life time, Karl Marx changed some of his views as conditions arose that contradicted them, but he never was able to join his beliefs to a world of natural selection, to absorb into his Marxist's Bible information that Malthus and Darwin had already published, to join his beliefs to a concrete past. Lenin, Stalin, and the other leaders that later came on the stage had an extremely difficult time explaining Karl Marx because they had to twist and turn and mash into the preconceived mold of communism, facts that could not be molded into a different shape. Each new fact that appeared to contradict Karl Marx, was even hidden by secrecy and censorship from the ruling class in the Russian Communist Party.

What the Communist Bible tried to do was give modern institutions a life that had no connection with the past. Its claim that how and by whom the goods were produced was the determining feature in our life, was like the claim in the Christian Bible that God created life just a few thousand years ago. In these two Bibles there is no room for human beings before an adduced time; there is no history, no connection with the millions of years of evolution. Wages, prices, surplus values and production miraculously appeared on the stage of history to become dominant in our relationships without a connection to the past. Mass production has only recently been introduced into the world, so it will not account for the history of the human primates before it was introduced. Stating that if the workers own the means of production, then there will be no competition, is too narrow a view and tends to separate us from not only the past, but from the other animals. The means of production does not cause all wars, all revolutions, all economic crises. What is more likely the cause of most of these phenomena are the rise and fall of the human population in two or more contending societies in relationship to the limited amount of resources they each need. Because the Communist states hold title to the land and own the means of production, it *does not lessen the competition by the individual* for his or her share. The modern means of production, however, *does increase* the human beings who can live off a defined area, and this can be seen in the drastic rise in the population, but it is the increase of the population and the relationship of land and the resources it produces, that creates most of the unstable cultures. The distribution of shortages is what creates class struggle; these classes will continually compete for a larger share of that shortage than would come with equal distribution. Until there are no more shortages, classes will continue to form and struggle against other classes for a share of the limited resources. When there is an expansion of the food supply in the animal kingdom, the consuming population expands until that surplus is used up. Just because human beings are able to engineer an expansion of their food supply, does not mean that they will react to it differently than other animals do, when they have a natural surplus. Left alone to breed, all species will fill their habitat until they meet a barrier. The barrier, through natural selection, will cause a culling to take place.

This can best be seen by studying and speculating on an island habitat, such as the 1.75 square mile Pitcairn Island, where in 1789, 28 people from the HMS Bounty arrived and settled 1,120 acres of uninhabited land. By the year 1856, there were 193 people living there, and today, in 1986, there are about 1500 living descendants from the original 28 people who landed there 197 years before. The population doubled about every 35 years. (This is not excessive when contrasted with some of today's population explosions in some nations.) Because there were other under-inhabited islands that the surpluses could disperse to, the culling was safely accomplished. Today we do not have that solution. There is no more surplus, uninhabited land. So, we come to the question, "By whom and by what means is the culling to be done?"

Infanticide was probably the most important inhibiting factor on population growth throughout most of human history. Then came the other population controllers: war, disease, accidents, starvation and natural catastrophes. War, a cultural culling method used successfully in the past by many governments, is also being curtailed. An imperialistic expansion war (by Communist or capitalist countries to take care of their surplus people) today, would need the extermination of the entire invaded nation's population to be effectual. This is caused by all nations now or in the near future, having a surplus population. So to invade a country for your expansion needs, for lebensraum (like Germany did in World War II), when the invaded country already has a surplus population, is not a practicable solution in today's world, unless you are willing to accept the policy of genocide. With the spread of modern medicine, today in many countries, nature is denied the natural culling methods of death by accident and disease. Starvation is another one of nature's remedies; it is a natural birth control, one of the ways that nature uses to cull. Trouble arises immediately when you feed the starving without controlling their birth rate. Every adult you save from starving produces more mouths to feed, cloth, and house. As relief food supplies expand, so does the population expand. The result is either death by starvation down the line, or you must control the population. Starving nations point to the food surpluses in the West and say it is just a question of distribution. But the West is growing, too; its population will eventually, like Pitcairn Island, reach its limit; and when the food surpluses are gone, and you deny nature its methods, then you can only be saved by artificial methods of birth control or resorting to the use of gas ovens to control the surpluses.

The division of bread and fishes, used in the Christian Bible, was and is strictly symbolism; it is a way to distinguish between realty and belief. For a time Mao Tse-tung abolished population controls in China. He was trying to bring symbolism to life by declaring that communism could support the increased Chinese population. He was declaring that Chinese Communism, like Jesus, could feed from a small amount of bread and fishes, a multitude of Chinese. This is not so, was not so, and will not be so in a future culture. Reality will always test all political and religious beliefs. They are always limited by mathematical laws, by the concrete resources obtainable.

Although hampered by their belief in the Communist Bible, the present leaders of China have realized that there has to be population control or there will be future mass starvation, which could lead to a temporary rejection of communism to solve the problems of the world. I am encouraged that China has now instituted the one child per family; that reality has caught up with a false belief. So far, the Chinese method of family planing and abortion is being run democratically; all families are subject to the same rules, so it has a chance to succeed. But, in many countries today, there is a belief that there can be no limit placed on birth, so that leaves immigration, starvation, disease, natural disasters, accidents, wars, and revolutions to do the culling. Many of these, however, are being curtailed, and the effectiveness of other natural population controls will be further curtailed, which will prove disastrous for the minority human beings in those cultures. I believe that this can be viewed as just more paving that will improve the road that must eventually lead to another Holocaust, to the genocide of the surplus populations. All minorities must understand that the majority will decide who that surplus is; and to point to a constitution that gives you equal rights will not save you. The minority's only hope is to control the population before the Holocaust begins.

It is interesting to speculate that if the Chinese are successful, they will also find that population controls will answer the question of what system will inherit the future. Can a capitalistic system of government solve the population problem? There is a possibility that it might work in Japan because the population is homogeneous in race and has a religion that can be modified. But the United States has a diverse population where the minorities look at methods that require them to control their growth as genocide. The United States also has a large, vocal group entirely opposed to family planing and abortion; the only practical methods left in our modern culture to control the birthrate. It can be proven statistically that unless you have the full cooperation of every single group, then family planning cannot be successful. The ruling class in the United States wishes to designate the poor and minorities as surpluses, but this will not work because a law controlling the population must be democratic for it to succeed. The poor and the other minorities are not about to take themselves out of the population race. We are stuck with our bid against communism that we can feed and house and clothe a greater amount of human beings than they can. The poor, the dispossessed, will always threaten capitalism with becoming Communist if they try to control their population in an unequal manner.

Like other countries, all wealth in the United States is the result of the utilization of the land and sea resources. So when the mainly Europeans came to the shores of America and arbitrarily occupied the Native American's land, they obtained the true wealth and true future wealth of those lands. Their inheritors claim that they have the right to this wealth because the labor of their ancestors produced it. However, I say, "If their ancestors had remained in their homeland and expended that labor a hundred fold, they would have produced nothing but poverty." In a small ecological period, the capitalists have raped and pillaged the North, South, and Central continent of America of its natural resources. They have spent in a few ecological years, an inheritance that took nature hundreds of millions of years to gather; and all I can do is to grieve at their folly because it cannot be reversed. Wealth is produced in the United States by its natural resources, and all the labor in the world will produce nothing if you do not have access to natural resources. You can cram 100,000 people on Pitcairn Island, but without the resources, and no matter how much they are motivated to work, or the system of government, all you will produce is death, not wealth.

Large nations are simply an expansion of the primate troop that holds by its strength in numbers a feeding and hunting environment. Before written language, possession of the land outside the physical domination of the group was unknown. Only with the arrival of writing has the individual been able to hold title to land that he or she previously had to occupy and hold by force. Our genes can tell us to fight someone who invades our territory, but they cannot tell us to go outside the perimeters of our controlled territory and attack a specified group because in some future time that group might be a threat. It takes language to do that.

A ruling class is a ruling class regardless of what you call the rulers. The dominant primates of a troop, also settle disputes among members, govern their territory, and expand by war their territory if the troop increases, and like all governments, punish and keep in line the discontented. We have just expanded the ruling class; only the names have been changed, not the purposes. All our activities and institutions can be traced to the past, and it can be carried back to prerecorded history by an examination of the actions and reactions of a troop of primates. We flatter ourselves when we think that our ruling system is something outside the bounds of nature; that it developed outside nature and has no past. We still, like a troop of monkeys, seek the primal needs of life — food; and have in recent geological time added shelter and clothing; all other acquisitions must be viewed as vanity. If the dominants in a troop of primates could express their views by using language, they would give the same reasons that they should govern, as our present rulers.

The Communist and capitalist nations find that they are in a consumer war for the loyalties of their people. They are competing to see who can support the greater number of people. This is foolishness! Decent food, housing, and clothing are essential, but as I have stressed, all else is vanity; and consumer goods, such as private automobiles, are extreme vanity. Hard, concrete numbers tell us that everyone cannot be equally provided with the equivalent of a standard of living enjoyed in the United States. The Communists have entrapped themselves; they all promised to improve their standard of living to match the United States to prove that they are an industrial giant; they equate consumer goods for everyone as proof of superiority, proof of being a civilized country. They prevent their citizens from migrating, believing that this would cast doubt on the ability of their system to provide. They do not understand that every worker who leaves, produces wealth; just as migration from Pitcairn Island allows those left to survive better. Size does not change the basic formula.

In a contending society, to form a classless society is an impossibility. Everyone does not seek the same goal; few are ever satisfied with their assumed or chance allotment. There will always be economic disputes in a culture because everyone in society represents his or her selfish interest; and few persons would relinquish their selfish needs. Because the ruling class has different needs than the ruled, all present governments preclude declaring a society classless. We continue to look for rulers who will be neutral, but they are always comprised of individuals, and there lies the conflict. No ruling class has ever given up its preferential treatment, its powers. It does not want to be regulated back to the common, to have someone else make the decisions on their share; they know that someone else will not make a neutral decision, that individuals cannot rid their minds of being biased. The proof of this statement is always with us; in our hearts, we each, know that we are biased in favor of ourselves, so we have a right to be afraid.

ESSENCE:

The significance of the above primer on populations is that I can now conclude that the "Grand Unified Engine" — which is continually running in the background and that I have been trying to formulate — can be entirely embodied in the simplified, natural process of too many primates (over population), singularly and in troops, contending for a limited environment. So, with this in mind, we can now predict that even with sufficient zeal and a willingness to sacrifice our life for a cause, that unless it is conducted in relationship to solving the Planet's excess population growth, then all we can do is to temporarily mitigate, alleviate, and relieve many of the problems of the world; but they cannot be permanently solved until their main cause is addressed —too many human beings competing for its limited habitats.

You can (like me) subscribe to *The Nation, In These Times, Z Magazine, The Progressive, Mother Jones, The Skeptial Inquirer, Free Inquiry, World-Watch Magazine, The Humanist, Journal of Palestine Studies, Against the Current, Monthly Review, Dollars and Sense, Utne Reader, Tikkun* and *The Socialist Review,* so you will be well informed and know what the problems are. And you can (like me) belong to Amnesty International/USA, The American Civil Liberties Union, The National Organization for Women, Southern Poverty Law Center,

Americans for Religious Liberty, Greenpeace, and The Simon Wiesenthal Center, but unless you also belong and believe what The Planned Parenthood Federation, Worldwatch Institute, and Zero & Negative Population Growth, Inc. are trying to tell you, you will not be able to solve the root cause of the world's problems: too many people.

What we are fighting against is not the different modes of government, not the different systems of production and distribution, not the different forms of religion, but our genes that tell us to produce as many descendants as possible. We can rant, rave, and scream how unfair life is. We can pray to Buddha, to Christ, to Allah, to Jehovah, to Stone Idols, to pictures of saints, or even to Karl Marx and Lenin, but unless we take action to reduce the population, the problems will still be there. We can donate our time and money to saving the whales, to stopping acid rain, to preventing the cutting down of the rain forests, to every conceivable ecological problem, but the demands of overpopulation, which put the pressures on the ecology of the world, will negate all the sacrifices that we make. We can give our time and money to try to control or eliminate poverty and world wide hunger, and to try to give everyone their social, religious, and civil rights, but these can only be temporarily mitigated until the population is reduced. The Catholic and Protestant problems in Northern Ireland, the Black, White, and Colored problems of South Africa, the Palestinian and Israeli problems in the Middle East, and on and on, cannot be permanently solved because they all involve an excess population fighting for a limited environment.

That is why, unless we recognize the truth, we are forced to solve our problems the same way that the primate troops solve their territorial disputes: by trying to subvert to our need, or if that fails, to kill off the primates occupying adjacent territory who limit our expansion, and so prevent us from doing what our genes demand — to produce as many descendants as possible. This "Grand Unified Engine" is sufficient to explain the conflicts among and between capitalism, socialism, fascism, and feudalism and their modes of production and distribution, and account for the history and prehistory of primates. If examined, all wars, revolutions, and migration are just variation on this theme. The finality — to a large extent — is that when analyzed, all human problems seem to be amendable to a reduced population.

Our success in nature confers nothing, other than the truth that we are the product of that success. The other primates cannot be judged because they retained their animal culture and developed differently; they also live, they are also successful. And because they are here in many more species and varieties, also convey nothing. No matter how we embellish our actions and try to give status to them by giving them divine sanction, all our actions still can be traced back to our animal origin. Every exhibited trait comes from an animal ancestor. Only an absurdity can be reached when you try to shape and fit an animal into a mythological creature with no ties to the rest of the animal kingdom. We are not perfected; we are not the final product; we are not the last design; we are just human beings, descendant from other primates, trying to understand a world with unperfected minds. Human beings, like the rest of the animals on earth, are all in transition; nothing is ever perfected. These questions will continually arise in each generation: "Will we ever understand the world, will we ever know what is Truth?" I personally believe that nature has unknowingly supplied us with the tools of language and mathematics to understand it; if we allow ourselves the time, we can deduce the correct formula; we can link the past, present, and future together; we can possess the Truth.

CHAPTER 30

NARRATIVE: CONJECTURE

To delve into some probabilities, inferences and afterthoughts, we must again go back to the time when I tried to convince Lili, while I was still at the DeWitt State Hospital, of the futility of my running away with her. I suspected that I did poorly. Time was the main interference. I had so little of it, so I was afraid of confiding and burdening her with what had brought us to this Y-in-the-road. Still, before being released from the hospital and returned to the Sacramento County Jail, I remember that the time we had, we used as constructively as we could; we tried to commingle our individual assortment of miseries into achieving for ourselves a temporary state of bliss amongst the backdrop of one of societies many crumbling structures.

Over and over, through the passing years, circumstances had brought to my attention that occult feeling, handed down generation after generation through the genes, that I should rely more on hunches and premonitions. I truly came to believe that I should be guided by the senses of the moment; by those senses that had served our now fossilized decedents so well in that evolutionary struggle that had taken place on those grassy savannas, so impressively long ago. My failure to heed that raw, basic feeling, would in time preoccupy my mind to a never-ending reappraisal of that decision of not informing Lili of the facts so she would not feel that I was abandoning her. Lili had confided in me that she, too, had this premonition that this would be our final parting if I did not take to the road with her. The problem: my mind could not ignore the danger I thought Lili would face if the forces aligned against me became aware I was in love with someone vulnerable to attack. There was a chance they might breach my wall of resistance by assaulting me through Lili's softer defenses. My hope was to be freed, first, then to rejoin Lili to see if we could not assemble from the diversities of our strengths and weaknesses, a more civilized entity. One that could exist in todays plundered and crumbling social structures; one that, regardless of the price paid, would try to change what others alluded to as unchangeable; one that would not be intimidated by meaningless rituals; one that would bring a new conversion, a new meaning, a new awareness to those who were still seeking, but not finding a righteous cause.

To understand what my fears were, we must return to my awaking in that bare, solitary cell in the Vacaville Medical Center. It is April of 1961 and the only fact I know for sure was I was being framed by an unknown group that had at their command this immense power. I could only speculate on how it was done and theorize on what coalition of FBI, CIA, and extreme right-wing groups were involved and what type of structure they were working under, but was unconditionally sure of why it was done. I was sure they wanted information from me, but could not understand why they did not just pull me off the street and resort to plain, old fashioned torture. My first thoughts were they might have wanted me to become a double agent and resorting to torture would be harmful to those plans; recruitment by torture does not produce a reliable agent. Much later, when reading books and magazine articles exposing the FBI and CIA's methods and ideas, I came to understand that I was not treated like that because they still, in 1961, retained this image that they were the "good-guy" pitted against the evil and corruption in the world. This image did not seem to fade or was not discarded completely until the Vietnam War unleashed them to perpetrate outright inquisitional torture on their Vietnam captives; and by doing this, they proved once again that by using immoral methods, human beings will succumb to and be transformed into what they claim they are fighting against.

Initially, I stayed at the Vacaville Medical Facility for three months. I was surprised and left unenlightened that nobody openly came to talk to me about making a deal for my cooperation. All the time I was there, I remained puzzled. Eventually I began to speculate that if they truly believed my story that I was unable to remember anything about the bank robbery, then they also might think they were safe. I would then not even know I was being framed, so they would not want to jog my memory by getting in touch with me. Information released (reluctantly) in the 1970s by the CIA and Army Intelligence on "Mind Control Experiments" would lead a person to believe this was a valid assumption. Through exposures in the news media, the public was informed about an Army Intelligence Team subjecting an American soldier, in 1961, to isolation, to injections of Sodium Pentothal, to being hypnotized, to being abused verbally and physically under interrogation, and finally he was administered LSD, without his knowledge, to determine whether he had taken classified documents for espionage. In that report, they also admitted that seven Asians and nine Europeans were illegally given LSD, without their consent, for experimental interrogation. (Note: the army thought it was a useful tactic, when employed as a duress factor, to call the subject's attention to his LSD influenced state and threaten to extend this state indefinitely, even to a permanent state of insanity.)

MK-ULTRA was a code word used from 1953 to 1964 for 130 research programs in prisons, hospitals, and universities. Sub-project h-68 was headed by an American psychiatrist named Dr. Cameron, who worked in the Allan Memorial Institute at the McGill University, in Montreal, Canada. These projects were secret CIA funded experiments, and those doctors involved were willing to do terminal (contributing to the end of life) experiments. These doctors were involved in studies that used the combination of LSD, forced isolation, and shock treatment; they were also into drug testing, into sensory deprivation, and into drug-induced sleep treatment, with a combination of hallucinogenic drugs and electric shock treatment. The CIA spent $25 million in 25 years to try to control human beings by brainwashing experiments. The results: many patients used as guinea pigs were left *emotionally crippled for life*. Some patients were given daily, intensive electroshock (using six times the normal current to introduce the brain seizures); some were given sleep therapy as long as 60 days, and forced to undergo Psyche Driving — the repetition of a recorded taped message up to one half-million times. They were then injected with curare that brought on temporary paralysis so they could not avoid the repeated messages. We were told these treatments caused hallucinations, distortions, permanent brain damage, and other long term aftereffects.

When exposed, those in charge of the CIA tried to destroy all documents to these experiments, but a few escaped being destroyed. Those found were stamped "Sensitive Intelligence Sources and Methods Involved," and admitted the experiments were to study the effects on human behavior of the repetition of verbal signals; they also told how they proposed to use LSD-25 and other similar agents as a way of breaking down the patient's ongoing patterns of behavior so they could substitute new behavior patterns. The experimenters' conclusions were that these experiments were ineffectual, caused "long-term memory loss" in some patients, and were not persuasive in obtaining information from the drugged patients.

In 1961 there was a memorandum that suggested that an initial experiment on amnesia and post-hypnotic suggestion should be carried out by the CIA. The object of the experiment was to find out if an unwilling subject could be quickly hypnotized, and whether once hypnotized, the victim could be made to undergo amnesia and long lasting and serviceable post-hypnotic suggestions. This would have been an expedient tool in the hands of an organization that was perverted enough to use it for unlawful purposes. Imagine what they could have done if they could have hypnotized someone such as Lee Harvey Oswald and made him think it was his idea to kill President Kennedy, and after the deed was done, he would have complete amnesia of who planted the original suggestion. Surely, it did not happen like that because we are told the experiments failed; and would our FBI, CIA, and Army Intelligence lie to us in such an important matter? Still, I would have been much more convinced if the Warren Commission and subsequent commissions had looked deeper into those classified experiments.

Later, in some circles interested in the constitutional safeguards of experiments in mind control, there was wide speculation on some of the happenings that had taken place at the Vacaville Prison Medical Facility before, during, and after I was there. There were drugs being used and tested on inmates that were nothing more than a form of torture using drugs instead of physical means. There were experiments in sensory deprivation in isolation cells, there were daily shock treatments being given, and doctors were doing experimental lobotomies on prisoners; and then there was the wild rumor (which might have had some basis in truth) that electrodes were being implanted in the brain of inmates to control their actions.

Everything happening in Vacaville would lead a rational person to assume that someone was trying to find the keys to mind control. Notations in my medical files at Vacaville show that I was given drug treatment before I was given shock treatment. This raises the question, "Could I have been used as a human guinea pig in mind control experiments?" It also raises the possibility that they could have retrieved information from me under drug-hypnoses and then erased from my mind, with drugs and shock treatment, the knowledge of their actions. So if they had reached my mind, and were able to cover it up, then they would have known I was innocent in the death of those I exposed; they could have gained all the information I had about their deaths, so would not have a reason to get in touch or bargain with me for information.

Early on, I discounted their ability to control my mind; where this theory breaks down is they would have had to know the pivotal words I used to put myself under deep self-hypnosis. If I had never before hypnotized myself, then under drugs, they might have been able to elicit information from me. But I had been conditioning myself for two years, so unless I recited a "code sentence" a prescribed number of times I could not be hypnotized, and nobody but I knew the sentence and how many times it had to be repeated. There was the possibility they could have developed a drug to overcome and bypass this mental block that I had implanted in my mind for my protection, but later revelations had shown they had little success against people unprepared for such a probe. So, although I do not believe they succeeded with me, where independently I had trained my mind to resist all such probes, still, there always remained in the back of my mind the possibility it could have happened.

Another interesting conjecture as to why they might have abandoned me, is my composition "The Word According to Thou." To a superstitious coalition of human beings, this might have influenced their judgement when they read it. Picture an undercover group of people, with ultra right Christian leanings, who have just completed a complicated series of events that had, through miscalculation, almost exposed them. Then confront them with evidence that they were either dealing with a mentally ill person who thinks he is talking to a Supreme Being or, because they are prone to believe in miracles, they are involved in a plot to crucify one of His Messengers. Although it is an interesting speculation, I also discarded this one as I simply do not think this was the reason I was abandoned.

Then there was a time when I came to believe they did not contact me because they had been sidetracked by the developments resulting from the "Cuban Crisis." The day I was arrested was the third day of the CIA backed Cuban invasion, and the losing of that battle, surely, must have drawn their attention away from such a small annoyance as me.

Another explanation could be that there was the chance they had received information about what had transpired down in the Los Angeles area and realized I could not be held accountable for the actions taken by others that I had no control over. I would have still been seen as an enemy, so they would not have tried to rectify their actions, but they might have stopped all covert operations against me.

For the full length of my incarcerations, I waited for a contact. For a couple of years after I was released and all charges were dropped against me, I waited. In the two years after my release, I set hair traps to inform myself if anyone had made an exploratory probe into my living quarters when I was absent. All results were nil. I mentally questioned all new acquaintances, but they consistently turned out to be above suspicion.

I personally made no overt move to contact anyone in the Los Angeles' area or, for that matter, anyone connected with my former experiences. I had completely cut myself off from my former life, and devoted myself to analyzing my past actions and studying the current movements that were taking place. This drop out, at times, worried me as it brought to my mind the suspicion that maybe this was not a voluntary act but a theatrical role planted by somebody's mind experiments.

It was only when I began to think about writing this book in 1979 that I began to believe it was the intervention of the natural, reciprocal law that if everything is going right for you, then it is going bad for your opponent, that guided me through to victory. The group allied against me and responsible for the events leading to my being charged with bank robbery, had completely overestimated their power to control events. I in turn had allowed myself to be deluded by what I thought was a major, all inclusive conspiracy, when it most likely only involved a small inconsequential group of retired and current working right-wing oriented FBI and CIA agents. Their operations were probably sponsored by the extreme right-wing, who thought the time was ripe for them to use their money to consolidate their position in the coming police state. Remember: These people surely believed McCarthy's propaganda that the Communists had possession of the United States Government. It would only be logical to form such a movement to fight outside the government. One can see how narrowly the believers in McCarthyism had missed coming to power by the actions of this group. They were there, waiting to make their stage entrance; only their bad luck of picking someone who understood how to manipulate the bureaucratic mind, had prevented me from being one of their first sacrificial victims.

Although theory, the original scenario probably read in this manner: Just before the bank robbery occurred, I was to be picked up on the beach and, along with my station wagon, transported to a prearranged safe-house that was somewhere close. I would then be given the choice of full cooperation with my captors or to be framed with a bank robbery which would then be in progress. I presume they would have allowed me to listen to the search for the suspect over a radio equipped to receive FBI and local police transmissions so I would hear the description of the suspect and the station wagon involved. Later — to convince me of the seriousness of their intentions — I would have been shown the license plates used in the robbery, the money derived from it, the clothing worn during the robbery, and newspaper accounts of it. But after all these years of thinking over and speculating on different confrontations I could have had with this group, I still cannot believe I would have believed them capable of framing me for bank robbery. Instead, I would have thought they were just trying to perpetrate a deception on me with phony electronic transmissions, fake newspapers, and imitation situations; all of which I knew they were capable of using to deceive me. Unless they have had a similar experience, nobody can understand the emotional shock I received at that Santa Rosa

Police Station when under the sedation of an unknown drug, I heard them discussing the finding of $10,000 in my station wagon, from a robbery that I knew that I did not commit.

They probably had the drug they used on me at the police station to use if I did not comply with their demands. If I did not cooperate with them, then they would have placed me, drugged, back into my station wagon, parked it back on the beach where they had abducted me, then phoned another police agency to report that there was a station wagon that met the description of the get-away car parked at the beach. The stolen money would have been placed in my motor vehicle and an untraceable .22 automatic pistol would have been substituted for my bb-gun when they realized there was not one in my automobile. (Eight months before, I had stopped in Arizona on my way to Arkansas and had bought the bb-gun and, at the same store, a .22 pistol, but because I was a convicted felon in California, I was afraid to bring it across the border, so I sold it before leaving Arkansas or there would have been a .22 pistol in that glove compartment.) They also would have planted the clothing used in the robbery; and the stolen license plate used in the robbery would have been found in the parked station wagon or freshly buried nearby; and I am sure my fingerprints would have been found impressed on that license plate. And when they found the contact lenses were not in the glove compartment, then their explanation would be that I threw them away after the robbery, but then how would they explain why I kept the solutions needed to place them in my eyes and the extra carrying case that should have held them? So to be consistent, they would have had to throw them away before calling the police, but they could not do this at the police station; and that is why someone there was worried and hoping that I might still have them in my eyes. (At one time, I did have two pairs. But within one week after buying them, one popped out of my eye and was lost in the grass, and one for the other eye was lost a couple of months later in Arkansas.) I had bought the contact lenses, the bb-gun, and .22 pistol on an International Credit Card, so, if they had access to those records, they might have known this, but they had no way of knowing I had sold the .22 pistol or lost one pair of contact lenses.

My response to the situation of waking up in a police station accused of bank robbery, would have been the same as when I woke up in the hospital in Vacaville. I could not tell the authorities I was being framed because I would have had to convince them I was guilty of a greater crime, which would have exposed the people that worked under me to prosecution for those crimes. The plotters would have known that if I did not tell them under duress what my involvement down south was, then they would have nothing to fear when I was arrested under the false charges of bank robbery; and their assessment would have been true.

Would I have faked being mentally ill? I am not sure because the condition would have been different. I would have expected to be arrested and would have already known by whom. To repeat myself, I would not have believed them when they had me in their grasp, but when I woke up in the custody of the FBI, I would have no choice but to believe. Furthermore, I would not have had the shock I experienced at the Santa Rosa Police Station of finding out I was being framed. So, the question is unanswerable.

My adversaries awe-inspiring plan had begun to disintegrate the day before they had chosen to put it into operation. My decision to shave and go into Santa Rosa to see the movie *Elmer Gantry* was based entirely on my purchasing a newspaper at a small local store — the first newspaper I had bought since arriving at the beach. The headlines of the Cuban Invasion had attracted my attention, but nobody could have known that I saw that advertisement in the newspaper and decided to go see that movie. Their failure to introduce someone to go to that beach, someone to get acquainted with me, someone to find out my daily plans, especially what I was planning to do on the day of the robbery, was the cause of all later dominos falling in disorderly fashion. Being a sociable person, I would have relished the company of anyone that showed up on that beach. I could have been taken in by anyone with or without a cover story, because I had no premonition that I was not safe and unknown at that off season camping beach. Since I had no communication with my people in the south, I thought nobody knew where I was. It could have been they did not want to bring more people into the plot then were necessary, but after prolonged browsing through the alternatives, I finally came to believe I was not supposed to leave that beach that morning of the bank robbery.

I cannot think of one logical reason of why I was not stopped from leaving the beach that day except something extraordinary and unexpected must have happened to prevent them from carrying out their plan. Unless they were distracted, they should have been alerted when, for the first time in two weeks, I shaved that morning. I could speculate for a thousand pages and still not be correct. It could have been that the California Highway Patrol had noticed the automobile of those who were watching me from the bluff above and decided to stop that day and ask them who they were, just as I was leaving to go into Santa Rosa, or it could have been as simple as a battery failure or a flat tire. Looking back, I cannot believe they would have allowed me to leave the beach that day unless something had come up that they were unprepared for. That left the possibility that I was not followed into Santa Rosa for the same reason. When I started up my station wagon and drove away from where I was camped, my watchers would not have been too worried as I had about every other day driven either up or down the coast for a few miles. They probably thought they could correct the problem they had and catch up with me in time to execute their plan. I had left the beach about a quarter of eleven and was in Santa Rosa about a quarter of twelve. The robbery did not happen, according to the newspapers, until 11:36 AM. That gave them plenty of time to call it off. However, because the bank robbery did take place, it must have been that by the time they realized they had lost control of me, it was too late to call off the bank robbery, or there was a mishap with their radio communications that did not allow them to call it off. I presumed they might have had a radio transmitter attached to my automobile and when it got out of range, they had no way to track me.

The reason the Exchange Bank of Cotati was chosen to be robbed was it had, according to the Santa Rosa Newspapers, already been robbed four times before. The FBI, the highway patrol, and local police officers had arranged that when the alarm was set off, it would trigger a prearranged roadblock. Only a person knowing where the roadblocks were to be set up could hope to escape it, and only the people that set it up could have that knowledge. Most likely, I was entering Santa Rosa when that alarm went off.

My 1950 Plymouth Station Wagon remained parked in that lot next to the Santa Rosa Police Station until I left the theater around 5:45PM and drove back to the beach. On my way back, I drove through a thunder shower that was so bad that I had to pull off the road halfway to the little town of Sebastopol, for about five minutes, because I could not see the roadway through my windshield. I am sure my safe arrival at the beach brought a sense of relief to them, but if they had not been able to follow me into Santa Rosa, then they had no way of knowing where I had spent the day, or if I had an iron clad alibi. They would have known though if I had been stopped and questioned about the robbery.

They must have had some hurried consultations during the night about what changes in their plans were needed; at least until they could find out where I had been when the robbery occurred. By arising at daybreak and starting my journey back south, I had probably put new "kinks" into their plans. The only thing they would have been able to do was follow me and hope I was not stopped and questioned; and if I was, hope that I would not have impeachable witnesses to swear I was with them at the time of the robbery. The first hope was not to be, as intervention came into the picture when I was stopped on Lakeville Highway, just east of Petaluma, California, by John Marchi, Special Agent of the FBI, who I believed had no knowledge of or was in anyway connected with the plot to frame me. I came to this conclusion because of his lack of preparedness and ineptness in handling the unexpected situation that confronted him. Still, there was always the chance that he was a supremely talented actor.

There were several questions I could not even begin to answer that came into my mind when I awoke in Vacaville, and a few more that came up when I read, in 1979, the newspaper accounts of the crime I was accused of committing. I will have to speculate on some of those questions because the answers are needed to understand what happened the day I was arrested for the bank robbery. The major question was why the money, about $10,000, was placed in a large thermos jug that was filled with water. The FBI explained to my aunt that I placed it there because I was under a delusion that I was going to start a new religion and thought the money was unclean, so this act was for the purification of the evil money. This was only speculation on their part, perhaps following from their discovery of the manuscript entitled *The Word According to Thou* and the monastery robe that I had made up by a Hollywood costume shop. They could not have known I had the robe made up to see the reaction it caused being worn in public and to evaluate whether it would be a good disguise if Party members had to go underground. I would have, unhesitatingly, used them in my defense, but I would have had the knowledge that it was entirely untrue. The only explanation I could fit into such an odd thing as them putting the money in a large thermos jug is they had no choice. If my assumptions were right, and they did not know where I had been the day of the robbery but they did follow me away from that beach on the morning I was stopped by the FBI agent, then they did not want to plant the money until they found out where I had been the day of the robbery. When they learned I had gone to the theater across the way from the Santa Rosa Police Station where they were interrogating me, they could calculate that I could have had the time to have committed the bank robbery at 11:36AM, changed my clothes, shaved, and still be in line for the opening of the theater's doors at 12:45PM.

I had a partial alibi because I had probably arrived in Santa Rosa about 11:45AM which was near the time the robbery was taking place. When I parked in the lot that was next to the Santa Rosa Police Station and across the street from the Roxy Theater, I remembered going to a cafe to get something to eat, as the theater did not open to sell tickets until 12:45PM, and the movie did not start until 1:00PM. There were people at the restaurant who might have remembered when I arrived, but I knew I could not depend on it as it was close to noon and they were busy. I believed I told them I had arrived a little before the first movie had started. They would not tell me the correct time of the robbery. All they would say was it was in the morning, so I told them I was probably on the road when it occurred.

When they knew where I was, they must have decided to plant the stolen bank money in my station wagon. But they had searched and probed and pulled apart, for at least two or three hours, every conceivable place that could hide that money. Every conceivable place except, maybe, the water jug. Some distraction for a few minutes and either the money was dumped into the thermos jug or a substitute replaced mine. After a suitable period, after everyone had given up on finding the money, behold, the water jug was opened and there was 10,000 dollars floating around in the water.

I thought about this and came to the belief that if you put the money into a thermos jug filled with water and drove around for a short time, when you opened the jug, all you would have was a mush of disintegrating paper. I made an experiment, when I began this book, to see the results of such an occurrence. I found out that paper money was protected by a waterproof coating and could take days of immersion in plain water without hurting it. However, I did find out that the green and black ink on paper money would come off new currency and stain the water a dirty green. Because I had used that water when I returned to the beach, and the next morning to shave and cook with, I knew after the test that the money had not been planted when I was in the theater as I would have noticed the color of the water. And as I slept in the station wagon the night of the bank robbery, they could not have planted it after I returned to the beach or the next morning when, on my journey South, I was arrested.

When I read, in 1978, the newspaper accounts of the robbery, they mentioned a fifty dollar bill was missing from the bank loot. It is well known, especially by professional criminals, that banks have a special bill in each teller's cage, usually a fifty or a hundred, to give to anybody who robs a bank or a government insured savings and loan company. The serial number of the bill is recorded and it is placed at the bottom of a pack of bills, under a holder so it is not given out unless there is a robbery. I had this information in 1961, and if I had robbed the bank, then I would have destroyed it if I had a way of distinguishing it from the other fifty and hundred dollar bills. But because I am denying I was involved in it, then the question comes up of, "Why the persons responsible for the crime would remove or destroy the fifty dollar bill that was missing?" Once again, I can only surmise. Perhaps if I had cooperated with them the vehicle used in the robbery would have been found with the stolen license plate still attached and the fifty dollar bill discarded in it as added corroboration that it was the correct station wagon. Evidently the missing fifty dollar bill was not at their disposal to be pulled out of my sock or to be thrown into the container where the money was found. Why it was not on hand, I cannot say. The question remains though, how, unless they had gained the information from the bank tellers after the robbery, did they know which bill was the planted one? I am going on the assumption that the missing bill was the planted one.

The most damaging evidence was that three out of four tellers, according to the newspaper accounts, had picked me out of a lineup as the robber. This is the easiest to explain away, especially to those familiar with experimentally staged robberies in classrooms and the discrepancies in the eyewitness accounts of those robberies. It being a Saturday, it took them all morning to arrange the lineup. When the people who were present at the holdup were brought in to the police station and told that the FBI had captured the bank robber, the witnesses would, by suggestion, anticipate seeing the person that had committed the crime. My station wagon would have been pointed out to them, they would have been informed that the money from the robbery had been recovered from it, then they would have been warned that I had changed my clothing, shaved, and removed my contact lenses to prepare them for a difference in my appearance. After all this, I was put in a lineup with people 15 years younger than me and with some that outweighed me by 50 pounds. The only thing not understandable was why the lone holdout?

Their plot had begun to melt away when they gave me that drug that mimicked mental illness. Unless they had very good communications, they must have been acting under their own initiative by then. There remained the possibility that the drug was not supposed to react the way it did on me. Experimental drugs, for that matter all drugs, are unpredictable, and results vary considerably from person to person. Maybe they thought the drug would scramble my brain to such an extent that I would be unable to point out some flaw in their plot; or perhaps they still thought they had a chance to make a deal with me if I were proven to be insane at the time of the robbery. The world of probability is so vast that the mind is unable to cope with the possible explanations of the unknown actions of a single person, let alone a group. I believe that whoever was running this group that framed me realized that the disintegration of their imprudent thought out plans, and the lack of control of the actions of everybody and everything that was happening around me, led them to completely abandon me to the mercy of the system they had thrust me into. What they had lost was more than made-up for by the lesson the group had learned. The invaluable lesson was that in a spy novel, the author has complete control over the actions of his characters and events, but in a nonfictional setting, all actions are uncontrollable. However, what hurt them most was they had no influence over other persons (like FBI Special Agent, John Marchi) integrating their unplotted roles into the staged event they were trying to control.

CHAPTER 31

NARRATIVE: INSIGHT

When I was released on my own recognizance, I euphorically dialed the DeWitt State Hospital to tell Lili that I might be free to join her in the close, intimate future. Although disappointed when informed she had signed out of the hospital, I was not distraught as I had pleaded with her not to write or contact me while I was in the Sacramento County Jail, not divulging to her that fear for her safety still strayed through my thoughts. I had memorized a few contacts in the San Francisco Bay Area where she might be reached, but her transient friends were as impermanent as the life they lived. The "Moving On" culture, that she had merged with, was so completely hiding her by its life-style that I was unable to reach her or even feel I was close to solving her disappearance. Because I had no permanent address myself, I could only tell them I would call back when I settled-in someplace permanently.

By using a ruse that I had learned from a former telephone operator, I managed to obtain the unlisted telephone number of Lili's mother. When I explained who I was, I was greeted by a silence that only the heavy breathing on the other end of the line and the absence of an audible click let me know I had not been disconnected. I could guess the scenario that was passing through her mind because the same scene, my refusal eight years ago to accept their offer, was also levitating out of my subconscious.

It is so easy to point the accusing finger away from ourselves, but the fact remains that many choices cannot be made without hurting another; and when that decision affect's someone you love, the regret will be immense if your original decision was not made with integrity, and so you find yourself unable to accept the consequences of your actions. We are lucky to be human beings and not immortals; an immortal would tend to accumulate an immense burden of regrets as the centuries passed. Although I accepted the blame for all my actions, the speculation of what could have been preyed on my mind.

Will the frost on the grass remember the relationship after the sun's rays have dispersed the frost back into the atmosphere? We are sure it does not, but we mortals, have the ability to remember our relationships and to exaggerate a natural occurrence of frost into a serene snowdrift that hides the rocky turf that lovers must traverse. When the sun's rays finally melt our imaginary snowdrift, we find it hard to explain to ourselves why we needed the deception. I was left in the position of holding a theory that if I had accepted the offer of Lili's parents and, as a result, had become a success in the business world, then it would have changed me and my views. I would have found myself defending what I formerly opposed and opposing what I previously defended. Because there would always be an exceptional few who would not change with success, my situation will always have to remain uncomputable as there were too many variables for the outcome to be known. So, I must always remain in doubt about whether I was strong enough to become an exception. However, I do not personally believe this was a deception, an imaginary snowdrift I created to break away from Lili.

Lili was important in my life not because of the short time we were together but for what she represented to me. As the years passed, she became in my mind a family, a stability, a mother to my children, someone who could reproduce my genes. Lili was an idea, a concept that represented home, symbolized tribal beliefs, manifested a reason for going back and rejoining the tribe from an imposed exile. She represented an entirely new course in my life, something to cling to in a world that was crumbling under the burden of its senseless expansion.

Home is past patterns ingrained on frail cells. When returning home, the disappointment is the new patterns can never match the old familiar patterns. With this understanding, I could not promise Lili's mother I could move Lili from the path that she was on, because paths do become familiar, do become old friends, and difficulties arise when you try to sell another path to someone when you know all too well that all paths will eventually reach the same destination. It is just that some paths are easier to traverse than others, especially when you have someone who has proceeded you and can lead you through the thickets. Not that I was so presumptive to claim I had the illumination to avoid all the pitfalls encountered in life, when I knew by then that all you can do is to postpone your cosmic future, but never eliminate it. So my agreement with Lili's mother was simply that she would try to locate Lili, and I, with financial help from her family, would try to persuade Lili to accept a new life-style.

The fate of all human beings, of all living things, is change; I soon realized that since we last met, Lili had not been immune to this biological law. I, myself, had been changed by time and my struggle. Some changes I approved of, but others: passive for long periods of time, withdrawn for even longer periods of time, a true paranoia (meaning a paranoia I was not faking, one I did not have under control), and a zest for life obliterated, was not to my approval. These I attributed to the random destruction of my brain cell connections that had been overloaded by an induced current, clogged by an experimental drug, or a combination of these mind disrupters. These personality changes I could only grieve over and ask myself, "As there seems to be no new sweet fruit being produced on my branches, where have all the pollinators gone to?"

If in the "Newtonian Sense" for every loss there is a corresponding gain, then I must weigh insight on the opposite side of the scale to see how they balanced out. I found vengeance missing when I found myself unmoved by the superficial inequities perpetrated on me. I had no interest in tracking down for retribution those who had wronged me. I came to understand how their fears, their ideas, their reasoning could lead them to form the group that had beleaguered me. Although their premises were (from my point of view) wrong, how could I find guilt and judge them unless I judged myself first. I had to find myself guilty of being a threat to their existence; and so, under the "No God Rule" they also could resort to whatever means they needed to preserve their lives. Self-preservation supersedes all other forms of law.

We are not surprised when a person grows up and learns to speak Chinese in China or English in England; and we can even see why most of the people in Italy become Catholics instead of Moslems; but we do not seem to see the same connection when the Russians produce a majority of atheists or the United States produces a majority of Christians. It is all learned behavior. Only a few will overcome their original indoctrination, but the few that find a variant in their society and adopt it, must be cautious or they will arrive at their new found religion, philosophy, or political science by the same method of reasoning that gave them their original belief. A switch in beliefs does not automatically mean the accepting of a new belief is better than the previous abandoned belief. The only thing different is you will have a little more control over information you allow to enter your realm of thought. Still, one should be wary because one should realize even the screening is formed from earlier accepted ideas.

As an example: I can make a personal judgment that the Russian writer, Aleksandr Solzhenitsyn, did a magnificent labor in exposing the illusions behind communism. The truth in his literary works on Russian

Communism will always be his monument, and because it is the truth, it will never be overthrown. But I also can make a judgment that he could not overcome his prejudices of accepting other beliefs just because they were in opposition to communism. After rejecting communism, he turned right around and accepted the illusions of the Christian religion and capitalism for reality. Solzhenitsyn did not realize (because the system he grew up in restricted his information) the United States had a uniqueness: a new, under-exploited land, rich in natural resources, and with a small population that allowed many freedoms to be fought for and won. But hear my warning, comes the exhaustion of those natural resources, and all those freedoms will become tumbleweed; just skeletons of their former existences.

A computer has an advantage over the human brain; when you put an inconsistency into it, it will not run the program. A human being is not so constructed. You should understand that if everyone was born equal, with the same amount of money and intelligence, there would still be room at the apex for only a selected few; therefore a lottery would be the only fair way of choosing our leaders, choosing those who will do the dirty work needed in a modern society. Still, even if this was not obtainable in the immediate future, it would not confer on me the right to place myself in the concentration camp's guard tower, guarding the wealthy within it. When I found I could not blame or condemn the poor, who in revolt were trying to rectify an inherited distribution of wealth and power that came through the unfair, blind lottery of birth, then how could I blame the wealthy, the winners of this lottery. They receive the gift just as blindly and accidentally as the disinherited. The rich are conditioned by their wealth just as much as the poor by their poverty. I satisfied myself that I was not going to make the world more civilized by becoming a concentration camp guard, because no matter who was inside, it came down to human beings guarding other human beings; and if I had a choice — and I do — it is closer to civilized behavior to be on the side of the guarded than on the side of the concentration camp guards.

Many times, I was reacquainted with and saddened to learn that the American Jew, the Black American, and the Chicano American, who have all been unjustly discriminated against, would be procurable to be guards in an American concentration camp if the other groups that they were taught to hate and despise were in that enclosure. Of course, most of the white Anglo-Saxons are happy to be a guard for anybody. Go to the places where white Anglo-Saxons gather and feel free to express their beliefs and you will find most of them are willing to solve our Jewish problem, our Black problem, and our Chicano problem by the same methods the Germans used under Hitler. We have not learned from the past that what you advocate will determine what the opposition can do to you without feeling guilty when they come to power. We are all a minority in some part of the world. So, if we take advantage of another group because they are small in number, how can we complain of our treatment if due to some unforeseen circumstance, we become a minority.

Human beings must understand that they have no preeminence over the other animals. The coyote is berated for eating the domestic sheep, the lion is berated for eating the domestic cattle, the shark is berated for eating human flesh; they all remain ignorant of the importance of and the superiority of human beings. These animals have no understanding of our assumption that our laws are valid when applied to them. From an interpretation of this, we can see our fault is the greater fault because we remain ignorant of their needs when we have the capability of knowing them, while they have not the endowment of knowing or responding to our needs.

Although it is history, I still cry for the North American Indians massacred at Sand Creek, at Wounded Knee, and all the other massacres perpetrated against the North, South, and Central American Indians. I cry for the brutality Americans expressed at MyLai; I shed tears over all the concentration camps that were ever erected, and become incensed that they are still with us; and yes, I even weep for those Midians killed on the plains of Moab. Five thousand years on paper is yesterday and so profoundly near for me. And I still shed tears for those two infiltrators I exposed, and whose death I fully accept responsibility for. You can see I have much to weep for, but if you do not cry for the dead of the past, then who will cry for you when you become the past. If you cannot shed tears, then you have not learned from the past and so will go on endlessly repeating its mistakes. Until everyone recognizes the need to shed those tears, then there is little hope of our world becoming civilized.

One day, Mr. Robert Maheu, a CIA paid consultant, met in a Miami Beach hotel room with members of what the news media call the Mafia, a secret organization accused of controlling many criminal activities. The object of the meeting was to negotiate a CIA contract to kill Fidel Castro. The CIA had convinced Mr. Maheu it was his patriotic duty to have Castro killed. This was not an isolated incident as the past shows there were people that were convinced, or were convinced by others, that it was their patriotic duty to assassinate President Kennedy, that it was necessary to the stability of the United States to kill Robert Kennedy, and it was in the interest of the United States to kill Martin Luther King. And back in 1940 a Communist took out a murder contract on Leon Trotsky because Stalin thought he was a threat to communism; thought that the inevitability of communism was in jeopardy; and the same thinking led in 1984 to some

Polish Secret Police coming together and agreeing it was their patriotic duty to kill the Catholic Priest, Father Jerzy Popieluzka. Those who did, or ordered the killings, believed the world is controlled by the ideas and actions of individuals, and if you killed the person then you also killed the ideas they expressed and represented. I presume Mr. Maheu and the CIA thought that if they killed Fidel Castro, millions of people would dance in the street, and by murdering him it would bring capitalism back to Cuba.

The common belief held by these assassins and their governments, is the same as holding the belief that by killing, torturing, or humiliating people you can eliminate or change the law governing gravity. They cannot grasp the principle that if you kill off all the people that know and teach the theory of gravity, and destroyed all the books where it is mentioned, that these acts will have no effect on gravity. Someone will always rediscover it again and again. The truth of gravity, or any other truth, cannot be killed or eliminated by killing people or destroying the books that describe that truth. How sad, that there are *Homo sapiens* who think they can control knowledge by resorting to those methods.

Even if they do not recognize it, all individuals surely create history through the choices they make from the true or false information they have chosen. We are handicapped in trying to control history because we have no control over most of the choices made by others. We have no way to control the material that each person has absorbed. We are further handicapped by those choices we think we make in a free and rational manner, but because of our acceptance of erroneous material as true, we make the wrong decisions. There also are individuals who believe if they can change the past records of what choices were made by individuals and groups to reflect the present point of view, then they can control history by channeling it into agreeing with what they see is the desirable channel. They say they do this to reach an inevitable end, which they claim to have the prescription for, sooner. These people then insult us by stating that this was the foreordained channel. They do not explain that if it is predetermined, if it is foreordained, then why the need for manipulation?

All through those waiting years — before I wrote this book — I remained an observer, a Darwinian Observer. My goal? My purpose? These were unknown to me. Only the passing of time would show me that I would seek to become an apprentice "Bridger" — a human being who unifies broken circles of thought. While I waited those many years, everyone I met was grist for my observation mill. Every friend, every foe had been dissected and observed for a hint they were different, that they were acting outside the bounds of animal behavior. I compared their words to their deeds, their declared goals with their actions, their actions with their motivations and only in a few isolated instances could I see anyone who was not, always, acting in their instinctive interest. I was pleased when I observed those few civilized acts; mightily pleased, because, they gave me bread, they gave me substance, they gave me hope. They showed that I, too, had a chance to overcome my selfish animal traits; that I could learn from the past; that I was not automatically doomed to always act in my innate interest if I could explain why those selfish traits were passed on, if I could explain why they benefited the individual. To believe we could not decipher, could not learn, is to deny we can ever understand our animal actions, the only excuse we have for our cruelties. All future analyzing will show we have not yet had the time to overcome by natural or human selection the blind education given by our selfish genes; genes put there by nature to protect the species by those personal acts of selfishness.

Men and women are engaged, like all other life, in survival of the fittest, using and adopting different creeds, religions, and political parties that they perceive will give them an edge in this struggle. I find I cannot condemn, outright, false religious or political beliefs. Belonging to the majority religion does give a benefit; belonging to the majority political party does give a benefit. You cannot condemn someone for believing something false if it does give their gene pool an edge. So, I no longer feel animosity toward religious people, toward other political beliefs. The religious believe that morality is set by something outside their minds, whereas I believe each person is responsible for their actions if they have the knowledge to recognize they are selfish animals. I recognize them as simply mammals in error, but error they cannot see because of their genes and false imprinting that mammals are heir to. I do not judge the actions of a lioness hunting and killing for her cubs or protecting them by killing a hunter because she cannot reason her imprinting and genes away. So how can I judge the human animal that also is deficient in its reasoning?

CHAPTER 32

NARRATIVE: UNIFYING

You plant; it grows; you harvest. You do not plant wheat and harvest oats; neither do you plant evil and harvest righteousness; nor do you plow injustice into the land and reap justice. If you plant lies, knowingly or unknowingly, you will not know the truth. And if you say, "I did not plant this crop!" know that a seed produces only its own kind. It cannot lie. Be assured, you will not be known by the seeds you claimed you planted, but by the crop your seeds produced.

Before we unite and unify the final broken circles of thought in this book, we will describe an event that coincided with the writing of it; an occurrence that someone suffering from a mental aberration might have readily dreamed up. To be truthful, I am not quite sure. This might be the result of having the patchy and hazy memory of a schizophrenic that Dr. Bromberg alluded to in his court testimony. However, the event, whether of the mind or a true incident, began when one Saturday morning there came to my door a young woman with a parrot, an extremely large parrot. She explained to me, using words that strictly conformed to a pattern and with precise English inflections, that I was about to see and hear what was prophesied would happen when the time was near. This was a supernatural revelation, granted from a unity with Him, that would astonish the modern world. I was chosen; yes, chosen by Him to have this religious experience which would confirm that the Christian Bible was the true word of God. She then proceeded, with a few urgings, to have the parrot recite diverse passages from the Christian Bible. Carefully interspersed in the selections being quoted were some innocuous interpretations of the meaning of the Christian experience such as: "God died for our sins. God is love. God loves the repentant sinners that come to Him." I could see she was very pleased by the stuttering, ill at ease, fidgeting parrot's performance; and I imagined she had spent many devoted hours teaching this large parrot its repertoire, but I remained unconvinced of its significance and informed her of my doubts. She became agitated and indignant when I pointed out to her that I was not impressed with the performance as I knew all along a parrot could be trained to speak, but it had no comprehension of what it was saying; it was just mimicking what she had taught it. I informed her that anyone could obtain the same results by just speaking into a tape recorder and playing it back. And although it was able to recite the Christian Bible in English, she could have taken the parrot to Iran and have taught it to recite the Koran in Arabic or have taken it to Russia and have taught it to recite the writing's of Karl Marx and Lenin, and I still would not have thought of it as anything unusual.

Then, trying desperately to rise above her diminutive form to intimidate me with her words, this woman, who I could see was intensely immersed in her religion, informed me, using all the control she was taught when speaking to a disbeliever, that this was no parrot, this was her 7-year-old son! Of course I was not fooled. I had noticed when I answered my door that it was dressed as a boy and had the features of one, but I knew somebody had gone to quite a bit of trouble to try to convince me that this parrot standing in front of me was a little boy. What gave the scheme away was the eyes; you cannot disguise the eyes. I could see by looking into them that it did not know what it was reciting; it was just a parrot disguised as a small boy.

The young parrot, masquerading as a boy, managed to hold back the tears until it reached my sidewalk gate where the woman had quickly dragged it. Her intention, I presume, was to see if she could ward off my contaminating influence — that I am sure she felt — by a quick and drastic separation from the contaminant: me. But it was too late; the mind had been contaminated with knowledge, with insight; so when he arrived at the gate, the tears gushed forth as the mother tried in vain to stem them by hugging him closely and telling him I was wrong, that anyone could see that he was a boy. Instinctively, the mind knew; it knew something was dreadfully wrong; it knew its world would never be the same again; it knew a veil had dropped exposing the parrot underneath. Yes, he knew he had been just repeating what had been taught him; repeating a meaningless monologue to please his mother.

I felt deeply saddened that I had been responsible for the revelations that had produced those tears; and in my youth, before those experiences that you have just read, there was a time when I would have liked a chance to have taught that parrot the truth about religions, about politics, about life. Now I am older, and realize that all I would have when I was through teaching everything I knew, was a parrot that could speak about secular humanism, about evolution, about atheism, about socialism, but it still would be a parrot. A parrot speaking in a different dialect, I will admit, but indistinguishable from the parrot that was brought to my door.

You might well ask then, "Is there no hope for us parrots; are we just to grow up to become adult parrots?" Yes, there is hope; there is a way that leads to a wonderful metamorphosis. It is called knowledge, it is called the truth, but all human beings must find it for themselves. What knowledge does is to give you the metamorphic ability to change yourself from a parrot into a human being. And "how," you might ask, "how will you know when you have become a human being?" The answer is simple: you will know it when you recognize you were "once upon a time in the past" a parrot; and that recognition is all one needs to become a human being. From that beginning, you can seek the knowledge of how to become a civilized human being.

For over 20 years there was silence from me. Who would have believed such a fantastic story as you have just read? Surely, if I, the author of this story, could have doubts when I knew it was true, then what could I expect from you, the readers, but skepticism, doubt, disbelief. But time had slowly moved the calendar forward, and as the planet earth continued to traverse its orbit, the old cliches of exposure began to merit a closer scrutiny as stories began to unravel about what the CIA, the FBI, and the CID were doing in the 1950s and '60s.

For years, we were informed by the news media that we should use Mr. J. Edgar Hoover as our role model; that he represented the true patriotic American; that he was sculptured out of the finest American marble obtainable. Then, after his death, we were informed that one way Mr. J. Edgar Hoover had kept control of the FBI through his later years was by blackmail. He had used the FBI's investigative powers to amass, in files kept at his residence, information about the private sexual lives of prominent senators, congressmen, business people, movie stars, and national figures who were engaged in movements that, he thought, were in opposition to the policies of the government in power.

From past records, we learn the CIA had hired people in organized crime to try to assassinate Fidel Castro and others who controlled regimes the CIA opposed. We were not informed of how many other attempts were successful on lesser government officials, nor do we know the price the CIA paid organized crime for those duties.

We read that our armed forces used live viruses in a test of biological warfare in San Francisco and other cities in the United States, in complete disregard for the safety and civil rights of fellow Americans they had pledged to protect.

We are treated to the CIA and CID using brutal torture and then, murdering captured soldiers and civilians in the Vietnam War.

We see a climate emerging where many people in the United States believe there could have been agencies in our government that were behind the assassinations of President John Kennedy, his brother, Robert Kennedy, and Martin Luther King.

We see a former president of the American Neurological Association, a former president of the American Psychological Association, and a former president of the American Psychiatric Association getting grants from the CIA to conduct experiments designed to manipulate human behavior without the knowledge of the recipient of this manipulation.

We see, in the prisons and mental hospitals in the United States and Canada, massive doses of tranquilizers administered, sophisticated hypnosis used, and electroshock and other techniques used to brainwash patients in federal and state drug addiction programs.

We are exposed to the CIA giving generous grants for research to remove from the human mind all memories, behavior patterns, and value judgments, and then reprogramming those empty minds to values and behavior patterns that agree with the experimenters.

Being constrained, what are we to make of the Iran-Contra hearings, where we have Oliver North, a self-confessed liar and forger, advocating piracy on the high seas, advocating terrorism, then trying to change history to show that he, as head of the American Government's anti-terrorism unit, was firmly against all acts of terrorism? We also catch the executive branch in collusion with other government bureaus forming a government unit outside the American Constitution's structure so they did not have to be bound by its rules. How did we gain this information? By accident; by luck; because out of thousands he destroyed, Oliver North missed one document and did not know how to permanently destroy the memos in his computer. Think about this: Now they do know; so never again will we know how accurately they will portray our future history; those who control the data banks will now write your history books, will now revise history to meet their needs, to reflect and coincide with their views of the truth.

We find that not only our government, but all governments are trying to control an illusion of their own creation; trying to rearrange, manipulate, substitute, and eventually bend the mind to fit a preconceived notion of free choice; trying to produce a mind unhampered by selfish genes by declaring it so; trying to divorce the mind from contamination with nature. They refuse to believe the truth: that we are animals living in a world of imperfection; so they deny they are like the rest of the animal kingdom — in transition.

Because I know I am an imperfect animal, then how can imperfection judge imperfection? I can see no way out of this contradiction, this dilemma; so all I can do is to declare my values and try to live by them. Time alone will be the judge, the blind judge; and the eventual acceptance by the living of my beliefs, and the surviving of my beliefs and values will be the proof of their righteousness.

The above description of the 1950s and '60s, is all documented; it is not speculation, not theory, but stark reality. In those 25 years of silence by me, our knowledge of how governments acted, continued to expand. By the 1970s, I realized I did not need, nor should I look for vindication for my actions and deeds, but instead I should write with the intention of exposing what we human beings were capable of doing to each other under the facade of saving the world from the menace of "them."

And you, the future, do not judge us harshly; all our vile and abhorrent acts toward each other are inherited traits that were programmed into us long before the coming of language, long before the adoption of a culture, and were meant to protect the individual's survival. It served its purpose; it produced us through natural selection, and it will remove, through natural and human selection, those traits when they no longer serve a purpose; when they produce death instead of life.

In the beginning, I asked you to suspend judgment on the truth of what you were about to read. All the evidence that I wish to present has been introduced. I am not going to ask for a show of hands, ask for yeas and nays; you should comprehend by now that 100 percent, either way, does not decide, does not define, does not represent the truth. From this you should see that your opinion of this book can only be your personal belief, and will, just like the beliefs of others, have no bearing on whether it is true or false. I will tell you, however, that this book was written for a minority; a dreadfully small minority; but still, it is my hope that they, in time, will represent the future. They know who they are, they will recognize the truth of what I have said, they will recognize me because we are united under a common banner that cannot fail, cannot be denied; they know it is the *message* that is important, not the messenger.

NARRATIVE: THE JOURNEY WE MUST ALL MAKE

Meanwhile, the disappearance of my Lili went unresolved; she remained missing. I kept in touch with her mother, and kept phoning her friends in the Bay Area. I gave them my permanent address in Grass Valley, where I had settled, and waited patiently to hear from her. Time passed, and once again the dice ricocheted off an unseen obstacle and came to rest on a number that was not and could not be covered. I find it intriguing that the information of cause and effect is denied to other mammals, and can only assume this curse must inadvertently be nature's punishment for developing our mental capabilities. Six months after having all charges dropped against me, I received through the mail a plain envelope without a return address on it. It was indistinguishable from the millions delivered daily, but a letter bomb would have been preferred, would have been more charitable to me. How can one adequately describe the slow penetration of a dagger into the heart without experiencing it? Inside the envelope was a newspaper clipping telling of the death of a young woman; a death that was attributed to an overdose of heroin. I did not know that printed words so simply written could carry so much pain, so much sorrow. The irony of, and the capricious actions of an overdose of pain reliever causing pain and mental anguish in someone that was entirely divorced from the injection, was not lost on me. Being devastated by a white crystalline powder that someone else injected, showed me the futility of not believing in a world where all acts are connected, of not believing that we are living in a completely entwined ecosystem.

Realistically, whom can I blame for the grief, the pain, all the suffering caused by that crystal powder? Surely not the fields of poppies swaying gently in the warm summer breeze; surely not the farmer in the field trying to make a living and trying to survive in a harsh habitat; surely not the knowledge of chemistry that benefits the living; and surely not the seller of dreams trying to compete in the marketplace against the religious and political dream sellers. No! All this can be rejected, and once again the path leads backward; once again we can trace the tapestry back to that first thread forming in that Alpha Sea; to the alignment of those first molecules into a chemical structure that can be destroyed by other chemical compounds. How can we control the future when we do not even acknowledge that the past, in the form described, ever existed? Invariably, the result of not being able to learn from the past is the present without references.

Lili, my lovable Lili! No longer would she have the chance to breathe in the scent of mountain wild flowers, run in the mountain meadows, make love in the warm summer grass; no more was I to hear Lili express our mutual desires. As for those tears you would have seen streaming down my cheeks that day, they were not for her, the departed, but for me, the living. She had died being loved, loved deeply by another person. From this harsh life, you can ask or expect no more than that. The tears were for me, for me the living, because I thought I had nothing to look forward to in my remaining time but an ever increasing void in an expanding universe.

There remained for me, a long period of reflection, and from that meditation, I perceived that this vacancy would only be true if I allowed it to be so. I still had to believe there was hope for me or I could not go on living in this, perceived by me, mean world that had deprived me of the love I so desperately needed. I still knew and understood that nature is benign; that it was not punishing me, it was not judging me, it was not a critic or reviewer of my actions. So out there someplace, somewhere there was still a cause worth not only dying for, but in my circumstance, one worth living for, and my goal was to try to find that cause. Then perhaps, the divine dice of life would allow me once again to have a long run at the table of life.

If we chance to meet on the road and you recognize me, give me the sign of the pyramid builders. It tells me you believe; it tells me you were mentally with me; it shows you believed that we protested in a just cause. Thus, when you have the time and the chance, chalk up the sign of the pyramid for my Lili and for all those other human beings that have died unknown, unnoticed, unsatisfied. All, dragging and hauling and chipping away and making smooth those enormous blocks of stone just so they can be fitted into place, fitted into place for the glorification of some mortal God. When you give the sign of a pyramid worker, be reminded that we are all just mortals, and so we have no right to have our names chiseled on the surface of a tomb, but must be content to be remembered for all time, collectively, as pyramid workers.

I am thankful that I was born with this affliction of always seeking, always reaching, always looking to see beyond the curve; and finally knowing that always seeking is the answer for me; yes, perpetually seeking, and knowing that your life will be devoted to it; that you must continually keep asking, "Why?" Looking forward, I hope time will judge me correct in seeking the unknown, instead of the choice that Lili's parents offered me. Looking back, I think that I can perceive that to see what others have not seen, he or she must, in the true sense, become alienated from the crowd, must always observe from the outside of a class, a culture; must be always a stranger, a visitor in their own country.

Soothing or discordant as the melody is, life's tune must eventually end for each of us. When it is all over, there will always be the peaceful, the restful blackness. Yes, I knew when my life's hamstring was bitten through and I was lying there waiting for nature's unpredictable, random, capricious predator — death — to consume me, there would be no intervention, no fairy godmother to intervene and postpone; just eternal blackness where not even an exploding nova would or could disturb that final rest.

Cosmically, when all the structures that man and woman have put together, are toppled and become dust, there will remain still, my love for

Lili. A love echoing, echoing across Einstein's curved space, forever and ever.

This book, if fate allows it, will be my contribution to the genetic pool. I now know my body genes will never be passed on to future generations because I find myself mentally impotent with women since the death of my Lili. Yes, I have tried. So I know that all my uniqueness as a human being, is going to come to a dead end. But I hope this book will take the place of those genes that were not passed on through Lili and me; that these ideas, expressed in this book, will multiply just as other gene pools in natural selection do; and that these written thoughts will produce a more civilized person who will inherit not only this world but the universe surrounding us.

THE END